ABORTION
POLITICS
IN
AMERICAN
STATES

ABORTION POLITICS IN AMERICAN STATES

MARY C. SEGERS   TIMOTHY A. BYRNES
Editors

M.E. Sharpe
Armonk, New York
London, England

Library of Congress Cataloging-in-Publication Data

Abortion politics in American states / editors, Mary C. Segers
and Timothy A. Byrnes.

p. cm.
Includes bibliographical references and index.
ISBN 1–56324–449–7. — ISBN 1–56324–450–0
1. Abortion—Political aspects—United States—States.
2. Abortion—Government policy—United States—States.
I. Segers, Mary C. II. Byrnes, Timothy A., 1958–
HQ767.5.U5A269 1995
363.4′6—dc20
94–27735
CIP

Printed in the United States of America

The paper used in this publication meets the minimum requirements
of American National Standard for Information Sciences—Permanence
of Paper for Printed Library Materials, ANSI Z 39.48–1984.

∞

BM (c)   10   9   8   7   6   5   4   3   2   1
BM (p)   10   9   8   7   6   5   4   3   2   1

Contents

Preface

Putting together a book such as this one is a little like participating in a nation-wide seminar conducted by phone, fax, and e-mail. As editors, we wanted to produce a volume that would capture the vitality and diversity of state-level abortion politics in the United States, and we felt the best way to do so was to commission a series of case studies from a representative sample of states. From that beginning we embarked on a process of conversation and argumentation that resulted in *Abortion Politics in American States*.

This is not, then, a collection of readings; we did not approach a publisher with a packet of articles and papers that we had found elsewhere. Instead, this is a collaborative volume, an original work by thirteen contributors. All but two of the chapters were written because we expressly asked the authors to do so. None has been published previously. We set out a number of themes we wished the contributors to address and a number of variables we wished them to assess. Then the contributors applied those themes and variables to the complex, partic-ular circumstances of their particular states. The result is a series of studies that we hope comprises a coherent and convincing whole.

We wish to thank Michael Weber of M. E. Sharpe for his initial support of this project and for his patience and guidance as it came to fruition. We also wish to acknowledge Thomas O'Hara for his help and his understanding and Dolores M. Byrnes for indexing the book.

Above all, we want to thank our contributors for making the process by which this book was produced so stimulating and, perhaps as important, so efficient. Over many conversations and exchanges of letters with them we have learned a tremendous amount about the states included in this volume and, of course, about the politics of abortion in the United States. We have also learned about the merits of collaboration and the value of collegiality. We sincerely hope that our work together has been as rewarding for them as it has been for us.

Mary C. Segers
Timothy A. Byrnes

MARY C. SEGERS AND TIMOTHY A. BYRNES

Introduction: Abortion Politics in American States

This is a book about the diversity and complexity of abortion politics in America in the 1990s and beyond. During the past thirty-five years, the issue of abortion has, at one time or another, confronted officials at every level of American government—from the White House, Congress, and the Supreme Court to governors, state legislatures, state courts, county boards, and county executives. Even at the local level, school boards have had heated debates over the place of abortion in sex education curricula, zoning boards have considered whether an abortion clinic should be allowed to operate in a community, and police and municipal courts have had to cope with clinic protests and clinic violence. Few issues in American politics have so intensely engaged citizens and public officials at all levels of the American political system.

To be sure, the abortion issue has not confronted officials at all levels simultaneously. The institutional venue for abortion policy has shifted in response to Supreme Court decisions clarifying aspects of abortion in federal law. It is the shifting character of American abortion law that is of deepest interest today to scholars of abortion politics and political scientists who specialize in state politics. After all, abortion was originally a subject of state jurisdiction within the American federal system, a matter of marriage and family law within each state's legal system. The Supreme Court's decision in *Roe v. Wade* changed this and made abortion a matter of both state and federal law. Thus, both historically and currently, the fifty states have been central players in the law and politics of abortion in the United States.

This introductory chapter provides a brief historical overview of shifts and stages in the abortion controversy in the United States. Except for the first

1

category, these stages are denoted by landmark cases that shifted the primary focus of abortion politics from one level of American government to another. Such stages include (1) the pre-*Roe* period (1800–1973); (2) from *Roe* to *Webster* (1973–89); (3) from *Webster* to *Casey* (1989–92); (4) *Casey* and beyond (1992 to the present). Basically, we argue that while abortion was an issue of state law and politics before 1973, the Supreme Court's decision in *Roe v. Wade* **federalized** abortion and made it a matter of state *and* federal policy. Although states responded in various ways to the Supreme Court's decision and some states continued to enact anti-abortion laws, *Roe* shifted the primary focus of abortion politics to the national level and to activities of the three branches of the federal government. Sixteen years later, a combination of changes at both state and national levels of government led to the Court's decision in *Webster v. Reproductive Health Services,* which **refederalized** abortion. In allowing state governments greater leeway to regulate abortion, *Webster* shifted the primary political emphasis once again back to the level of state politics. As a result of *Webster* and of the Court's 1992 ruling in *Planned Parenthood of Southeastern Pennsylvania v. Casey*, the abortion struggle continues to be waged fiercely at *both* national and state levels, a situation that will prevail for the foreseeable future.

The Pre-*Roe* Period: 1800–1973

Legally permissible in 1800, abortion was illegal in all states by 1900. Beginning with an 1821 anti-poison statute in Connecticut, state governments restricted abortion in response to pressure from newly professionalized "regular" physicians, who sought to eliminate competition from midwives and other medical "irregulars."[1] As the Connecticut example indicates, doctors were concerned about the dangers of poisonous abortifacients and the risks of surgical abortion in a nonantiseptic age. Nativist concerns about the threat of European immigration to the power and status of native-born Protestant Americans also fueled the drive to restrict abortion. By 1900 every state had enacted severely restrictive laws, with the result that abortion went underground or, to use the classic phrase, into the "back alleys" of illegal practice. In reality, a double standard developed concerning access to abortion. Wealthy women went to private physicians who discreetly interpreted legal exceptions for therapeutic abortions broadly enough to satisfy their patients. Less fortunate women faced more risky alternatives. Most abortions, and a particularly high percentage of abortions performed on poor women and on women in rural areas, were performed illegally, with grave risks to maternal health. Gradually, physicians and social workers who saw firsthand the consequences of illegal abortions began to call for liberalization of the nation's restrictive abortion laws.

The Movement for Abortion Reform

The abortion reform movement, begun in the 1930s, gathered momentum in the 1950s and 1960s. Led by physicians who feared prosecution for performing illegal therapeutic abortions, the movement included demographers worried about overpopulation, public health officials concerned about maternal mortality from illegal abortions, social workers concerned about family poverty, and police officials worried about illegal abortionists' defiance of, and public contempt for, anti-abortion laws.

This unusual coalition of reformers was influenced by several events. In 1962 the case of Sherri Finkbine drew nationwide attention to the dilemma of an Arizona housewife who had taken thalidomide, a tranquilizer that caused birth defects, in the early stages of pregnancy. Since abortion for fetal defects was not permissible under Arizona law, Finkbine and her husband flew to Sweden, where she had an abortion. The national attention this case drew worked to change public opinion and so made the reformers' campaign slightly easier. The reform cause was similarly influenced by a 1964 rubella epidemic (rubella also poses the threat of birth defects to pregnant women) that again called into question the severity of most state abortion laws. In 1965, the Supreme Court's use of constitutional privacy rights to invalidate a Connecticut birth control statute in *Griswold v. Connecticut* led reformers to wonder whether they could logically extend a woman's constitutional privacy to protect abortion as well as contraception. By 1967 the movement had founded the Clergy Consultation Service on Abortion, a major referral network that began in New York City and rapidly spread nationwide. The reform movement also realized its first state victories in 1967 when Colorado, California, and North Carolina liberalized their abortion laws.

Indeed, between 1966 and 1973, restrictive nineteenth-century abortion statutes were reformed by fourteen states and repealed by four others. Together these eighteen states represented about 42 percent of the nation's population in 1970. Reform states (Mississippi, Colorado, California, North Carolina, Georgia, Maryland, Kansas, Delaware, Arkansas, New Mexico, Oregon, South Carolina, Virginia, and Florida) generally followed the restrictive guidelines suggested in 1959 by the American Law Institute. The ALI model statute permitted abortion in cases of rape, incest, fetal deformity, and to protect the physical and mental health of the mother. Reformers used the ALI statute as the basis for their proposal of moderately permissive abortion laws in many states.

It soon became evident, however, that reform laws did not significantly reduce the number of illegal abortions. These moderately permissive laws contained many provisions, such as state residency requirements and approval by hospital review committees, that made it difficult for young, poor, and rural women to obtain abortions. Moreover, these laws did not reduce the cost of abortion. Thus the effect of abortion reform was to perpetuate traditional, long-standing discrimination against poor and minority women who could not afford private physician or hospital abortions the way more privileged women could. A two-tiered, class-based system of reproductive health care continued in which wealthy women could have abortions while poor women in rural areas resorted to unsafe, "back alley" abortions.

In the late 1960s, therefore, abortion reformers shifted their efforts from lobbying for moderately permissive abortion laws to supporting repeal of all criminal laws banning or severely restricting abortion. This shift from reform to repeal stemmed from the realization that reform laws did not work; it was also influenced by the resurgence of the women's rights movement in the United States in the late 1960s. Women's liberation activists were crucial in transforming what had been an abortion reform effort led by doctors and population controllers into a movement that argued for the right to legal abortion as an essential ingredient of women's moral autonomy and freedom. Abortion reformers, assisted by women's rights advocates, began to insist that abortion be completely decriminalized and become purely a medical decision between doctor and patient.

In 1970 four states (Hawaii, New York, Alaska, and Washington) repealed their anti-abortion statutes and legalized abortion as an elective, not merely a therapeutic, procedure. In the context of the 1960s, this development seemed to be radical rather than incremental or gradual change. The chief difference between reform and repeal laws was that repeal laws lodged decision making with women themselves (abortion on request) whereas reform laws placed ultimate authority with physicians. Interestingly enough, however, these repeal laws permitting elective abortion contained many restrictions, such as residency requirements, spousal consent, and parental consent.[2]

Setbacks in the Reform Movement

These victories marked the high point for abortion rights advocates in the pre-*Roe* period. By 1972 the movement for reform of the states' abortion laws was slowing as it encountered growing opposition from a nascent right-to-life movement. In 1967 the Arizona state legislature rejected an ALI-type reform statute. In Michigan, a Cincinnati physician, Dr. John Wilke, worked with the recently formed National Right to Life Committee to defeat a 1972 referendum that would have legalized abortion in the first twenty weeks of pregnancy. A 1972 referendum on abortion reform in North Dakota also went down to defeat. Repeal efforts were defeated in Iowa and Minnesota. Only Florida in 1972 enacted liberalized abortion reform based on the ALI model. And in December 1972, after a campaign in which the Pennsylvania State Catholic Conference and Philadelphia Cardinal John Krol actively opposed liberalization, the Pennsylvania state legislature passed a highly restrictive bill (SB800 would have banned all abortions except those to save the life of the woman) only to have it vetoed by the governor.

By 1973, then, on the eve of the Supreme Court's ruling in *Roe*, a patchwork quilt had developed of various state-level statutes and regulations having to do with abortion. Four states offered "abortion on request," and fourteen states had moderately permissive laws. The remaining thirty-two had highly restrictive statutes, permitting abortion only to save the woman's life. Moreover, women's access to abortion services was severely limited; in twenty-three states, every woman seeking an abortion had to go out of state to obtain one.[3] The stage was set for the Court's dramatic ruling in *Roe v. Wade*.

From *Roe* to *Webster* (1973–89)

In *Roe* the Supreme Court, by a 7–2 vote, ruled that the right of privacy, grounded in the Fourteenth Amendment's concept of personal liberty, "is broad enough to encompass a woman's decision whether or not to terminate her pregnancy." At issue in *Roe* was an 1857 Texas statute that made it a crime to "procure an abortion" except to save the woman's life. Writing for the majority, Justice Harry Blackmun found this statute unconstitutional and, in effect, declared a fundamental constitutional right to abortion. Nevertheless, this right was not held to be absolute; it had to be balanced against the state's legitimate interest in maternal health and potential human life. Blackmun elaborated a trimester framework to balance these competing interests. During the first three months (or first trimester) of pregnancy, abortion is a matter between a woman and her physician. During the second trimester, government may intervene and regulate abortions in order to preserve and protect the woman's life and health. But during the third trimester, after the point of fetal viability, government may regulate or even prohibit abortion in order to protect fetal life. The lone exception in the third trimester is that states may not prohibit abortions performed to preserve the life or health of the woman.[4]

The Court's decision to legalize abortion had a transforming effect on American law and politics. *Roe* invalidated forty-six of fifty state laws and superseded repeal laws in the remaining four states. In legalizing abortion, the justices inaugurated a national public debate and transformed political discourse about abortion policy. The Court's decision also triggered the rapid development of the right-to-life movement in the United States and lulled abortion rights supporters into a false sense that women's access to abortion was secure.[5] Above all, *Roe* federalized abortion policymaking, shifting the primary focus of abortion politics and political initiative on abortion policy to the federal government in Washington. State governments became reactive, enacting measures to test the limits of the Supreme Court decision and to carve out some degree of state autonomy and control. After *Roe*, however, the center of power shifted to the institutions of the federal government, especially the Supreme Court and Congress in the 1970s and all three branches of government in the 1980s.

Needless to say, *Roe* was not a resolution of the abortion controversy. Indeed, as Glen Halva-Neubauer has pointed out, the battles over abortion in state legislatures increased in number and intensity after *Roe v. Wade*.[6] The struggle within the federal government also intensified throughout the 1970s and 1980s. Abortion became an issue in the presidential election of 1976 and in congressional debates from 1973 on. Congress considered human life constitutional amendments, human life statutes, conscience clauses, and measures restricting abortion funding. In the 1980s Presidents Reagan and Bush campaigned on Republican Party platforms that supported a constitutional amendment to ban abortion, the reversal of *Roe*, and the appointment of pro-life judges to the federal courts. The Supreme Court ruled in several major abortion cases post-*Roe*, including *Maher v. Roe, Planned Parenthood v. Danforth, Bellotti v. Baird, Colautti v. Franklin, Harris v. McRae, Thornburgh v. American College of Obstetricians and Gynecologists*, and the *Webster* and *Casey* decisions.

Thus, in the years from 1973 to 1989, abortion politics continued at *both* state and federal levels, with emphasis and final determining authority located at the national level. States might pass laws, but the Supreme Court would review their constitutionality. As a result, interest groups directed their attention primarily to the national institutions of American government. At the same time, the abortion struggle continued within state governments as state legislatures sought to define state law in relation to the federal judicial standard enunciated in *Roe*. "Challenger states"[7] such as Illinois, Massachusetts, Minnesota, Missouri, and Pennsylvania enacted new laws both to test the limits of *Roe* and to restrict access to abortion within their boundaries. These laws and regulations concerned everything from abortion advertising and promotion, licensing and reporting requirements for clinics, fetal protection statutes, consent and notification laws, regulations on public funding and the use of public facilities. *Roe* had left so many questions unanswered that it stood as an open invitation to states to regulate and litigate.

Thus, despite the Court's ruling in Roe, shifting the primary focus of abortion politics to the federal level, the fifty states did not withdraw from the abortion debate. Over time, state legislative enactments and test-case challenges, combined with changes in the composition of the Supreme Court, worked to undermine the Roe decision. In its 1989 decision in the Webster case, the Court signaled to the states that increasing state regulation of abortion was constitutionally permissible.

From *Webster* to *Casey* (1989–92)

Webster v. Reproductive Health Services, Inc., presented an abortion clinic's challenge to a restrictive Missouri abortion law. The Missouri law included a ban on the performance of abortion in public institutions, even when the woman would be paying her own bill; a statutory preamble declaring that "the life of each human being begins at conception"; a provision prohibiting public funding of abortion counseling; and a regulation requiring doctors to determine whether any fetus of twenty or more weeks' gestation was viable, that is, could potentially survive outside the womb. On 3 July 1989 Chief Justice William Rehnquist, writing for a three-member plurality, found the Missouri statute constitutional.

Webster was important because of changes in the political climate of the country and in the composition of the Supreme Court during the 1980s. Both the state of Missouri and the Bush administration asked the Court to use *Webster* as an occasion to reconsider its decision in *Roe v. Wade*. Moreover, by the time this case arrived at the Supreme Court, the composition of the Court had changed dramatically from the nine justices present for the original *Roe* decision. All five justices who retired in the Reagan-Bush era—Potter Stewart, Warren Burger, Lewis Powell, William Brennan, and Thurgood Marshall—were members of the original seven-member majority in *Roe v. Wade*. Their retirement from the Court gave President Reagan the opportunity to appoint three justices (Antonin Scalia, Anthony Kennedy, and Sandra Day O'Connor) and President Bush the chance to name two justices (David Souter and Clarence Thomas). An anti-abortion strategy to alter the complexion of the federal judiciary bore fruit in *Webster* when a more conservative Court, by a 5–4 vote, upheld the Missouri law.

The key finding in *Webster*, in terms of the politics of abortion in the United States, was the acceptance of viability or, put another way, the recognition of the state's interest in potential human life, at twenty weeks (reduced from the definition of twenty-eight weeks in *Roe*). This was a break with the trimester formula established in *Roe* and an invitation to states to enact laws similar to the Missouri statute that would challenge other portions of the *Roe* ruling. In other words, *Webster* sent a clear signal to state governments that the Court was willing to consider abortion restrictions that did not, strictly speaking, adhere to the governing judicial precedent.

Webster thus **refederalized** the abortion issue in American politics. The Court's decision allowed state legislatures more flexibility in regulating abortion. As a result, the attention of pro-choice and pro-life groups shifted immediately away from the Court and back to the grassroots to marshal public opinion in support of their respective positions and to carry on their advocacy in the halls of state legislatures. At the same time, *Webster* spawned renewed efforts at the federal level to "codify *Roe*" and thereby preserve the legal right to abortion in the event the Court reversed *Roe* in the future. In short, the battle over abortion policy continued after *Webster* on *both* the federal and state levels of government, even though the primary focus of political struggle shifted to the states.

The impact of *Webster* was dramatic, unleashing a flurry of activity in state elections, state legislatures, and state courts. From July 1989 to July 1990, some

351 bills concerning abortion policy were introduced in state legislatures. Abortion immediately became a major issue in the November 1989 gubernatorial election campaigns in New Jersey and Virginia; pro-choice candidates became governors in each state. *Webster* also resulted in renewed activism among pro-choice groups. Alarmed at the *Webster* ruling and convinced that the Supreme Court was only one vote away from overturning *Roe*, pro-choice advocates mobilized their supporters for state election campaigns and increased lobbying efforts in state legislatures. Pro-life adherents, on their part, supported passage of restrictive state laws in Louisiana, Pennsylvania, and Utah but ran into political roadblocks in other states (Florida in 1989, Idaho in 1990). Pennsylvania and Louisiana legislators intended these strict anti-abortion statutes to be test cases, to be occasions for the newly constituted Supreme Court to overturn *Roe*. Finally, with the return of abortion to state politics, legislators and governors could no longer hide behind *Roe* and avoid taking a position. Voters insisted that politicians go on record declaring their position on legal abortion and on the specific restrictions they would or would not support.

Perhaps the best indication of the significance and impact of *Webster* is the realization that, in two cases, state laws invalidated by the Supreme Court before *Webster* were upheld by the Supreme Court after *Webster*. In *Thornburgh v. American College of Obstetricians and Gynecologists* (1986), the Court struck down a Pennsylvania law requiring (1) women to be advised of medical assistance and that the natural father is responsible for child support; and (2) physicians to inform women of the detrimental effects and risks of abortion.[8] In *Planned Parenthood of Southeastern Pennsylvania v. Casey* (1992), the Court upheld similar informed-consent and physician-counseling requirements. Ohio provides an even clearer illustration of the impact of *Webster*. With minor changes, Ohio now has the kind of law—informed consent, mandatory twenty-four-hour waiting period, and parental notification with option of "judicial bypass"—that the Court invalidated in its 1983 ruling in *City of Akron v. Akron Center for Reproductive Health*.[9] Before *Webster*, these provisions did not pass Supreme Court scrutiny; after *Webster*, they were held to be legal.

Casey and Beyond: 1992 to the Present

If *Roe* federalized abortion politics and policy, *Webster* refederalized it. That is, it returned the primary focus of abortion politics and policymaking to the states. In 1992 *Casey* continued the refederalization process, when it both reaffirmed a woman's right to abortion and permitted states to restrict that right. The political result of this is a continuation of the struggle over abortion policy at both federal and state levels of American government.

In *Planned Parenthood v. Casey*, a badly splintered Supreme Court issued a complicated ruling that both upheld a woman's right to abortion and upheld state restrictions on that right. *Casey* presented yet another challenge by abortion providers to a restrictive state statute. At issue were provisions of the 1989 Pennsylvania Abortion Control Act, which amended the state's abortion law to include additional restrictions: abortion counseling by a physician before obtaining a woman's informed consent; a mandatory twenty-four-hour waiting period; parental consent; spousal notification; and reporting and public disclosure requirements. As in *Webster*, the Bush administration joined *Casey* with an *amicus* brief, urging the Court to overrule *Roe*. Once again, a period of heightened public debate and anxious anticipation preceded oral argument and announcement of the Court's decision. A total of thirty-two *amicus* briefs were filed in the case (compared with the seventy-eight briefs filed in *Webster*). On the last day of the Court's term, in July 1992, the justices delivered their ruling. A plurality of three justices (Souter, Kennedy, and O'Connor) staked out a middle position, reaffirming *Roe* but also upholding most of the challenged provisions of the Pennsylvania law. On 20 March 1994, five years after the legislation was first enacted and two years after *Casey*, the Pennsylvania Abortion Control Act finally went into effect.

Controversy immediately developed over how to interpret the Court's complicated ruling in *Casey*. Pro-choice advocates declared that "*Roe* was dead" and that most people did not understand how deeply *Roe* had been dismantled. By contrast, pro-life activists said that *Casey* was a victory for abortion rights advocates. A more modest assessment was voiced by one of the principals in the case, Pennsylvania governor Robert Casey: "The decision, while not overturning *Roe*, clearly returns to the people the power to regulate abortion in reasonable ways, so as to protect maternal health and reduce the number of abortions in our country."[10]

Appealing to the rule of precedent (*stare decisis*) and to "principles of institutional integrity," a plurality of the Court concluded that "the essential holding of *Roe* should be retained and once again reaffirmed." According to Justices Souter, Kennedy, and O'Connor, that essential holding consisted of three points: a woman's right to abortion before viability, the state's power to restrict abortions after fetal viability (except in life- or health-threatening pregnancies), and the state's legitimate interest throughout pregnancy in protecting maternal health and potential life. While the *Casey* joint opinion reaffirmed *Roe*, however, it seems equally clear that it significantly redefined much of what *Roe* stood for. The plurality rejected *Roe*'s trimester framework for balancing the interests of the woman and the government. The plurality also rejected *Roe*'s argument that the right to abortion is a fundamental right that can be restricted only in the light of "compelling state interests." Instead, O'Connor, Kennedy, and Souter redefined the central principle of *Roe* as guaranteeing the woman a liberty interest under the Fourteenth Amendment "to choose to terminate or continue her pregnancy before viability." This meant that state restrictions on the right to abortion need not withstand the Court's strict scrutiny but were permissible as long as they had a "rational basis," a standard easily met by most state statutes. In fact, the plurality replaced *Roe*'s analysis with an "undue burden" standard first enunciated by Justice O'Connor in *City of Akron v. Akron Center for Reproductive Health*. According to this test, "an undue burden exists, and therefore a provision of law is invalid, if its purpose or effect is to place a substantial obstacle in the path of a woman seeking an abortion before the fetus attains viability."[11] Using this standard, the Court announced that it did not find unduly burdensome Pennsylvania's abortion counseling, informed-consent, mandatory waiting period, and parental-consent provisions.

In the final analysis, the Court's decision in *Casey* allowed states to impose more conditions on the availability of abortions, particularly after the first trimester. At the same time, the justices' reaffirmation of *Roe* meant that states were not free to recriminalize abortion. Thus the highly restrictive state laws passed by Utah and Louisiana immediately after the *Webster* decision would probably not withstand constitutional scrutiny. Other laws, such as parental consent, parental notification, informed consent, and waiting periods were viewed as moderately restrictive provisions and were permissible. But this portion of the *Casey* decision was unacceptable to abortion rights advocates, who began collecting data on the effects of the waiting period and other requirements with a view to challenging the Pennsylvania law as unduly burdensome in practice.

Four months after the *Casey* decision, Governor Bill Clinton, Democrat of Arkansas, defeated President George Bush in the 1992 presidential election. Once again, the national context of abortion politics changed. President Clinton campaigned on a Democratic Party platform supportive of abortion rights. Immediately after his inauguration in January 1993, he signed five executive orders reversing restrictive abortion policies inherited from the Bush administration.[12] He proposed a national health insurance plan that included abortion as part of its basic health coverage. He appointed Janet Reno, an outspoken critic of clinic violence, to be attorney general. He named Dr. Joycelyn Elders, a strong supporter of legalized abortion, to be surgeon general. Perhaps most important, President Clinton was presented with an opportunity to change the complexion of the Supreme Court on abortion law. In his first year in office, he appointed Ruth Bader Ginsburg, a firm abortion rights advocate, to fill the seat vacated by Justice Byron White. In 1994, he nominated Judge Stephen G. Breyer of the U.S. Court of Appeals for the First Circuit in Boston to replace retiring Supreme Court Justice Harry Blackmun. Breyer, a moderate liberal, is regarded as generally sympathetic to the abortion rights position. In short, the composition of the U.S. Supreme Court is shifting once again, from the 5–4 majority in *Webster* to at least a 6–3 and possibly a 7–2 majority in future abortion rulings.

At the same time, the struggle over abortion policy continues at the state level. Issues of parental consent, informed consent, mandatory waiting periods, clinic access, and abortion funding continue to be debated in state legislatures and state courts. Taken as a whole, abortion politics in the fifty states can be likened to a steaming cauldron of activity ranging from legislative statutes and gubernatorial vetoes to initiatives, referenda, and court rulings. It is clear that the abortion controversy will continue at *both* state and federal levels of American government for the foreseeable future.

The Case for Case Studies

This book focuses clearly on the states. We have included chapters on the national right-to-life and pro-choice movements and how they have responded to the "refederalization" of abortion. But the locus of legal and political activity concerning abortion has shifted predominantly to the fifty state capitals, and we set out in this collaborative project to depict and explain the diversity and complexity of that activity. There are, of course, a number of ways one could go about this task. We have decided to approach the matter through the use of a representative sample of ten case studies. Unlike an aggregate, fifty-state approach, the case-study method allows us to explore both the particularities of individual states and the significant patterns that emerge across the country.

More specifically, the case-study method affords us the opportunity to examine in detail the historical, cultural, and political contexts in which contemporary abortion policy is made. Just as abortion has had a complex history at the national level, so each of the fifty states has had its own historical development in this regard. Some states significantly liberalized their laws before *Roe v. Wade*; some did not. Some later "challenged," through state legislative action, the rights established in *Roe*, whereas others either "acquiesced" in them or "codified" them.[13] Whatever the facts of an individual case, these historical backgrounds seem to us to be keys to understanding what is going on in the states after *Webster* and *Casey*. In many of the case studies that follow, our contributors ask whether this past has been a prologue to current and future abortion law.

Similarly, the case-study method allows close examination of a state's political culture, another factor that might well serve as an important context in which abortion policy is shaped. Elazar defined political culture as "the particular pattern of orientation to political action in which each political system is embedded," and one of our tasks here is to discover the degree to which these cultural "patterns" relate to a given state's approach to abortion.[14] In addition, many of the contributors to this volume go beyond Elazar's formal definition to assess broader aspects of state cultural life, such as the diversity of the state's organized interests or the role of religion and religious institutions in the state's political processes. What is it about a state's political profile and style, they ask, that leads to varied outcomes on abortion?

Finally, in terms of context, our cases also examine the role that public opinion plays in setting state policy on abortion. Here we are not so interested in the direct relationship between opinion (as an independent variable) and policy (as a dependent variable). Instead, we are more interested in public opinion as a contextual factor setting the stage for the political relationships and political processes that might or might not transform that opinion into concrete policies.

Indeed, these political relationships and processes are just what we think our case-study approach is best suited for analyzing. We asked our contributors to look deeply into the political life of their individual states with an eye toward identifying and exploring the ways in which the central political actors interact with each other on this issue. Based on our reading of the relevant literature, we asked our contributors to consider four political factors in particular: the strength and effectiveness of abortion-related interest groups, the views and activities of the state's governor, the nature of party politics within the state, and the particular role played in abortion politics by the state's female legislators. Our hope was that these dimensions or variables would allow us to plunge into the thicket of abortion politics in ten states and emerge at the end not only more knowledgeable about those states but also equipped with a kind of map of abortion politics that would allow us to draw more general conclusions.

We have set for ourselves, then, two main tasks. First, we want to *describe* the contemporary politics of abortion in the United States. How varied are abortion policies from state to state? How varied are the political processes that produce these policies from state to state? And, more generally and perhaps most significantly for the longer term, what do these variations say about the nature of American federalism in the latter years of the twentieth century? How much initiative do states have to set their own agendas and match their own social policies to their particular historical, demographic, cultural, and political circumstances?

Second, we want to use these case studies, and the descriptive knowledge derived from them, to *explain* the differences in abortion law across the states. What accounts for these differences? We asked the contributors to use the contextual and political factors outlined above as their guides through the politics of abortion in their states. We asked them to identify what it was about their state that led to its current politics on abortion. It is not surprising that the case studies offer several different answers to this central question. It is, one might say, a very diverse political system we are examining. But as the cases also show, a number of rather clear patterns emerge. We return to those patterns in the conclusion.

Choosing the Cases

In any project like this, one of the most important matters is the original choice of cases. Any claim of representativeness must be backed up with clear and persuasive criteria of selection. In choosing the states to be included in this volume we used two central criteria and a number of supplementary ones. First, we sought geographic scope. If we are to review abortion politics in the American states, we have to capture the regional and geographic distinctiveness found across the United States. To that end, we included California, Washington, and Arizona from the West; Minnesota and Ohio from the Midwest; Louisiana and North Carolina from the South; and Pennsylvania, Massachusetts, and Maryland from the East. In addition to their regional breadth, these states differ in a number of demographic categories including the size, relative diversity, and religious affiliations of their populations. They afford us a diverse and representative sample.

Second, we looked for states that had taken varied approaches to the issue of abortion before *Roe v. Wade*. We hoped that this one specific difference would subsume within it a number of state-level political and legal differences that might well relate to contemporary policy on abortion. We hoped it would serve as an indication of a particular state's general approach to the issue of abortion. We included Washington, one of four states that repealed their abortion laws prior to *Roe*; California, Maryland, and North Carolina, three of fourteen states that reformed their abortion laws before *Roe*; and Arizona, Louisiana, Massachusetts, Minnesota, Ohio, and Pennsylvania, six of the remaining thirty-two states that retained restrictive anti-abortion policies in the years before the Court established in 1973 a woman's fundamental right to an abortion.

We found, once we had chosen the states, that this sample also varied on a number of other dimensions that we asked the contributors to deal with. The sample of states, for example, represents a broad array of different political cultures, as defined by Elazar. It includes very different levels of partisan competition, different roles for the states' chief executives, and very different levels of female representation in state legislative bodies. All in all, we feel the sample is representative of the American states and well suited to illuminate the complexity of contemporary abortion policy.

Finally, and somewhat less rigorously, we relied on a supplemental criterion that we came to call our "surprises" or "paradoxes." These were states we wanted to include because in one way or another they did not run in the direction that nonprofessional observers of American politics and American abortion policy might expect. We were sure to include North Carolina, for example, because it is a southern state with a very permissive abortion policy. Similarly, we were particularly interested in Minnesota because it is a generally progressive state that houses one of the country's most effective pro-life movements. And we sought out a study of Arizona that might account for a famously conservative state, with a long anti-abortion tradition, refusing to tighten its abortion law when given the opportunity by *Webster* to do so.

We felt that the inclusion of these states might draw our attention not only to the regional, historical, and cultural contexts *within which* policy is made but also to the complex and sometimes confounding political processes *through which* policy is made. Policy on abortion, no less than on other matters, is a result of the political interplay among public opinion, interest groups, public officials, election campaigns, the media, and any number of other actors and relationships. This complexity is not cause to throw up our hands in despair; our job, after all, is to make sense of political relationships and processes and to work toward generalization. This complexity, however, is cause for caution and perhaps some humility. Before we try to explain too much, before we rush to generalization, we should be sure we have looked carefully at relevant cases. That is what our contributors do in the chapters that follow.

Notes

1. For the history of abortion in the United States, see David J. Garrow, *Liberty and Sexuality: The Right to Privacy and the Making of Roe v. Wade* (New York: Macmillan, 1994); James Mohr, *Abortion in America* (New York: Oxford University Press, 1978); Kristin Luker, *Abortion and the Politics of Motherhood* (Berkeley: University of California Press, 1984); Rosalind Pollack Petchesky, *Abortion and Woman's Choice* (Boston: Northeastern University Press, 1984); Marian Faux, *Roe v. Wade* (New York: Macmillan, 1988); Lawrence Tribe, *Abortion: The Clash of Absolutes* (New York: Norton, 1990); Daniel Callahan, *Abortion: Law, Choice, and Morality* (New York: Macmillan, 1970); and R. Tatalovich and B.W. Daynes, *The Politics of Abortion: A Study of Community Conflict in Public Policymaking* (New York: Praeger, 1981).

2. The specific restrictions of the Hawaii repeal law included the following: abortions had to be performed by a licensed physician, in an accredited hospital, prior to fetal viability, upon request of any adult woman who was a resident of the state for a minimum of ninety days immediately prior to the abortion. See R.J. Pion, R.G. Smith, and R.W. Hale, "The Hawaii Experience," *The Abortion Experience*, ed. Howard J. Osofsky and Joy D. Osofsky (New York: Harper & Row, 1973), 177–87. Washington's repeal law also contained some restrictions: (1) that the physician be a licensed practitioner; (2) that except in medical emergencies the abortion take place in an accredited hospital; (3) that the woman have her husband's consent if she resides with him; (4) that a woman have a parent's or legal guardian's consent if unmarried and under eighteen years of age; (5) that the woman be a resident for ninety days prior to the abortion; and (6) that no one is required to participate in a termination of pregnancy if the individual cannot do so in good conscience. See Byron N. Fujita and Nathaniel N. Wagner, "Referendum 20—Abortion Reform in Washington State," in Osofsky and Osofsky, eds., *The Abortion Experience*, 232–60.

3. Barbara Hinkson Craig and David M. O'Brien, *Abortion and American Politics* (Chatham, N.J.: Chatham House, 1993), 77.

4. This was held in the companion case to *Roe*, a case from Georgia, *Doe v. Bolton* 410 U.S. 179 (1973).

5. See James R. Kelly, "Learning and Teaching Consistency: Catholics and the Right to Life Movement," in *The Catholic Church and the Politics of Abortion: A View from the States*, ed. Timothy A. Byrnes and Mary C. Segers (Boulder, Colo.: Westview Press, 1992), 152–68.

6. Glen A. Halva-Neubauer, "Abortion Policy in the Post-*Webster* Age," *Publius: The Journal of Federalism* 20 (1990): 27–44. See also Glen A. Halva-Neubauer, "The States after *Roe*: No 'Paper Tigers,' " in *Understanding the New Politics of Abortion*, ed. Malcolm L. Goggin (Newbury Park, Calif.: Sage, 1993), 167–89.

7. Halva-Neubauer categorized states by their policymaking approaches—challenger, codifier, acquiescer, or supporter—based on the number of restrictions each passed between 1973 and mid-1989 (before the *Webster* decision). Challengers demonstrated the greatest hostility toward *Roe*, passing numerous statutes; codifiers were willing to pass restrictions deemed constitutional by the U.S. Supreme Court; acquiescers largely ignored the issue or engaged in a debate on a limited scope of abortion restrictions; and supporters embraced *Roe* and did little to disturb the abortion status quo.

8. 476 U.S. 747 (1986).

9. 462 U.S. 416 (1983).

10. *Harrisburg Patriot-News*, 30 June 1992, as quoted in Craig and O'Brien, *Abortion and American Politics*, 326.

11. *Planned Parenthood of Southeastern Pennsylvania v. Casey*, 112 S.Ct. 2791 (1992).

12. In five executive orders on 22 January 1993, President Clinton reversed the ban on abortion counseling in federally funded family planning clinics; overturned the moratorium on federally funded research involving the use of fetal tissue; ordered a study of the current ban on import of RU-486, the French abortion pill, for personal use; revoked the prohibition on abortions in military hospitals; and voided the "Mexico City policy," which forbade U.S. foreign aid funds to agencies promoting abortions. See *Origins* 22, no. 34 (4 February 1993): 574.

13. Glen Halva-Neubauer, "Abortion Policy in the Post-*Webster* Age."

14. Daniel J. Elazar, *American Federalism: A View from the States*, 2nd ed. (New York: Crowell, 1984), 84–85.

ROSEMARY NOSSIFF

1 | Pennsylvania: The Impact of Party Organization and Religious Lobbying

The contemporary abortion reform movement began in the United States in the mid-1960s in the aftermath of the 1965 Supreme Court decision in *Griswold v. Connecticut*.[1] In the eight-year period between *Griswold* and *Roe v. Wade*, fourteen states reformed their abortion laws to permit therapeutic abortions, and four states repealed them.[2] A striking exception to this trend was Pennsylvania, which passed a bill in 1972 to outlaw all abortions except in cases where the mother's life was endangered. Although that bill, HB800, was vetoed by Governor Milton Shapp, Pennsylvania has continued to lead the nation in restrictive abortion legislation since *Roe* with the passage of four abortion-control acts and various other bills in the past twenty years.

The campaign to restrict Pennsylvania's abortion legislation began in the late 1960s. Anti-abortion groups led by the Pennsylvania Catholic Conference (PCC) triumphed over pro-abortion forces for a variety of reasons that this chapter explores.[3] Chief among them was the failure of the municipal reform movement in Pennsylvania to wrest control of the parties from the political machines. As a result, challengers such as the abortion reformers were unable to obtain the party support they needed to challenge the PCC. This, in turn, enabled the PCC to use its organizational and financial resources to create the abortion policy discourse in the state beginning in the late 1960s.

By discourse I mean talk,[4] the definition of an issue and the policy response to it. In the war over abortion policy, discourse can be seen as a political resource used by interest groups to win public support for their definition of abortion and for the polices they support to regulate or deregulate its practice. Public dis-

16

course shapes the way we think about an issue. Nowhere is this truer than in abortion policy, where the subject was until very recently taboo, despite the fact that thousands of women were getting abortions, even going abroad to avoid local constraints.

In the wider context of political development, the clash over abortion policy discourse reflects the stormy federalist relationship between the national government and the states, which is characteristic of social regulatory policy. The legal discourse established by *Roe* collided with the moral one advanced by pro-life forces at the state level. This clash can be analyzed by examining the development of abortion policy discourse in Pennsylvania, the state that has had the most successful history in establishing a pro-life legislative agenda.

Pennsylvania's abortion policy can be broken down into four distinct stages. In stage 1 (1965–72) the PCC deflected attempts to create support for abortion reform by creating a discourse that defined abortions as infanticide and cast moral aspersions on women who sought them. The abortion discourse created by the 1973 *Roe v. Wade* decision, however, which held that unrestricted access to abortion in the first trimester of pregnancy was a constitutional right, rendered this moral discourse immaterial.

During stage 2 (1973–80), pro-life forces in Pennsylvania passed the first Abortion Control Act as well as a myriad of bills designed to limit the impact of *Roe*. Much of this legislation was successfully challenged in the courts by pro-choice forces, and, as a result, pro-life forces altered their strategy. In stage 3 (1981–88) pro-life forces passed two additional abortion-control acts, designed both to work within the framework established by *Roe* and to push back its boundaries. In stage 4 (1989–92) the aftermath of the Supreme Court's decision in *Webster v. Reproductive Health Services* was played out in Pennsylvania when the legislature passed the 1989 Abortion Control Act. Three years later, in *Planned Parenthood of Southeastern Pennsylvania v. Casey*, the Court upheld three of the main provisions of the 1989 act.

To understand why political conditions in Pennsylvania were more conducive to the success of pro-life forces than those of their pro-choice opponents it is necessary to examine the political developments that preceded them. In the period under discussion Pennsylvania was a strong party state with traditional party structures that regularly nominated candidates for public office.[5] For this reason, the failure of the municipal reform movement to change the way the party system worked so that new political forces could be included played a crucial role in shaping the political resources and opportunities available to such outside groups as abortion reformers.[6]

To become part of the policy process, challengers need institutional support: legislators who are willing to sponsor bills; partisan resources, which can range from inclusion in various policy coalitions and party caucuses to access to lists of donors and active party members; and the political opportunities provided by a regime open to new policy demands.[7] Unlike their counterparts in New York, who succeeded in repealing New York's abortion law in 1970 with the help of the reform wing of the Democratic Party, abortion reformers in Pennsylvania did not have similar resources or opportunities available to them. A brief examination of the municipal reform movement in Pennsylvania in the 1950s may explain why.

Municipal Reform

The modern history of municipal reform in Pennsylvania began in the late 1940s with the failed mayoral campaign of Democratic reformer Richardson Dilworth. Charges of municipal graft and corruption were the bases of Dilworth's campaign against the Republicans in the 1947 Philadelphia race. Throughout his campaign Dilworth leveled specific attacks against Republican incumbents, accusing them of being associated with organized crime.[8] Although the Republicans denounced Dilworth in the press, he had established a large personal following, which became his future campaign base.[9]

Realizing the political support that municipal reform attracted in the campaign, the Democrats in 1949 drafted Dilworth to run for city treasurer; his former campaign manager, Joe Clark, ran for city controller in the off-year election. Both men won easily.[10] Two years later, the Democrats nominated Clark to run for mayor and Dilworth for district attorney; once again both were elected.

Despite the support of the Democrats, Clark and Dilworth primarily considered themselves to be *municipal* reformers. Once in office, they were more concerned with controlling city government than in reforming the Democratic Party. Clark and Dilworth underestimated the party's power at the precinct level, and as a result they did not attempt to take control of the party apparatus from the regulars or replace it with mechanisms that would ensure that party reform would endure.

As we shall see, their disinclination for party reform had significant implications for the future of party politics in Pennsylvania in the 1960s. For example, had Clark and Dilworth institutionalized changes in the 1950s, the reform wing of the Democratic Party may have regularly sponsored abortion reform bills and helped abortion reformers to create a broad-based coalition to generate the support they needed to change the abortion laws in the decade that followed.

The absence of lasting reform was exacerbated by Clark and Dilworth's departure from Philadelphia politics. In 1956 Clark successfully ran for the U.S. Senate; in 1962 Dilworth unsuccessfully ran against Bill Scranton for governor. In a neat twist, Scranton and his running mate, Raymond Shafer, incorporated the theme of municipal reform (minus the program) into their successful campaign against Dilworth. Both developments enabled the Republican machine to temporarily reassert its control at the state level and the Democratic machine to dominate city politics once again.[11] Within fifteen years of their ascendancy, municipal reformers had effectively lost their power base.

Against this backdrop, abortion reform forces in Pennsylvania began their campaign to change the laws. When the contemporary abortion movement in Pennsylvania is viewed in this context, it becomes clearer why the party access and resources needed by abortion reform forces to challenge the PCC were not available to them, as well as why the PCC had a head start on its opponents even before the battle began.

Stage 1 (1965–72): Griswold to HB800

The right to privacy articulated in the 1965 *Griswold* decision was used by abortion reformers across the country to begin campaigns to change restrictive abortion laws. Since the Court had found that the right to privacy protected married couples' access to contraceptives, the reformers reasoned that constitutional protection might also extend to another contraceptive: abortion.[12]

In 1965 abortion reformers in New York linked up with the reform wing of the Democratic Party and began a campaign to change the state's restrictive abortion laws. In 1966, Reform Democrats introduced an abortion bill based on the American Law Institute's model for abortion legislation, which allowed for abortions in cases of rape, incest, fetal deformity, or to protect the physical and mental health of the mother. One year later, in neighboring Pennsylvania, a similar bill, Senate Bill 38 (SB38), was sponsored by a bipartisan group of legislators as part of a larger effort to update the state's penal code.

Partly as a result of the failure of the municipal reform movement, the mechanisms needed to place new policy demands on party platforms had not been established, and therefore there was no organized support for SB38, which died in committee. Had party support existed in 1967 for abortion reform, SB38 may have made it out of committee and onto the assembly floor for debate. Pro-abortion forces in Pennsylvania could then have used it in the same way their counterparts in New York had used the early abortion bills sponsored by the reform Democrats in Albany: to build support for abortion reform gradually by speaking about it at political clubs around the city.

The introduction of SB38 marked the beginning of abortion reform in Pennsylvania and the active opposition of the PCC. Although the bill had little chance of passing, the PCC nevertheless began a campaign to shape the public discourse concerning abortion policy. The PCC's strategy was to remain on the offensive as long as possible and to go on the defensive when necessary. To that end, it sought the assurance of Governor-elect Shafer that he would honor his campaign pledge to oppose abortion reform legislation. In addition, the PCC issued a public statement opposing SB38 on two grounds: that there were no objective medical standards to judge when the physical or mental health of the mother was in jeopardy, and that however tragic rape and fetal deformity were, they did not constitute justifiable grounds for abortion.[13]

The underlying message of the PCC's position, outlined in a draft of its public statement against SB38, was that physicians and women were not to be believed:

> We are not unmindful of, or without compassion towards, the *totally* deformed, the *true* victims of rape, the possibility of the *true* impairment of physical or mental health of the mother, or in general, of the social and personal ills which the proponents of this legislation seek to remedy. We submit, however, that the act of deliberately taking innocent life can never be warranted as a remedy even for *actual* personal misfortune. . . .[14]

The absence of any previous discussion about abortion reform played into the hands of the PCC. From the start, it recognized the importance of establishing an anti-abortion discourse, which is why it responded so swiftly and vigorously to SB38. The PCC adopted Vatican II's definition of abortion as infanticide to establish the future parameters of the debate. By doing so, it was able to define the issue in the moral and religious terms it supported. Because the PCC was the only public voice heard on abortion policy until 1969, it was able to define the issue without challenge.

By any comparison, the organizational and financial resources of the PCC dwarfed those of the abortion reformers. In addition to direct and regular access to millions of Catholic parishioners, the PCC could also draw on the church's active political lobby at the national level, the U.S. Catholic Conference (USCC). In 1967 the PCC established an ad hoc committee on abortion, based on guidelines suggested by the Family Bureau of the USCC, to prevent further changes in the existing state abortion statutes. In the late 1960s it also created a grassroots organization, Pennsylvanians for Human Life, to generate legislative support for restrictive abortion legislation throughout the state.

Despite this disparity in resources, abortion reformers in Pennsylvania organized to challenge the PCC. In 1969 they formed the Abortion Justice Association (AJA) to press for the passage of unrestrictive abortion legislation, and in 1970 and 1971 the AJA worked with Representative Gerald Kaufman (D-Pittsburgh) to introduce two bills along the lines of the New York legislation. Because of the absence of widespread support for changes in the abortion laws, as well as the vigorous opposition of the PCC, neither bill made it out of committee. The New York abortion reformers had initially encountered similar obstacles, but they were able to overcome them with the support of the reform Democrats, who had annually supported abortion reform legislation from the start of their campaign.

The election of Milton Shapp in 1970 provided abortion forces with another opportunity to challenge the PCC. The governor was an avid supporter of abortion repeal, and in 1971 he created a commission on abortion law to recommend changes in the laws. The recent success of the New York abortion repeal campaign had encouraged pro-abortion activists in Pennsylvania. As one of the commission's members recalled:

> The Commission was influenced by the New York law. New Yorkers came down and testified (at the hearings). New York made it feasible for us to make a recommendation that was quite liberal, given Pennsylvania's composition (with) the Catholic Conference being very strong.[15]

For pro-abortion forces, the statewide hearings held by the commission represented a major victory. First, they legitimated the issue. This was especially critical given that the PCC had continually defined abortion as murder. Second, the hearings represented the first public debate on the issue. Despite Governor Shapp's support, however, pro-abortion forces in Pennsylvania were not sufficiently organized to forestall their opponents.

During this first stage in Pennsylvania, abortion policy was a function of interest groups, such as the PCC, rather than political parties. The failure of the municipal reform movement to take control of the party from the regulars had closed party channels to such challengers as the abortion reformers. Unlike New York's Governor Nelson Rockefeller, who was supported by a bipartisan abortion coalition that triumphed over the New York Catholic Conference, Governor Shapp was reduced to reacting to policy through the use of his veto, rather than creating it within his party.

In terms of the wider development of abortion policy in Pennsylvania, the chief importance of the pro-abortion legislation and Governor Shapp's commission was that they provided the PCC with an opportunity to go on the defensive. The PCC responded with HB800, one of the most restrictive abortion bills in the country.[16] That anti-abortion forces were able to do this in the midst of a national campaign to relax abortion bills indicated the strength of the PCC. So powerful was the anti-abortion discourse it created that Governor Shapp's role in the abortion battle was limited from the start and became more marginal in his second term.

Stage 2 (1973–80): *Roe v. Wade* and the Abortion Control Act of 1974

The extremity of the 1973 Supreme Court decision in *Roe v. Wade* astonished abortion activists on both sides of the issue. In addition to making abortion legal, the chief significance of *Roe* was that it established a national discourse on abortion based on women's constitutional rights. The Court's decision in *Roe* permanently altered the conflict over abortion policy by rejecting the moral absolutism that had previously characterized the issue and replacing it with a legal discourse. After *Roe*, abortion policy became a national issue. It propelled the women's movement onto the national level and did the same for the pro-family movement, which was the precursor of the pro-life movement. The new "rights discourse" established by *Roe* was reflected in the new names that activists on both sides of the struggle adopted: pro-choice and pro-life.

In the majority of states where most abortions were prohibited, *Roe* shifted the discourse away from prohibition *toward* limited restrictions beginning in the second trimester of pregnancy. The impact of *Roe* was especially significant in Pennsylvania, where the legislature had recently passed HB800.

The Abortion Control Act of 1974 (SB1318) was Pennsylvania's answer to *Roe*. The act centered on the notion of consent and state funding for abortion. In addition to the requirement that a woman requesting an abortion be informed about the procedure, the act stipulated that she obtain her husband's consent before having an abortion; if she was a minor, she had to secure one parent's consent. The other main provision prohibited state funding for "unneeded and unnecessary" abortions.[17]

The punitive nature of the funding and consent provisions reflected the attempts of pro-life forces to retain the moral imperative they had in the pre-*Roe* period and to continue to control the abortion discourse. As noted earlier, in the late 1960s one of the main legislative strategies of the PCC was to cast doubt on the legitimacy of claims of rape, incest, and mental health as grounds for therapeutic abortions. The consent provisions of SB1318 cast a similar shadow on women's trustworthiness and their ability to decide if they wanted an abortion without a state-prepared explanation of the procedure.

Both houses passed SB1318 by large margins and, as expected, Governor Shapp vetoed the bill, as he had done with HB800. This time, however, pro-life forces were prepared. After the legislature adjourned for the summer, the PCC organized a campaign that led to the legislative override of Shapp's veto in the beginning of the 1974 fall session. Going into his second term, Shapp did not want to squander any more political credit on an issue that clearly would be settled in the courts. The following year, the district court held that the spousal and parental consent requirements as well as the funding provisions of the act were unconstitutional; however, the court sustained other provisions, including the states' regulation of medical, administrative, and commercial practices.[18]

In contrast to the meticulous campaign carried out by pro-life forces to override Governor Shapp's veto, pro-choice groups in Pennsylvania were unable to mobilize an effective countereffort against SB1318. This partly reflected the complexity of the bill, which restricted access to abortion as opposed to prohibiting it outright. In addition, various pro-choice groups had disbanded after *Roe* because they had concluded that access to abortion was guaranteed. As one activist recalled, "[There was] nothing more that we had to do . . . [we] were sort of at a loss [after *Roe*]."[19] After the passage of SB1318, pro-choice forces recovered and concentrated their efforts in the courts. But it was not until the late 1970s that they emerged in Harrisburg to lobby against cuts in state-funded abortions.

In a sense the *Roe* decision was a double-edged sword for pro-choice groups. While it gave them an undeniable victory by legalizing abortions, it also lulled them into a false sense that women's access to abortion was no longer an issue. Nowhere was this truer than in Pennsylvania, where pro-life forces interpreted *Roe* as the *beginning* of the battle over abortion, not the end. The absence of an organized legislative challenge by pro-choice forces after *Roe* enabled the PCC to continue shaping abortion discourse at local and state levels with the constant introduction of anti-abortion bills and amendments in the 1970s. This was especially critical in Pennsylvania, which was one of the leading states in introducing pro-life legislation before and after *Roe*. Although *Roe* established a national discourse on abortion, pro-life forces in Pennsylvania continued to operate on the basic premise that abortion was a local issue, one to be regulated by the states, not the federal government.

The mid-1970s was a transitional period for pro-life forces across the country. The national campaign to convene a constitutional convention to add a human life amendment to the Constitution reflected the uncertainty of an emerging social movement struggling to articulate a discourse in response to *Roe*. The success of the Hyde Amendments in the late 1970s, which limited federal funding of abortions, suggested the direction pro-life forces at the state level needed to take if they were to regain the upper hand in establishing the abortion discourse. The moral absolutism that had characterized the pre-*Roe* period would have to be replaced with an approach better suited to the legal discourse established by *Roe*.

Increasingly it became clear that the struggle could be won by enacting restrictions that articulated the doubts many people had about the unrestricted access to first-trimester abortions allowed by *Roe*. Pennsylvania's Abortion Control Acts of 1982 and 1988 incorporated this new approach and began a new era in state abortion politics.

Stage 3 (1981–88): More Abortion-Control Acts

The emergence of a national pro-life movement in the late 1970s affected the development of abortion politics in Pennsylvania in several ways. Whereas abortion bills introduced in the second stage (1973–80) sought to challenge *Roe* directly, the abortion-control acts of the 1980s attempted to establish the parameters of states' rights to regulate abortions. This shift in emphasis was largely accomplished through a public discourse that defined these restrictions as ways for the states to control a practice imposed on them by the federal government—hence the name, abortion-control acts.

During this stage, Martin Mullen, the chief legislative leader for HB800 and

SB1318, was replaced by Stephen Freind, whose legal approach was better suited to the post-*Roe* period.[20] Mullen's passionate style and moral arguments against abortion had worked well in the pre-*Roe* era in Pennsylvania when the PCC had controlled the discourse. In the 1980s, however, abortion was a national issue and pro-life forces in Harrisburg increasingly relied on organizations such as Americans United for Life to create comprehensive legislation that could also withstand constitutional challenge.[21]

As a result of this shift, the role played by legislative leaders such as Freind was elevated at the expense of interest groups and the governor's office. In the first stage, before *Roe*, abortion policy was virtually dictated by the Pennsylvania Catholic Conference. In the period after *Roe*, the national government and the courts largely created abortion policy. By the 1980s, state legislators had reclaimed control over the issue. Because of the size of its constituency and its links to grassroots organizations around the state, the PCC remained the leading interest group in the abortion struggle in Pennsylvania in this stage, but it no longer masterminded legislative strategy.

This trend was also seen in the organization of grassroots groups. In the 1970s grassroots organizations such as the Pennsylvanians for Human Life and People Concerned with the Unborn Child coordinated activities with the PCC. The increasing nationalization of the pro-life movement saw a proliferation of independent grassroots groups across Pennsylvania, however, as well as throughout the rest of the country. By the 1980s several grassroots groups had joined the Pennsylvania Pro-Life Federation, an independent umbrella organization that coordinated their efforts to build support for restrictive abortion legislation. Other organizations emerged, such as the Pennsylvania Family Institute, which addressed a range of issues considered to have an impact on family life, including abortion and homosexuality.

The election of two governors who were more sympathetic to abortion restrictions than was Milton Shapp—Dick Thornburgh and Robert Casey—may have expedited but did not significantly alter the progress of pro-life forces in Pennsylvania in the 1980s. Both governors vetoed abortion-control acts on constitutional grounds, the same reasons cited by Shapp. Although each later helped draft abortion-control acts, neither of those acts differed significantly from the ones introduced by Representative Freind. Thornburgh and, to a lesser degree, Casey were mainly responding to political demands articulated by pro-life leaders in the legislature and not specifically creating support for restrictive abortion legislation. In short, abortion politics in Pennsylvania in the 1980s became more professional and less local in orientation, with each segment of the coalition contributing its strengths to the overriding goal of passing restrictive abortion legislation.

The strategy used by Freind in the 1980s was a gradualist one that sought to build support for state restrictions on abortion by introducing bills based on old restrictions and adding new ones that went one step beyond what the courts deemed constitutional. Hence, a package of bills introduced by Freind and Gregg Cunningham in 1981 incorporated altered provisions of the 1974 Abortion Control Act, which the federal court had struck down, as well as new regulations concerning parental consent and postviability abortions.[22] Although Governor Thornburgh vetoed the 1981 bills, the following year he signed the Abortion Control Act of 1982, which deleted some of the most controversial provisions of the 1981 bills but retained informed and parental consent and public funding limitations.[23]

In its 1986 decision in *Thornburgh v. American College of Obstetricians and Gynecologists*, the Supreme Court affirmed the decision made by the court of appeals to overturn six of the provisions of the 1982 act.[24] In the following year pro-life forces drafted a new abortion-control act that attempted to rectify specific requirements that the Court had found objectionable. Despite his personal pro-life sentiments, the newly elected governor, Robert Casey, did not squander his political credit on a bill that was likely to be overturned; he vetoed the 1987 bill on constitutional grounds. Several months later, his office drafted the 1988 Abortion Control Act, which was similar to the 1987 version with the exception of the parental notice provision, which it deleted.[25] As expected, the 1988 bill was challenged in court, but full consideration of the act was delayed, pending the outcome of *Webster v. Reproductive Health Services*.[26]

Stage 4 (1989–92): *Webster* to *Casey*

In terms of the wider conflict over abortion policy, the main importance of the restrictions implemented by the Pennsylvania abortion-control acts was the element of doubt they articulated concerning the virtually unrestricted access to first-trimester abortions established by *Roe*. A decade's worth of pro-life activity was vindicated by a 1989 Supreme Court decision. *Webster* was for pro-life forces what *Roe* had been for pro-choice advocates: both decisions established constitutional frameworks that the respective sides were invited to embellish. The crucial difference between the decisions was the Court's changing view of abortion.

In *Roe*, a majority of the Court interpreted abortion to be a fundamental constitutional right; in *Webster*, a new majority disagreed. As a result, *Webster* created a states' rights discourse that gave states more control over the use of public funds, medical personnel, and facilities for performing abortions. In addition, the balance between a woman's right to an abortion and a state's interest in protecting potential human life shifted more in favor of the state than a strict interpretation of *Roe* would have allowed. As she did in *Akron*, Justice O'Connor suggested that an approach based on a standard of "undue burden" should replace the trimester framework established by *Roe* to determine if a given restriction impeded a woman's constitutional rights.[27]

This deference to the states resonated in Pennsylvania, where pro-life forces interpreted the decision as an invitation to enact as many restrictions as the legislature saw fit. As expected, Pennsylvania was the first state to draft legislation based on *Webster*. The pattern of building on past successes as well as forging new ground prevailed in the provisions of the 1989 Abortion Control Act. In addition to an informed-consent provision, which was in the 1988 act, the 1989 act added regulations including a spousal notification provision and a twenty-four-hour waiting period before an abortion could be performed.[28] Pro-choice forces filed suit, and the case was eventually appealed to the Supreme Court.

The Court's 1992 ruling on the 1989 act held that restrictions that did not place an "undue burden" on the right to abortion were constitutional. Specifically, in *Planned Parenthood of Southeastern Pennsylvania v. Casey* the Supreme Court found that the informed-consent provisions and the twenty-four-hour waiting period were constitutional, but ruled that spousal consent was not.[29] After several years of litigation, the 1989 act took effect in March 1994.

Conclusion

Throughout the twenty-five-year war over abortion policy in Pennsylvania, the focal point of the struggle has been the battle to control the discourse. This is why the PCC began creating an abortion discourse six years before *Roe*. The failure of the municipal reform movement in the 1950s to change the way the Democratic Party worked precluded the political opportunities and resources that abortion reformers needed to challenge the PCC's definition of abortion in the legislative arena effectively. For most of the period under discussion, pro-life forces in Pennsylvania have retained control of abortion policy discourse.

The main legislative bills in this period, the Abortion Control Acts of 1974, 1982, 1988 and 1989, have sought to place restrictions on women's access to abortion. Their main impetus, however, has lain not in the restrictions themselves but in the wider effort to control the terms of the discussion. The 1973 Supreme Court decision in *Roe v. Wade* established the national discourse on abortion. In its 1989 decision in *Webster*, the Court invited the states to participate in the national dialogue by allowing them to place restrictions on women's access to abortion.

More than twenty years after *Roe*, the issue of abortion policy has returned to the states. For pro-choice forces, the main goal has been to retain *Roe*'s definition of abortion as a constitutional right. Pro-life forces, on the other hand, have organized and made substantial gains in limiting women's access to abortion by enacting restrictions that were constitutionally grounded by *Webster* and *Casey*. Restrictions on abortion do not prevent most women who want abortions from getting them. What they do is articulate the doubts and anguish that the issue of abortion policy evokes in the general public. Such misgivings have been used successfully by pro-life forces in Pennsylvania and in several other states to generate support for limiting the reach of *Roe*. Whereas pro-choice forces won the first round; pro-life forces won the second. The future of abortion policy in Pennsylvania lies between the ability of pro-life forces to create more restrictions along the lines of those upheld in *Casey* and the ability of pro-choice forces to enforce the discourse established by *Roe* to stop them.

Notes

1. In *Griswold v. Connecticut*, 381 U.S. 471 (1965), the Supreme Court ruled that a Connecticut law that prohibited the sale of contraceptives to married couples was unconstitutional because it violated citizens' rights to privacy as found in the First, Third, Fourth, Fifth, and Ninth amendments to the Constitution.

2. Barbara Hinkson Craig and David M. O'Brien, *Abortion and American Politics* (Chatham, N.J.: Chatham House, 1993, 75).

3. Until 1973 the terms "pro-abortion" and "anti-abortion" were used to describe the positions of actors on both sides of the issue. This chapter follows this distinction. The main anti-abortion group in Pennsylvania is the Pennsylvania Catholic Conference, one of thirty state Catholic conferences in the United States. The conferences represent the views of the church on a wide range of public issues; the PCC is considered to be one of the strongest and most active ones in the country.

4. Erving Goffman, *Forms of Talk* (Philadelphia: University of Pennsylvania Press, 1981), 70–71.

5. For a detailed discussion of the factors that constitute a strong party state as opposed to a weak one, see David Mayhew, *Placing Parties in American Politics* (Princeton, N.J.: Princeton University Press, 1986), 19–20.

6. Both parties in Pennsylvania could have been reformed but because the municipal reform movement in Pennsylvania was waged by reformers aligned with the Democratic Party, this discussion is limited to the opportunities reform would have provided for that party.

7. For a discussion of the factors that influence a regime's receptivity to new policy demands, see Herbert P. Kitschelt, "Political Opportunity Structures and Political Protest: Anti-Nuclear Movements in Four Democracies," *British Journal of Political Science* 16 (1986): 57–85, esp. 63.

8. Robert L. Freedman, *A Report on Politics in Philadelphia* (Cambridge: Joint Center for Urban Studies, MIT/Harvard, 1963), pt. 2, p. 21.

9. Ibid.

10. James Reichly, *The Art of Government* (New York: Fund for the Republic, 1959), 10–13.

11. Although the reform wing of the Democratic Party continued to challenge the machine in the 1960s and 1970s and succeeded to some degree in shaping the party platform, the regulars succeeded in electing machine candidates for mayor of Philadelphia from 1963 to 1978. For an alternative interpretation of the reformers' influence during this period, see Richard A. Kreiser, "The Rise of a Biracial Coalition in Philadelphia," in *Racial Politics in American Cities*, ed. Rufus P. Browning, Dale Rogers Marshall, and David H. Tabb (New York: Longman, 1990), 51–52.

12. This is not to suggest that no distinction was made between routine contraceptives such as the birth control pill and abortion, but that, based on *Griswold*, pro-abortion

activists thought the Court might include abortion as an activity to be protected by marital guarantees of privacy. For further elaboration of this point, see Lawrence Lader, *Abortion II* (Boston, Mass.: Beacon Press, 1973), 12.

13. Draft Statement of Pennsylvania Catholic Conference on Senate Bill, 20 February 1967, 2–4.

14. Ibid., 3–4. Italics added.

15. Interview with Elizabeth Shipley, member of the Pennsylvania Abortion Law Commission, Narberth, Pa., 15 July 1992.

16. HB800 prohibited all abortions except in cases where the mother's life was endangered.

17. Glen Halva-Neubauer, "Legislative Agenda Setting in the States: The Case of Abortion Policy" (Ph.D. dissertation, University of Minnesota, 1992), 275.

18. *Planned Parenthood Association v. Fitzpatrick* 401 F.Supp 554 (1975). See also Nancy Nolan, "Toward Constitutional Abortion Control Legislation: The Pennsylvania Approach," *Dickinson Law Review* 87 (Winter 1983), 380–81.

19. Telephone interview with Sandra Harmany, founding member of AJA, 30 January 1993.

20. Mullen lost his seat as a result of legislative redistricting.

21. The following discussion concerning the impact made by legislative leaders and interest groups on the pro-life campaign in Pennsylvania in the early 1980s is based on Halva-Neubauer, "Legislative Agenda Setting," 295.

22. The altered provisions that the Court had struck down in *Planned Parenthood Association v. Fitzpatrick* included parental consent and state funding. See Halva-Neubauer, "Legislative Agenda Setting," 297–98.

23. The other main provisions of the 1981 act retained by the 1982 act included the second-physician rule for postviability abortions and restrictions on the performance of abortions in state-owned facilities. See Halva-Neubauer, "Legislative Agenda Setting," 304. The parental-consent provision of the 1982 act was addressed in *American College of Obstetricians and Gynecologists v. Thornburgh*, 737 F.2d 283 (1984), where the Court ruled it should remain enjoined until the Pennsylvania Supreme Court could write rules to protect the confidentiality of minors. See Court opinion, 297.

24. In *Thornburgh v. American College of Obstetricians and Gynecologists*, 476 U.S.747 (1986), the Supreme Court struck down provisions concerning informed consent, printed information, and reporting requirements for individuals, as well as those connected to physicians' responsibilities concerning viability, degree of care required in postviability abortions, and the second-physician requirement. See Court opinion, 758. See also Eva R. Rubin, *Abortion, Politics, and the Courts*, rev. ed. (Westport, Conn.: Greenwood Press, 1987), 148.

25. Halva-Neubauer, "Legislative Agenda Setting," 321–22.

26. Ibid., 324. *Webster v. Reproductive Health Services* 109 S.Ct. 3040 [1989].

27. Justice O'Connor first made this observation in her dissenting opinion in *City of Akron v. Akron Center for Reproductive Health, Inc.* 462 U.S. 416 (1983). See Rubin, *Abortion, Politics, and the Courts*, 143. See also Craig and O'Brien, *Abortion and American Politics*, 236–37.

28. Craig and O'Brien, *Abortion and American Politics*, 329.

29. The parental-consent provision, which was also upheld in *Casey*, was in the 1974 Abortion Control Act, but had been delayed for twenty years due to a series of legal challenges. *Planned Parenthood v. Casey* 112 S.Ct. 2791 (1992).

GLEN A. HALVA-NEUBAUER

2 | # Minnesota: Shifting Sands on a "Challenger" Beachhead?

Minnesota abortion politics is rife with paradox. In a state that adopted liberal policies, produced liberal luminaries such as Walter Mondale, Hubert Humphrey, and Donald Fraser, and led Gloria Steinem to quip that she spent more time doing feminist benefits there than in New York,[1] anti-abortion organizations and sentiment have flourished. Even before the 1973 *Roe v. Wade*[2] decision, Minnesota Citizens Concerned for Life (MCCL)—among the nation's oldest, largest, and most sophisticated state anti-abortion organizations—numbered 10,000 members. Between 1973 and 1989 (after *Roe* but before *Webster v. Reproductive Health Services*,[3] which granted states greater regulatory authority over abortion), the Minnesota legislature passed eleven abortion restrictions and anti-abortion resolutions.

In earlier work,[4] I classified the Minnesota legislature's response to *Roe* as that of a challenger. Challenger states were those that demonstrated the greatest antipathy to *Roe* by enacting restrictions that undercut the decision or implemented it in the narrowest form possible. Why Minnesota, the liberal lodestar, pursued a restrictive abortion policy is our initial paradox.

The second paradox is equally intriguing. Since the 1989 *Webster* case, Minnesota has passed no abortion restrictions. In fact, no significant constraint on abortion access has been enacted since the 1987 fetal-disposal law—the longest drought for MCCL in its twenty-six years. The legislature refused to include abortion on its 1989 special-session agenda and rejected a highly publicized "ban on birth control abortions" in 1990. Moreover, in 1993 the legislature passed clinic access legislation over MCCL's objection, while spurning that group's initiatives. While a peculiar set of circumstances brought an informed-consent bill to the floor of both houses in 1994, the bill ultimately failed. Since *Webster*, other challenger states (notably Louisiana, Utah, and Pennsylvania) have continued to pursue restrictive abortion policies. Curiously, Minnesota has not.

To unravel both paradoxes, we first discuss the state's abortion policy from the early 1960s to the present. Throughout that discussion, the role of political culture, interest groups, legislative leaders and governors, and electoral politics is examined. Second, we evaluate these explanations to determine what best accounts for North Star abortion policy. We then conclude by noting the importance of the Minnesota case for the study of state-level abortion politics and policy.

Abortion Policy in the North Star State, 1963–94

Despite a long history of hostility against *Roe*, Minnesota pursued a cautious approach toward abortion restrictions after 1989. This shift is the result of the changing fortunes of the state's abortion interest groups, the emboldening of pro-choice legislative leaders, and the election of a pro-choice governor in 1990. The story begins with how Minnesota established itself as a pro-life beachhead.

*Pre-*Roe *Deliberations: The Rise of MCCL*

Minnesota's progressive tradition and activist politics often led the state to be a policy innovator; therefore it was not surprising that the North Star State tackled the abortion issue in the early years of the contemporary debate. Unlike other innovative bellwethers (e.g., Colorado and California), however, Minnesota did not enact abortion reform legislation. Beginning in 1963 and reaching its apogee during the 1967 and 1969 legislative sessions, lawmakers considered bills that permitted abortions in certain cases: rape, incest, gross fetal abnormality, or when a board of physicians approved the procedure. After those efforts failed, pro-choice groups sought to repeal the state's abortion statute in 1971.

Interest groups provide the best explanation as to why Minnesota pursued a restrictive pre-*Roe* policy. In 1967 Minnesota was close to joining North Carolina, California, and Colorado in enacting the nation's first wave of reform laws. But opposition to reform legislation by the Minnesota Medical Association and the Catholic Church (approximately one-fourth of the state's residents are Catholics)[5] sank the bill during that session. A fledgling pro-choice group, the Minnesota Council for the Legal Termination of Pregnancy (MCLTP), could not counteract the opposition of those two groups.

Minnesota's penchant for enacting liberal policies (reinforced by the 1967 legislative discussions), coupled with the growing national movement for abortion reform, led to the formation of MCCL in 1968. With MCCL in place, the Catholic Church assumed a less visible presence in legislative deliberations. Yet

MCCL cannot take credit for the defeat of the 1969 legislation—it failed when those favoring repeal disrupted legislative hearings on a reform bill. That defeat, however, gave MCCL an additional biennium to organize the anti-abortion faithful.

Besides MCCL, another hallmark of Minnesota's abortion politics is scope of conflict. True to its issue-oriented political culture, the state's abortion debate was not confined to the legislature but was infused into electoral and party politics. In 1970, Senator Gordon Rosenmeier (Conservative-Little Falls),[6] chair of the Senate Judiciary Committee, was targeted by MCCL because he allowed the 1969 bill to be reported from that committee.[7] Abortion rights organizations, notably MCLTP, urged both the Democratic-Farmer-Labor (DFL) and Republican parties to support repeal of the state's abortion statute in their 1970 platforms. Although the DFL obliged, Republicans supported reform legislation. Legislators later would acknowledge that abortion foes were more successful in 1970 electoral politics than were their abortion rights counterparts.[8]

The defining moment of the period arrived during the 1971 session when MCCL hosted a dinner for legislators and their spouses. Orchestrated by a public relations firm, the gala was the first show of political sophistication by the anti-abortion movement. One veteran lawmaker claimed that the event was "the most massive and effective lobbying effort" he had witnessed during his tenure.[9] MCCL officials reported that approximately 125 legislators were in attendance and eight busloads of anti-abortion supporters came from greater Minnesota.[10]

Minnesota's reputation for open politics made it easy for the abortion issue to be discussed as well as for single-issue groups to form. While Minnesotans were not substantially more opposed to abortion reform than the nation as a whole, the state's political culture provided fertile ground for the expression of anti-abortion sentiment. Moreover, once the 1967 and 1969 bills failed, the scope of conflict could no longer be contained. The issue was not controlled by professional elites but was a debate among citizens organized at the grassroots level. Thus, abortion conjured up a more highly charged set of symbols than those encountered by legal and medical professionals.

The abortion issue gained significantly more attention in Minnesota than in some states where reform efforts were successful, notably Colorado and California. In Colorado, abortion reform was linked with former Colorado governor Richard Lamm (a first-year House member at the time), who carefully navigated the reform bill through the legislature. Colorado's debate was quiet in comparison with Minnesota's noisy, well-publicized dispute. The extensive media coverage prompted one early Minnesota anti-abortion activist to say, "There were prime-time television debates between McCoy [Robert McCoy, long-time abortion rights activist and a founding member of the National Abortion Rights Action League] and Marjory Mecklenburg [one of the founders of MCCL and first president of the National Right to Life Committee] in 1970."[11] This stood in stark contrast to the 1967 California debate, which received scant media attention.

Minnesota's nineteenth-century abortion law remained intact prior to *Roe*; the prowess of the pro-life movement in electioneering and lobbying tactics made it difficult for pro-choice supporters to succeed. To defeat MCCL in 1971 would have required an equally well organized pro-choice movement, the support of legislative leaders or the governor, or the existence of a legislative champion. While legislative leaders did not block the pro-choice movement's agenda, neither did they advance it. Moreover, unlike Colorado, North Carolina, and California, where individual legislators were associated with reform bills, no lawmaker emerged as a champion of abortion reform in Minnesota.[12] After *Roe*, however, legislative leaders would not always be hospitable toward MCCL's goals. It is to this story that we now turn.

Post-Roe *Deliberations: MCCL versus Legislative Leaders*

Following *Roe*, MCCL and committed anti-abortion lawmakers began pointed discussions with the federal judiciary over state regulation of abortion. Sixteen anti-abortion restrictions and resolutions were introduced in St. Paul between 1973 and 1989; eleven became law. While abortion foes won lopsided victories, the size of these votes belies the difficulty in moving legislation to the floor. At certain junctures, the anti-abortion movement faced hostile legislative leaders and committee chairs.

While the legislature passed a comparatively large number of abortion restrictions, Minnesota lawmakers did not adopt the more extreme versions of the pro-life agenda (for instance, calling for a constitutional convention on the Human Life Amendment). In general, MCCL did not advocate abortion restrictions that flew in the face of *Roe* or its progeny. In short, MCCL exhibited a strong pragmatic streak in dealing with the legislature. Consequently, anti-abortion bills not only passed but most were implemented (even though all were challenged in state or federal court).

The post-*Roe* era began when the 1973 legislature overwhelmingly passed a resolution condemning *Roe* and asking Congress to propose a Human Life Amendment. Such action was taken only after several members delivered stinging comments about MCCL and its tactics.[13] While passage of this resolution was a symbolic effort, lawmakers failed to enact any substantive revision of the state's abortion law.

In 1974 the legislative logjam was removed, and the state adopted its only comprehensive abortion law of the post-*Roe* period. The law was the first of many that would be challenged in state and federal courts. Among its many provisions, the law prohibited abortions after the fetus was potentially viable (defined as twenty weeks). If the fetus were potentially viable, an abortion was permissible only when necessary to preserve the life or health of the woman. In essence, the law proscribed abortions in the second half of pregnancy. The federal court invalidated that provision of the law along with several others in 1976.[14] After the Supreme Court's ruling in *Planned Parenthood of Central Missouri v. Danforth*,[15] which struck similar provisions of Missouri's abortion law, no attempt was made to reinstate the law.

In the mid-1970s, MCCL turned its attention toward initiatives that would curb public funding of abortions for indigent women. The issue already had been brewing because several county welfare boards refused to pay for abortion services even though the state required it. The debate reached its zenith in the summer of 1977 when the U.S. Supreme Court held that states were not required to pay for elective abortions.[16] In view of these events, MCCL proposed legislation permitting publicly funded abortions only when two physicians certified it necessary to save the woman's life and in cases of promptly reported (forty-eight hours) rape or incest.

To enact the public funding bill, MCCL squared off against Senator George Perpich (DFL-Chisholm), chair of the Senate Health and Welfare Committee, during the 1978 legislative session. Although Perpich blocked the MCCL-backed legislation in his committee, Majority Leader Nick Coleman (DFL-St. Paul) kept his word that the funding question would be debated on the Senate floor. Federal challenges to this law proved unsuccessful, and the law was implemented.[17]

Senator Perpich blamed MCCL for his brother Rudy's 1978 gubernatorial loss (even though Rudy opposed abortion).[18] As a result, the senator engineered the defeat of several pieces of anti-abortion legislation during the 1979–80 legislative session, the most important being an attempt to make abortion an optional rather than required service at health maintenance organizations (HMOs). After Perpich's retirement, the HMO bill passed in 1981.

In addition, the 1981 session produced the most litigated abortion statute in the state's history: parental notification. The law required that both biological parents of a minor seeking an abortion be notified within forty-eight hours of the abortion or that a judge waive that requirement if the minor were mature enough to make the decision on her own. MCCL hoped that the law would be deemed constitutional without the judicial bypass option (since the law required notification, not consent). The federal district court allowed the law to be implemented, but only with the bypass provision intact.

In 1986, the American Civil Liberties Union (ACLU) brought another suit against the law.[19] This time, the federal district court found the law in practice to be unconstitutional; however, this decision was reversed by the Eighth Circuit Court of Appeals.[20] In 1990, the U.S. Supreme Court agreed (5–4) with the appellate court that the law (with the bypass option intact) met constitutional muster.[21]

With a parental-involvement statute in place and public funding prohibited, abortion foes pursued more novel means to restrict abortions. During the 1980s, they did not challenge Supreme Court dictates directly but championed peripheral legislation designed to keep the issue alive in St. Paul. A statute prohibiting wrongful birth and wrongful life suits was enacted in 1982. Wrongful life suits are brought by children against their parents alleging that the parents should have aborted them; wrongful birth suits are brought by couples against physicians who failed to recommend medical tests (such as amniocentesis) that may have led the couple to choose abortion. This statute, challenged in Minnesota courts, was upheld by the state supreme court.[22]

Following a December 1985 ruling by the state supreme court that a fetus was not a person, hence could not be a homicide victim, lawmakers sought legislative relief. While abortion rights legislators attempted to make feticide a crime against the mother, abortion foes wanted the crime to center on the fetus. The pro-choice view held sway with the Senate Judiciary Committee, but a pro-life substitute was adopted on the floor. The bill passed despite attempts by Majority Leader Roger Moe (DFL-Erskine), a pro-choice sympathizer, to restore the original language. The law was challenged and upheld by the state supreme court.[23]

Legislation was introduced in 1987 calling for the humane and sanitary disposal of fetal remains after members of Pro-Life Action Ministries and Citizens for Community Action (both direct-action, anti-abortion organizations) displayed fetal parts allegedly found in a dumpster outside a suburban Minneapolis abortion clinic. The legislation passed by wide margins in both houses. In August 1987 the law was struck down, but it was reinstated by the Eighth Circuit Court of Appeals in 1990.[24] This bill represents the last significant piece of anti-abortion legislation passed in the North Star State.

While abortion foes clearly held the upper hand in St. Paul from 1973 to 1989, abortion rights advocates were organized and active throughout the post-*Roe* period. Led by the Minnesota Abortion Rights Council (ARC), successor organization to MCLTP, the pro-choice lobby favored legislation that restored Medicaid funding for abortion, regulated pregnancy counseling clinics, and condemned abortion clinic violence. While the effort to return Medicaid funding to its pre-1978 status was symbolic, the other two proposals were debated on the Senate floor. In 1987, ARC claimed that pregnancy counseling centers used deceptive practices to lure naive, confused clients into their facilities. ARC's legislation made counseling centers culpable for a variety of deceptive practices, such as falsely informing a woman she was pregnant. The bill failed on the Senate floor, 32–31.[25] In 1988 pro-choice forces scored their only post-*Roe* victory when the Senate passed (37–23) a resolution condemning abortion clinic violence. Nearly filibustered to death by pro-life senators, the measure was never entertained in the House. Nevertheless, it illustrated the changing fortunes of the pro-choice lobby.

On the eve of *Webster*, abortion foes were stymied in their effort to pass a fetal viability bill (similar to the provisions at issue in *Webster*) that would have restored portions of Minnesota's invalidated 1974 law. While the House approved the legislation, it languished in a hostile Senate committee.[26] Key committee chairs occupied by pro-choice sympathizers and a pro-choice majority leader assisted in blocking the pro-life agenda. Even so, 108 of Minnesota's 201 legislators signed a petition asking the U.S. Supreme Court to use the *Webster* case to reverse *Roe*.[27]

No other topic gained more prominence than abortion in Minnesota electoral and party politics during the post-*Roe* period. Precinct caucuses, political party conventions, and the ballot box became battlegrounds over the issue. Pro-life candidates generally were the victors. From the late 1970s to 1990, Minnesota's congressional delegation was dominated by pro-life sympathizers, and the anti-abortion contingent in the Minnesota House grew to 70 percent.[28] The success of abortion foes in the electoral trenches was attributed largely to MCCL's superior grassroots organization.

The abortion issue wreaked havoc on the DFL Party. In 1978 Minneapolis congressman Donald Fraser was defeated in the U.S. Senate Democratic primary by Robert Short, a Minneapolis businessman, DFL maverick, and pro-life supporter. In 1976 Minnesota's delegation provided more votes to Ellen McCormack (an anti-abortion presidential candidate) than any other state. Nor did Vice-President Walter Mondale's favorite-son status deter sixteen delegates from casting first-ballot votes for noted abortion foe Senator Thomas Eagleton (D-Mo.) at the 1984 Democratic National Convention.

Meanwhile, Minnesota Independent-Republicans (IR)[29] renounced their moderate abortion plank of the early 1970s and became more conservative on the issue. This change, brought about by the mobilization of Protestant evangelicals, left few social liberals in office by the mid-1980s. Those who did remain, such as Congressman Bill Frenzel, faced frequent criticism by party members.[30] Today, it is impossible for a pro-choice statewide IR candidate to gain the endorsement of his or her party.

The post-*Roe* period firmly placed Minnesota's abortion law in the anti-abortion category. Minnesota's affinity for abortion restrictions was achieved largely through the efforts of MCCL; tenacious, grassroots lobbying coupled with indefatigable electioneering made the group a formidable political power. Yet Minnesota also produced a strong, well-organized pro-choice movement. While the state passed many abortion restrictions, it did not go as far as other challengers. In part, this can be explained by the presence of committed pro-choice lawmakers who held key committee or other leadership positions. Pro-choice forces contributed as well. In short, while MCCL's successes were impressive, they were not achieved without important opposition. The post-*Webster* emboldening of pro-choice lawmakers, the mobilization of new pro-choice converts, and the election of Minnesota's first pro-choice governor, however, signaled the dawn of a new day in Minnesota politics.

Post-Webster *Deliberations*

Minnesota's failure to pursue the anti-abortion agenda aggressively in view of *Webster* poses a second paradox. MCCL, one of the pro-life movement's most respected state-level organizations, stood ready to steer a sweeping anti-abortion measure through the legislature, yet lawmakers balked. We focus next on the role of legislative leaders, elections, governors, and MCCL's lobbying tactics in accounting for the reluctance of Minnesota lawmakers to endorse the post-*Webster* anti-abortion agenda.

1989 Special Session

During the 1989 session, then-Governor Rudy Perpich vetoed a bill designed to provide property tax relief. A special session was needed to correct problems in the law. Even before the Supreme Court announced its *Webster* decision, MCCL lobbyist Jackie Schwietz acknowledged that her organization would push for additional abortion restrictions during the special session.[31] After *Webster*, MCCL representatives still appeared confident that the legislature would add abortion to the special session's agenda.

　　Governor Perpich, an abortion foe, refused to call a special session until an agreement was reached with legislative leaders regarding the abortion issue. Either the issue would not be considered or the language of new restrictions would be hammered out in advance. Senate Majority Leader Moe, an MCCL adversary, was opposed to any discussion of abortion restrictions during the special session. House Speaker Robert Vanasek (DFL-New Prague), an abortion foe who owed his speakership in part to MCCL support, eventually agreed to keep abortion out of the special session.

　　Pro-choice spokespersons claimed that a two-day special session did not provide sufficient time to consider new abortion restrictions. MCCL said such talk was merely a dilatory tactic. Just prior to the session's opening, however, MCCL announced that it would not pursue abortion restrictions at that time. Schwietz argued that new regulations would require hearings that could not be accommodated in the short special session.[32] With the governor and legislative leaders opposed to addressing the subject, MCCL realized that it could not obtain its goal. Whether pro-choice pressure superseded legislators' desire to avoid this issue during a special session remains unclear. In any case, MCCL's original position did not prevail.

1990: Banning "Birth Control" Abortions

The most celebrated legislative spectacle of the post-*Webster* era occurred in 1990 when MCCL introduced a measure banning "birth control" or convenience abortions. The bill limited abortions to cases of rape, incest, gross fetal abnormality, or when necessary to save the mother's life. Key legislators, such as Speaker Vanasek, believed that MCCL hurt its cause by refusing to circulate drafts of its bill before the session.[33]

Sponsor Senator Gene Waldorf (DFL-St. Paul), requested that the bill's hearing be canceled, since the addition of newly elected senator Carol Flynn (DFL-Minneapolis) to the Health and Human Services Committee stacked it in favor of pro-choice legislators. Waldorf wanted to postpone the hearing to explore other means of bringing the bill to the Senate floor. The Senate DFL caucus, however, refused Waldorf's request, providing further evidence of the growing hostility against the anti-abortion agenda in the Senate.[34] Anti-abortion organizations believed that the House Health Committee (with an anti-abortion majority) would report the bill to the floor. Such success would bring additional pressure to bear upon senators to consider the legislation. If, however, the bill stalled there, it was unlikely that a vote would come before the House.

Both Senate and House committees held hearings in late February 1990. Some 1,500 pro-choice supporters rallied on the Capitol steps prior to the House hearing. Throughout the day, opponents and supporters held impromptu rallies at the Capitol. A St. Paul columnist chronicled the day's events as a circus:

> . . . throngs of abortion partisans faced off in the hallways, chanting at each other. "Pro-life!" one side would chant. "Pro-choice!" the other side would retort. The spectacle resembled a beer commercial where the crowds chant, "Tastes Great!" or "Less Filling!" And it was about as meaningful.[35]

More significant was the Senate hearing. After six hours of testimony, the Health and Human Services Committee defeated the bill on a tie vote (8–8).[36] Senator Flynn's assignment to this crucial committee two weeks earlier had sealed the bill's fate. One analyst would later fault MCCL for not paying more attention to her appointment to that committee.[37]

House leaders had agreed not to schedule a committee vote until the legislation moved in the Senate; thus the bill appeared dead. Extraordinary measures to move the bill onto the Senate floor failed in that chamber's Rules Committee. Schwietz, MCCL's lobbyist, would later charge that IR members of the Rules Committee acted in concert with Majority Leader Moe to sink the banning of birth control abortions.[38]

1990 Electoral Politics

Political pundits believed that *Webster* would cause abortion to take on additional prominence at the 1990 precinct caucuses. Those predictions did not come true. The real fireworks came at DFL and IR endorsing conventions where several prominent pro-life DFLers, including Senator Waldorf, were denied party endorsement by pro-choice supporters;[39] and anti-abortion delegates to IR party conventions denied endorsements to six southeastern Minnesota incumbents, including Senate Minority Leader Duane Benson (IR-Lanesboro). Benson, a stalwart anti-abortion supporter, was denied endorsement for his role in stopping the birth control legislation from reaching the Senate floor. Following the endorsement meetings, Benson reacted angrily by calling Schwietz a "DFL hack" (referring to her role as a member of the DFL State Central Committee) and, along with other prominent IRs, called for her resignation as MCCL lobbyist.[40] Schwietz and Benson would later appear before a group of IR anti-abortion activists in Benson's district to clarify their differences. While Schwietz downplayed the importance of the dispute, Benson promised to work with MCCL as long as the group did not employ partisan tactics.[41]

Abortion also played an important role in the 1990 gubernatorial race. While the DFL endorsed Governor Rudy Perpich for an unprecedented fourth term, IR delegates chose Jon Grunseth, an executive with St. Paul–based Eco-Labs. Perpich easily defeated pro-choice Mike Hatch, commerce secretary and former DFL state party chair, in the September primary.

More intriguing was the IR race, where Grunseth, an anti-abortion proponent, faced two pro-choice supporters, Doug Kelley, a former federal prosecutor, and Arne Carlson, the state auditor. Carlson did not seek the IR endorsement because his pro-choice position made it impossible to secure the support of convention delegates. Carlson, however, was the only Republican state officeholder; polls indicated that he would trounce Grunseth in the September primary.[42] With an extraordinarily low turnout and an enthusiastic campaign organization, it was Grunseth who trounced Carlson. Anti-abortion forces were elated—both gubernatorial candidates were abortion foes.

To say the general election was unusual is an understatement. Grunseth, plagued by allegations of sexual impropriety, withdrew from the race with only fifteen days left in the campaign. Carlson then was named the Republican nominee. His narrow victory over Governor Perpich signaled a change in the abortion position of the state's chief executive officer. For the first time since 1973, Minnesota abortion rights advocates had a committed pro-choice governor. In addition, pro-choice Paul Wellstone defeated U.S. Senator Rudy Boschwitz, a popular, well-funded, anti-abortion incumbent.

Abortion advocates claimed that the elections laid to rest the notion that a pro-choice candidate could not win a statewide contest. Schwietz argued that the election had little to do with abortion. She claimed that Lieutenant Governor Marlene Johnson's pro-choice position had hurt the Perpich ticket.[43] Tracking polls showed that middle-ground abortion supporters (those morally opposed to abortion but who believe it is a decision best left to the woman and her family) gave their support to Carlson in the waning days of the campaign. Exit polls indicated that abortion played a greater role in the Carlson/Perpich race than in the Wellstone/Boschwitz election.[44]

The 1991–92 Session: Legislative Stalemate

In 1991 pro-choice organizations went on the offensive while MCCL pursued a defensive strategy. The election of Governor Carlson and changes in the Senate's membership favorable to pro-choice supporters made the 1991 legislature more hostile toward MCCL's goals. Hence the roles of abortion proponents and opponents became reversed.

At the beginning of the session, pro-choice organizations unveiled a package of proposals designed to prevent rather than prohibit abortion. These proposals included increasing state funding for family planning services, revamping the parental notification statute, funding abortions for indigent women, and codifying the principles of *Roe* into state law.[45] Only legislation amending the state's parental notification law generated significant attention.

Sponsored by Senator John Marty (DFL-Roseville), the "trusted adult" bill altered the parental notification law to permit abortions when the minor notifies a trusted family member (parent, grandparent, cousin, etc.) or seeks counseling from a psychiatrist, psychologist, practical nurse, minister, or clinical social worker.[46] Marty's legislation was tabled in a Senate committee. An amended version requiring only one-parent notification, but containing a bypass provision, was reported from that committee. The amended bill failed on the Senate floor.

The legislative stalemate continued during the 1992 session. Each side could block the opponent's initiatives, but not pass its own. As long as the House remained solidly anti-abortion, a pro-choice governor and sympathetic Senate leaders could not enact the abortion rights agenda. The Senate Health Committee did report a Freedom of Choice Act in 1992, but it was not debated on the Senate floor. Few anti-abortion initiatives were even introduced during the 1991–92 session.

1992: Pro-Choice Victories

The 1992 campaign season saw significant internal squabbles over the abortion issue in both parties. Anti-abortion DFLers sent five delegates to the national convention after having no representatives in 1988.[47] DFL state convention delegates waved "pro-choice" placards during pro-life Eighth District Congressman James Oberstar's address. Senator Don Frank (DFL-Spring Lake Park), again denied endorsement in his district, epitomizes the difficulty in securing party support as an anti-abortion DFL candidate. During the campaign season, several prominent anti-abortion DFLers switched from a pro-life to a pro-choice stance, notably Congressmen Gerry Sikorski and Bruce Vento.[48]

Pro-choice IRs fared no better. Long-time Rochester senator Nancy Brataas was denied party endorsement by IR abortion foes for the second time.[49] And as a result of Governor Carlson's support of abortion rights, a resolution expressing appreciation for him was tabled by convention delegates in southwestern Minnesota.

Fall elections brought the Senate within a few votes of having a pro-choice majority. Pro-choice leaders announced they had thirty-two solid votes in the sixty-seven-member Senate. A concerted effort by abortion rights groups to win in suburban districts yielded significant victories. MCCL representatives noted that many pro-life members had resigned and that the 1991 redistricting plan adopted by the legislature placed many others in hostile districts.[50]

1993–94: Carpe Diem

Despite pro-choice victories in the 1992 elections, the House remained in the hands of abortion opponents. The stalemate that characterized the 1991–92 session seemed destined to remain intact for another two years.[51] The status quo was altered, however, when Operation Rescue (a militant, direct action, anti-abortion group that blocks entrances to abortion clinics) revealed it would hold a training session in the Twin Cities during summer 1993. Operation Rescue's announcement created an opportunity for pro-choice lawmakers and organizations to enact legislation protecting access to abortion clinics;[52] this legislation had been introduced in the 1991–92 session, but had not received serious attention.

MCCL opposed the bill, saying it restricted free-speech rights. The legislature disagreed and made it illegal to interfere physically with people entering or leaving medical facilities, including abortion clinics.[53] Pro-choice forces had seized the moment. Ironically, Operation Rescue provided the impetus pro-choice forces needed to pass this legislation.

MCCL found that proposals it favored, especially informed-consent legislation with a twenty-four-hour waiting period (validated in *Planned Parenthood of Southeastern Pennsylvania v. Casey*)[54] received scant attention from lawmakers in 1993. It now appeared that pro-choice advocates could not only block pro-life initiatives but occasionally pass their own legislation. As the 1994 session convened, most political observers thought the year would yield little action on the abortion conundrum.

Conventional wisdom held true until the last month of the session when the House appended an informed-consent proposal onto a welfare reform bill. This provision required women seeking abortions to wait twenty-four hours after receiving information from a physician about alternatives to abortion, fetal development, and risks associated with abortion. Women or their partners were allowed to sue physicians who failed to provide such information.[55] The amendment passed, 82–50, amid familiar charges that MCCL, rather than lawmakers, was running the House.

Pro-life forces also capitalized on a changing environment. Election-year politics, especially those surrounding the governor's race, were shaping House members' behavior. Governor Carlson was facing a serious challenge from former representative Allen Quist (IR-St. Peter), a champion of socially conservative issues. Quist garnered significant support in IR precinct caucuses; as a result, many House members, particularly Republicans, were anxious to appease his followers. Not only did the House pass an abortion restriction, it also advanced legislation promoting silent prayer in school, protecting gun ownership, banning flag burning, and prohibiting promotion of homosexual behavior in schools.[56]

Even more important, a socially conservative Democrat, Representative Irv Anderson (DFL-International Falls), had replaced pro-choice representative Dee Long (DFL-Minneapolis) as House Speaker. While Long would have determined that the anti-abortion amendment was not germane to the welfare reform bill, Anderson deemed otherwise.[57] Without his ruling, the informed-consent initiative would not have advanced.

Speaker Anderson, too, seized the day. Known for his rabid partisanship, Anderson may have favored the informed-consent proposal because it would create additional strain between Carlson and social conservatives.[58] The bill placed the governor in an awkward position—alienate his pro-choice supporters or estrange himself from the Christian Right. Continued squabbling in the IR party could only benefit the DFL gubernatorial candidate.

On the Senate side, Majority Leader Moe attempted to steer the bill to a conference committee where the abortion provision could be deleted. Despite the tradition of resolving differences in major pieces of legislation in conference, senators voted 34–33 to accept the House version and send the bill to Governor Carlson.[59] Election-year politics also may have influenced this vote. Several anti-abortion DFL senators who normally would be expected to vote with Moe were running for governor; hence the chance to place an anti-abortion bill on the governor's desk also may have affected their decisions. It now appeared that MCCL had seized the moment.

That moment passed quickly, however. After the Senate's decision, Senator Linda Runbeck (IR-Circle Pines) asked that the vote be reconsidered. Two days later, Runbeck and seven other IR senators changed their previous votes, thus tabling the legislation.[60]

Several IR senators (including Senator Joanne Benson [IR-St. Cloud], Carlson's running mate) crafted a compromise proposal that removed physician liability as well as allowed ancillary clinic personnel to provide the required information. Meanwhile, Attorney General Hubert H. Humphrey III stated that the legislation would not meet *Casey*'s undue burden standard. While Governor Carlson said he would sign the revised version into law, MCCL vehemently opposed such a compromise. The diluted version of the bill was rejected overwhelmingly, 47–19.[61] Hence, in the end, no legislation reached the governor's desk.

One long-time observer of Minnesota politics noted that the Republican proposal on informed consent probably reflected public opinion in Minnesota. Nevertheless, MCCL was thought to oppose any legislation deviating from the
language crafted by its Washington, D.C., attorneys. In short, MCCL appeared
more interested in advocating legislation designed to obtain a specific legal
challenge than in passing an informed-consent bill.[62]

Minnesota's reluctance to enact further abortion restrictions after 1989 is
explainable. Even before *Webster*, the Senate was becoming less receptive to
MCCL-backed initiatives; the ruling only hardened the resolve of that chamber's
pro-choice contingent and gave Majority Leader Moe greater ability to block the
anti-abortion agenda. Moreover, Moe's position was strengthened by the election
of a pro-choice governor and senators following the 1990 and 1992 elections.
Failure of informed-consent legislation to win final approval during the 1994
session, however, illustrates the independent impact of the governor. Without
Carlson (or another pro-choice chief executive) in office, Minnesota would have
enacted an informed-consent law.

MCCL's hardball tactics after 1989 do not account for its failure to win
approval for the anti-abortion agenda. From its inception, MCCL has been controversial. Its problems with IR senators and some anti-abortion lawmakers come
at a time when the pro-choice movement has its largest contingent of supporters
ever. Despite the charges made against Schwietz and the organization, MCCL
successfully maneuvered the 1994 informed-consent bill onto the floors of both
houses. Even in its weakened state, MCCL continues to be a player in Minnesota
politics—it still controls the pro-life legislative agenda. In the next section we
investigate interest-group politics as well as other explanations for the dynamics
of North Star abortion politics.

Explaining Minnesota's Abortion Policy and Politics

Minnesota has displayed amazing fluidity in its abortion policy. In the late
1960s, it appeared poised to pass reform legislation; from the early 1970s to the
late 1980s, Minnesota's status as a "challenger" was well established; currently,
the state has pursued an ambiguous policy that leans pro-choice. We examine the
role of political culture, legislative leaders and governors, and interest groups as
factors that offer the greatest explanatory power in accounting for Minnesota's
abortion policy and politics.

Political Culture

Political culture, the notion of which was formulated by Daniel Elazar in the mid-
1960s, has long been a standard independent variable in comparative state politics
literature. Elazar argues that a state's politics are a function of the political orienta-

tion of the original settlers; hence, political culture shapes the conception of politics and governance in a particular state. He classifies Minnesota as having a moralistic political culture by virtue of its Yankee and Scandinavian heritage. In such cultures, politics is viewed as a positive force in people's lives, is issue oriented, and its political parties are dominated by amateurs.[63] In sum, politics in moralistic cultures is devoted to discussions of what constitutes the "good life."

Political culture helps us to understand the Minnesota story. Elazar notes that Minnesota is the consummate exemplar of moralistic political culture. He argues that Minnesotans accept the "legitimacy, efficacy, and desirability of politics."[64] The acrimonious, prolonged abortion debate in Minnesota's politics and the issue's infusion into its political parties seem consistent with the state's political culture. The state's citizens have faith in finding a political solution to most problems, even those considered seemingly irresolvable. It is little wonder that people on both sides of the issue seek governmental solutions to the abortion question. Typically, political culture helps explain political behavior—in this case, why political parties became forums for the abortion debate (even before *Roe*) and why the state is a breeding ground for abortion activists. Likewise, the persistent salience of the abortion issue among the state's electorate is consistent with moralistic political culture: campaigns are substantive and voters focus on issues more than party labels.

Culture is less good at explaining policy outcomes. Moralistic states have pursued a variety of abortion policies, from being supporters of *Roe* to staunch opponents of the decision. Such a finding is not surprising; in theory, moralistic political culture can account for a state's pursuit of either restrictive or liberal abortion policies. The fundamental theoretical problem is predicting what a moralistic culture's pursuit of the good society demands. Does it protect what some consider to be the most vulnerable members of society—the unborn—or does the good society protect individual liberties, including those associated with abortion?

Minnesota vacillates between these two perspectives. Until recently, it was solidly in the anti-abortion camp, but it now appears to be assuming an individual liberties stance. In addition to being less willing to regulate abortion, the 1993 legislature enacted a gay rights statute. Therefore, the swinging of the pendulum indicates the ambiguity that "hot button" issues create for moralistic cultures. Such ambiguity is accentuated by the support socially conservative issues (flag burning, gun control, school prayer) received during the 1994 session.

Legislative Leaders and Governors

A second explanation for Minnesota's abortion policy focuses on a much narrower concern: the abortion position legislative leaders and governors hold. Scholars have noted the profound affect leaders have in shaping legislative agendas.[65] Leaders can provide a sympathetic ear, display hostility, or show neutrality toward an issue. Their willingness to lend support to an issue may catapult it into the legislative limelight.

Legislative leaders (including committee chairs) played an important role in Minnesota's abortion story, particularly during the post-*Roe* and post-*Webster* periods. No legislative leader stands out as an enthusiastic supporter of the anti-abortion cause, but many leaders did vote pro-life. More important, however, is that without legislative leaders (especially in the Senate) who opposed the anti-abortion agenda, Minnesota may have passed more stringent policies. Legislative leaders were a major obstacle to overcome. Until Governor Carlson took the helm in 1991, Minnesota chief executives played a small role in abortion policymaking. All were abortion foes, with only Albert Quie (1979–83) being ardently pro-life. Carlson's promise to veto anti-abortion legislation has made it much more difficult to generate enthusiasm for restrictive abortion proposals. Indeed, his failure to support MCCL's version of the 1994 informed-consent bill was the singularly most important reason the legislation did not pass.

The hostility of Senate leaders, particularly Majority Leader Moe, provides the greatest support for the leadership hypothesis. Moe's predecessor, Senator Nick Coleman, also had been unwilling to lend much support to the anti-abortion agenda. While Coleman did ensure a debate on the 1978 funding bill, he refused to quell Senator Perpich's furor against MCCL during the late 1970s; the anti-abortion agenda languished as a result. In his early days as majority leader, Moe did not use his power to block MCCL-backed initiatives. Over time, however, he became increasingly hostile toward the anti-abortion cause. The fetal viability bill died in 1989 largely as a result of his lack of support.

After 1989, Moe became an ardent pro-choice proponent. Most state capitol observers credit his pro-choice zeal for the legislature's failure to enact abortion restrictions soon after *Webster*. Yet Moe's power was not always so sweeping. In the mid-1980s, a pro-life feticide bill passed despite his objections. With the growing number of pro-choice senators following the 1990 and 1992 elections, Moe had even more power to block anti-abortion bills; one anti-abortion senator said that only three members of the DFL caucus listed abortion as a high priority for the 1991 session.[66]

Moe has significant influence over the Minnesota legislative process because of the institution's relatively short session. Among a leader's most important duties is to control the flow and pace of bills—in short, to set priorities. The pressure to consider priority legislation severely limits the number of discretionary measures that can be heard. A bill that will consume many hours and is likely to fail is not a good use of time. Hence the failure of legislative leaders to recognize an item as a priority is an important obstacle for a bill's proponents to overcome. MCCL found that a sympathetic leader, such as Speaker Anderson, could have a profound impact on its ability to move legislation—his decision to allow the informed-consent amendment to be added to the welfare reform bill was a major coup for the group.

During the post-*Roe* period, legislative leaders opposed to MCCL achieved limited success in controlling the abortion agenda. They did block legislation on several occasions, which likely had the effect of making MCCL increasingly cautious in its proposals. Moreover, these leaders made it more difficult for MCCL to enact its agenda than might otherwise have been the case. As Moe became more hostile toward MCCL, he appeared willing to use his power to obstruct the group's initiatives.

The leaders/governors hypothesis appears to have validity in explaining the Minnesota case. Hostile or supportive legislative leaders can make a difference, but they cannot transform an overwhelmingly supportive legislature into a hostile one. Moreover, when determining its legislative priorities, MCCL was aware of the power that leaders held. Since 1989, the election of a pro-choice governor and senators has amplified a trend begun several years earlier—an emboldened Senate majority leader willing to take on MCCL.

Interest Groups

Throughout this chapter and the abortion politics literature, the role of interest groups has been well documented. In Minnesota, no analysis of abortion politics can be made without an extensive examination of MCCL. In this section we are especially interested in charting changes in interest-group tactics that may explain why Minnesota has not continued to be an anti-abortion haven in the post-*Webster* era.

Grau's 1987 survey of Minnesota legislators and lobbyists found MCCL to be one of the most effective lobbies in the state. MCCL is given especially high marks for its work at election time.[67] Only Missouri's pro-life organization was found to command such stature among a state's interest groups. While the political culture explanation offered earlier helps to account for the rise of MCCL, it does not reveal why the group was unable to take advantage of the *Webster* decision. Two tactical reasons may account for MCCL's failure.

One explanation is that MCCL may have worn out its welcome in the statehouse. A bitter fight over a living-will bill in the 1989 session resulted in passage of legislation that was not acceptable to MCCL. Many legislators, including anti-abortion sympathizers, were angry at MCCL over its uncompromising attitude. Schwietz, MCCL's lobbyist, was the subject of legislative criticism for her use of coercive tactics during the 1990 "birth control" debate. She not only took on rank-and-file members but challenged Senate IR leaders as well. In her defense, Schwietz said that MCCL was only asking legislators to carry out their pledges to the group. Why, then, were members surprised to be asked to support an MCCL-backed measure that would significantly reduce the incidence of abortion?[68]

Criticism also was lodged against Schwietz from inside the pro-life movement. Two legislators thought that MCCL wielded too much control over the pro-life agenda.[69] One implied that MCCL could use some competition, since it operated largely as an anti-abortion monopoly. The organization should not be considered the final word on what was pro-life, but needed to recognize the efforts of legislative supporters as well. These concerns were raised indirectly during the 1994 debate: Why should MCCL's version of informed-consent legislation be the only one considered? Was MCCL more concerned about garnering national attention for its innovative legislation or passing a bill that would place restrictions on abortion? Such concerns from lawmakers lead to our final point: the limits of a grassroots movement.

MCCL's strong grassroots base is undoubtedly a great strength, but it also may be contributing to its current fall from grace. While MCCL consults with lawmakers and briefs them on its legislative proposals, the group largely determines the agenda for a specific session. Anti-abortion legislators, therefore, play a less prominent role in abortion policymaking than does MCCL. No one in St. Paul speaks about the importance of a given anti-abortion lawmaker; rather, interviewees acknowledge the strength of Schwietz or MCCL. The failure to develop a strong, independent, legislative champion may have led to the demise of the anti-abortion agenda in recent years.

Of the explanations investigated for the shifting sands of North Star abortion policy, the most compelling evidence concerns the importance of legislative leaders and governors. The landscape of Minnesota abortion policy may have looked very different if lawmakers hostile toward the pro-life movement had not occupied key committee and leadership positions (witness the change in policy with Speaker Anderson). MCCL clearly has been the moving force behind abortion restrictions in St. Paul, but it has often had to fight a leadership opposed to or uninterested in its agenda. The election of a pro-choice governor in 1990 provided an additional barrier (and a particularly important one) for the anti-abortion movement—it had not faced such an obstacle during its history.

While MCCL may have committed tactical errors during the past six years, that does not adequately account for the legislature's failure to pass abortion restrictions. The virulence of the leadership's opposition, more than MCCL's gaffes, has led to the ambiguous course of abortion policy since *Webster*. The 1994 session provides an especially important piece of evidence to support this statement. Finally, while political culture offers an explanation for the fluid nature of Minnesota's abortion policy, it better accounts for why the state is a hotbed for abortion activism.

Conclusion

For more than three decades, Minnesota lawmakers have navigated the turbulent waters of abortion policy. The state has pursued policies that, at first blush, appear paradoxical. Why a state with a liberal tradition also would be a leader in enacting restrictive abortion policies puzzles most political analysts. If, however, one considers that the state's activist culture spawns movements of many political orientations (including a significant pro-life movement), the legislature's actions become more understandable.

The legislature's retreat from its historical opposition to *Roe* largely has been orchestrated by legislative leaders and solidified by the election of a pro-choice governor. Pro-choice mobilization after *Webster* has not been inconsequential—undoubtedly, it has assisted in electing more pro-choice senators—but the growing impatience of the Senate leadership with MCCL predates *Webster*. The threat to abortion rights posed by that decision required and received a firm response from legislative leaders. As a result, the anti-abortion agenda has stalled in Minnesota. This is not to say that the state will not return to its anti-abortion predilections. A change in the Senate leadership, the election of an anti-abortion governor, or the rise of a committed legislative champion could alter MCCL's fortunes. The 1994 session may be a harbinger of renewed anti-abortion sentiment or an election-year fluke. Nevertheless, the key variables to consider in assessing the case remain unchanged.

The Minnesota story wonderfully illustrates the dynamic nature of abortion policymaking. By analyzing this case over a thirty-year period, we see how changes in key variables, such as legislative leaders, governors, and interest-group tactics, can reshape abortion policy. While the decisions reached in the late 1960s set the stage for subsequent action, they did not dictate Minnesota's future abortion regulations. Examining abortion policymaking in other challenger states that pursued ambiguous post-*Webster* courses (e.g., Missouri and Illinois) will test the generalizability of ideas discussed in this chapter. Such an investigation will allow us to see if there has been a shifting of sands or a full-scale erosion on challenger beachheads.

Notes

The author wishes to thank Tim Byrnes for his helpful comments on this essay and Jeanine Halva-Neubauer, as always, for her editorial expertise.

1. Gloria Steinem, "Barnstorming on Feminist Air Force One," *Ms.*, December 1981, 79–86.

2. 410 U.S. 113 (1973).

3. 492 U.S. 490 (1989).

4. Glen A. Halva-Neubauer, "Abortion Policy in the Post-*Webster* Age," *Publius: The Journal of Federalism* 20 (Summer 1990): 27–44.

5. John Kelly, "Abortion Reform Gaining," *St. Paul Pioneer Press*, 24 January 1968.

6. Minnesota's legislators were elected on a nonpartisan ballot until 1972, but caucused as Conservatives or DFLers (also known as Liberals).

7. "Abortion as a Campaign Issue," *Minneapolis Tribune*, 22 October 1970.

8. Finley Lewis, "Abortion-Reform Backers Cautioned," *Minneapolis Tribune*, 24 February 1971.

9. From *The Guardian*, MCCL Southern Minnesota Regional Office Newsletter, February 1971, found in the MCCL file, Katherine Wood Taylor Papers, Minnesota Historical Society.

10. Howard Erickson, "Legislators Wooed by Foes of Abortion," *Minneapolis Tribune*, 13 January 1971.

11. Confidential interview, 15 August 1981.

12. Jain and Hughes credit the leadership of Assemblyman Anthony Beilenson (D-Los Angeles) for the success of abortion reform in California. See Sagar C. Jain and Steven Hughes, *California Abortion Act 1967: A Study in Legislative Process* (Chapel Hill, N.C.: Carolina Population Center, 1968).

13. Robert Whereatt, "Bill Urging Amendment to Ban Abortion Gains," *St. Paul Pioneer Press*, 22 March 1973.

14. *Hodgson v. Lawson*, 542 F.2d 1350 (1976).

15. 428 U.S. 52 (1976).

16. *Beal v. Doe*, 432 U.S. 438 (1977); and *Maher v. Roe*, 432 U.S. 464 (1977).

17. *Hodgson v. Board of Commissioners, Hennepin County*, 614 F.2d 601 (1980).

18. Gerry Nelson, "To Senator Perpich, the MCCL Is Not Too Formidable a Foe," *St. Paul Pioneer Press*, 2 November 1979.

19. *Hodgson v. Minnesota*, 648 F.Supp. 756 (1986).

20. *Hodgson v. Minnesota*, 853 F.2d 1452 (1988).

21. *Hodgson v. Minnesota*, 497 U.S. 417 (1990).

22. *Hickman v. Group Health Plan, Inc.*, 396 N.W.2d 10 (1986).

23. *State v. Merrill*, 450 N.W.2d 318 (1990).

24. *Planned Parenthood of Minnesota v. Minnesota*, 910 F.2d 479 (1990).

25. Sharilyn Bankole, "Bill Addresses Deceptive Pregnancy Counseling," *Minnesota Daily* (Minneapolis), 26 February 1987.

26. Gregor W. Pinney, "Bill to Curb Abortions of 'Viable' Fetuses Unlikely to Pass," *Star Tribune* (Minneapolis), 19 May 1989.

27. Gregor W. Pinney, "Most Legislators Urge Overturning of *Roe v. Wade*," *Star Tribune* (Minneapolis), 21 April 1989.

28. Linda Kohl, "Abortion Opponents Keep Legislators in Line," *St. Paul Pioneer Press and Dispatch*, 6 April 1986.

29. Since 1975, Minnesota Republicans have referred to themselves as Independent-Republicans, believing that the new name would help them to garner support among the significant number of Independents in the state's electorate.

30. Beth Spring, "Born-Again Minnesotans Play Political Hardball," *Christianity Today*, 21 September 1984, 68–70.

31. Jack B. Coffman, "Abortion Foes Eye Special Session," *St. Paul Pioneer Press Dispatch*, 7 June 1989.

32. Jack B. Coffman, "Anti-Abortion Group Drops Special Session Plan," *St. Paul Pioneer Press Dispatch*, 23 September 1989.

33. Kurt Chandler, "Abortion Bill Introduced; Vanasek Doubts Its Chances," *Star Tribune* (Minneapolis), 13 February 1990.

34. Kurt Chandler, "DFL Caucus Overrides Sponsor, Wants Hearing on Abortion Bill," *Star Tribune* (Minneapolis), 27 February 1990.

35. Nick Coleman, "Abortion Circus Full of Clowns," *St. Paul Pioneer Press and Dispatch*, 1 March 1990.

36. Jack B. Coffman, "Restrictive Abortion Bill Defeated," *St. Paul Pioneer Press Dispatch*, 1 March 1990.

37. Kurt Chandler, "Abortion Battle Lost before Session Began," *Star Tribune* (Minneapolis), 1 March 1990.

38. Kurt Chandler, "Jackie Schwietz's Fight against Abortion Leaves Little Room for Subtleties," *Star Tribune* (Minneapolis), 14 April 1990.

39. Dan Oberdorfer, "DFLers Refuse to Endorse Waldorf," *Star Tribune* (Minneapolis), 2 April 1990.

40. Jack B. Coffman, "Benson Latest Victim of 'Abortion Politics,' " *St. Paul Pioneer Press*, 25 April 1990.

41. Jack B. Coffman, "Benson, Schwietz Patch Up Abortion Differences," *St. Paul Pioneer Press*, 23 May 1990.

42. Bruce Orwell, "Politicians Declare Opinion Polls the Loser in Primary Elections," *St. Paul Pioneer Press*, 13 September 1990.

43. Jack B. Coffman, "Effect of Abortion-Rights Stands in Elections Disputed by Activists," *St. Paul Pioneer Press*, 8 November 1990.

44. Kurt Chandler, "Abortion Rights Advocates Claim Support of Voters," *Star Tribune* (Minneapolis), 8 November 1990.

45. Kurt Chandler, "Abortion-rights Activists Offer Sweeping Proposals," *Star Tribune* (Minneapolis), 9 January 1991.

46. Kurt Chandler, "Abortion Agenda Includes Notification Law, Funding," *Star Tribune* (Minneapolis), 7 March 1991.

47. Jack Coffman, "Anti-Abortion DFLers Gain Five National Delegates," *St. Paul Pioneer Press*, 8 June 1992.

48. Nick Coleman, " 'Evolution' in Abortion Politics Can be Sudden, Dramatic," *St. Paul Pioneer Press*, 25 February 1993.

49. Jack B. Coffman, "Abortion Issue Heats Up; Battles Brewing within Minnesota Party Ranks," *St. Paul Pioneer Press*, 28 June 1992.

50. Jack B. Coffman, "Abortion-Rights Groups Claim Gain in Elections," *St. Paul Pioneer Press*, 5 November 1992.

51. Jack B. Coffman, "Usual Fireworks Expected to End in the Usual Stalemate," *St. Paul Pioneer Press*, 3 January 1993.

52. Jack B. Coffman, "Senate Bill Sets New Penalties for Blocking Clinics," *St. Paul Pioneer Press*, 1 May 1993.

53. Kurt Chandler, "Clinic-Access Bill Clears Senate, 41–24," *Star Tribune* (Minneapolis), 1 May 1993.

54. 112 S.Ct. 2791 (1992).

55. Jean Hopfensperger, "Abortion Foes Get Victory in House," *Star Tribune* (Minneapolis), 13 April 1994.

56. John Myers, "Conservatives See Trend in Victories in the Legislature," *St. Paul Pioneer Press*, 14 April 1994; and Dane Smith, "It's Premature to Say Conservative Tilt Will Leave Mark," *Star Tribune* (Minneapolis), 14 April 1994.

57. Confidential interview, 24 May 1994.

58. Confidential interview, 24 May 1994; and Hopfensperger, "Abortion Foes."

59. Dennis J. McGrath, "Senate OKs Abortion Restriction, Holds It for Tinkering," *Star Tribune* (Minneapolis), 15 April 1994.

60. Jack B. Coffman, "Senate Shelves Abortion-Waiting Bill," *St. Paul Pioneer Press*, 16 April 1994.

61. Jack B. Coffman, "Senate Defeats Diluted Abortion Bill," *St. Paul Pioneer Press*, 27 April 1994.

62. Confidential interview, 24 May 1994.

63. Daniel Elazar, *American Federalism: A View from the States*, 3rd ed. (New York: Harper & Row, 1984).

64. Daniel J. Elazar, "A Model of Moralism in Government," in *Minnesota in a Century of Change*, ed. Clark E. Clifford, Jr. (St. Paul: Minnesota Historical Society, 1989), 329–59.

65. John Kingdon, *Agendas, Alternatives, and Public Policies* (Boston: Little, Brown, 1984); and Jack Walker, "Setting the Agenda in the U.S. Senate: A Theory of Problem Selection," *British Journal of Political Science* 7 (October 1977): 423–45.

66. Confidential interview, 1 March 1991.

67. Craig H. Grau, "Minnesota: Labor and Business in an Issue-Oriented State," in *Interest Group Politics in the Midwestern States*, ed. Ronald J. Hrebenar and Clive S. Thomas (Ames: Iowa State University Press, 1993), 145–64.

68. Chandler, "Jackie Schwietz's Fight."

69. Confidential interviews, 1 March 1991 and 4 March 1991.

ELIZA NEWLIN CARNEY

3 | Maryland: A Law Codifying *Roe v. Wade*

If we can have a decisive victory for this bill in Maryland it will put the issue behind us, not only in Maryland but nationwide. It will be a test of public sentiment. And in that sense, whether or not it survives the Supreme Court, the Roe v. Wade concept will be adopted in the vast majority of our states.

—Maryland State Senator Howard A. Denis

When the Maryland General Assembly passed a ground-breaking law in 1991 that guaranteed a woman's legal right to an abortion, state legislators had one grueling political battle behind them and another yet to come. The law, which essentially codified the Supreme Court's 1973 *Roe v. Wade* ruling that legalized abortion, was passed only after an eight-day filibuster in 1990 that became one of the most divisive stalemates in state history. No sooner had Democratic governor William Donald Schaefer signed the bill into law on 18 February 1991 than it was petitioned to a referendum by a well-organized coalition of abortion foes. What followed was a high-dollar lobbying battle on the scale of a major electoral campaign.

In theory, a state as heavily liberal and Democratic as Maryland should have had little trouble passing an abortion rights bill. In fact, abortion opponents were surprisingly successful at setting the legislative agenda in Annapolis and defining public opinion statewide. The fireworks surrounding the abortion issue in Maryland from 1990 to 1992 were sparked largely by two key factors: the influence of the Catholic Church and the increasing sophistication of anti-abortion lobbyists. In a trend reflected nationally, Maryland's Catholic hierarchy renewed its anti-abortion activism, responding in part to weak leadership from traditional pro-life groups.

At the same time, anti-abortion organizers in Maryland experimented with a new, more moderate image. Repeating a strategy that had been successfully tested in other states, the legislation's opponents claimed to support abortion rights in general, but painted Maryland's new law as an extremist exception.

Ultimately Maryland voters upheld the abortion rights bill, which appeared on the ballot as Question 6, by an impressive 62–38 percent margin. Despite heavy spending by the anti-abortion "Vote kNOw Coalition," which poured some $3 million into its campaign to defeat the bill, abortion rights advocates retained the upper hand. In part, the so-called Maryland FOR Choice coalition proved that nothing beats an old-fashioned, get-out-the-vote campaign. While the Vote kNOw Coalition was bankrolling sensational television ads and billboards, Maryland FOR Choice was knocking on doors, leafleting county fairs, recruiting volunteers, and working the polls on election day.

More important, the referendum's outcome reflected where Maryland voters had stood all along: in favor of abortion rights. The real lesson taught by Maryland's referendum is that public opinion is not as ambiguous as many polls would indicate. Maryland voters have long been and are likely to remain abortion rights advocates. Even the Vote kNOw Coalition's slogan—Make Them Get It Right—appeared to acknowledge that the group was forcing its views on the Maryland electorate.

As it unfolded in the backyard of the nation's capital, the Maryland referendum was carefully watched by political leaders bracing for larger-scale battles over abortion. In 1993 Congress yet again took up the Freedom of Choice Act, a bill that mirrored the Maryland law in its attempt to codify *Roe v. Wade*. Lawmakers also struggled over whether to include abortion services in the Clinton administration's national health-care plan. In many ways, the fight over Question 6 provided a microcosm—and a preview—of upcoming national abortion debates.

The Maryland referendum also offered a glimpse of what other states will be up against as pro- and anti-abortion rights bills continue to test public opinion. In Maryland, many legislators who fought abortion rights in 1990 were voted out of office. In Maryland as elsewhere, a strong anti-abortion platform remains a risky stance for state legislators seeking reelection. What follows is an account of one of the stormiest chapters in Maryland's political history and a look at how the new law changed the terms of the statewide abortion debate.

Maryland: Liberal Voters, Liberal Laws

Maryland's political landscape positioned the state as an ideal candidate to test abortion rights legislation. The state's history of religious and racial tolerance is matched by a diverse population that runs the gamut from white-collar workers in Washington's upscale suburbs to crab fishermen on the Chesapeake Bay.[1]

Democrats dominate among registered voters, in part reflecting the state's sizable black population—just under 25 percent in 1992.[2] (This percentage is the highest in any state outside the Deep South.)[3]

With Democrats boasting 61 percent of registered voters, compared with 29 percent Republicans,[4] it is not surprising that Governor Schaefer has enjoyed consistent popularity and a dominant role in state politics since his election in 1986. Democrats Paul A. Sarbanes and Barbara A. Mikulski also have strong statewide support. Sarbanes beat his Republican opponent, Alan L. Keyes, with 62 percent of the vote in 1988. In 1992 Keyes challenged Mikulski with even less success; she won 71 percent of the vote.[5]

Maryland's Democratic predelictions also have surfaced clearly in presidential elections throughout the 1980s. In 1984 Walter Mondale won 47 percent of the vote compared with Ronald Reagan's 53 percent.[6] Four years later, Maryland missed picking Michael S. Dukakis by a hair; he won 48 percent of the vote, compared with George Bush's 51 percent.[7] Bill Clinton won 50 percent of the vote in Maryland in 1992, compared with 36 percent for George Bush and 14 percent for Ross Perot.[8] Clinton's strong showing in Maryland was topped only in the District of Columbia and in his home state of Arkansas.[9] Clinton's popularity in Maryland was to become an important factor in tilting voters toward Question 6.

Not surprisingly, given their party leanings, Maryland voters tend to voice views supportive of abortion rights. Polls taken in 1989, the year of the Supreme Court's landmark *Webster v. Reproductive Health Services, Inc.*, ruling, show that Maryland was fertile territory for activists seeking a state guarantee for abortion rights. One poll by Columbia, Maryland–based Mason-Dixon Political/Media Research showed that 54 percent of Marylanders surveyed described themselves as "pro-choice," 35 percent said they were "pro-life," and 11 percent were "not sure." A much larger number—64 percent—agreed with the statement: "During the first three months of pregnancy, the decision to have an abortion should be left entirely to a woman and her doctor." (Twenty-eight percent disagreed, and 9 percent said they were not sure.)[10]

By contrast, only 29 percent of American voters surveyed by the Gallup Organization in July 1989 said that abortion should be legal under any circumstances. Fifty-one percent said abortion should be legal only under certain circumstances, and 17 percent said it should be illegal in all circumstances.[11]

More important, poll results showed that a majority of Marylanders disagreed with the Supreme Court's *Webster* ruling, which gave states greater leeway to restrict abortion rights. Some 55 percent of respondents told Mason-Dixon in a separate 1989 poll that they disapproved of the *Webster* ruling. (Thirty-five percent approved and 10 percent were not sure.)[12] Maryland NARAL took full advantage of voters' anxiety about *Webster*, arguing that the state needed a law to guarantee abortion rights in case the Supreme Court overturned *Roe v. Wade*.

Maryland has a history of initiating laws that were less restrictive of abortion than the national norm. In 1968, five years before the *Roe* ruling legalized abortion, Maryland passed a law that allowed abortions in cases of reported rape, severe fetal deformity, or when a woman's life or health was in serious danger.[13] At the time, the Maryland law was hailed as a liberal, national model. With the passage of *Roe*, the 1968 law was declared unconstitutional. But political leaders pushing for a new, more permissive law in the post-*Webster* era issued dire warnings that this 1968 statute would spring back into place if *Roe* were over-turned. Ironically, Maryland's once liberal law was decried as draconian and overly stringent two decades after its passage.

Maryland did pass three somewhat restrictive abortion statutes in the 1970s. A 1975 law forbade abortion referral agencies to receive fees, or "kickbacks," for referring women to abortion providers. This law was nullified by a later Maryland statute that outlawed medical referral fees of any kind. A parental notification law passed in 1977 was found unconstitutional and never enforced because it contained no provision for a bypass, such as approval from a judge. A third law passed in 1979 required that a woman seeking an abortion must receive a pamphlet in advance, informing her of such alternatives as adoption. A key provision of Question 6 was that it repealed this "information before abortion" law.

In 1989 Maryland became a pace setter again, approving the nation's first clinic-access bill.[14] Adopted in response to escalating clinic violence statewide, the bill protected legal access to all medical facilities. Four years later, House and Senate leaders introduced the Freedom of Access to Clinics Entrances Act, a bill that again applied the principles of the Maryland statute on a national scale.[15]

Maryland's most ground-breaking abortion legislation was the abortion rights law signed by Governor Schaefer in 1991. That law, which essentially barred the state from interfering with a woman's decision to have an abortion in the early stages of pregnancy,[16] dominated Maryland politics for three years, from 1989 to 1991. Known simply as Senate Bill 162 (SB162), the 1991 law made and broke political careers; it dragged the state Senate through its most bitter political showdown; and it sparked a multimillion-dollar lobbying fight.

From Prayers to PACs: A Bill Painfully Becomes Law

The year 1989 had both promise and peril for the abortion rights movement in Maryland. On the plus side for abortion rights advocates, Maryland NARAL, the state affiliate of the National Abortion Rights Action League, was riding high. Under the leadership of Karyn Strickler, a gifted grassroots organizer who took the helm of the organization in 1986, membership grew from 700 to 12,000 over a six-year period. Emphasizing frequent fund raisers and high-profile media events such as an emotional "speak out" by Maryland women who said they had been harmed by restrictive abortion laws, Strickler launched a grassroots drive that picked up steam following the *Webster* ruling.

Planned Parenthood of Maryland also anchored the abortion rights community by spearheading a statewide coalition dubbed Marylanders for the Right to Choose. The group, which now represents some eighty organizations, was founded in the early 1980s to lobby for greater access to Medicaid-funded abortions. (Language added to Maryland's annual budget in 1978, and made more stringent in 1981, requires women to meet one of four fairly narrow medical conditions before receiving Medicaid funding for an abortion.)[17]

Also favoring the abortion rights camp was nominal representation by the Maryland Right to Life Committee. Preoccupied by presidential politics, the state's affiliate of the Washington, D.C., National Right to Life Committee did not even open a full-time office in Annapolis until 1992—well after the SB162's passage was all but certain. On the flip side, the Maryland Catholic Conference was emerging as an aggressive and visible anti-abortion player. Headed by long-time Catholic lobbyist Richard J. Dowling, the Annapolis-based conference would lead a vigorous charge against Question 6 in 1992.

In the meantime, abortion rights activists turned to two prominent female state senators—Barbara A. Hoffman (D-Baltimore) and Paula C. Hollinger (D-Baltimore County)—to champion abortion reform. In 1990 Hoffman and Hollinger cosponsored an early version of the abortion rights bill that sought in simple terms to codify the principles of *Roe.*

Though a vote count showed majority support in both the House and Senate, tepid support from two key Democratic leaders paved the way for a legislative fiasco. Adopting an unusual stance, Schaefer refused to take a public position on the issue of abortion. Senate president Thomas V. ("Mike") Miller, Jr., also failed to endorse the Hoffman-Hollinger bill, attempting to remain neutral. A devout Catholic, Miller had personal reasons for trying to remove himself from the fray. He also miscalculated the abortion issue's political potency; before the 1990 legislative session opened, Miller told the *Baltimore Sun* that abortion was just not going to be an issue.[18] He was wrong.

Anti-abortion Republican senators, urged on by a small but hardy community of pro-life activists, took full advantage of this leadership void. When the bill was introduced in March 1990, it passed the House with ease but met quickly with a filibuster on the Senate floor. Sixteen senators joined forces to block action on the bill. The remaining thirty-one members of the Senate voted to cut off the filibuster, but they were one vote short of the two-thirds majority needed for an override.

The filibuster dragged on for eight days, tearing the Senate apart and stopping work on all other legislation. With each day, tempers got shorter, the theatrics got more extreme, and the name-calling got uglier. Calling the shots for the anti-abortion side was Dowling, of the Maryland Catholic Conference, who barely left his Annapolis office during the course of the filibuster. Dowling took some heat from Senate leaders who questioned whether the church should have such a loud voice in the legislature, but he showed no sign of intimidation. "The bill which we're opposing is testimony to why we need to be involved," Dowling said at the time. "From the moral point of view, it's an outrage."[19]

An intense and vocal band of anti-abortion organizers effectively set the tone for the Senate debate, contributing to what some legislators called an almost cultlike atmosphere in Annapolis. The leadership of this fluid, grassroots network was not obvious at the time, but it undoubtedly included Clifford J. Gannett, a Bowie, Maryland–based activist affiliated with Operation Rescue, and Alan L. Keyes, a former Republican senatorial candidate who had helped organize three "March for Life" protests in Annapolis early in the year. (Gannett later headed CARAL, the Committee against Radical Abortion Laws, which lobbied against Question 6.)

With prayer vigils and "survival packages" of food sent in for pro-life senators, these activists helped drive a wedge between opposing Senate camps. On St. Patrick's Day, they sent in cupcakes decorated with fake fetuses. Exacerbating the tension was an anti-Semitic undertone. As Jewish women, Hoffman and Hollinger found themselves painfully singled out. On day 7, Maryland senators came to work to find a sensational leaflet comparing abortion to the Holocaust on their desks. The leaflet, which featured photos of corpses piled at concentration camps, bore a Taylor, Arizona, post office box number and the name of a mysterious group called The Precious Feet People.[20]

"It was perhaps [during] my 15 years in the legislature, the lowest point of my career," Hollinger later said of the filibuster. "It took the Senate a long time to heal."[21]

Maryland Jewish organizations were deeply offended. So were the voters. The filibuster tainted the public's view of the Maryland Senate and had heavy political fallout. The Senate ended its 1990 session with no consensus on abortion. (Senators had adopted an eleventh-hour compromise measure that was loaded down with amendments and died in the House.) In statewide elections later that year, abortion rights advocates moved aggressively to capitalize on public disgust.

Maryland NARAL entered the 1990 election season with a clear mandate: to create a filibuster-proof "supermajority" in the state Senate. The group set up a political action committee (PAC) to target three anti-abortion senators who had helped lead the filibuster: Margaret C. Schweinhaut (D-Montgomery), Frank J. Komenda (D-Prince Georges), and S. Frank Shore (D-Montgomery). Shore had clowned his way through the filibuster, turning up each day in the same plaid suit and brandishing a football to dramatize his role in what he dubbed "the super bowl for life."[22]

A separate Baltimore abortion rights group dubbed Choice PAC, headed by former Planned Parenthood lobbyist Steve Rivelis, targeted Senator Francis X. Kelly (D-Baltimore County), a key filibuster leader. Choice PAC backed Janice Piccinini, the popular former head of the state teachers union, who campaigned largely on an abortion rights platform to defeat Kelly in the Democratic primary.

NARAL's primary candidates fared equally well. House Delegate Patricia R. Sher won her primary challenge against Schweinhaut with two-thirds of the vote. Delegate Gloria Gary Lawlah narrowly defeated Komenda in the Democratic primary. And Delegate Mary Boergers won by 2–1 over Shore.[23] Like Piccinini, all three Democratic winners had made abortion a central campaign theme. Abortion rights candidates were helped by some $40,000 in contributions from Choice PAC, and another $50,000 from Maryland NARAL, according to the groups' leaders.

Despite these primary wins, the sought-after supermajority was never achieved. In the general election, Democratic incumbent Senator Edward Kasemeyer, an abortion rights advocate, lost to Republican pro-life challenger Christopher J. McCabe. In raw numbers, abortion rights groups were little better off than they had been in 1990. In political terms, however, the elections had a decisive impact. "What we had created was a perception [among state legislators] that you could be next," said Strickler, of Maryland NARAL. "Any one of you could, in fact, be defeated on the abortion issue."[24]

Maryland Democratic leaders got the message. Schaefer broke his long silence soon after the elections, announcing that while he personally deplored abortion, he opposed government intrusion and endorsed the passage of abortion rights legislation. Senate President Miller also underwent a conversion, making the passage of a bill that guaranteed abortion rights his number-one priority in 1991.

What caused the Catholic Miller to reverse his position after twenty years as a pro-life legislator? Perhaps it was the fact that his family, including his five children and his mother, all lobbied him to support the abortion rights bill. (As Miller's chief of staff John R. Stierhoff put it: "Mike listens to his Mom.")[25] Perhaps it was the embarrassment of watching a gut-wrenching filibuster disrupt order in the Senate under his watch. Perhaps it was the calculated pragmatism of a politician with one eye on the governor's mansion.

Whatever the reason, Miller became the prime architect of the Senate's abortion rights bill in 1991. Miller personally lobbied every member of the Senate and defused the gender issue by placing the bill in the hands of Senate Majority Leader Clarence W. Blount (D-Baltimore), Deputy Majority Leader John A. Pica, Jr. (D-Baltimore), and Senator Walter M. Baker (D-Cecil).[26] The bill's previous female sponsors took a back seat. "If you care about the issue, you get out of the firing line," said Hoffman at the time.[27]

Maryland abortion rights lobbyists also made important concessions to smooth the bill's passage. Maryland NARAL and others had strenuously opposed a parental notification clause in 1990, but relaxed their opposition in 1991. The final version of Senate Bill 162 required parental notification for minors seeking an abortion, with the caveat that a doctor may waive the notification requirement if a minor is mature enough to offer "informed consent" or if notification is not considered to be in her best interests.[28]

The bill's backers also acknowledged that the parental notification clause would help the bill survive a referendum challenge, which was widely regarded as inevitable. According to political science professor Herbert C. Smith at Western Maryland College in Westminster, this was a savvy move. In an April 1990 poll, Smith stated:

> During the debate in the Maryland State Senate, pro-choice legislators amended the omnibus bill to include a parental consent provision. In light of our survey findings, this was prudent. A 63 percent statewide majority would support such a limitation. This illustrates the cross-pressuring nature of this most emotional public policy to many citizens. While many support choice in abstract or even an applied sense, a considerable proportion would impose conditions and limits to abortion policy.[29]

As it turned out, SB162's supporters did well to appease Maryland's more moderate voters. The bill passed both the House and Senate with little controversy, less than halfway through the legislative session. Yet Schaefer's signature was barely dry when the bill's opponents petitioned it to a referendum. Anti-abortion forces gathered close to 144,000 signatures in a three-week period in 1991—more than four times the 33,000 they needed to get it on the ballot.

Both sides approached the referendum as a critical test of American abortion policy. It was the first such referendum since the Supreme Court's June 1992 ruling in *Planned Parenthood of Southeastern Pennsylvania v. Casey* that set a new standard for state abortion restrictions, namely that they could not place an "undue burden" on women seeking abortions. Question 6 was also one of only two state proposals in 1992 that asked voters to decide on abortion. (The other was an Arizona ballot initiative seeking to ban all abortions except in reported cases of rape and incest or when the mother's life was in danger; see Chapter 5.) For Maryland Democratic leaders who had ushered the bill through, the real test had just begun.

The Maryland Referendum: A Matter of Definition

A visitor walking into the Vote kNOw Coalition's offices in Columbia, Maryland, in 1992 would have seen no clue associating the group with the Catholic Church. The subdued decor included anti-abortion messages but no Christian icons or literature. "We really are just a bunch of people who have come together for this issue," insisted communications director Frederica Mathewes-Green in an interview several weeks before the referendum. Mathewes-Green said the group was spawned by several Bowie-based lawyers who came together because SB162 is "frankly so bad" that "even thoughtful, pro-choice people are not comfortable with it."[30] While the Vote kNOw Coalition's core staff was not necessarily Catholic—Mathewes-Green, for example, has a Master of Theological Studies from the Virginia Episcopal Theological Seminary in Alexandria— the vast bulk of the group's budget came from Catholic Church fund raising.

In addition to Mathewes-Green, the group's most visible leader was executive director Ellen Curro, the former head of a postabortion counseling service based in Washington, D.C., called Project Rachel. Curro and Mathewes-Green worked hard to promote the group's image as a grassroots, pro-woman organization out to protect young women's best interests. The group deliberately cultivated a friendly, homespun image by keeping its political operatives in the background, according to one Vote kNOw insider. As the group's press secretary Tom Berriman told a reporter at the time, "We are cash poor and people rich."[31]

As it turned out, the Vote kNOw Coalition had plenty of cash. The coalition's primary vehicle for communicating with voters was an affiliate organization called the Pro-Life Education Foundation, which received a steady infusion of funds from Catholic dioceses in the Baltimore/Washington region. A Mother's Day collection at Catholic churches statewide pulled in some $216,000 for the anti-abortion cause.[32] On the weekend of 12–13 September, some 300 Catholic churches statewide took up a second collection just for the Vote kNOw Coalition, raising considerably more than on Mother's Day, according to Dowling, who declined to give an exact figure. (Conveniently, Dowling was also chairman of the Vote kNOw Coalition.)

In one sense, Catholic leaders saw little alternative but to take the lead. The Maryland Right to Life Committee had virtually disengaged itself from the referendum battle. The group did not help gather signatures to put SB162 on the ballot and had no budget set aside for the referendum campaign. Though Maryland Right to Life distributed several thousand brochures and church program inserts on Question 6, the group did not work at all with the Vote kNOw Coalition. The reason, said executive director Roger Stenson, was that the Maryland Right to Life needed to devote all its resources for George Bush's reelection campaign.

"The most important issue in Maryland and in any other state in the country right now is the reelection of President Bush," said Stenson at the time. "If we lose him, we lose the whole world. And it doesn't matter what we do on the referendum if we lose a pro-life president."[33]

A key element of the Vote kNOw Coalition's strategy was to eschew the inflammatory, baby-killer rhetoric of traditional activist groups, opting instead for a middle-of-the-road message aimed at moderate voters. Vote kNOw carefully distanced itself from CARAL, the Coalition Against Radical Abortion Laws, which represented a group of anti-abortion activists who had cut their teeth on pickets and clinic blockades—what CARAL's leader Clifford J. Gannett dubbed "direct intervention."

CARAL eventually invested some $50,000 in the campaign against Question 6—a pittance compared with the close to $3 million spent by Vote kNOw. Still, CARAL rustled up between 200 and 300 volunteers to drop anti–Question 6 literature at homes throughout the state and conducted a limited ad campaign on local cable television and radio stations. CARAL also carried out a voter identification and registration drive, a traditional grassroots networking tactic that was largely missing from the Vote kNOw campaign.

The heart of Vote kNOw's message, which according to Dowling was defined with the help of political consultants who had worked on anti-abortion campaigns in other states, was that the coalition was not actually anti-abortion, but simply objected to extremist measures in Question 6. In sophisticated videos and television ads, the group argued that Question 6 provided "no effective parental notification" because doctors could use their discretion to bypass the parental consent requirement.

The coalition portrayed Question 6 as removing protections for young women because it did not require health and safety regulations for clinics. (In fact, the bill did empower the state to adopt such regulations.) Vote kNOw also criticized Question 6 for repealing Maryland's 1975 law banning kickbacks for abortion referral agencies. (Abortion rights groups said these arguments were misleading, since the bill required licensed physicians to perform abortions, and all medical referral fees are illegal in the state.) Notwithstanding, Vote kNOw's literature painted a dire picture of what would happen to Maryland if Question 6 became law:

> This law positions Maryland as an aggressively pro-abortion state, ready to attract industry driven out of abortion-free states, with guarantees of civil and criminal protection that will be tempting to abortionists in trouble elsewhere. With no health or safety regulations for clinics, and all barriers removed to profitable "counseling" services which funnel women in, the industry will be drawn to our state like a magnet.[34]

According to Mathewes-Green, the Vote kNOw Coalition took no official position on *Roe v. Wade*. Pressed for their own views, however, Vote kNOw members typically denounced the *Roe* ruling. Mathewes-Green, for example, admitted that she "would like eventually to see there be laws that protected unborn life."[35]

Maryland abortion rights leaders were highly critical of the Vote kNOw Coalition's approach. Jim Guest, president of Planned Parenthood of Maryland, called them "wolves in sheep's clothing." Maura Keefe, who became communications director for a pro–Question 6 coalition, summed up the Vote kNOw campaign this way:

What we are seeing happening here is a revived political strategy on the part of the pro-life movement. What they are doing, and it's very clever, is that they are going after what we call the "mushy middle" by saying, "We are pro-choice too, but this is a bad law and it goes too far."[36]

Question 6 advocates were unnerved by the Vote kNOw Coalition's approach, but they were not unprepared. Maryland abortion rights groups had watched with alarm the outcome of a similar referendum in Washington State in the fall of 1991 (see Chapter 8). Despite polls showing that 75 percent of Washington State voters supported abortion rights, a statewide abortion rights measure was defeated on election night and squeaked by only after absentee ballots were counted, with a margin of just 4,222 votes.[37]

Anticipating an uphill fight, abortion rights groups joined forces in a statewide coalition dubbed Maryland FOR Choice. The chair was Jim Guest, head of Planned Parenthood of Maryland. Members of the Steering Committee included Maryland NARAL, the Maryland State Teachers Association, and the American Civil Liberties Union of Maryland. More than fifty religious, education, and health-care groups signed up as endorsing organizations or members of the coalition's leadership council. This broad-based network gave Maryland FOR Choice a solid fund-raising base and gave the group access to a diverse array of Maryland voters. For both sides, the Baltimore region was crucial; some 50 percent of Maryland voters still live within the traditional boundaries of the greater Baltimore metropolitan area.[38]

Like the Vote kNOw Coalition, Maryland FOR Choice hired professional consultants to help define its message. These included Democratic pollster R. Harrison Hickman, of Hickman-Brown Research in Washington, D.C., and Washington media consultant Carter Eskew. Eskew had helped backers of a Maryland gun-control law survive a similar referendum challenge in 1988. Not unlike the Vote kNOw Coalition, the National Rifle Association had spent millions on what turned out to be a fruitless campaign to defeat the law. Eskew helped Maryland FOR Choice boil its message down to a simple slogan that proved effective with voters: "Privacy, Safety, Choice."

Maryland FOR Choice also hired Stacie Spector, a Democratic political consultant who had extensive experience on statewide electoral and issue campaigns, to run the coalition. In addition to fund raising and advertising—the group eventually invested $1 million in television, radio, cable television, and newspaper ads—Spector established an impressive grassroots organizing network. An early strategy was neighborhood "house parties"—Maryland FOR Choice organized 126 of these in a single week after the *Casey* ruling in July—to inform voters about the referendum. The "house parties" also helped the coalition identify a pool of volunteers for help later in the campaign. On election day, Spector estimated, some 7,000 to 10,000 volunteers turned out to man the polls and lobby for Question 6.

Maryland FOR Choice also set up phone banks to target and identify voters sympathetic to abortion rights. This voter identification drive allowed Maryland FOR Choice to mail literature to the undecideds and to call voters back on election day to remind them to vote. The group also blanketed the state with appearances at flea markets, county fairs, festivals, and concerts. In addition, Maryland FOR Choice drummed up publicity by tag-teaming with numerous abortion rights legislators, including Senator Mikulski and Representative Constance Morella (R-Md.). An important ally as the election approached was the state's Democratic Committee, which recommended a vote *for* Question 6 on its sample ballot.

Fund raising was also nonstop, including a $500-a-plate dinner hosted by Planned Parenthood of Maryland in honor of feminist author Gloria Steinem; based on turnout, the dinner raised a minimum of $20,000. Maryland FOR Choice ultimately spent some $2 million on the Question 6 campaign.

Notwithstanding, polls taken as the referendum approached showed public support for Question 6 slipping. Between July and October 1992, the number of voters who told pollsters they would vote for Question 6 dropped from 71 percent to just 51 percent.[39] For a time, it appeared that Vote kNOw Coalition was defining the message more effectively than Maryland FOR Choice. Vote kNOw started its television advertising earlier, the group's yard signs were everywhere, its press conferences incessant. Maryland pollsters also issued warnings that voters tend to vote no on referenda, since there is a natural inclination to support the status quo.

A high point for Vote kNOw came in early September when Dr. Ben Carson, a well-known pediatric neurosurgeon from Baltimore, appeared in an anti–Question 6 television ad. "Let us be understanding and kind," Carson told television viewers. "But let us not be duped." The ad generated considerable attention, in part because as a black physician Carson was in a unique position to reach black voters, considered by both sides to be a key constituency.

Ironically, the Ben Carson ad turned into a major embarrassment for the Vote kNOw Coalition. Pressured by colleagues to explain his position more fully, Carson called a press conference on 1 October, in conjunction with Maryland FOR Choice, to revise his stance. "My intention was not to make a campaign commercial and, in fact, I did not understand that the tag-line 'vote against Question 6' would be included in the ad," Carson said in a prepared statement. Carson concluded by stating: "My message is not to vote 'for' or 'against' Question 6, but to educate yourself."[40]

Two major Baltimore television stations also challenged the wording of the ad, in which Carson had stated that the law "fails to provide any health or safety regulation, it legalizes profit making referral fees, and physicians would not have to notify parents." WMAR (Channel 2), an NBC affiliate, asked Vote kNOw officials to change the text that flashed on the screen to read "Parental notification, up to doctors' discretion," instead of "No parental notification." At ABC affiliate WJZ (Channel 13), station managers pulled the spot entirely after a short time on the air because of the reference to referral fees. "To the best of our knowledge, those referral fees are illegal under existing law," said station vice-president and general manager Marcellus W. Alexander in a statement.[41]

The Ben Carson ad soon disappeared from the airwaves (Vote kNOw officials said the spot had simply run its course), but some political observers said the damage had been done. "It came at a really critical . . . juncture," said Stierhoff, of Miller's staff. "And it made the anti-abortion people look like liars, in part."[42] Maryland FOR Choice was quick to accuse Vote kNOw of deliberately confusing the issue, and apparently some voters agreed. At least one anti–Question 6 flier was potentially misleading. The flier, which warned, among other things, that Question 6 "takes away your right to a safe abortion," claimed to be put out by a group called "Marylanders For Safe Choices"—a name strikingly similar to that of the Maryland FOR Choice coalition.

The last two weeks of the campaign proved crucial for the Question 6 camp. Money was freed up for a flurry of television ads, the phone banks began to work their magic, and on election day the polls were swarming with Question 6 supporters. By contrast, the Vote kNOw Coalition was virtually invisible on election day. According to one Vote kNOw insider, the group was following the advice of consultants to keep abortion rights activists away from the polls. "Absence of political experience on our side was detrimental," Dowling admitted later.[43]

Also tilting the balance toward Question 6 was solid support from political leaders statewide. Democratic lieutenant governor Melvin A. Steinberg, a staunch abortion rights supporter, traveled around the state to receptions, public events, and grassroots meetings to stump for Question 6. Mikulski, Morella, Schaefer, and many others endorsed it. Two highly visible black leaders—Baltimore mayor Kurt L. Schmoke and Democratic congressional candidate (now Representative) Albert Wynn—endorsed Question 6 in the crucial constituencies of Baltimore and Prince Georges County.

In the end, Question 6 won in forty-four out of forty-seven state legislative districts, with the highest margins in Baltimore and Montgomery counties. (These awarded the initiative 77 and 78 percent of the vote respectively.)[44] The 62–38 margin in favor of Question 6 placed Maryland solidly in the forefront of states that support abortion rights. The referendum's passage made Maryland one of only four states to guarantee abortion rights in the early stages of pregnancy, the others being Connecticut, Nevada, and Washington State.

Both sides had lobbied furiously to define the terms of the debate. As it turned out, many Maryland voters had their minds made up from the start. "The right-to-lifers were trying to swim against the current of Maryland politics and Maryland opinion," said Herbert Smith of Western Maryland College. "And the numbers just weren't there for them."[45]

After the Referendum: Abortion Politics
in Maryland Today

Did the passage of Question 6 help the abortion rights movement in Maryland? Ironically, the answer is no. Just as the election of Bill Clinton as the first pro-choice president in twelve years has put national abortion rights groups on the defensive, the success of Question 6 has shifted the balance of power in Maryland abortion politics. (Clinton's election appears to have left many Americans under the impression that abortion rights are no longer at risk in the United States. At the same time, national groups like NARAL face a greater challenge than ever as the abortion debate moves beyond simple questions of legality to more complex issues such as federal funding and parental consent.)[46]

Similarly, Maryland abortion rights advocates, who have renewed their fifteen-year campaign to relax restrictions on Medicaid-funded abortions, face an electorate that sees little urgency in the abortion issue. "We are finding that the people who voted for Question 6 really felt like they were 'fixing' this,"[47] said Gloria A. Totten, the new executive director of Maryland NARAL. State legislators, too, are eager to put the abortion debate behind them. In Maryland, as elsewhere, notes former Democratic state senator Catherine I. Riley, who left office in 1991, many lawmakers simply want the abortion issue to go away. Says Riley: "Most politicians fear an abortion debate more than any other issue there is. Because there is no convincing the other side. And compromise is extremely hard to find."[48]

At the same time, the success of Question 6 has reinvigorated Maryland's anti-abortion movement, which is better organized than ever. As soon as the Vote kNOw Coalition closed down, its leaders organized a transition group with an eye toward forming a statewide anti-abortion coalition. What emerged was a younger, more politically savvy cadre of anti-abortion activists that held several statewide meetings in the summer of 1993 and elected two delegates to represent the group from each of Maryland's forty-seven legislative districts. The group, which is supported by the Maryland Catholic Conference and serves as an umbrella organization for some twenty anti-abortion groups throughout the state, has set out to increase anti-abortion representation substantially in both the state House and the Senate.

Given modest Republican gains statewide in 1992, the anti-abortion movement may well find itself on firmer political territory in coming years. (Republicans in Maryland won three county executive posts and two close congressional races in 1992.)[49] Given legislators' painful memories of the 1990 filibuster and 1991 Senate races, however, dramatic shifts in Maryland's abortion politics appear unlikely in the near term.

For abortion rights advocates, the Maryland referendum cleared the way for a new agenda that includes unrestricted Medicaid funding for poor women seeking abortions and reproductive health coverage for women. This once again positions Maryland as a potential leader in terms of challenging the limits of abortion rights legislation.

Maryland's role in promoting ground-breaking abortion rights legislation was illustrated clearly in 1993 when the state legislature moved to include a full range of reproductive services for women, including abortion, in its health-care reform package. In another parallel to national politics, the Maryland legislature passed a health-care reform bill aimed at improving care for employees at small businesses.[50] Responding to concerns that employees at small businesses were being squeezed out of the health-care system, the legislature required that Maryland businesses with fifty workers or fewer offer a standard benefits package at low cost. (The package may cost no more than 12 percent of the average Maryland worker's salary.)

As in the debate over President Clinton's proposed Health Security Act, the abortion question placed a potentially controversial stumbling block in the path of health-care reform. Based on their experience with the 1992 abortion referendum, however, state lawmakers were not eager to reopen the abortion debate. The legislature adroitly sidestepped this issue by establishing a seven-person Health Care Access and Cost Commission charged with determining which benefits the plan should cover. Maryland lawmakers were thus able to approve a health-care bill without getting bogged down in benefits controversies, including abortion coverage.

The commission, then, became the target of lobby groups wanting to keep abortion in or out of the benefits package. Again, Governor Schaefer proved helpful to abortion rights advocates, appointing what turned out to be a largely pro-choice roster of members to the commission task force dealing with abortion. (It should be noted, however, that Schaefer picked only one of the candidates recommended by abortion rights groups, and his other appointments were not necessarily driven by abortion considerations.)

Led by two Planned Parenthood affiliates serving Maryland and the Greater Metropolitan Washington area, abortion rights advocates brought a host of witnesses before the commission to argue that abortion should be included in the standard benefits package. Their premise was virtually identical to that forwarded by advocates pushing for reproductive coverage in President Clinton's plan. That is, most private insurers cover abortion already, so leaving it out would effectively rob women of an existing service; and abortion is properly seen in the context of overall reproductive health, including contraceptive, prenatal, and baby care.

While Maryland's Catholic leaders also produced witnesses to argue against abortion coverage, their campaign was less aggressive than it had been during the Question 6 referendum. Catholic organizers may also have been hurt by their position that standard benefits should not cover family planning. For Maryland abortion rights advocates, the passage of a health-care package that included abortion, along with an impressive range of gynecological services, was a significant victory.

In Maryland, as on Capitol Hill, the vocabulary of the abortion debate is changing. For the recently renamed National Abortion and Reproductive Rights Action League and for other abortion rights groups, the new rallying cry is adequate health care for women. The standard political debate over legality has been replaced with a call for comprehensive reproductive health coverage, with equal weight given to abortion, contraception, prenatal care, and other women's health services.

Whether this strategy proves effective nationally remains to be seen. Unlike the Maryland legislature, the U.S. Congress is far from reaching a consensus on the abortion issue. Despite the election of a pro-choice president, abortion advocates failed in 1993 to secure passage of the Freedom of Choice Act, which effectively would have codified *Roe v. Wade*, or to overturn the Hyde amendment, which bars public funding for poor women seeking abortions. These losses bode poorly for the inclusion of abortion services in a national health benefits package, and reflect the renewed strength of the anti-abortion lobby in the wake of Clinton's election.

If national health-care reform fails to guarantee reproductive services for women, it will represent a serious setback for the abortion rights movement. (Once resolved, the national health-care reform debate will not be revived in the near term.) It will also place Maryland squarely on the leading edge of states that not only protect abortion's legality but ensure women's *access* to abortion services. In all this, the 1992 referendum played a critical role.

For Maryland legislators, the referendum provided a clear reference point for where voters stand on this explosive political issue. For all the finger pointing, electioneering, and lobbying incited by Maryland's struggle to enact an abortion rights law, many lawmakers now see the referendum in positive terms. "In retrospect, the referendum was good," said Lieutenant Governor Steinberg. "It was good for the system, it was good for the people. They had an opportunity to speak."[51]

Notes

1. Michael Barone and Grant Ujifusa, *The Almanac of American Politics 1992* (Washington, D.C.: National Journal, 1991), 539.
2. Michael Barone and Grant Ujifusa, *The Almanac of American Politics 1994* (Washington, D.C.: National Journal, 1993), 572
3. Ibid., 568.
4. Ibid., 572.
5. Ibid., 573, 574.
6. Barone and Ujifusa, *Almanac of American Politics 1992*, 572.
7. Ibid.

8. Barone and Ujifusa, *Almanac of American Politics 1994*, 572.

9. Ibid., 571.

10. The poll was commissioned by Maryland NARAL, the state affiliate of the Washington, D.C.–based National Abortion Rights Action League, and was published by Mason-Dixon Political/Media Research of Columbia, Md., on 18 July 1989.

11. "Abortion: Presidential Politics," *American Enterprise*, May/June 1992, 99.

12. "Survey Says Majority of Maryland Voters Back Legal Abortion," *Daily Record: Business and Legal News of Maryland*, 20 July 1989, A1.

13. *Abortion: A Legislator's Factbook*, published by Marylanders for the Right to Choose. Under the 1968 statute, abortions had to be performed in a hospital, following approval by a hospital review committee.

14. Ibid.

15. S636, introduced by Senator Edward M. Kennedy (D-Mass.), on 23 March 1993. Companion bill, HR796, introduced by Representative Charles Schumer (D-N.Y.).

16. SB162. The main provisions of the law were as follows: It prohibited the state from interfering with a woman's abortion decision before viability (typically defined as 18–22 weeks); it required a physician to notify the parent or guardian of an unmarried minor seeking an abortion, except when it was not in the minor's best interests or when the minor was mature enough to give "informed consent"; it repealed legislation on the books that required women seeking abortions to receive information about alternatives such as adoption in advance; it repealed laws barring abortion referral fees; it required abortions to be performed by licensed physicians; it protected doctors from civil damages or criminal penalties for performing abortions; and it authorized the state to adopt abortion health and safety regulations.

17. A woman may receive Medicaid funding for an abortion in Maryland if her life is in danger, if she is a victim of rape or incest, if the fetus is deformed, if there is substantial risk to her present or future physical health, or if there is medical evidence that continuing the pregnancy would endanger her present and future mental health.

18. "Abortion: Same Issue but New Year," *The Sun*, 24 February 1989, G1.

19. "Leaflet Likens Abortions to the Holocaust," *Washington Post*, 22 March 1990, D1.

20. Ibid.

21. Interview with Paula C. Hollinger, August 1993.

22. "Maryland Abortion Battle Moves from Senate Floor to Ballot Box," *Washington Post*, 16 July 1990, B1.

23. "Maryland Assembly; Abortion-Rights Candidates Poised to Make Senate Filibuster-Proof," *Washington Post*, 12 September 1990, B1.

24. Interview with Karyn Strickler, August 1993.

25. Interview with John R. Stierhoff, August 1993.

26. "Male Senators in Maryland Push Abortion Rights," *Washington Post*, 7 February 1991, B1.

27. Ibid.

28. SB162.

29. The poll was conducted by Herbert C. Smith for WBAL-TV in Baltimore, a CBS affiliate, in April 1990.

30. Interview with Frederica Mathewes-Green, September 1992.

31. Interview with Tom Berriman, September 1992.

32. "Local Parishes Mobilize to Defeat Abortion Referendum," *Catholic Standard*, 27 August 1992.

33. Interview with Roger Stenson, September 1992.

34. "Maryland's Referendum on SB162: The Text of the Law and Commentary." Distributed by the Vote kNOw Coalition of Maryland, Inc.

35. Interview with Frederica Mathewes-Green, September 1992.

36. "Abortion-Rights Test," *National Journal*, 10 October 1992, 2304.

37. "Look Out—Here Comes the Right to Lie," *Baltimore City Paper*, 8 May 1992.

38. Barone and Ujifusa, *Almanac of American Politics 1994*, 568.

39. Confidential tabular report prepared for Maryland FOR Choice by Hickman-Brown Public Opinion Research. Dated October 1992.

40. Statement of Dr. Ben Carson, 1 October 1992.

41. Interview with Marcellus W. Alexander, September 1992.

42. Interview with John R. Stierhoff, August 1993.

43. Interview with Richard J. Dowling, August 1993.

44. Analysis of general election results conducted by Baltimore-based Planned Parenthood of Maryland.

45. Interview with Herbert C. Smith, August 1993.

46. "Tough Choice," *National Journal*, 15 May 1993, 1176.

47. Interview with Gloria A. Totten, August 1993.

48. Interview with Catherine I. Riley, August 1993.

49. Barone and Ujifusa, *Almanac of American Politics 1994*, 568.

50. HB1359, the Maryland Health Care and Insurance Reform Act.

51. Interview with Melvin A. Steinberg, August 1993.

CHRISTINE L. DAY

4 | Louisiana: Religious Politics and the Pro-Life Cause

When the Louisiana state legislature passed the nation's most restrictive abortion law over the governor's veto in 1991, it was continuing a strong anti-abortion tradition dating back to the years preceding *Roe v. Wade*. The 1991 law outlawed all abortions except to save the woman's life, and in cases of rape and incest reported to police and medical authorities before the woman could know she was pregnant. The state continued to defend the law, appealing all the way to the Supreme Court, even after the Court had laid out the "undue burden" requirement in *Planned Parenthood of Southeastern Pennsylvania v. Casey*. In March 1993 the Supreme Court declined to review a lower court ruling that Louisiana's anti-abortion law is unconstitutional.

During the next legislative session, in 1993, pro-life legislators made no move to pass a new state law that might pass judicial scrutiny; nor did most pro-life political organizations actively press for such a law. Although the issue is likely to be revisited soon, there were several reasons for not doing so in 1993. For one thing, the legislature was preoccupied with fiscal and budgetary problems; economists projected a large deficit, and the debt had grown to such proportions that Louisiana ranked fourth in the nation in the amount of interest paid annually on a per capita basis. In addition, some of the most stalwart pro-life legislators opposed any law that would permit any abortions except to save the woman's life. Moreover, state officials and Louisianians in general were simply worn out from a long and tumultuous fight over abortion restrictions after the 1989 Supreme Court decision in *Webster v. Missouri Reproductive Health Services*.

The politics of abortion in Louisiana since *Webster* can be characterized as "dysfunctional politics." Elizabeth Cook, Ted Jelen, and Clyde Wilcox[1] present three possible scenarios for the politics of abortion as the courts have opened the door to state restrictions: normal politics, dysfunctional politics, and empowerment politics. Normal politics involves reflection, debate, and compromise among competing values; dysfunctional politics entails heated, emotional conflict and the inability to compromise; and empowerment politics mobilizes previously apolitical citizens, promoting widespread participation. Although many observers may perceive much of Louisiana politics to be outside the "normal" range by national standards, political activities surrounding the abortion issue—variously described in press accounts as a "brawl," an "embarrassment," and a "three-ring circus"—have been dysfunctional even by Louisiana's standards. At the same time, the abortion debate in Louisiana also involves empowerment politics. On the pro-life side, for example, many religious leaders and their followers turned out to protest abortion in large numbers for the first time,[2] while many previously inactive people on the other side were "trained" by the pro-choice movement for political activism on abortion rights and other issues.[3]

The background of the abortion debate in Louisiana, including the political and religious culture, public opinion, and the restrictive laws prior to *Roe v. Wade*, is discussed in the first section of this chapter. Next comes an account of the events following the 1989 *Webster* decision, including the passage of the 1991 law and the activities of pro-choice and pro-life groups. The third section describes the aftermath of the 1991 legislative session, including the court battles, the legislative and gubernatorial elections, and continued pro-choice and pro-life activism. Finally, the future prospects for abortion restrictions in Louisiana are discussed. Much of what happens at the state level will depend, of course, on developments at the national level, including the fate of the Freedom of Choice Act in Congress, the possible licensing of the abortifacient pill RU-486, and the inclusion of abortion coverage in future national health-care reforms. Meanwhile, despite the Supreme Court's decision, access to abortions in Louisiana remains restricted by the small number of abortion providers, the enforcement of parental-consent laws, the lack of public funding for nearly all abortions, and, more broadly, a long tradition of abortion restrictions.

Political Culture and Public Opinion

Louisiana's anti-abortion tradition dates at least as far back as the 1855 criminal abortion statute that state officials tried to reinstate after the *Webster* decision. Thus, when it came to predicting which states would be most likely to impose abortion restrictions after *Webster*, Louisiana was one state that topped everyone's list.[4] Before *Roe v. Wade*, Louisiana was one of three states, along with New Hampshire and Pennsylvania, that prohibited all abortions; in 1989, the year of the *Webster* decision, it was one of several states that enforced parental-consent laws for minors and funded abortions for indigent women only to save the woman's life.[5] Louisiana was also one of three states, along with

North Dakota and South Dakota, with "no hospitals, public or private, which performed abortions" in 1976; this lack of facilities coupled with lack of public funding placed Louisiana among the states with the lowest abortion rates three years after *Roe v. Wade*.[6]

Religion and culture intersect in Louisiana to produce this strong tradition of abortion restriction. The southern part of the state is predominantly Roman Catholic, while the northern part is predominantly evangelical Protestant. Northern Louisiana is culturally similar to the rest of the Deep South, Southern Baptist and socially conservative. It is the southern part of the state that distinguishes Louisiana from the rest of the South. The Catholic majority there traces its roots to various groups: Catholic Creoles of French and Spanish descent living there at the time of the Louisiana Purchase in 1803; French-speaking Cajuns who immigrated after being expelled from Canada by the British in 1755; and later immigrants of Irish, Italian, German, and other national origins through the Port of New Orleans.[7] Louisiana Catholic and evangelical Protestant activists have clashed on a number of political issues, including Catholics' support for public funding of nonpublic schools and evangelicals' opposition to sex education. Opposition to abortion has united these religious groups.

Religious composition alone does not determine a state's abortion policies, of course; many states with the highest proportion of Catholics also have the most liberal abortion laws. Susan Hansen notes that, unlike Louisiana, most of the states with large Catholic populations have relatively high abortion rates:

> A state-by-state analysis suggests one explanation: Catholic influence in a state, rather than the absolute proportion of Catholics. The urban, industrialized states of the Northeast with large Catholic populations are characterized by religious and ethnic diversity, active women's groups, and strong demand for abortion from large numbers of black and poor residents. In Louisiana, the percent of Catholics is about the same as New York's or New Jersey's. Since the Catholic Church is in a politically more dominant position in that conservative, rural state, however, abortion facilities are very scarce.[8]

Similarly, many other states that are, like Louisiana, relatively rural, conservative, and predominantly evangelical Protestant also have relatively restrictive abortion policies, but not as restrictive as those in Louisiana. No state has Louisiana's unique combination of Catholicism, evangelicalism, and rural conservatism.

Public opinion in Louisiana reflects the state's cultural tradition. The majority of Louisianians are like the majority of Americans, favoring neither a total ban on all abortions nor a lifting of all restrictions. Surveys indicate, however, that Louisianians tend to favor more restrictions than people in the rest of the country. In 1988, for example, 27 percent of respondents in Louisiana, but only 17 percent of U.S. respondents, said that abortion should be illegal in all circumstances. In Louisiana, 15 percent favored legalizing abortion under all circumstances, compared to 24 percent in the nation as a whole.[9] Louisianians are also less supportive of legalized abortion under specified conditions, as can be seen by comparing 1990 state and national surveys. Similarly high percentages of Louisianians and Americans (90 to 93 percent) support legalized abortions when childbirth would seriously endanger the woman's health; over 85 percent of both groups favor making abortion legal if the woman is raped. But only two-thirds of Louisianians, compared to 81 percent of all Americans, support legalized abortion if there is a strong chance of a serious defect in the baby. And only one-third of Louisianians, compared to nearly half (48 percent) of all Americans, would make abortion legal for women who cannot afford any more children.[10]

Evangelical Protestants and Catholics in Louisiana,[11] as in the United States generally,[12] are more likely to oppose legalized abortion than are mainline Protestants and those with another or no religious affiliation. Some studies indicate that strength of religious commitment—often measured by frequency of church attendance or particular doctrinal beliefs—is an even stronger source of opposition to abortion than religious affiliation.[13] While the Louisiana public opinion data examined here contain no measure of religiosity, Mary Holland Benin found in her analysis of national-level data that an interactive variable combining religious affiliation and age was significantly related to support for abortion restrictions.[14] She attributes this interaction effect to greater religiosity among older people, greater salience and personal relevance of abortion to younger people, or both. A multivariate analysis of Louisiana public opinion data found evidence of the same interaction effect: the difference in attitudes between Catholics and evangelical Protestants on the one hand, and mainline Protestants on the other, was greater among middle-aged and older Louisianians than among younger adults.[15]

In the same analysis of Louisiana public opinion data, conservatives, those with less formal education, and African Americans were also found to be more opposed to legal abortion than liberals, the more highly educated, and white people. Although it is risky to draw aggregate conclusions based on individual data, this analysis may help to explain why Louisiana, with its relatively low levels of education and high levels of conservatism along with the predominance of Catholic and evangelical Protestant religions, tends to be more pro-life than the nation as a whole.

Post-*Webster* Politics and the Passage of the 1991 Law

Religion, culture, and politics combined to throw Louisiana into the spotlight in 1990, during the first legislative session after the Supreme Court opened the door to more state restrictions on abortion with its *Webster* decision. Demonstrations and debates among pro-choice and pro-life advocates were intense, and colorful and impassioned speeches on the floor of the legislature—including the use of plastic fetuses and a short speech about the value of incest for producing championship horses—were recorded with glee by national and international media. That year, the legislature passed two anti-abortion measures, the first of which outlawed all abortions except to save the woman's life and the second of which added exceptions for rape and incest. The legislature failed to override the governor's veto in both cases, but in 1991 another law containing only those three exceptions was finally passed over the governor's veto.

Glen Halva-Neubauer has suggested that state abortion policies "are functions of the strength and professionalization of the state's anti- and pro-abortion organizations, the position of legislative leaders and the governor on the issue, and the presence of a legislative champion (a passionate, committed advocate)."[16] An examination of these factors in Louisiana helps explain why Louisiana passed the nation's most restrictive post-*Webster* law.

Organized interests on both sides of the abortion issue are key players in the policymaking process, as they are on most moral issues.[17] Interest groups tend to be particularly active when they have suffered a perceived loss in the political process. Thus, in Louisiana as elsewhere, the mobilization of pro-life forces increased after the *Roe v. Wade* decision effectively invalidated state anti-abortion laws. Pro-choice groups stepped up their activities toward the end of the 1980s as Reagan and Bush appointees increased the conservatism of the Supreme Court, and especially after the 1989 *Webster* decision. Activists on both sides geared up for the post-*Webster* legislative battles as pro-life legislators sought to test the boundaries of permissible abortion restrictions.[18]

The National Right to Life Committee was formed in 1966; the Louisiana Right to Life Federation was founded just four years later, and now has over twenty chapters statewide. The founding president, Robert Winn, who currently sits on the national board of Right to Life, organized the Louisiana federation three years before the Supreme Court handed down its decision in *Roe v. Wade* because, he said, he "saw it coming." Although not officially affiliated with the Louisiana Catholic Conference (LCC), Louisiana Right to Life often coordinates its lobbying and educational efforts with the LCC and the Louisiana Pro-Life Council, which is affiliated with the Archdiocese of New Orleans.[19]

Other pro-life organizations that are more closely affiliated with the evangelical Protestant churches include the Louisiana chapter of the Eagle Forum and its Louisiana Family Lobby, strongest in the northern part of the state; Operation Rescue (OR); and local organizations affiliated with OR such as United for Life, a coalition of Protestant and some Catholic churches. Operation Rescue began blockading abortion clinics and protesting at physicians' homes in Louisiana as early as 1988.[20]

Nationally, the pro-life alliance between Catholics and evangelical Protestants has been an uneasy one, with the evangelical Christian Right generally taking more conservative positions on many other social and economic issues.[21] In Louisiana, activists from both camps presented an unusually united front as the 1990 legislative session got under way. After Governor Charles ("Buddy") Roemer vetoed the first, no-exceptions anti-abortion bill, however, the coalition split over whether to accept exceptions for rape and incest. Louisiana Right to Life, the Louisiana Catholic Conference, and the Louisiana Pro-Life Council all pushed for these exceptions, arguing that a highly restrictive law was better than no anti-abortion law at all; many evangelical Protestant activists refused to support any exceptions. There are also some differences over tactics, with lobbyists from the Right to Life and Catholic-affiliated organizations distancing themselves from the more militant, protest-oriented actions of such groups as Operation Rescue.[22]

Divided or united, pro-life organizations are a powerful political force in Louisiana, but they are not without substantial opposition. Planned Parenthood of Louisiana is generally acknowledged by friend and foe alike as the strongest and most consistent proponent of abortion rights; its executive director, Terri Bartlett, has been called "*the* voice of choice."[23] The League of Women Voters and the National Organization for Women have also been active in lobbying the state government, supporting pro-choice state candidates, and organizing grassroots demonstrations. The American Civil Liberties Union has taken an active role in litigation, fighting abortion restrictions in court. Louisiana Choice, an affiliate of the National Abortion Rights Action League, was formed before the Supreme Court's *Webster* decision. Aside from occasional abortion defense actions, however, the pro-choice movement was largely dormant until mobilized by the *Webster* decision to oppose new anti-abortion legislation. The Louisiana Coalition for Reproductive Freedom coordinated the activities of these organizations during the legislative battles of 1990 and 1991. The Coalition to Reclaim Our Abortion and Reproductive Rights (CROARR) was formed in May 1992 to defend abortion clinics from actions by Operation Rescue. Pro-choice groups, like those on the pro-life side, have been divided over political strategy, with CROARR and other clinic defense groups advocating the more militant approach.[24]

The pro-life movement in Louisiana had a lot to lose when the *Roe v. Wade* decision invalidated state anti-abortion laws and a lot to regain when a more conservative Court signaled a willingness to validate some abortion restrictions with the *Webster* decision. The 1855 state law that was still on the books in 1973 banned all abortions and imposed criminal penalties of up to ten years at hard labor for those performing abortions. Within a few months after *Webster*, attorneys for the state attorney general and the New Orleans district attorney were in federal court asking that the injunction against that law be lifted. The federal court refused to reinstate the law in 1990, and when the legislature convened that year, pro-life legislators were ready to pass a similar bill, hoping to provoke a court case that would lead to the overturning of *Roe v. Wade*.[25]

The first bill proposed in 1990, banning all abortions except to save the woman's life, sailed through both houses by large margins but was vetoed by Governor Roemer. The House voted quickly to override the governor's veto, but the Senate failed to override by three votes. The following day, with only two days left in the legislative session, both houses overwhelmingly passed a second bill with added exceptions for rape and incest. Governor Roemer, despite having expressed support for anti-abortion legislation containing rape and incest exceptions, vetoed the second bill, objecting to the stringency of the rape reporting requirements and to the procedures behind the bill's passage. Rather than call a special session for another veto override attempt, pro-life legislators decided to wait until 1991 to pass another anti-abortion bill.

The bill they passed in 1991, this time over the governor's veto, outlawed all abortions except to save the woman's life; in cases of incest when the crime is reported to the police and the abortion is performed within thirteen weeks of conception; and in cases of rape when the crime has been reported to the police within seven days, the woman has been examined within five days by a doctor other than the doctor who performs the abortion, and the abortion takes place within thirteen weeks of conception. The law imposes penalties of up to $100,000 and ten years at hard labor for those performing illegal abortions.

Legislative committee and floor leaders, passionate anti-abortion advocates within the legislature, savvy pro-life lobbyists, and grassroots supporters combined efforts to pass all three anti-abortion bills. While both pro-choice and pro-life advocates lobbied the legislature and held demonstrations outside, pro-lifers were generally more numerous and visible. The abortion issue is generally more salient to abortion opponents than to supporters of legal abortion.[26] Religious organizations, heavily pro-life, are particularly adept at mobilizing grassroots support because of their large committed memberships. More Americans are members of religious groups than of any other kind of group, and organized religion provides a major forum for political participation.[27] Activists and journalists at the state capitol described "corridors filled with an unlikely alliance of Roman Catholics and Bible-toting Protestant fundamentalists," with "pro-choice lobbyists either voluntarily retreating in the face of overwhelming odds, or being deliberately hampered by state officials."[28]

Pro-life organizations employ several other political resources beyond their grassroots support. Several professional and well-informed lobbyists and activist attorneys enjoy easy access to key legislators, counting them among their close personal friends. The Louisiana Catholic Conference confers highest priority to the abortion issue on its policy agenda, by unanimous consent of the Louisiana bishops. Legislators and activists cite LCC lobbyists, along with those from Right to Life and the Louisiana Pro-Life Council, as the most influential. Their willingness to compromise on the rape and incest exceptions strengthened their position with the legislature. Although some legislators denounced the apparent inconsistency in defining abortion as murder while allowing exceptions, not even Louisiana is likely to pass an anti-abortion law with no exceptions at all. Thus the strategy of fighting for the strictest law possible has been more effective than that of other pro-life groups, such as the Eagle Forum, who are reluctant to support any exceptions beyond saving the life of the woman.[29]

Another pro-life strength is the ability of officials in the Catholic Church hierarchy to exert some influence on church members. No politician wishes to be perceived as taking direct orders from the church, and there is little evidence that Catholic politicians change their positions under pressure from church officials.[30] Nevertheless, church members may be sensitive to official pronouncements from bishops and priests, and this may be significant in a legislature that is half Roman Catholic. Anecdotes from newspaper accounts and interviews relate stories of Catholic legislators called before their own church committees or entire congregations to answer for their votes, prohibited by church officials from speaking publicly at any church-sponsored forum, and even threatened with excommunication for voting against abortion restrictions. Senate president Sammy Nunez even received a petition from his mother's church, and a letter and phone call from his mother at the urging of her church's priest.[31]

Some of the most visible and effective pro-life advocates in Louisiana are legislators themselves. One of the major factors cited by Halva-Neubauer as contributing to restrictive state abortion policy is the presence of a "passionate, committed advocate" in the legislature. The most prominent such leader is Representative Louis ("Woody") Jenkins, an evangelical Protestant political leader who has led the fight against anti-abortion exceptions and has appeared in nationwide media clutching his trademark plastic fetus models. Some pro-life and pro-choice activists attribute even more influence to Representative Sam Theriot, an ordained deacon in the Roman Catholic Church who has been instrumental in writing and passing bills containing rape and incest exceptions while Jenkins and a few others have refused to support those exceptions.[32]

Passage of all three anti-abortion bills in 1990 and 1991 was facilitated by the acquiescence, and usually the active support, of key committee chairs and floor leaders. The most dramatic example occurred at the end of the 1990 session, after the governor vetoed the first, no-exceptions, bill. With only two days remaining to push through a bill containing rape and incest exceptions and lacking time to send a new bill through committee, Catholic pro-life senators searched for a bill pending on the floor that could be reworked into an anti-abortion bill. They found one: a bill that would have amended the state criminal code to make assault on anyone burning a U.S. flag punishable by a maximum twenty-five-dollar fine. This "beat-the-flag-burner bill" had passed the House by a large margin, but it stood little chance of passing the Senate. Senators John Saunders and John Hainkel, with the help of Catholic and Right-to-Life lobbyists, removed all references to assaulting flag burners and replaced them with language criminalizing abortion. Senate president Nunez, also a Catholic, ruled that the amendment was germane, and the revamped bill passed the Senate and then the House. Only the governor's veto stopped it from becoming law.[33]

Half the Louisiana legislature is Catholic and one-third is evangelical Protestant, but religious composition alone does not explain the legislature's overwhelming support for the anti-abortion legislation of 1990 and 1991. Although Catholics and evangelicals were somewhat more likely to vote for these bills, even large majorities of mainline Protestants supported the legislation. Democrats and Republicans were also equally likely to vote in favor. Female and African American legislators were much more likely than white males to oppose the abortion restrictions, but there were too few of them in 1991 (20 blacks and 4 women in a legislature of 143) to make much difference. In a multivariate analysis, the variable found to be most significant in distinguishing the bill's supporters from its opponents was urbanism; legislators from rural, small-town, and suburban areas were much more likely than those from the state's three largest cities to support the anti-abortion legislation.[34] This pattern affirms, once again, the importance of religious values in state politics within a largely rural, socially conservative political culture.

It would seem, since Governor Roemer vetoed all three anti-abortion bills, that the only major pro-life element missing from Louisiana politics in 1990 and 1991 was a staunchly pro-life governor. Roemer, however, was no champion of the pro-choice position; by national standards he belongs in the pro-life camp. As a representative in the U.S. Congress, Roemer took consistently pro-life positions, and as governor he indicated a willingness all along to sign a strict anti-abortion bill. His only objections to the 1991 bill, as he stated in his veto message, were that the rape reporting requirements were too narrow, the law appeared to criminalize intrauterine devices and the termination of tubal pregnancies, and he preferred another exception for severe fetal deformities. After vetoing that bill, he made little attempt to persuade legislators to sustain the veto, and the legislature's veto override became the first in Louisiana in the twentieth century.[35]

In sum, the conditions listed by Halva-Neubauer as important to the passage of restrictive abortion laws—strong and professional pro-life organizations, supportive or acquiescent legislative leaders, committed pro-life activists within the legislature, and a governor who could be considered pro-life despite his three vetoes—were active and effective in post-*Webster* Louisiana.

The Morning After: Electoral, Judicial, and Political Consequences

In the aftermath of the passage of the nation's most restrictive anti-abortion law, the politics of abortion in Louisiana moved to the judicial and electoral arenas.

The day after the 1991 bill became law, the American Civil Liberties Union filed suit in federal court, challenging the law's constitutionality and obtaining an injunction against its enforcement. By the time the case, *Sojourner T. v. Roemer*, reached the Supreme Court, the Court had already affirmed the unconstitutionality of any state law placing an "undue burden" on women seeking abortions in *Planned Parenthood of Southeastern Pennsylvania v. Casey* and had refused to uphold Guam's strict anti-abortion law. Nevertheless, the state attorney general continued to defend Louisiana's law in federal court, noting that Guam's law was in some ways stricter (omitting rape and incest exceptions, but permitting the termination of pregnancies that would gravely impair a woman's health). The attorney general was banking further on Louisiana's status as a state and on the fact that Guam's law missed review by the Supreme Court by only one vote. The Court dealt Louisiana's law a final blow in March 1993, however, when it let stand the lower court ruling that the law was unconstitutional.[36]

As *Sojourner T. v. Roemer* wound its way through federal court, the law was challenged simultaneously in the state courts in a case filed by Planned Parenthood and several abortion providers. The basis for the legal challenge at the state level was the explicit provision for right to privacy in Louisiana's state constitution. Ironically, the delegate to the 1973 constitutional convention who argued most forcefully for making privacy a fundamental right was legislative pro-life champion Woody Jenkins. The case was dismissed when federal courts deemed the anti-abortion law unconstitutional, leaving some to wonder whether future strict anti-abortion laws could be successfully challenged in state courts should the U.S. Supreme Court ever overturn *Roe v. Wade*.[37]

Meanwhile, toward the end of 1991, state elections threw Louisiana into the international spotlight once again. Governor Roemer was defeated in his bid for reelection in the first primary, leaving former governor Edwin W. Edwards and former American Nazi and Ku Klux Klan leader David Duke to face each other in the runoff. Determining the role of the abortion issue in Roemer's defeat is difficult because there were many other factors involved, including Louisiana's deteriorating economy. In an analysis of Louisiana public opinion surveys leading up to the election, Susan Howell and Robert Sims found the issue's electoral influence to be highly conditional and specific. Among whites, abortion attitudes affected the electoral choices of Protestants more than those of Catholics. Abortion attitudes were also most likely to affect the choices of advocates feeling the most threatened: pro-life advocates in 1990 after both anti-abortion bills had been successfully vetoed, and pro-choice advocates in 1991 after the governor's veto was overridden. In general, however, the electoral impact of abortion attitudes had begun to fade in the gubernatorial race between 1990 and 1991. By the time of the 1991 election, publicity surrounding Duke's candidacy had enhanced the relative importance of Duke's racism as a campaign issue.[38] Still, pro-life activists and legislators, unhappy with Roemer's perceived abandonment of their cause, suggested that his narrow loss in the first primary could have been avoided if he had signed the anti-abortion bill instead of "talking out of both sides of his mouth" on the issue.[39]

Abortion was not a prominent issue in most of the 1991 state legislative races, but it did affect a few of them. Seven pro-choice women challenged seven anti-abortion male incumbents, and three of them won—not a bad record for challengers. One of the four losers was Sandy Ashby, a former head of the Louisiana Coalition for Reproductive Freedom, who challenged the legislature's most visible pro-life advocate, Woody Jenkins. Although Ashby lost by 54 to 46 percent, she did force Jenkins into a runoff after he failed to capture a majority of the vote in the first primary.[40]

The salience of the abortion issue seems to have declined among the Louisiana public since the legislative battles of 1990 and 1991; constituency mail on the issue has dropped off, and many mainstream activists have temporarily curtailed their activities and turned their efforts to other issues.[41] Many observers expected the legislature to propose new abortion restrictions during the 1993 legislative session, after the 1991 law was struck down in federal court, but the legislature was quiet on the issue as it dealt with pressing economic crises. Pro-life lobbyists held back from pressing hard for new restrictions as they waited for the legislature to address fiscal problems, directing more of their effort to fighting the national Freedom of Choice Act in Congress. Meanwhile, some of the most passionate anti-abortion advocates in the legislature, including Representative Jenkins and Senator Mike Cross, refused to introduce legislation containing any exceptions beyond saving the life of the woman.[42] The only legislative action on the issue in 1993 was the passage of a nonbinding resolution urging Congress to oppose the Freedom of Choice Act and to prohibit all government funding of abortions.

Most of the abortion-related political action in Louisiana since the 1991 law was struck down has revolved around protests at abortion clinics and doctors' homes by pro-life organizations such as Operation Rescue, and clinic defense by pro-choice groups such as the Coalition to Reclaim Our Abortion and Reproductive Rights. The issue is far from dormant in the capital, however; most expect the controversy to regain momentum by the time the state legislature convenes in 1994.

Future Prospects

Several abortion restrictions are on the 1994 legislative agenda for pro-life activists and legislators. Proposed restrictions include requiring the consent of both parents instead of just one for minors seeking abortions, requiring waiting periods of perhaps twenty-four or forty-eight hours between the time a woman signs up at a clinic and the time she obtains an abortion, and the licensing and regulation of abortion clinics for sanitary and safety standards. Most observers feel that

Governor Edwin Edwards would sign any such legislation, although he steers clear of active involvement in the issue. Nevertheless, advocates of such restrictions would face opposition not only from pro-choice advocates but also from legislators such as Representative Jenkins and Senator Cross, who do not support anti-abortion laws containing exceptions. Both Jenkins and Cross contend that the Supreme Court would uphold a law containing no exceptions beyond saving the woman's life because such a law would treat all fetuses equally and consistently.[43]

Much of what happens in Louisiana, and in other states, depends on developments at the national level. The Freedom of Choice Act, if passed by Congress, would invalidate most state anti-abortion laws. Debates over coverage of abortion under the proposed national health-care reforms, and the possible licensing and distribution of the abortion pill RU-486, may significantly change women's options and transform the abortion controversy nationwide. Thus, many pro-choice and pro-life activists have shifted their attention back to the national level, after having shifted to the state level following the *Webster* decision. Most of the members of the Louisiana delegation in the U.S. House of Representatives and Senate—with the exception of the two urban liberal representatives, William Jefferson and Cleo Fields—have taken consistently pro-life positions on issues ranging from abortion rights bills to abortion funding and inclusion of abortion coverage in national health-care reforms.[44]

Meanwhile, regardless of the status of anti-abortion laws, access to abortions in Louisiana continues to be problematic for women seeking them. Abortion clinics are currently operating in only two metropolitan areas—New Orleans and Shreveport—since the closing of the Delta Women's Clinic in Baton Rouge after its doctor retired, although the Baton Rouge clinic plans to reopen when a new doctor is found.[45] This situation is not unlike that in the nation as a whole; 83 percent of the counties in the United States have no abortion providers.[46] Abortion availability and abortion rates tend to be lowest in states with no Medicaid funding for abortion, few hospital services, and smaller proportions of the population in urban areas;[47] thus Louisiana is likely to remain one of the states with the lowest availability of abortion facilities.

The politics of abortion in Louisiana in future years will probably continue to fit the "dysfunctional" and "empowerment" scenarios described by Cook, Jelen, and Wilcox.[48] Like Louisiana politics in general, political activity surrounding the abortion issue is likely to remain largely polarized, boisterous, and rarely dull.

Notes

I am grateful to all the interviewees for lending their valuable time and expertise, and to Jun Yin for her research assistance.

1. Elizabeth Adell Cook, Ted G. Jelen, and Clyde Wilcox, *Between Two Absolutes: Public Opinion and the Politics of Abortion* (Boulder, Colo.: Westview Press, 1992).

2. Christine L. Day, "Abortion and Religious Coalitions: The Case of Louisiana," in *The Catholic Church and the Politics of Abortion: A View from the States*, ed. Timothy A. Byrnes and Mary C. Segers (Boulder, Colo.: Westview Press, 1992); interview with the Reverend Bill Shanks, director of United for Life and regional director of Operation Rescue, 1 September 1993.

3. Interview with Julie Schwamm-Harris, grassroots coordinator for the Louisiana Coalition for Reproductive Freedom and chair of Citizens for Personal Freedom, 20 August 1993.

4. Barbara Hinkson Craig and David M. O'Brien, *Abortion and American Politics* (Chatham, N.J.: Chatham House, 1993), 281; Glen Halva-Neubauer, "Abortion in the Post-*Webster* Age," *Publius* 20 (Summer 1990): 27–44; National Abortion Rights Action League, *Who Decides? A State-by-State Review of Abortion Rights*, 3d ed. (Washington, D.C.: NARAL Foundation, 1992).

5. Craig and O'Brien, *Abortion and American Politics*, 75, 86, 95.

6. Susan B. Hansen, "State Implementation of Supreme Court Decisions: Abortion Rates since *Roe v. Wade*," *Journal of Politics* 42 (1980): 372–95. Quote appears on 380.

7. Christine L. Day, "State Legislative Voting Patterns on Abortion Restrictions in Louisiana," *Women and Politics* (forthcoming); Charles D. Hadley and Ralph E. Thayer, "Louisiana: The Unfolding of Its Political Culture," paper presented at the annual meeting of the American Political Science Association, Washington, D.C., 1988; Arnold R. Hirsch and Joseph Logsdon, eds., *Creole New Orleans: Race and Americanization* (Baton Rouge: Louisiana State University Press, 1992).

8. Hansen, "State Implementation of Supreme Court Decisions," 385. See also Mary C. Segers, "Abortion Politics Post-*Webster*: The New Jersey Bishops," in Byrnes and Segers, *The Catholic Church and the Politics of Abortion*, 27–47.

9. The Louisiana data are from Susan E. Howell, "Louisiana Presidential Election Survey, October 21, 1992," report issued by the Survey Research Center, University of New Orleans, 1992. The national data are from the Gallup poll, reported in Malcolm L. Goggin, "Understanding the New Politics of Abortion: A Framework and Agenda for Research," *American Politics Quarterly* 21 (1993): 4–30.

10. The Louisiana data come from a survey conducted by Mason-Dixon Research of Columbia, Md., 1–5 September 1990 and reported in "Poll: Louisiana Supports Roemer's Vetoes of Abortion Bans," *New Orleans Times-Picayune*, 9 September 1990. The national data come from the National Opinion Research Center, reported in Craig and O'Brien, *Abortion and American Politics*, 254.

11. The analysis of Louisiana public opinion data described below appears in Day, "Abortion and Religious Coalitions." The data were collected by Susan E. Howell and the Survey Research Center, University of New Orleans, September 1990.

12. Mary Holland Benin, "Determinants of Opposition to Abortion," *Sociological Perspectives* 28 (April 1985): 199–216; Cook, Jelen, and Wilcox, *Between Two Absolutes*; Kenneth D. Wald, *Religion and Politics in the United States* (New York: St. Martin's Press, 1987), 75–76.

13. Cook, Jelen, and Wilcox, *Between Two Absolutes*; Ross K. Baker, Laurily K. Epstein, and Rodney D. Forth, "Matters of Life and Death: Social, Political, and Religious Correlates of Attitudes on Abortion," *American Politics Quarterly* 9 (1981): 89–102; Charles H. Franklin and Liane C. Kosaki, "Republican Schoolmaster: The U.S. Supreme Court, Public Opinion, and Abortion," *American Political Science Review* 83 (1989): 751–71.

14. Benin, "Determinants of Opposition to Abortion." The relationship between abortion attitudes and age by itself is complex. Many studies have found that older people tend to oppose legalized abortion somewhat more than younger people do. On the other hand,

Cook, Jelen, and Wilcox found that white people who reached adulthood after the 1960s were less supportive than older people of legal abortion, perhaps because younger people may take abortion availability more for granted and thus focus more on moral objections to legal abortion. See Elizabeth Adell Cook, Ted G. Jelen, and Clyde Wilcox, "Generational Differences in Attitudes toward Abortion," *American Politics Quarterly* 21 (1993): 31–53.

15. Day, "Abortion and Religious Coalitions."

16. Halva-Neubauer, "Abortion Policy in the Post-*Webster* Age," 33.

17. Kenneth J. Meier and Deborah R. McFarlane, "The Politics of Funding Abortion: State Responses to the Political Environment," *American Politics Quarterly* 21 (1993): 81–101.

18. Craig and O'Brien, *Abortion and American Politics*, chap. 2.

19. Interviews with Emile Comar, executive director of the Louisiana Catholic Conference, 12 February 1993; Peg Kenny, executive director of the Louisiana Pro-Life Council, 14 July 1993 and 5 February 1991; Sharon Ryan-Rodi, president of the board of the Louisiana Right to Life Federation, 8 September 1993.

20. Interview with the Reverend Bill Shanks; Rebecca Theim and Sheila Grissett, "Local Clergy Arrested in Clinic Protest," *New Orleans Times-Picayune*, 28 January 1989.

21. James L. Guth, Corwin E. Smidt, Lyman A. Kellstedt, and John C. Green, "The Sources of Antiabortion Attitudes: The Case of Religious Political Activists," *American Politics Quarterly* 21 (1993): 65–80; Clyde Wilcox and Leopoldo Gomez, "The Christian Right and the Pro-Life Movement: An Analysis of the Sources of Political Support," *Review of Religious Research* 31 (1990): 380–89.

22. Day, "Abortion and Religious Coalitions"; Doug Myers and Bill McMahon, "New Anti-Abortion Bill OK'd," *Baton Rouge Advocate*, 9 July 1990; Dawn Ruth, "State's Catholics, Protestants Join Forces in War on Abortion," *New Orleans Times-Picayune*, 26 June 1990; interviews with Terri Bartlett, executive director of Planned Parenthood of Louisiana, 1 February 1991 and 10 February 1993; Peg Kenny, 5 February 1991; Louisiana state representative Mitchell J. Landrieu, 7 February 1991; Emile Comar, 12 February 1993.

23. Interview with Julie Schwamm-Harris; also, interviews with Susan Ferron, activist with the Coalition to Reclaim Our Abortion and Reproductive Rights, Sharon Ryan-Rodi, the Reverend Bill Shanks, and Robert Winn.

24. Interviews with Susan Ferron and Julie Schwamm-Harris.

25. Craig and O'Brien, *Abortion and American Politics*, 293–95; Halva-Neubauer, "Abortion Policy in the Post-*Webster* Age," 31.

26. Jacqueline Scott and Howard Schuman, "Attitude Strength and Social Action in the Abortion Dispute," *American Sociological Review* 53 (1988): 785–93.

27. Alen D. Hertzke, *Representing God in Washington: The Role of Religious Lobbies in the American Polity* (Knoxville: University of Tennessee Press, 1988).

28. Ruth, "State's Catholics, Protestants Join Forces in War on Abortion," A4; see also Day, "Abortion and Religious Coalitions"; Day, "State Legislative Voting Patterns on Abortion Restrictions in Louisiana."

29. Interviews with Terri Bartlett, Emile Comar, Peg Kenny, Sharon Ryan-Rodi, Robert Winn, and State Representatives Mitchell Landrieu and James Donelon. See also Day, "Abortion and Religious Coalitions."

30. Timothy A. Byrnes, "The Politics of Abortion: The Catholic Bishops," in Byrnes and Segers, *The Catholic Church and the Politics of Abortion*; Wald, *Religion and Politics in the United States*, 236–38.

31. Doug Myers, "Abortion Override Fails," *Baton Rouge Advocate*, 8 July 1990; Iris

Kelso, "Lots of Fallout from Legislative Abortion Bombshell," *New Orleans Times-Picayune*, July 15, 1990; Day, "Abortion and Religious Coalitions," 109; interviews with Terri Bartlett and Representative Mitchell Landrieu.

32. Interviews with Terri Bartlett, Sharon Ryan-Rodi, and Robert Winn.

33. Myers and McMahon, "New Anti-abortion Bill OK'd"; Kelso, "Lots of Fallout from Legislative Abortion Bombshell"; interviews with Terri Bartlett and Representative Mitchell Landrieu.

34. Day, "State Legislative Voting Patterns on Abortion Restrictions in Louisiana." See also Stephanie L. Witt and Gary Moncrief, "Religion and Roll Call Voting in Idaho: The 1990 Abortion Controversy," *American Politics Quarterly* 21 (1993): 140–49, on the importance of religion and political culture in legislative votes on abortion in another state.

35. Peter Nicholas and Ed Anderson, "Roemer Didn't Twist Arms to Get Votes," *New Orleans Times-Picayune*, 19 July 1991.

36. Ed Anderson, "Louisiana to Pursue Abortion Ruling," *New Orleans Times-Picayune*, 2 December 1992; Doug Myers, "Court Kills Louisiana Abortion Law," *Baton Rouge Advocate*, 9 March 1993; interview with Robert Winn.

37. Robert Baudouin, "The Other Abortion Case," *Louisiana Political Review*, September/October 1991, 39–40.

38. Susan E. Howell and Robert T. Sims, "Abortion Attitudes and the Louisiana Governor's Election," *American Politics Quarterly* 21 (1993): 54–64.

39. Interviews with Peg Kenny, Emile Comar, Sharon Ryan-Rodi, and Representative James Donelon.

40. Peter Nicholas, "Abortion-Rights Candidates Win Three, Lose Four," *New Orleans Times-Picayune*, 20 October 1991; John Maginnis, Richard Baudouin, and Jim Leggett, "Survivors," *Louisiana Political Review*, November/December 1991, 18–22.

41. Interviews with Susan Ferron, Julie Schwamm-Harris, and Representative James Donelon.

42. Ed Anderson and Hayes Ferguson, "Bills Push Tougher Child-Care Rules," *New Orleans Times-Picayune*, 13 April 1993; Jack Wardlaw, "From Special to Regular, Legislative Session Evolves," *New Orleans Times-Picayune*, 24 March 1993; interviews with Peg Kenny, Sharon Ryan-Rodi, Robert Winn, and Representative James Donelon.

43. Doug Myers, "Court Kills Louisiana Abortion Law"; interviews with Terri Bartlett, Peg Kenny, Sharon Ryan-Rodi, Robert Winn.

44. John McQuaid, "Health Reform Carries Thorny Abortion Issue," *New Orleans Times-Picayune*, 3 October 1993; interviews with Terri Bartlett, Representative James Donelon, Peg Kenny, Julie Schwamm-Harris, Sharon Ryan-Rodi, and Robert Winn. For an analysis of the importance of ideology in congressional voting patterns on abortion, see Raymond Tatalovich and David Schier, "The Persistence of Ideological Cleavage in Voting on Abortion Legislation in the House of Representatives, 1973–1988," *American Political Quarterly* 21 (1993): 125–39.

45. "Delta Women's Clinic Closes after Fifteen Years in Operation," *Lafayette Advertiser*, 5 September 1993; interview with Terri Bartlett.

46. Alissa Rubin, "The Abortions Wars Are Far from Over," *Washington Post National Weekly Edition*, 21–27 December 1992, 25.

47. Susan B. Hansen, "State Implementation of Supreme Court Decisions: Abortion Rates since *Roe v. Wade*."

48. Cook, Jelen, and Wilcox, *Between Two Absolutes*.

DANIEL J. O'NEIL

5 | Arizona: Pro-Choice Success in a Conservative, Republican State

This chapter examines the attempt to limit abortion in Arizona by means of a constitutional referendum voted on in the 1992 presidential election. The study examines the story of the contest, the Arizona political culture, the arguments of proponents and adversaries, and the campaign and its outcome. It attempts to explain the result and scrutinize its implications.

The Story

On 1 July 1992, shortly following the *Casey* decision, Arizonans for Common Sense presented 255,667 petitions to the secretary of state for the purpose of initiating a constitutional referendum that would severely restrict abortion.[1] The petitions greatly exceeded the 158,000 required to place a proposition on the ballot and ensured that the referendum would be voted on in the upcoming presidential election. Arizonans for Common Sense was headed by former legislator Trent Franks, who concurrently served as executive director of the Arizona Family Research Institute, a conservative organization committed to traditional family values and suspicious of the cultural revolution. A group of anti-abortion Chicago lawyers, Americans United for Life, advised on preparing the petition. An Encinitas, California, organization, National Voter Outreach, orchestrated the collection of signatures, and a Dallas-based firm, Tyler and Associates, helped with the fund raising. The supporters of the referendum—entitled the Preborn Child Protection Amendment—believed that Arizona could serve as a model for anti-abortion campaigns in other states.

The referendum, known as Proposition 110, read as follows:

Section 1.   No public funds shall be used to pay for an abortion, except when that procedure is necessary to save the life of the mother.

Section 2.   No preborn child shall be knowingly deprived of life at any stage of biological development except to save the life of the mother. However, the Legislature shall provide for exceptions only in those circumstances which result from an act of either reported sexual assault or reported incest.

Section 3.   This amendment shall not subject any woman to criminal prosecution or civil liability for undergoing an abortion.

Section 4.   Any court of competent jurisdiction, upon request, shall appoint a licensed attorney as a special guardian to represent preborn children, as a class, for the purpose of protecting their rights under this amendment from deprivation by any person.

Section 5.   This amendment shall not affect contraceptives or require an appropriation of public funds.[2]

Supporters of the proposal labeled it a moderate, compromise measure to deal with a complex problem; opponents charged that it was an extremist effort to outlaw virtually all abortions.

Immediately, a counterorganization called Pro-Choice Arizona appeared to defeat the proposition. A tent operation, it represented such groups as Planned Parenthood, Arizona Right to Choose, the American Civil Liberties Union (ACLU), the National Organization for Women (NOW), and the League of Women Voters.[3] Its clientele extended beyond the expected liberal Democrats to include large numbers of upper-middle-class persons. Individuals having some link with Planned Parenthood were especially visible throughout the campaign.

Both sides engaged in the usual networking and mobilization of forces. Opponents contacted members of the tent organizations, while proponents contacted the churches.[4] For the latter, the most active response came from evangelical churches, although the Catholic bishops released a letter urging "serious, prayerful and favorable consideration" for Proposition 110. Catholic activists seemed divided; some accepted the measure as a compromise and others contended that it conceded too much. Throughout the campaign the most visible and vocal supporters of the proposition seemed persons with an evangelical link. In many respects the campaign seemed to be a battle between the evangelicals and Planned Parenthood.

Both sides predicted that substantial funding existed for the campaign, suggesting that as much as $3 million might be spent.[5] The petition's supporters expected to spend $750,000 to $2 million, while the opponents expected to spend about $1 million. These sums seemed excessive for an Arizona referendum and indicated out-of-state involvement.[6] They would ultimately prove exaggerations.

Each side released polls indicating support for its position.[7] Poll results seemed to relate to the wording of the question and the definition of the issue. Pro-life polls produced pro-life responses, and pro-choice polls produced pro-choice responses. Actually the proposition had been designed with close attention to the polls and concern for the kind and degree of abortion acceptable to the public.

The week before the ballots were to be printed, the Arizona League of Women Voters and a Tucson academician attempted to have the judiciary remove the question from the ballot.[8] They charged that the proposition, contrary to the constitution's "single-subject requirement," forced the voter to vote on two separate questions with one vote. The proposition linked denial of public funds for abortion, which was one question, with banning abortion, which was another question. Proponents argued that there existed a "coherent scheme" and "reasonable relationship" linking the issues and that the protest was filed too late. Judge Elizabeth Stover of the Maricopa County Superior Court ordered the proposition removed from the ballot, but was later overruled by the Arizona Supreme Court on the grounds that the protest had been filed too late.

In early October the proponents would be confronted by organization problems and negative polls. This resulted in changing the organization's name, replacing its chairman, and reorienting its focus.[9]

The popular campaign was short, lasting no more than the two final weeks of the 1992 presidential race. It was intertwined with numerous other electoral decisions and was but part of a total campaign scenario. It was greatly overshadowed by the presidential, congressional, and legislative races. The campaign consisted primarily of television commercials and countercommercials, with the surprise intervention of elder statesman Barry Goldwater in opposition to Proposition 110.[10] Three of the four major newspapers opposed the measure, while the fourth endorsed it. The arguments utilized were essentially a rehash of the national arguments, except for the emphasis on the petition as a compromise, middle-of-the-road measure. There were charges and countercharges concerning deceit and misrepresentation. The outcome was a landslide victory for the opponents of Proposition 110.

The Arizona Political Culture

Arizona, part of the sunbelt, in many respects lies between California and the South.[11] It enjoys the growth and boom associated until recently with California linked with the relaxed, laid-back lifestyle associated with the South. Arizona had been colonized by Spain and had remained part of New Spain for approximately 300 years. With Mexican independence in 1821, Arizona was claimed by Mexico, although contact with Mexican authority remained precarious. Arizona had never been effectively controlled and populated by the Spanish or Mexicans, primarily because of the ferocious Native American resistance. Following the Mexican-American War (1846–48), most of Arizona was annexed by the United States; the southern sector was purchased in 1853. The earliest nineteenth-century English-speaking settlers came disproportionately from Utah and Texas. During the Civil War considerable Confederate sympathy existed in the territory with at least one battle recorded. Arizona finally achieved statehood on 14 February 1912, becoming the forty-eighth state. Population growth would greatly accelerate following World War II and continues to the present. Currently, Arizona has a population of 3,665,228.[12] Phoenix, the largest city has a population of 983,000, and Tucson, the second-largest city, is home to 405,000. Maricopa, the most populous county, has a population of 2,122,101. In all there are fifteen counties, most of them rural, but state politics tend to be dominated by the urban areas. Racially, contemporary Arizona divides as follows: whites constitute 80.8 percent; blacks, 3 percent; Native Americans, 5.6 percent; Asians, 1.5 percent; other races, 9.1 percent. Persons who identify as Hispanic without regard to race number 18.8 percent. The age distribution is 26.8 percent under eighteen years and 13.1 percent over sixty-five years; the median age is 32.2.

Religiously, Arizona conforms to the national pattern with a few exceptions. The Protestant-Catholic ratio matches the national pattern with Catholics representing 22 percent of the population. But a high percentage of Catholics are Hispanic and are only nominally Catholic. Evangelical/fundamentalist Protestants form a somewhat higher percentage than at the national level. Also, given the state's proximity to Utah, the 5 percent Mormon population is not without significance. Jews, close to the national percentage, have been prominent in Arizona since the nineteenth century. Currently even the traditional, non-Christian Native American religions are being absorbed into the civil creed. Traditionally, Arizona has not been characterized by religious conflict or politicized religion. Religion has been viewed as a private and personal commitment. Usually the religion of a candidate is not offered or solicited. Akin to many border regions, Arizona has fostered a live-and-let-live attitude combined with substantial religious syncretism.

Manufacturing is Arizona's most important industry, followed by the service sector, and retail trade. Agriculture continues to be of significance. The main manufacturing items include electrical, communications, and aeronautical products. Traditionally, the copper industry was vital, with Arizona producing over half the nation's copper. The leading agricultural activities are cattle, cotton, dairy products, and lettuce. Federally owned lands, representing 43.6 percent of Arizona land, continue to have an impact on the economy.

Politically Arizona is one of the most conservative states, although there are pockets of liberalism; the more liberal Tucson is often pitted against conservative Phoenix. During Democratic ascendancy (1912–52), conservative Democrats, called Pintos, who were indistinguishable from Republicans, controlled the state. The politics resembled that of the Solid South. Today Republicans outnumber Democrats in registration and the state has not voted for a Democratic presidential candidate since 1948. Although the current congressional delegation is evenly split, the state legislature is Republican, as is ordinarily the case. Arizonans often demonstrate a certain independence by electing Democratic governors and Republican legislatures, although at the present time both governor and legislature are Republican. There is little hesitancy for most voters in crossing party lines; party identity is a very nominal loyalty. Successful Arizona Democrats usually win by focusing on state and local concerns and minimizing the national Democratic link. Arizona notables who move to the national level often dichotomize their state and national images. Morris Udall in Arizona was considerably more conservative than Morris Udall in Washington, D.C. The same will no doubt prove true of Bruce Babbitt. Arizonan conservatism was also manifested in the career of Barry Goldwater, leader of the GOP right-wing uprising, 1964 presidential candidate, and elder statesman. During the Goldwater period the state also had a strong and visible John Birch Society, which considered Goldwater less than orthodox.

Only a minority of Arizonans were born within the state. Numerous transplants feel that they have fled the severe weather and urban problems of the North and East. They have left the insecurity, the crime, the crowds, the smog, the graffiti, and the competitiveness for a more relaxed lifestyle in the Arizona sun. Seldom are they sympathetic to the concerns of northern and eastern inner cities. It took three elections, a united establishment effort, and a national boycott to secure a positive vote for a Martin Luther King holiday. For thousands, Arizona is the end of the rainbow. It attracts affluent winter visitors, fly-by-night speculators, down-and-out transients, and middle-class folks seeking a new environment. It is no accident that it has the highest bankruptcy rate in the United States.[13]

Arizona conservatism sounds more Lockean than Burkean, more libertarian than social/organic. It stresses the claims of the atomized individual against authority. It views government, especially national government, with suspicion. It demands maximal freedom and space for the individual. But it expects the individual to carry his or her weight and not become a dependent. It is "anti-big," whether bigness is represented by big government, big business, or big labor. It is exceptionally patriotic with the cult of the flag manifested throughout Arizona and little sympathy shown conscientious objectors or flag burners. It preserves the romanticized values of the cowboy and early settler with the paradoxes and inconsistencies seldom conceded.

The Arguments

The advocates of Proposition 110 presented their position as a "common sense" compromise to a difficult question. It was a middle-ground solution to a human problem that had divided the country for twenty years.[14] Supposedly it appealed to the great middle that rejected a total ban on abortion as well as abortion on demand. It sought the support of those who rejected both "always" and "never." It conceded the exceptional need for abortion in hardship cases but condemned abortion as a means of birth control. Advocates presented Proposition 110 as a deterrent to the abortion industry that supported some thirty abortionists and encouraged abortion for financial gain. Advocates bemoaned permissive abortion as well as the failure to warn women of the physical and psychological ramifications of abortion. They promised that the petition would remove the question from gutless politicians incapacitated by interest groups and would allow the voters to settle the matter.

Toward the end of the campaign, the emphasis changed somewhat.[15] Public statements de-emphasized abortion and stressed the civil rights nature of the petition. It was a civil rights measure for the unborn. Advocates stressed the vulnerability of the unborn and the proposition as a remedy. They emphasized that it did not prohibit abortion, allowing it when the mother's life was threatened, and charging the legislature to cover the hardship exceptions. But the sanctity of human life was crucial and the unborn the most exposed. Advocates cited the dangerous precedent of abortion in compromising that sanctity and charged that abortion also posed a threat to the family and its integrity. Throughout they tried to avoid a sectarian stance that would identify the effort with the Religious Right. They eschewed scriptural quotes and church manifestoes. They sought a common denominator that might attract a broad base of support.

Advocates expended much of their effort in answering charges of the opposition that this was an extremist, sectarian effort of religious enthusiasts who wanted to bring government into the bedroom and ultimately outlaw all abortion. They also had to cope with the charge of deceit—that the petition was tendentious and its real objective was cleverly concealed.

The antireferendum forces utilized the usual pro-choice arguments.[16] They focused on choice rather than abortion, contending that the real question was who would make the decision—a woman or the government. They cited a woman's constitutional right to privacy and the "back alley" alternative to safe, legal abortion. They noted that twenty years of progress were threatened by this backward proposal. They labeled supporters as extremists committed to a sectarian agenda.

Opponents critiqued the contents of the referendum, citing a variety of objections.[17] They noted that the prohibition on public funding was redundant since public funding was presently illegal in Arizona. They contended that there was no exception for rape and incest, only the possibility of legislative action, and legislatures were unpredictable. Opponents charged that the references were to "reported" rape and incest, and one-third were never reported. They cited the failure to allow abortion for mental health reasons. They charged that the provision for legal assistance for the unborn would be economically disastrous and a lawyer's bonanza. They speculated that the proposition might even outlaw a variety of birth control devices. They threatened that should the petition pass, they would turn to the judiciary because the petition would clearly conflict with *Roe v. Wade*. Finally, they charged that Proposition 110 would give Arizona the most restrictive abortion law in the United States.

The Campaign and Outcome

The referendum campaign occurred simultaneously with the 1992 presidential election. The electorate had to vote on national, state, local, and referendum questions. There were numerous propositions on the ballot, dealing with such issues as hunting restrictions and a Martin Luther King holiday. Abortion was but one of many topics to be decided in a campaign dominated by the presidential election. Judging by news coverage and letters to the editor, abortion was probably the most controversial proposition, but it was still a minor consideration for most voters, obscured by the many other issues and candidates. Proposition 110 (P110) seemed overwhelmed by the amount of decision making demanded of the electorate.

The proposition's supporters relied primarily on short television commercials shown during the last two weeks of the campaign. Employing a professional actress, they presented P110 as a rational, pragmatic compromise to a complex problem. One representative commercial had an actress speak as follows:

> What should have been a very personal reasonable debate has been turned into a shouting match between two extreme groups speaking only for themselves.
>
> Most of us defy simplistic labels like "pro-choice" or "pro-life."
>
> We know there are times when abortion is the best choice, but we still revere the sanctity of life.[18]

The commercial then urged support for P110 as a solution to the problem. The ambiguity of the commercial led some to assume this was a pro-choice ad. Another commercial employed the same actress contending that "the politicians only pander to the extremists on both sides, leaving no one to speak for the majority of us here in the middle." "We regret the idea that the only choice is between always and never."[19]

In addition to the television commercials, supporters sent letters to churches and to state newspapers. The church correspondence addressed to "Dear Co-

Laborers in Christ" urged ministers to witness against "the horrible sin of abortion" by prayer and the distribution of a brochure and assured them that involvement would not threaten the church's tax-exempt status.[20] Supporters also enjoyed the usual pamphlet access to all voters provided by the state.

Similarly, opponents of P110 utilized television commercials, worked through their networking organizations, and countered by means of the state pamphlet. They stressed the choice/privacy factor, constitutional rights, fear of governmental intervention, and the extreme, fanatical nature of P110. Representative of their commercials was one that used the Statue of Liberty as a prop. A male voice intoned:

> Our ancestors came to America because of a promise of freedom, liberty and choice. But now in Arizona, extremists want to take away our freedom of choice!
>
> Proposition 110 is a radical ban on virtually every abortion in Arizona. It forces the government and politicians to meddle in a family's life. And it wants to use millions of taxpayers' money to pay for it. Keep government out of private lives. Vote no on Proposition 110.[21]

The strong libertarian stance of the opponents led some to question their overall philosophy of government. Who were they, and what was their motivation?

Supporters of P110 changed organization name, chairman, and strategy during the last month of the campaign.[22] Arizonans for Common Sense became Arizonans for Proposition 110, Mac Magruder replaced Trent Franks, and civil rights for the unborn replaced abortion limitation in the public statements. These changes coexisted with the television commercials that seemed to reflect the original strategy. They were justified as an attempt to reach out to the business community and broaden the appeal, but no doubt related to the negative polls predicting defeat.

The mass campaign, waged primarily by television, lasted less than two weeks, with Barry Goldwater, elder statesman and former presidential nominee, emerging as a crucial actor.[23] An Episcopalian of Jewish extraction and an economic libertarian, Goldwater had never been comfortable with the Religious Right and its social agenda. His first wife had founded Planned Parenthood of Central and Northern Arizona, and he maintained contact with numerous persons associated with the organization. Goldwater attended a widely publicized fund raiser for the opposition to P110 and stated: "I feel as a man that a man shouldn't be overreactive on abortion. It's not a man's business, but if he behaved himself he wouldn't have to worry about it. I'm a great believer in a woman's choice."[24] He volunteered to make an oppositional commercial, which was widely used, and urged a negative vote on grounds of freedom and choice. In the commercial, the highly respected

Goldwater said: "We Americans share a heritage of freedom guaranteed us by our Constitution. Some of those freedoms, particularly the freedom of choice of a woman, are being threatened today particularly by P110. 110 is not good for our freedom. It's not good for Arizona. Vote against 110."[25] An announcer concluded by saying: "Keep government out of our private lives. Vote no on P110."

Supporters of P110 questioned Goldwater's integrity, noting that during his tough 1980 senatorial election, he had endorsed the right-to-life amendment. This amendment would have outlawed abortion, except to save the life of the mother. Supposedly, Goldwater had urged the right-to-life people to wait until his wife's departure before coming to his home for a signature.

Goldwater's intervention in the 1992 election was not limited to the abortion conflict. He shocked many by endorsing a Democratic congressional candidate over a Republican with strong Religious Right credentials.[26] The Republican candidate, a recent migrant to Arizona and associate of the Bakker evangelist team, had served for twenty years as an evangelical minister. He had worked for the Bush White House but had been relieved reportedly because of opposition to a White House invitation to homosexual leaders. The Goldwater intervention proved especially embarrassing in that the Republican candidate had campaigned as a Goldwater Republican. After the election, Republicans charged that the Goldwater endorsement was crucial, costing the Republican candidate some 7 percent of the vote. The Democratic victor stated that "I've got a lot of people to thank, and Barry Goldwater is right at the top of the list."[27]

Missing actors or the minimal participation of groups usually associated with the anti-abortion effort characterized the Arizona campaign. The Catholic Church and the right-to-life organization were primary among these.[28] Arizona is 22 percent Catholic, and the Catholic Church has an unambiguous anti-abortion stance and a sophisticated chain of command. The proponents of P110 seemed to assume that Catholic support would be available without effort and cultivation. Catholics would have no alternative to supporting the compromise petition. Actually, the P110 commercials seemed to portray the Catholic opposition to abortion as extremism and the right-to-life label as sloganeering. The Catholic bishops did release a letter of support but that seemed to represent the extent of Catholic involvement.[29] A Catholic organization—Catholics United for the Faith (CUF)—opposed the proposition, and some clergy referred to it as sanctioning "a little bit" of abortion. The Catholic effort manifested in many other states failed to materialize. Similarly, the right-to-life organization had minimal involvement. It did not participate in soliciting the signatures necessary to get P110 on the ballot. After ballot space was secured, it did endorse the proposition but committed itself primarily to electing sympathetic candidates, not promoting the referendum.[30] After the election, right-to-life leaders charged that the compromise had caused the defeat.

A variety of private and media polls tracked public opinion throughout the campaign. The presidential race assured ample polling that also covered the nonpresidential races.[31] The polls uniformly and constantly reported numbers similar to the actual outcome.[32] Evidently the emotional nature of the question did not deter a candid response on the part of those polled. The polls seemed to encourage change in leadership and strategy on the part of the proponents but did not encourage complacency on the part of the opponents. Even with the polls, the opponents ran scared, fearing that the confused nature of the proposition and the ambiguous advertising would lead many voters to believe that a vote for P110 was a pro-choice vote.

In the campaign both sides united in opposition to government. Both presented government as incompetent and potentially hostile to the individual. The proponents initially faulted government (i.e., politicians) for failure to deal with abortion and vulnerability to special-interest groups. They contended that now the people could take the initiative and act. The adversaries anathematized P110 as governmental intrusiveness into a private realm and governmental violation of a sacred individual right. Both sides sounded quite conservative.

A sample of statements by P110 opponents reveals the reliance on antigovernment sentiment to defeat the proposition. Gloria Feldt, executive director of Planned Parenthood of Central and Northern Arizona, wrote concerning the single major newspaper endorsement: "How ironic that a newspaper whose other editorial positions favor minimal government intervention supports a measure that would place the government squarely into our most personal decisions about childbearing."[33] Mary Crisp, head of the National Republican Coalition for Choice, told a fund-raising crowd: "This is a conservative issue. We need to keep government out of our lives. No one likes abortion, but it's the ability to choose that matters."[34] Similarly, an American Bar Association apologist, in a letter explaining the ABA position, wrote: "The resolution reflects classic conservative political doctrine: it urges the ABA to keep government out of the private lives of American women."[35] Finally Jeff Robinson, campaign manager for Pro-Choice Arizona, asserted that "Arizonans are independent, they are anti-government, and they don't want government intrusion."[36] "It [P110] would place government and politicians between a woman and her physician."[37] "It's outrageous to think that Arizonans would turn a private decision over to politicians, lawyers and the courts."[38]

Obviously the referendum battle was not a left-right, liberal-conservative contest. Arizona, at the same time that it voted overwhelmingly against P110, voted for Bush and strengthened the Republican forces in the legislature. Jay Nenninger, executive director of Arizona Right-to-Life, in a different context, characterized pro-abortion volunteers as "the country club set" and "members of the upper class."

The outcome was an overwhelming victory for the opponents of P110. The electorate voted 69–31 percent in opposition to the proposition. It lost in every county except the two rural counties of Apache and Graham. It lost with every category of citizen except for white evangelicals. Women and men voted virtually alike, as did mainline Protestants and Catholics, Republicans and Democrats, the different economic categories, and the different age groups.[39] It proved a disastrous defeat for the supporters and meant that it was improbable that the Arizona legislature would further restrict abortion. It also meant that the P110 trial run would not serve as a model for limiting abortion elsewhere. Gloria Steinem predicted that the defeat would prevent similar campaigns in at least twelve other states.

Explaining the Outcome

How to explain the one-sided outcome despite the conservatism of Arizona, the pro-life polls, and the financial resources available to the proponents? Given the present lack of survey research, explaining the outcome involves an impressionistic exercise. Some seven factors—without regard to hierarchy of significance—would seem to account for the result.

1.   The ability to define the issue seemed vital to success. The advocates of P110 stumbled in their effort. First they spoke of rational pragmatic compromise on a delicate matter and later they spoke of civil rights for the unborn. More successful anti-abortion efforts have focused on abortion, what it is, and what it does. By contrast, opponents of the proposition concentrated on choice and who makes it. It was a question of freedom and privacy and opposition to governmental and authoritarian intrusion. Abortion as an issue subsided. One could oppose abortion per se but support the right to choose. The ability to define the issue and control the language of discussion is crucial.
2.   The organizational confusion of the advocates hurt the effort. The change in leadership and strategy indicated problems in planning as well as the failure to think through the mechanics of a serious campaign against viable opposition.
3.   The anti-abortion effort suffered from the continuous charges of deception about P110, what it intended, and what it would accomplish. Voters seemed confused about what it would legislate. In such a situation, the rational response for many is to remain with the status quo, vote no.
4.   The advocates failed in their attempt to convince the electorate that the opponents were extremists. Goldwater in Arizona is no extremist but an arch-establishment notable. Opposition to P110 by such establishment organizations as the League of Women Voters, the YWCA, and the ABA legitimized the opposition. Meanwhile, the limited base of the supporters left them appearing as extremists.

5. The failure to establish coalitions, especially with the large Catholic sector, and to link with nonevangelicals probably made the effort appear sectarian despite claims of nonsectarianism. In American politics, the tent approach is the winning formula.

6. The advocates had to cope with unsympathetic media. Three of the four major newspapers endorsed the opposition, and media research indicates that media people are overwhelmingly liberal on the social issues.[40] The advocates lacked the skills and resources to communicate over the established media.

7. The supporters were at an initial disadvantage in that they were attempting to deprive people of a right that they have been told for twenty years was theirs. The electorate had learned, even in Arizona, to live with abortion.

Implications: The Catholic-Evangelical Alliance

This case demonstrates the difficulty of forging an anti-abortion coalition. The expected Catholic-evangelical collaboration never materialized. Somehow the two traditions, despite similar opposition to abortion, never formed a united effort. The evangelicals, who orchestrated the campaign, failed to communicate with the Catholics. Socialized to be suspicious of Catholicism, evangelical leaders seemed uncomfortable in approaching Catholic authorities and the Catholic laity. Consequently, Catholic leaders and clientele were never attracted to the campaign; only token support appeared.

A Catholic-evangelical alliance is the dream of many neoconservative intellectuals.[41] It would bring together the largest American denomination—Roman Catholicism—and the most dynamic and fastest-growing Protestant sector. It would link traditions that stress the need for a cohesive family orientation and entertain similar views on such social questions as divorce, homosexuality, abortion, and pornography. It would mesh traditions that are basically conservative.

But the legacy of history thwarts such a coalition. The evangelicals trace their origin to the sixteenth-century Protestant Reformation. The Reformation generated two explosions. The first involved the political break, centering on the attempt to nationalize and control the medieval church. The church *in* England would become the Church *of* England. Thus the reformed churches of England, Germany, and Scandinavia retained much that was traditional and catholic. They maintained significant continuity with the past, but eliminated the papacy and accepted integration into the machinery of state. These churches would be active in the twentieth-century ecumenical movement and would reestablish contact with the Catholic Church.

The second reformation explosion involved those who charged that the original reformers had not gone far enough. These dissenters advocated dogma revolution usually associated with simplicity of worship, congregationalism, egalitarianism, and self-interpretation of Scripture. They rejected the new state churches as well as Catholicism and suffered persecution throughout Europe. Later they played a major role in the settlement and development of North America. It is with this "low church," dissenting tradition that contemporary evangelicals identify. Consequently, to forge a link with Catholicism—even Vatican II Catholicism—involves considerable adjustment.

While Catholicism and evangelicalism espouse similar views on family and social issues, they differ adamantly in interpreting Christianity. Evangelicals are the most Protestant of the Protestants, and Catholicism is the religion they have traditionally protested against.[42] They advocate a Bible-oriented commitment and a simplicity of worship in an attempt to reconstruct the religion of first-century Christianity. They remain faithful to the old Protestant dogmas of Scripture alone and faith alone. Traditionally they have abjured much of Catholicism as nonbiblical, corrupted by pagan accretions, and somewhat foreign.

By contrast, Catholicism perceives itself as organic, incarnational/sacramental, and international.[43] It views the New Testament as the seed or beginning, rather than the model for all time. Christianity must be inculturated in every culture and the fruits of each integrated with the creed. Religion should have an aesthetic aspect in that the material world has been redeemed and must participate in worship. Thus many Catholics view evangelicals as Puritans, frozen in history, and having a manichean fear of culture. They perceive their "lecture as worship" as an unhistorical remnant of frontier religion.

Catholics and evangelicals differ in ethnic background, date of arrival in the United States, and geography of location. They also differ in recent historical memory. For Catholics, evangelicalism is the religion of the South and the Bible Belt, the areas most hostile to Catholicism. Evangelicals were the people most inclined to question Catholic patriotism during the presidential elections of 1928 and 1960. They are the people who, while supporting quasitheocracy in the Bible Belt, are constantly warning that Catholics are subverting the separation of church and state. Evangelicals are the ones expending vast sums to proselytize traditional Catholic countries while ignoring the inner cities that purport to be Protestant. They are most inclined to stereotype Catholicism and have little commitment to ecumenism. Their churches are seldom perceived as "sister churches."

Evangelicals countered by noting that Catholicism is an unbiblical religion that often condoned persecution of evangelicals in Catholic countries. They cited the corrupt politics and unhealthy environment of large Catholic cities and the clout exercised by the church hierarchy. Also they faulted Catholics for a permissive lifestyle (e.g., smoking, drinking, dancing, gambling). They seldom perceived Catholicism as part of the Body of Christ.

Economic differences also complicate the potential for a Catholic-evangelical alliance. While Catholicism is conservative on sexuality and certain social issues, on economics it moves to the left of the American spectrum. A series of papal encyclicals from *Rerum Novarum* (1881) to *Centesimus Annus* (1991) place the Catholic Church far closer to European social democracy than to American liberal capitalism. Catholic authorities have consistently condemned communism for its atheism and materialism, but also capitalism for its individualism, competitiveness, and materialism. Always there was hope for a third way, a Christian alternative to the extremes of communism and capitalism. The evangelical tradition, with its individual salvation emphasis and American flavor, seems much more reconcilable with capitalism than does the Catholic tradition.

Still, while mainline American Protestantism moves in a modernist direction and mass secularization continues, Catholics and evangelicals could be forced to de-emphasize their differences and examine their points of convergence. Despite the historical legacy and the numerous differences, both are firmly trinitarian and christological. Both appeal to Scripture, accept the primacy of the spiritual and the reality of salvation and damnation. Within the context of a comparative religious perspective, they seem more related than unrelated. The reforms of Vatican II—the biblical emphasis, the vernacular in the liturgy, the emphasis on the laity—make Catholicism less foreign and unintelligible to the evangelicals. Also, the evangelicals have mellowed somewhat in their apologetics and seldom view Catholicism as a monolith. There have been limited Catholic-evangelical ecumenical contacts, and stranger alliances have been fashioned in religion and politics.[44]

Implications for the Republican Party

The referendum campaign indicates a major problem for the Republican Party. It is represented by the class nature of the abortion controversy. How can the party reconcile the concerns of the religiously motivated with its silk-stocking base? The evangelicals—who voted 65 percent for Bush in 1992—identify with the GOP on social issues, but are not obviously and traditionally Republican in terms of class status. Catholics also have been moving away from their strong Democratic tradition, especially in presidential politics. How much of this relates to economic mobility and how much to social issues is difficult to determine. Protestant evangelicals and conservative Catholics seem ripe for Republican conversion. But the more affluent core Republicans, due to educational orientation and lifestyle, while cognizant of their economic interests, often are unsympathetic toward traditional social values. Can the church and the country club be reconciled?

In Arizona many upper-middle-class Republicans did not feel affected by the social concerns of the lower middle class. Affirmative action, quotas, mandated busing, abortion, and homosexual reform were abstract ideas that they might even embrace. It was quite respectable to be economically conservative and socially progressive. One could protect one's economic base but still embrace some features of the cultural revolution. Planned Parenthood, the ACLU, and the various women's organizations attracted many such individuals. In the United Kingdom such persons are labeled "Hampstead Liberals," while in France they are characterized as wearing their "hearts on the left and pocketbooks on the right."

Ronald Reagan moved the Republican Party beyond its silk-stocking base and appealed to large numbers of traditional Democrats.[45] His background—part ethnic, self-made, lower middle class—plus his commitment to patriotism and traditional values and his communication skills attracted many who did not identify with the Republican Party. The *macho* factor, Reagan's suspicion of communism, and his rejection of liberal guilt exercises endeared him to many who were not economically Republican. On social issues, he spoke the language of the old working-class, ethnic-oriented Democratic Party that had elected Roosevelt, Truman, and Kennedy. He stressed traditional values, being pro-family, anti-abortion, and antipornography. One Catholic politician interviewed called him "the closest we've had to a Catholic president."

Reagan Democrats were people who often contended that the national Democratic Party left them as of 1972. They could not comprehend how the "new class," the "wine and cheese crowd," had come to dominate their party. They personally did not live in security enclaves, send their children to elite academies, or travel extensively abroad. They were concerned with personal safety, criminal violence, and urban decay, and they fled the cities by the millions. They were working people who resented welfare, food stamps, and preferential treatment for the advantaged. They distinguished sharply between the deserving and nondeserving poor. Deeply patriotic, they failed to understand the rejection of patriotism by the more privileged, and they saw no excuse for draft dodging or flag burning. In protest, they turned by the millions to vote for Ronald Reagan. But these people were not economically conservative. In a homogeneous society, uncomplicated by racial division and the cultural revolution, they would probably be loyal social democrats.

These people are crucial to Republican electoral success. The problem is how to hold them for a party whose economic stance is not clearly in their interest. What can the Republican Party offer these Reagan Democrats? If the GOP switches on social issues, what motivation would the Reagan Democrats have to remain apart from their ancestral home, the Democratic Party? The great communicator has retired and communism/anticommunism is no longer a factor. What then can attract the nonaffluent to the party of the affluent?

Implications: Abortion and the Liberal-Conservative Spectrum

This study indicates the difficulty of placing the abortion issue within the context of the liberal-conservative spectrum. Arizona, one of the most conservative states, which rejected Democratic presidential candidates for over forty years, and now has a Republican governor and legislature, voted overwhelmingly pro-choice. The same electorate that voted against P110 strengthened the Republican position within the legislature. How can one reconcile this with conventional wisdom that labels pro-choice as liberal and pro-life as conservative? How account for the fact that in this conflict the pro-choice people, when compared with the pro-life people, seemed the more affluent? Conventional wisdom identifies liberalism with the less affluent and conservatism with the more affluent. Perhaps in the case of abortion, conventional wisdom has simplified a complex issue.

Not all persons of liberal orientation perceive abortion reform as a liberal issue. Liberalism has a complex history and draws on many sources. There are liberals who entertain reservations about the recent liberal endorsement of abortion, seeing it as inconsistent with liberal philosophy, faddish, and a concession to Yuppie consumerism. They argue that the central issue is the definition of life and its boundaries rather than the elevation of individual choice. In a tribal world of callousness and brutality, the sanctity of life must be asserted. Pro-life liberals contend that, traditionally, liberalism generously embraced life in all its variety. Liberalism urged concern beyond family, tribe, and nation to encompass all humanity. Liberalism was unapologetically international and cosmopolitan. Later liberals even extended concern and sympathy to animal life and the realm of nature. Whales and other endangered species must be respected and their link with humanity acknowledged. Now to exclude the most vulnerable—unborn humans—is not liberal but reactionary. It means limiting and contracting the definition of authentic life. It is not progress but regression to a more barbaric, more selfish era. It is a rejection of liberal humanism, especially when justified for the convenience of the atomized individual. It is more akin to the liberalism of the nineteenth century than to the social variety of the twentieth century. Obviously, this pro-life liberalism is quite minoritarian and generally unrecognized. It is found primarily among persons of a religious orientation who appeal to the "seamless garment" argument in affirming life in opposition not only to abortion but also to capital punishment and war.

On the other hand, many conservatives feel quite comfortable with abortion reform. They see conservative association with anti-abortion efforts as an aberration and a too-generous concession to the Religious Right. It is an embarrassment to be explained away in terms of *realpolitik*. They perceive conservatism as a very modern ideology stressing individualism, maximal freedom, and minimal government. They perceive government and governmental intrusion as the major problems. Consequently, arguments that stress individual decision making and limited government in all areas, including abortion, appeal to them. Also, they are not unaware of the changing demography as well as the racial/ethnic composition of the 1.6 million abortions performed yearly.

The dominant strain of American conservatism, which is really nineteenth-century Lockean liberalism, differs greatly from the more European, Burkean conservatism.[46] The latter does not defer to atomized individualism, maximal freedom, or minimal government. It is far more organic and social, stressing such values as family, community, the chain-of-being, tradition, and continuity. Philosophically, it provides a much stronger base for resisting permissive abortion. For the Burkean conservative, breaking the organic chain-of-being for convenience's sake is blasphemy with all sorts of dire ramifications. Minimizing the claims of family, father, and community and ignoring the religious heritage for one person's "right to choose" is selfish and ultimately disastrous. American conservatism, however, is not Burkean but is the liberalism of an earlier period. Barry Goldwater is a nineteenth-century liberal, and the Burkean concerns and priorities carry little weight in our ever-changing, very modern society. So in Arizona, the most conservative of states, conservatives who cherished atomized individualism, maximal freedom, and minimal government responded to the pro-choice campaign. Barry Goldwater and Gloria Steinem met and embraced.

Notes

1. *Arizona Republic*, 3 July 1992, 1.
2. *Phoenix Gazette*, 20 October 1992, C1.
3. *Phoenix Gazette*, 3 July 1992, B1.
4. *Phoenix Gazette*, 9 October 1992, 6.
5. *Phoenix Gazette*, 3 July 1992, B1.
6. Interviews with an ex-Tucson mayor, Thomas J. Volgy, 8 June 1993, and with State Senator Peter Goudinoff, 9 May 1993.
7. *Arizona Republic*, 3 July 1992, 7, and 29 October 1992, 1.
8. *Arizona Republic*, 18 September 1992, 1.
9. *Phoenix Gazette*, 13 October 1992, 1.
10. *Phoenix Gazette*, 22 October 1992, B1.
11. Arizona political culture is a neglected area of research. Consequently one must resort to histories of the state and the recent voting behavior. See Lawrence C. Powell, *Arizona* (New York: Norton, 1976); George Babbitt, *Arizona* (Scottsdale: B & H Publishing, 1977); and Robert Woznicki, *History of Arizona* (Phoenix: Woznicki, 1992).
12. For the basic demographic and industrial statistics on Arizona, see Michael Barone and Grant Ujifusa, *The Almanac of American Politics 1992* (Washington, D.C.: R.R. Donnelley & Sons, 1991); Edith R. Hornor, ed., *Almanac of the Fifty States* (Palo Alto, Calif.: Information Publications, 1993); and *Statistical Abstract of the United States, 1992* (Washington, D.C.: Government Printing Office, 1992).
13. Interview with attorney J.B. Stroud, 17 July 1993.
14. *Arizona Republic*, 19 September, 2; *Arizona Daily Star*, 25 October 1992, F1.
15. *Arizona Republic*, 10 October 1992, B4; *Arizona Daily Star*, 25 October 1992, F1.
16. *Arizona Republic*, 19 September 1992, 2; *Arizona Daily Star*, 25 October 1992, F1.
17. *Phoenix Gazette*, 20 October 1992, C1; *Tucson Citizen*, 22 October 1992, 11.
18. *Arizona Republic*, 20 October 1992, 1.
19. *Arizona Daily Star*, 21 October 1992, B1.
20. *Phoenix Gazette*, 9 October 1992, 6.

21. *Arizona Republic*, 27 October 1992, B1.

22. *Arizona Republic*, 10 October 1992, B4; *Phoenix Gazette*, 13 October 1992, 1.

23. *Phoenix Gazette*, 30 October 1992, 1.

24. *Arizona Republic*, 4 October 1992, C5.

25. *Phoenix Gazette*, 22 October 1992, B1.

26. *Phoenix Gazette*, 30 October 1992, 1.

27. *Phoenix Gazette*, 4 November 1992, 9.

28. *Phoenix Gazette*, 13 October 1992, 1, and 5 November 1992, 1.

29. This represented an interesting change, since the Catholic Church and bishops had been the primary opponents of the abortion reforms first introduced in the Arizona legislature in the late 1960s. See Daniel J. O'Neil, *Church Lobbying in a Western State* (Tucson: University of Arizona Press, 1970).

30. Interview with right-to-life representative Dennis S. Wikfors, 16 July 1993.

31. *Arizona Republic*, 3 July 1992, 7, and 28 October 1992, 1; *Phoenix Gazette*, 16 October 1992, 2, 29 October 1992, A10, and 30 October 1992, 2.

32. Interview with pollster Henry C. Kenski, 10 August 1993.

33. *Arizona Republic*, 30 October 1992, 17.

34. *Arizona Republic*, 4 October 1992, C5.

35. *Arizona Republic*, 13 October 1992, 10.

36. *Arizona Republic*, 18 October 1992, A10.

37. *Arizona Republic*, 28 October 1992, 1.

38. *Arizona Republic*, 18 October 1992, A10.

39. *Arizona Republic*, 4 November 1992, 15.

40. See Robert S. Lichter and Stanley Rothman, *The Media Elite: America's New Powerbrokers* (Bethesda, Md.: Adler and Ader, 1986).

41. Most prominent among these neoconservatives would probably be Michael Novak and Richard Neuhaus. See also the journals *Crisis* and *First Things*.

42. The best introduction for nonevangelicals to the tenets and contemporary thinking of evangelicals is the popular journal *Christianity Today*.

43. The best description of the Catholic ethos continues to be Newman's classic: John Henry Newman, *An Essay on the Development of Christian Doctrine* (Garden City, N.Y.: Doubleday, 1960).

44. For an interesting ecumenical effort linking conservative Catholics and evangelicals, see William Ball, ed., *In Search of a National Morality* (San Francisco: Ignatius Press, 1992).

45. *New York Times*, 5 November 1992, B9.

46. See Louis Hartz, *The Liberal Tradition in America* (New York: Harcourt, Brace, 1955).

RUTH ANN STRICKLAND

6 | North Carolina: One Liberal Law in the South

North Carolina was officially dubbed a "megastate" when the 1980 census revealed it as the tenth-most-populous state in the nation. Its population grew by 13 percent in the 1980s and continues to expand and diversify.

North Carolina settlers were typically not as wealthy as those in neighboring southern states, fostering a populist political environment. Traditionally, North Carolina experienced little in-migration, except for the importation of slaves prior to 1808. Yet as North Carolina becomes headquarters for NationsBank, the nation's fourth-largest bank, and Nucor, the nation's leading minimill steelmaker, more in-migration has occurred, particularly in Charlotte and in Raleigh-Durham's Research Triangle.[1]

In the 1960s North Carolina employed the highest percentage of workers in manufacturing in the nation. In the 1990s manufacturing constitutes 30 percent of the state's workforce while service industries provide 65 percent of the state's gross product. Because much of the industry in North Carolina is textiles, furniture, and tobacco, it also has the lowest level of unionization in the country. Low wages and poor working conditions once characterized many jobs in North Carolina, and in some sectors of the state's economy this is still true. But in the 1980s and 1990s wages rose, unemployment declined, and professional and high-tech jobs moved in rapidly.[2]

In the eastern, coastal part of North Carolina, politics was shaped by British Anglican settlers who became Methodists and Confederate slaveholders and identified with the Democratic Party. In the Piedmont region the settlers were Scots-Irish Presbyterians who were Union supporters and voted Republican. The less populous western part of the state, settled primarily by the English, Germans, and Scots-Irish, has been a traditional Republican stronghold. Unlike the eastern part of the state, which still votes almost solidly Democratic, the Piedmont and the western regions have witnessed increased party competition in the 1980s and 1990s. Piedmont cities have become more Democratic because of the influx of professionals and blacks; yet the rural counties in the Piedmont remain heavily populated by white Born-Again Christians who vote Republican. In the 1980s and 1990s, the state has been torn politically between traditional and modernizer politics, symbolized by the rivalry between Democratic governor Jim Hunt and Republican senator Jesse Helms.[3]

In 1982 more than 3 million North Carolinians (about 54 percent of the population) were affiliated with one of fifty-six religious denominations. Baptists are the state's largest religious group, followed by Methodists, Presbyterians, and Roman Catholics. Many North Carolinians espouse fundamentalist beliefs, claiming that the Bible should be taken as the literal truth. Conservative evangelicals who have their roots in North Carolina, such as Billy Graham, have preached to mass audiences.[4] The evangelical spirit of the state, combined with an identification with fundamentalism, has provided a spawning ground for anti-abortion groups, such as right-to-life committees, Operation Rescue, and the North Carolina Christian Action League. Despite the religiosity of the state, in recent years the Baptist membership has declined and churches have faced competition from secular and modernizing forces. The strength of the anti-abortion groups has been diluted by pro-choice groups, such as the North Carolina Religious Coalition for Abortion Rights and the National Abortion Rights Action League chapters of North Carolina.

The Abortion Debate

Common ground between those who favor choice and those who are against choice on the issue of abortion is difficult to achieve. The debate surrounding access to abortion is often framed in bimodal terms with opponents taking intense, mutually exclusive positions. These positions are illustrated by the fundamental dispute over when life begins: either the fetus is a person at conception or not; therefore, either the fetus has rights as a person or not. The moral arguments add intensity to this issue and make compromise difficult if not impossible.[5]

The abortion debate is a political and increasingly a religious battle. It pits well-intentioned groups against one another as opponents disagree fundamentally about the scope and role that government should play in determining access to abortions or in protecting the rights of the fetus. Religious conflict is evident as the Catholic Church and some fundamentalist Christian denominations characterize abortion as the "unjustifiable killing of innocent human life." Beyond this, it is an issue that potentially embodies gender conflict as pro-choicers argue for reproductive choice and modifications of patriarchal control of female social and gender roles in society and anti-abortionists argue for continuance of traditional gender roles.[6]

When the issue of public funding of abortion is raised, morality politics and redistributive policy questions make compromise and consensus even more unlikely. Studies that compare state policies on public funding of abortion have indicated that advocacy groups and political forces in the state play the dominant role in shaping outcomes in this policy area.[7] This chapter examines the historical and political forces that led to the passage of liberal abortion legislation, especially the State Abortion Fund, in North Carolina.

The Hyde Amendments and the Public Funding Debate

In 1977 Congressman Henry J. Hyde (R-Ill.), sponsored the Hyde Amendment, which limited the use of federal Medicaid funds for abortions to those instances when the mother's life would be endangered should the fetus be carried to term. The U.S. Supreme Court upheld this restriction on access to abortions for poor women in *Harris v. McRae*, 448 U.S. 297 (1980), ruling that *Roe* did not institute a new entitlement that would guarantee equal access to abortion.[8]

Since 1977, the Code of Federal Regulations has specified differing guidelines funding Medicaid abortions, varying from abortions only in cases of medical necessity to including rape and incest to endangerment of the mother's life. The most restrictive interpretation of the Hyde Amendment prevailed until December 1993, allowing Medicaid abortions only if the mother's life was endangered. Given this restriction on funding at the federal level, state governments that desired to guarantee low-income women equal access to abortion had to subsidize elective abortions with state funding.[9] In December 1993 the Health and Human Services Department of the Clinton administration issued a directive[10] requiring states to pay for abortions of low-income women in cases of rape or incest.[11]

Arguments against Public Funding

The debate over public funding is characterized by morality and redistributive issues. The opponents of public funding of abortion typically rely on moral arguments and are opposed to most or even all abortions, holding that the fetus is a human being and therefore deserving of protection. Moreover, opponents assert that taxpayer money should not be used to fund the taking of an innocent life and that if a person cannot afford an abortion, other options, such as adoption, should be considered. Instead, government should be neutral and restrain itself from rendering any dictates about reproductive choices.[12]

Other, more moderate opponents claim that public funding encourages a procedure that should be used as rarely as possible and not as a means of birth control. Using public funds to pay for abortions is tantamount to endorsing them. Scarce public monies should be used to fund prevention programs, not to fund sexual recreation that leads to pregnancy. The more extreme opponents argue that abortions constitute mass murder at the taxpayer's expense.[13]

Arguments for Public Funding

Those in favor of publicly funded abortions claim that *Roe v. Wade* gave women the right to obtain abortions. They also argue that it is immoral to deny someone access to a right simply based on income.[14] They further claim that a right is worthless unless one has the means or capacity to exercise it. An examination of women who sought therapeutic abortion under a very restrictive state law (which permitted abortions if pregnancy threatened the mother's life) revealed that under psychiatric evaluation, 79 percent lacked emotional support from the man responsible for the pregnancy and the majority experienced great stress from the interplay of existing problems and an unwanted pregnancy.[15] Such studies verify the need for less restricted access to funded abortions.

Some argue that if other medically necessary procedures are funded under Medicaid, abortions should also be funded—to single out abortion is unconstitutional. Others claim that the Hyde Amendment is unconstitutional on the grounds that government expends monies for the costs of childbirth, but not for abortion. Since pregnancy is a condition that requires medical care, there are two ways to handle pregnancy: abort or carry the fetus to term. Under the *Roe* decision, the government is to ensure privacy, and under this reasoning it has no legitimate interest in whether the woman chooses abortion or childbirth. Its primary interest is to protect the health and safety of the mother, and if she gives birth, then it should protect the child as well.[16] To remove abortion from the medical choices open to poor women places government on the side of pregnancy continuance, not in a neutral position.

Others cite the commitment of time, energy, and emotional support needed to raise a child and assert that the mother who is forced to carry an infant to term may harbor resentment and withhold time, energy, and emotional support from the child. If there are no public funds for abortion, low-income women, especially teenagers, would be forced into a long-term commitment that they may not be ready to handle. Many proponents fear that low-income women, unable to procure an expensive private abortion, will resort to cheaper methods in dollar terms but costly in public health terms—the coat hanger, the "back alley" abortion.[17]

Public Funding of Abortions in the South

At present, thirty states publicly fund abortions only if the life of the mother is at stake. Twelve states fund abortions in most or all circumstances; eight states will fund abortions only in cases of rape, incest, or fetal deformity. North Carolina is one of twelve states that provides funds for abortion in most or all circumstances. It is the only southern state to provide funding for elective abortions.[18]

All other southern states restrict access to abortion using a variety of techniques. Before the *Roe v. Wade* ruling, six southern states—Alabama, Arkansas, Louisiana, Mississippi, Oklahoma, and Texas—had laws on the books prohibiting virtually all abortions. Today, most southern states retain a number of restrictions on abortion. For example, five southern states—Alabama, Arkansas, Georgia, Louisiana, and South Carolina—require that minors notify one or both parents or obtain consent. In addition, Alabama, Florida, Kentucky, Louisiana, Mississippi, Tennessee, and Virginia require women to be counseled on abortion and many women must wait twenty-four hours or more before obtaining abortion services. Three states—Florida, Kentucky, and South Carolina—require that women obtain consent or notify their husbands prior to obtaining an abortion.[19]

Kentucky and Louisiana prohibit the use of public facilities and/or personnel in the performance of abortions. In 1992, four southern governors (those in Alabama, Louisiana, Mississippi, and South Carolina) advocated criminalizing abortions. Louisiana prevents health-care providers from giving advice or referrals on abortions. All southern states except North Carolina—Alabama, Arkansas, Florida, Georgia, Kentucky, Louisiana, Mississippi, Oklahoma, South Carolina, Tennessee, and Texas—refuse to fund abortions unless the woman's life is imperiled by continuing the pregnancy; Virginia also will not fund abortions unless a woman's life is in danger, but will fund them if rape or incest is involved in the pregnancy.[20]

In a study conducted by Halva-Neubauer comparing state abortion policies after the *Webster* ruling was issued, North Carolina is labeled an "acquiescer state."[21] The National Abortion Rights Action League (NARAL) characterized North Carolina as a battleground state, although of these states it poses the lowest risk for loss of abortion rights should *Roe v. Wade* be overturned. In 1992 NARAL ranked North Carolina the seventh-most-likely state in the nation to keep abortion services safe and legal.[22] In the area of public funding of abortions, North Carolina might be labeled a "supporter state." Counting the number of restrictions enacted by state legislatures may not take into account the stringency or leniency of the measures enacted. Also, some restrictions place greater burdens on access to abortion than others. This should be taken into account when considering abortion legislation in North Carolina, the state with the most liberal abortion policy in the South.

Creating and Expanding North Carolina's
State Abortion Fund, 1977–84

With the passage of the 1967 abortion statute, North Carolina's General Assembly became the second state legislature (following Colorado's) to enact a liberal abortion law, permitting the women of North Carolina to terminate a pregnancy at twenty weeks or less if continued pregnancy impaired health or imperiled life, or in the case of rape, incest, or a grave birth defect.[23] In subsequent years, North Carolina has established a state fund for low-income women seeking elective abortions, once again distinguishing itself as a relatively liberal state.

Before the enforcement of the Hyde Amendment (fiscal year 1976–77), $1.8 million—90 percent of it federal funds—funded elective abortions for poor women in North Carolina.[24] When federal funds were eliminated by the Hyde Amendment, state aid for abortions in North Carolina was temporarily suspended from August 1977 to January 1978. In response to the Hyde Amendment, Human Resources secretary Sarah Morrow recommended that state monies be used to assist poor women who could not afford elective abortions.

In January 1978 the North Carolina Department of Human Resources shifted $442,000 from other purposes to continue funding state abortions. At a state Social Services Commission meeting, Dr. Morrow recommended that North Carolina begin paying for these abortions by 1 February 1978. Dr. Morrow based her request on the *Roe v. Wade* decision and the idea that all women, not just the wealthy, should have access to elective abortions.[25] By February 1978, the Department of Human Resources of the state of North Carolina had set up a State Abortion Fund.

Abortions for eligible low-income women were funded totally by state monies but at a lower rate than that sponsored by Medicaid funding. The average abortion payment of $442.30 for poor women in 1976–77 was reduced to $201.[26] Governor James B. Hunt in May 1978 gave his support for state funding of abortions for low-income women. At a press conference, he stated: "I don't think it's fair for the rich to have [access to abortions] and the poor not to have it." The $442,000 of public abortion funds set aside in February was exhausted by 30 June 1978 and consequently the department requested additional funds from the legislature. With Governor Hunt's approval, Dr. Morrow recommended that the General Assembly appropriate $1 million for a State Abortion Fund.[27]

During the short legislative session in the summer of 1978, state funding of abortions became one of the hotly debated issues. Numerous groups mobilized to protest for and against state funding of abortions.[28] Interest-group and citizen testimony was emotionally charged. Ms. J.C. Honneycutt of Charlotte testified that access to abortion saved her from giving birth to a child that would have been severely retarded and deformed and that approving public funding for low-income women was not just a moral or legal issue but a question of survival. A Greensboro insurance man, David Osteen, characterized state-funded abortions as similar to genocide under Nazi Germany. Anti-abortion foes sent a wave of letters asking legislators not to fund abortions.[29]

By a 46–39 vote, the Joint Base Budget Committee voted to defeat a motion to remove $1 million of state funding for elective abortions. Senator Ollie Harris

(D-Cleveland), who led the effort to eliminate the appropriation, asked, "Is the North Carolina General Assembly becoming more liberal than the Congress of the United States?" Despite strong protest from anti-abortion groups, the measure prevailed with the support of black legislators and key committee leaders. Representative Harold L. Kennedy (D-Forsyth), in response to Senator Harris, stated that it was not a matter of liberality but a question of whether North Carolina was going to discriminate against low-income women who could not afford abortions.[30]

Later in 1978, the State Abortion Fund came under attack from Paul Stam, Jr., then an Apex attorney who was acting president of the Wake County Right to Life Association. Stam filed a lawsuit challenging the constitutionality of state funding of elective or medically unnecessary abortions for poor women. Stam, a right-to-life proponent, claimed that a fetus is a person, and he asserted that counties were not authorized to collect revenues (via taxes) to fund elective abortions. In particular, he was concerned about the use of Wake County funds, his home county, to supplement the State Abortion Fund. The North Carolina Supreme Court held in March 1981 that state funding of elective abortions was constitutional but that county governments could not levy taxes to supplement funding of such abortions because no specific statute authorized such activity. State and local officials in reaction to the ruling stated that it would have little effect on state funding of abortions because only Wake, Guilford, and Mecklenburg counties had some kind of supplemental program.[31] As a result of the ruling, counties are now reimbursed for the cost of providing abortion services to poor women.[32]

In the 1981 North Carolina General Assembly session, opponents of state-funded abortions launched another attack on the State Abortion Fund. Senator Harris, one of the most outspoken abortion foes, tried to cut $900,000 out of the proposed $1 million budget for elective abortions. His motion to reduce appropriations to the State Abortion Fund from $1 million to $100,000 was narrowly defeated in a vote taken in the Joint Base Budget Committee. His proposal also specified that the $100,000 be used only for abortions involving rape, incest, or where the mother's life was threatened. Although some members called for a show of hands on the committee voice vote, the committee co-chairperson, Senator Robert Jordan, used the rules to prevent this by claiming that the request came after he had announced the vote (legislative rules hold that request for a show of hands must occur before the committee chair announces the voice vote results). The loss was the second and most critical one suffered by abortion opponents. At that time Senator Harris decided to desist in his efforts to delete abortion money from the state budget.[33]

In July 1982 the state legislature increased annual State Abortion Fund appropriations from $1 million to $1,374,500. Between 1982 and 1984, there was a brief lull in the abortion funding controversy. The gubernatorial administration of Democrat Jim Hunt (1976–84), sympathetic to the issue of public funding of abortion, was replaced by that of a Republican governor, Jim Martin. With the national mood clearly more conservative and a president who avidly opposed abortion rights, the atmosphere was ripe for conflict at the state level over this divisive issue.

Retrenchment of the State Abortion Fund, 1985–92

During his 1984–92 administrations, Governor Martin publicly advocated ending state abortion funds for abortions except in cases of rape, incest, or endangerment of the mother's life. In 1985 abortion funding became a contentious issue again. Under the Martin proposal, more draconian cuts in the State Abortion Fund were suggested than those proposed earlier by Senator Harris, reducing the fund from $1.3 million to $50,000 a year.[34]

In the 1985 legislative session the governor and members of his political party (and some Democrats) in the General Assembly squared off against prominent Democratic leaders on the issue of publicly funded abortions. Those against funding for abortion, such as Representative Coy Privette (R-Cabarrus), Senator Ollie Harris (D-Cleveland), Representative Frank J. ("Trip") Sizemore III (R-Guilford), Representative Theresa H. Esposito (R-Forsyth), and Senator Wendell H. Sawyer (R-Guilford), voiced moral opposition to abortions and also asserted that they had the strength (the votes) sharply to reduce state funding of abortions. Pro-choice advocates, such as Representative Liston Ramsey (D-Madison), Representative Daniel T. Blue (D-Wake), Representative Margaret Keesee-Forrester (R-Guilford), Lieutenant Governor Robert B. Jordan III, and Senator Anthony E. Rand (D-Cumberland), publicly opposed cutting the fund and argued that abortion access should be equal, not based on class distinctions.[35]

Interest groups were quite vocal. Paul Stam, still active in the Wake County Right-to-Life Association, dismissed arguments that poor women should have equal access to abortion stating: "The difference between having money and not is that the person with money can pay for things that others can't. We don't have a Cadillac fund. The choices in transportation are limited. Their choices all over the lot are different."[36]

Supporters of the abortion fund believed not only that poor women should have the same medical rights as their more affluent sisters but that eliminating the fund would cost millions of dollars. According to the Reverend Deborah J. Steely, coordinator of the North Carolina Religious Coalition for Abortion Rights, an estimated $40 million in additional services for newborns and infants, including welfare services, would be drawn from North Carolina taxpayers if the State Abortion Fund was reduced dramatically.[37]

Ultimately the State Abortion Fund was reduced in the 1985 legislative battle, and compromises were made. The Joint Base Budget Committee narrowly voted to maintain funding. Funding was set at $924,500 (a 30 percent decrease in funding), and additional eligibility requirements were levied. Not only must recipients be North Carolina residents receiving Title XX Health Support Services but they must meet one of the following criteria: impairment of health as a result of pregnancy, victimized by rape or incest, mentally retarded, or younger than eighteen years of age.

Much debate ensued later when there was a sharp decline in access to and delay in obtaining abortion services for poor women as a result of the "health impairment" stipulation. Although doctors' statements certifying health impairment were not difficult to obtain because most doctors interpreted this phrase broadly to include mental and physical health, many women were confused and did not try to overcome the extra obstacle.[38] The health-impairment stipulation was worded vaguely and did not state that health impairment must be physical. The state Department of Human Resources, in its list of possible diagnoses that might warrant a state-funded abortion, listed such things as "acute anxiety reaction" or "acute subrational reaction," inferring that emotional and mental disturbances in health are as impairing as being physically unable to carry a fetus to term.[39]

In July 1989 the U.S. Supreme Court upheld parts of a restrictive Missouri abortion law in *Webster v. Reproductive Health Services, Inc.* (109 S.Ct. 3040), permitting restrictions on the use of public facilities and personnel in the performance of abortions and requiring viability tests on the fetus if the woman is twenty or more weeks pregnant. North Carolina legislators and interest groups reacted strongly to the decision. Representative Paul B. "Skip" Stam (R-Wake) stated that the North Carolina General Assembly would probably adopt a Missouri-type law. In fact, before the ruling, Representative Stam had already introduced a bill similar to the Missouri law and had anticipated passage in the short 1990 legislative session. A North Carolina Right to Life lobbyist expressed hope that momentum was on their side in the funding debate but also believed that passing a law similar to the Missouri law would be very difficult. Representative Sharon A. Thompson (D-Durham) responded that the Supreme Court ruling would activate pro-choice groups and would force a major battle to guard against eroding North Carolina's liberal abortion law.[40] Pro-choice groups, including the National Women's Political Caucus, National Organization for Women, WomenElect, and the National Abortion Rights Action League, reacted by targeting North Carolina state legislative campaigns and lobbied strongly to prevent the passage of more restrictive abortion legislation.[41]

By 1989, state funds for abortions were cut from $924,500 (1985–88) to $424,500 (1989–92). Pro-lifers, particularly on the House Appropriations Committee, wanted to slash the fund by 78 percent, from $924,500 to $200,000, but the Senate voted to cut the fund to $424,500. Leading the charge to reduce the abortion fund budget was Representative Paul Stam. At his urging, the House

Appropriations Committee version would have drastically altered access to abortion services for poor women because it would have limited abortion to victims of rape or incest and those whose "lives" (not health) were imperiled if they tried to carry the fetus to term. It was estimated that under these criteria only 100 women would be eligible per year for state-funded abortions.[42]

In the 1989 extra session, access to abortion was limited but not as severely as Stam hoped. The General Assembly reduced the gestation time from 135 days to 112 days, thus limiting a state-funded abortion to pregnancies of 112 days or less. It also passed a provision that adult women would be eligible for a state-funded abortion once in a lifetime obtained under the reason of health impairment. The more liberal Senate version became the law and allowed eligible women to receive state-funded abortions if they were victims of rape or incest or if continuing their pregnancies would "endanger their health." These regulations went into effect in July 1990. For fiscal year 1991–92, the General Assembly appropriated $424,500 for the budget of the State Abortion Fund, and regulations and restrictions remained the same as those enacted in 1989.

A Return to Expanding State Abortion Funds, 1993

In the legislative session of 1993, the North Carolina General Assembly once again revisited the issue of state funding of abortions. In the reconciliation between the House and Senate Appropriations Committees, this issue became contentious. The Senate proposed to increase the State Abortion Fund from $440,000 to $1 million, whereas the House plan sought an increase up to $1.4 million.[43] In the compromise that emerged from the conference committee, the State Abortion Fund was almost tripled, from $424,000 to $1.2 million for fiscal year 1993–94.[44]

Interviews conducted in June 1993 with various representatives and senators in the North Carolina General Assembly indicated that some prior restrictions on access to abortion were removed, notably the "one abortion in a lifetime per adult woman" stipulation and the requirement that a woman visit a state-certified physician, rather than the doctor of her choice, when determining health impairment.

Of those state legislators who favored public funding of abortion for low-income women, many claimed that minors in particular are harmed by families who have a punitive outlook on unplanned, unwed pregnancies and that the tendency to punish, not assist, young women who are pregnant brings about great costs to society in the long run. Others who favored public funding argued that the abortion fund is a small investment when compared to the number of unwanted pregnancies that would occur, the Aid to Families with Dependent Children (AFDC) and other welfare costs that would be incurred, and the abuse of children by frustrated mothers that might occur.[45]

State legislators opposed to public funding of abortions often cited public opinion in North Carolina as one reason (the fact that 61 percent of North Carolinians polled opposed the use of taxpayer's money for funding of abortions for low-income women). They also stated that public monies should not be used to fund private recreational activities and that such funding, if available at all, should be for cases of rape, incest, or if the mother's life is at stake due to a continued pregnancy. Others who oppose public funding of abortions argue that abortion constitutes murder of an innocent human being and public monies should not be used for this purpose.

When asked if future restrictions (i.e., parental notification/consent or a twenty-four-hour waiting period) seemed likely, most state legislators felt that restrictions would be introduced but that none would pass. Most cited the presence of Governor Hunt's administration as a force responsible for the continuation of a liberal abortion law and public funding of abortions in North Carolina. (For a brief history of the State Abortion Fund in North Carolina, see Table 6.1.)

Possible Restrictions on Access to Abortion Services

Since the passage of the liberal abortion law in 1967, numerous efforts have been launched unsuccessfully to place limits on access to abortion services in North Carolina. Table 6.2 presents a brief summary of some bills that have been introduced and referred to committees for consideration. At this point, none of these bills have become law. By far the most frequently supported, yet unsuccessful, proposed restriction by legislators is the requirement that unemancipated minors receive parental consent before obtaining an abortion. Arising in almost every legislative session, this restriction garners the most sponsors; if any additional restriction will gain passage in the future, this appears to be the most likely one.

Political Climate and Fluctuations in Abortion Funding

Several factors account for the fluctuations in the State Abortion Fund over the years. Among these are political party divisions on abortion funding, the tension between modernizer and traditional politicians, public opinion of North Carolina's citizenry, the presence of women legislators in North Carolina's General Assembly, and the mobilization of pro-life and pro-choice interest groups.

Political Party Divisions

The State Abortion Fund was reduced between 1985 and 1989 because the political climate had undergone a metamorphosis. In 1984 an anti-abortion Republican governor ascended to office. Before James G. Martin's governorship, James B. Hunt, a Democrat, was pro-choice. In subsequent state legislative elec-

Table 6.1

History of the North Carolina State Abortion Fund, 1967–93

Date	Event
1967	North Carolina abortion law limits elective abortions to the first twenty weeks of pregnancy.
1973	*Roe v. Wade* ruling is issued by U.S. Supreme Court.
October 1975	Family planning becomes a mandatory service in North Carolina under Title XX, and abortion services are available as a resource.
August 1977	Federal funding for elective abortions (or 90 percent of the total cost of providing abortion services) is eliminated under Medicaid and Title XX programs, thus ending elective abortions as an option for low-income women in North Carolina.
January 1978	Department of Human Resources shifts $442,000 from other purposes to continue providing abortion services to low-income women.
February 1978	The State Abortion Fund is set up, utilizing only state money to reimburse low-income women for abortion services ($150 in first-trimester and $500 for second-trimester abortions).
June 1978	The General Assembly appropriates $1 million to support the State Abortion Fund for fiscal year 1978–79.
July 1979	Income eligibility level is lowered to contain costs within the $1 million appropriation.
March 1981	The state supreme court upholds the use of state monies for elective abortions but strikes down county expenditures for that purpose.
February 1982	A four-month shortfall occurs in the State Abortion Fund budget.
July 1982	The General Assembly raises the annual State Abortion Fund appropriation to $1,374,500.
July 1985	The General Assembly lowers the annual State Abortion Fund appropriation to $924,500 and adds more eligibility requirements.
July 1989	The General Assembly reduces the annual State Abortion Fund appropriation to $424,000 for fiscal year 1989–90.
July 1990	The General Assembly limits access to abortion for low-income women by reducing the gestation time under which abortions can be obtained from 135 days to 112 days; the number of abortions that can be obtained due to health impairment are limited to one in a lifetime for women aged eighteen or older.
July 1993	The General Assembly raises the annual State Abortion Fund appropriation to $1.2 million; restrictions on access to abortion services for low-income women are reduced.

Table 6.2

Sample of Restrictive Abortion Bills Introduced in North Carolina General Assembly since 1979

Bill	Description
HB246 (1979) SB214 (1979)	A bill prohibiting the appropriation or expenditure of public funds for the purpose of providing or defraying the costs of abortions.
SB690 (1981)	A bill to prohibit use of state funds for abortions.
HB917 (1985)	A bill to require parental or judicial consent for an unemancipated minor's abortion.
HB1055 (1985)	A bill to require that advertisements of abortion facilities contain suitable health warnings.
HB918 (1985)	A bill to enact the unborn children's civil rights act by limiting the use of funds for abortions.
HB1267 (1987)	A bill to allow taxpayers to contribute to the State Abortion Fund when filing their income tax returns, and to provide that no state funds may be appropriated for the State Abortion Fund.
HB1068 (1987)	A bill to require parental or judicial consent for an unemancipated minor's abortion.
HB157 (1987)	A bill to prohibit any state funds being used for elective abortions.
HB1231 (1989)	A bill to establish an abortion control act (similar to the Missouri abortion law).
SB122 (1989)	A bill to provide counseling and educational services to adolescent parents and their families and for adolescents that terminate their pregnancies and to provide family-oriented procedures for notification of pregnancy termination.
HB93 (1989)	A bill to require the consent from a parent or a county department of social services for an unemancipated minor's abortion.
HB1040 (1991)	A bill to require the Social Services Commission to adopt specific rules to make replicas of a fetus in its developmental stages available to State Abortion Fund clients on request.
HB236 (1993)	A bill to allow taxpayers to contribute to the State Abortion Fund when filing their income tax returns, to use these contributions along with other contributions to replace state appropriations for abortions, and to codify the guidelines used in determining who is eligible for assistance from the State Abortion Fund.
HB1026 (1993)	A bill to require informed consent of the pregnant woman before abortion may be performed.
HB1024 (1993)	A bill to require parental or judicial consent for an unemancipated minor's abortion.
HB872 (1993) HB985 (1993)	A bill to protect a person's access to health-care facilities.

Sources: Printed Bills Office, Legislative Building. North Carolina General Assembly; Debora W. Whitley, Department of Cultural Resources, State Library of North Carolina.

tions, Republicans, most of whom were pro-life, won seats in the General Assembly. At the same time, various strong pro-choice advocates, such as Lieutenant Governor Robert Jordan and Senate Majority Leader Anthony Rand, were replaced by abortion opponents such as Lieutenant Governor James Gardner and Senate president pro tempore Henson Barnes.[46]

Modernizers versus Traditionalists

North Carolina state legislators can be placed in two categories: modernizers and traditionalists. Traditionalists tend to represent rural small towns in North Carolina, whereas modernizers represent cities with a more cosmopolitan outlook. The fluctuating fortunes of the State Abortion Fund may be attributed to the basic differences between traditionalist and modernizer legislators. Traditionalist legislators on social issues stress the importance of the patriarchal family and typically oppose public funding of abortions.[47] Traditionalist legislators, particularly on abortion rights, can be found predominantly in the Republican Party but also among some conservative Democrats. Although the Democratic leadership has endorsed the State Abortion Fund, it has encountered opposition from socially conservative traditionalist Democrats on important committees, such as the Senate Human Resources Appropriations Committee.

In 1985 when a vote on whether to continue the abortion fund was held in the state senate, there was a tie, with all twelve Republican senators opposing the bill and twelve of thirty-eight Democrats also voting no. All but one of the opposing male Democrats came from a rural area; the three black senators and the four women senators all supported the funding of abortions.[48] This illustrates that if Republicans can ally themselves with social traditionalist Democrats, the State Abortion Fund can be challenged and its budget dramatically reduced. It also implies that if this alliance can be formed, restrictive abortion legislation can be proposed and possibly passed.

Public Opinion

When North Carolina residents were polled in June 1989, 50 percent supported the *Roe v. Wade* decision, and 52 percent believed abortions should be legal.[49] Sixty percent personally viewed abortion as wrong, yet 58 percent of those questioned opposed a constitutional amendment that would outlaw abortions.[50] When asked whether they would like to return to the pre-*Roe* days and allow each state to decide whether abortions should be legal, 54 percent opposed and 39 percent favored such a scenario. When asked who they would most likely vote for between a pro-choice and pro-life candidate, 49 percent would vote for the pro-choice candidate, whereas 41 percent would vote for the pro-life candidate; 10 percent were not sure who they would support.[51]

When polled again in March 1990, 60 percent of North Carolina residents agreed that abortion should be legal under certain circumstances; 25 percent believed it should be legal under all circumstances, and 13 percent opposed it under all circumstances. Over 80 percent agreed that the state should require a parent's permission for abortion if the prospective mother is a minor. This attitude is comparable to that held nationwide. In a 1989 *Newsweek* national poll, when respondents were asked whether teenagers must obtain parental consent before obtaining an abortion, 75 percent supported the idea and only 22 percent opposed it.[52]

In the March 1990 poll of North Carolinians, 61 percent opposed the spending of North Carolina tax money on abortions, whereas 31 percent supported it.[53] In this poll 98 percent supported abortions if the woman's health was endangered and 90 percent favored the procedure in cases of rape and incest. Support declined for abortion under other circumstances, such as allowing abortion if a child would be deformed or retarded (64 percent) and abortion for an unmarried teenager who would be seriously affected by a pregnancy (34 percent). Overall, North Carolinians favor legalized abortion under certain circumstances and were not prone to reversing all abortion rights.[54]

Although most North Carolinians (61 percent) oppose public funding of abortion, the abortion fund has survived. Rarely has the issue of public funding of abortion been separated from the current operations budget. Typically, state-funded abortions are part of the general appropriations bill, and the public therefore is not able to disaggregate a legislator's support for publicly funding abortions from a vote for the general appropriations bill. Consequently, legislators can protect themselves from a potentially unpopular direct vote on whether public monies should be appropriated for the purpose of state-funded abortions for low-income women.

Presence of Women Legislators

There has been much debate about whether women in positions of political power would behave differently than men. Typically, women legislators have placed greater emphasis on social and family issues than on economic or business concerns.[55] Studies show that female legislators are much more likely to be pro-choice on abortion than their male counterparts.[56] It has also been shown that at the aggregate level, female state legislators, if represented in state legislatures in large numbers, can have an impact on abortion parental notification policies at the state level but not on public funding of abortions.[57] This seems to apply to North Carolina in particular.

Historically, women have not been represented in large numbers in the North Carolina General Assembly.[58] In 1967 there were only 5 women (out of a possible 170 members) in the General Assembly, making up 2.9 percent of that legislative body. By 1973 the number of women doubled as women gained approximately 6 percent of the legislative seats. Twenty-four women were elected to office in 1977, constituting 14 percent of the General Assembly. Women made modest gains in 1989, winning twenty-six (or 15.3 percent) of the legislative seats. They made their largest gains in 1993, obtaining twenty-eight (or 16.3 percent) of the legislative seats.

On restrictive abortion bills introduced since 1979, North Carolina's women legislators have been divided. Republican female legislators are more likely than Democratic female legislators to sponsor restrictive abortion bills. Except for 1979, however, women legislators in the North Carolina General Assembly have not sponsored bills that would end public funding of abortions for low-income women.

In 1979, for example, two Republican women and one Democratic woman were listed as sponsors on bills that would have prohibited appropriations of public monies for providing or defraying the costs of abortions. These women were Representative Edith Lutz (D), Representative Mary N. Pegg (R), and Senator Anne Bagnal (R). The North Carolina state Senate in 1979 had five female senators, four Democrats and one Republican. The North Carolina House of Representatives had fourteen female representatives, thirteen Democrats and one Republican. In the Senate, Anne Bagnal constituted 20 percent of the female vote and was the only female senator overtly to sponsor a bill that would end public funding of abortions for low-income women. In the House, one Republican woman and one Democratic woman were listed as sponsors for such a bill, constituting 14.3 percent of the support in the House for this restriction.

In 1985 six women in the state House of Representatives, two Democrats and four Republicans, were listed as sponsors on a bill that required parental consent or judicial consent for an unemancipated minor's abortion. The following female legislators supported this restriction: Representative Betsy Cochrane (R), Representative Theresa Esposito (R), Representative Jo Graham (D), Representative Edith Lutz (D), Representative Charlotte A. Gardner (R), and Representative Doris R. Huffman (R). At this time there were fourteen women legislators in the House, seven Democrats and seven Republicans. Approximately 43 percent of the female delegation in the House supported the parental-consent restriction.

In 1987, when the consent for a minor's abortion bill arose again, six female sponsors in the House of Representatives were found: Representative Betsy Cochrane (R), Representative Theresa H. Esposito (R), Representative Charlotte A. Gardner (R), Representative Doris H. Huffman (R), Representative Edith Lutz (D), and Representative Beverly M. Perdue (D). Of the nineteen women legislators in the House during 1987, 31.5 percent were sponsors of the parental-consent restriction.

By 1989 eleven female sponsors in the House were listed as supporting the parental-consent bill—eight Republicans and three Democrats. Many of the same women tend to support the parental-consent bill from year to year. Altogether there were eleven Democratic women and ten Republican women. In total, there were twenty-one women legislators in the House during 1989—52 percent of these women sponsored the parental-consent provision; 48 percent were not overt sponsors, but some of these female legislators could have also supported the provision.

In 1992 Representative Doris Huffman (R-Catawba), an abortion rights moderate, argued that the North Carolina Women's Legislative Caucus is divided on the abortion issue and has maintained an "unspoken rule" to turn its attention to issues other than abortion. As a result, issues such as parental consent and other restrictions on abortion have remained on the back burner in her opinion.[59]

In 1993, one female Republican of twenty women in the state House of Representatives (constituting 5 percent of the female delegation) sponsored a bill that would require informed consent of the pregnant woman before an abortion could be performed. Four female Republicans of the twenty women (or 20 percent of the female delegation in the House) sponsored parental-consent legislation. Fourteen of the twenty women are Democrats. Five Democratic women sponsored legislation to protect a person's access to health-care facilities, a bill ostensibly aimed at anti-abortion protesters who block access to abortion clinics.

Women in the North Carolina General Assembly have not been characterized as strongly feminist.[60] The women's delegation in the state legislature has been divided on the abortion issue along party lines, although Democratic women are just as likely as Republican women to support parental-consent/notification restrictions. One indicator of a stronger feminist movement among the female legislators is that they pushed for and obtained passage of legislation that prevents anti-abortion protesters from blocking access to abortion clinics. They were also able to get the state's marital rape exemption repealed during the 1993 summer session.

Interest Group Influences

Various interest groups have been vocal and have periodically lobbied the legislature for or against access to abortion in North Carolina. Groups that have worked toward pro-choice causes include African Liberation Support Committee, Women's Health Organization, Planned Parenthood and its local affiliates, North Carolina Religious Coalition for Abortion Rights, the National Abortion Rights Action League (NARAL) of North Carolina, National Women's Political Caucus, WomenElect, North Carolina Coalition for Choice, and the National Organization for Women (NOW) and its local affiliates. Many pro-choice groups have opted for a national strategy. In particular, NARAL, Planned Parenthood, and NOW have publicly stated that the federal Freedom of Choice Act and the Reproductive Health Equity Act are their top priorities.[61]

Despite recent trends indicating that pro-choice groups are taking more of a national strategy, numerous abortion rights groups have staged demonstrations to urge maintenance of a liberal abortion law in North Carolina. In 1978, for example, about 100 pro-choice marchers held a demonstration urging the state to approve public funding of abortions. Several speeches were given at Capitol Square. Dr. Paul Fleming of the Fleming Center (an abortion clinic in North Raleigh) argued that motherhood should not be made mandatory and called for public funding of abortions to prevent this from occurring. Doug Gillis of the African Liberation Support Committee was concerned that without public funding rich, white women would have easier access to abortions than poor black women.[62] In 1983, marking the tenth anniversary of *Roe v. Wade*, nearly 100 anti-abortion protesters marched in front of the North Carolina General Assembly's Legislative Building. Sponsored by North Carolinians for Life, the marchers carried roses to the governor's mansion. In response, the North Carolina Coalition for Choice delivered apple pies to all state legislators to symbolize the all-American nature of abortion rights and freedom of choice. Candlelight vigils were sponsored around the state by both pro-life and pro-choice groups.[63]

In 1989 WomenElect and the National Women's Political Caucus targeted North Carolina to subsidize legislative campaigns of pro-choice candidates and to support female Democratic candidates who were for choice.[64] In April 1990 an abortion rights demonstration drew approximately 2,500 people to Raleigh. The North Carolina Coalition of Choice sponsored the event to call attention to abortion issues coming before the General Assembly in May 1990.[65]

Anti-abortion groups that have sought to eliminate or restrict abortion services include right-to-life committees, North Carolina Christian Action League, Operation Rescue, Students for America, Action League for Life, National Right to Life, North Carolinians for Life, Women Exploited by Abortion, and Life Advocates. In 1983 Representative Henry J. Hyde (R-Ill.) came to North Carolina to address more than 200 members of the North Carolina Right to Life in Raleigh. He asked them to continue their opposition to abortion and lashed out against the pro-choice movement, terming the anti-abortion movement "a bloody civil rights battle." Chris Kremer of Carolina Students for Life conducted a workshop on how to picket a clinic and asked potential picketers to be sensitive to the feelings of patients and to remember that "women are victims of abortion as much as the babies." The North Carolina Coalition for Choice, a Charlotte-based group, argued that the tactics developed by right-to-life organizations were designed to harass and psychologically coerce women who already faced a frightening and difficult situation.[66]

In January 1984 a rally protesting eleven years of legal abortions was sponsored by North Carolinians for Life—an umbrella group that encompasses a number of organizations opposed to abortion. At this protest, speeches were heard from various religious leaders and a march was held. A spokeswoman for

North Carolinians for Life stated that their goal was to unify opposition to abortion through prayer. Donna Turner, director of the North Carolina chapter of Women Exploited by Abortion, denounced *Roe v. Wade* and stated that it is responsible for a "bitter trail of dead babies and broken women in our nation."[67]

Students for America, a conservative group based in Raleigh, stated in 1985 that its goal was to close down the Fleming Center. According to the director of the group, Ralph E. Reed, its membership numbered around 7,000 people spread across 130 campuses in 35 states. This group reportedly modeled its tactics after the civil rights movement by regularly picketing abortion clinics and holding mock funerals to protest abortion. Its director was eventually arrested for trespassing after staging a one-man sit-in.[68]

In 1985 the tactics of some anti-abortion sympathizers seemed to be working. Because of a series of bomb threats, the Women's Pavilion Clinic in Greensboro, North Carolina, closed down. Clinic administrators had received harassing calls at home and verbal insults as they entered the building, as well as threats. From 1982 to 1984, thirty abortion clinics across the nation were attacked. Ann Hardin of the Women's Pavilion Clinic stated that workers were afraid their luck would run out and that they too would be bombed.[69]

Operation Rescue, a New York–based pro-life organization, started blocking access to abortion clinics on 19 July 1988 in Atlanta during the Democratic National Convention. North Carolina was also targeted for these demonstrations. In Chapel Hill, three of twenty protesters were arrested after refusing to leave the Triangle Women's Health Center. Eight anti-abortion protesters were charged with trespassing after preventing the access of six patients to the Raleigh Women's Health Organization. More than seventy anti-abortion demonstrators were arrested for trespassing on 19 October 1988 as Operation Rescue sought to block access to a Charlotte-based abortion clinic. On 3 December 1988, twenty-five abortion protesters participating in an Action League for Life demonstration were arrested at the Charlotte Women's Clinic. Later that day, a pro-choice rally sponsored by Planned Parenthood of Greater Charlotte at a church was interrupted by a bomb threat. Pro-life sponsors responded that they did not condone violence and hated that some people would even think of threatening violence.[70]

At least two members of the General Assembly were executive directors of one of the groups. Representative Paul Stam (R-Wake) was director of Wake County Right to Life and Representative Coy C. Privette (R-Cabarrus) was executive director of the North Carolina Christian Action League. Both legislators were opposed to the public funding of abortions and were active in introducing additional restrictions on access to abortion. In interviews, when asked if interest-group activity influenced their opinions on abortions, legislators claimed that their views on abortions were fixed and not affected by the materials distributed by or lobbying of pro-life or pro-choice interest groups.

Most Liberal Law in the South

In conclusion, a confluence of factors explains why North Carolina has maintained a relatively liberal and almost restriction-free abortion law. The most important factor is a Democrat-controlled legislature led by a governor who has remained pro-choice. Except for the years of Governor Martin and the cuts in the abortion fund that occurred during that time, North Carolina's General Assembly has not pushed through any of the expected restrictive legislation that many states enacted after *Webster v. Reproductive Health Services*. This could reflect the presence of social modernizer legislators who have countered the traditionalists and have voted down measures such as parental notification.

The liberal abortion law could also be attributed to public opinion polls that indicate that North Carolinians largely view abortion as a right and do not wish to see the *Roe v. Wade* decision reversed. Public opinion polls in other southern states (such as Tennessee) show that North Carolinians are more supportive of abortion rights than their neighbors. A poll taken in fall 1991 revealed that only 47 percent of Tennesseans believed the state's law on abortion should stay as it is, whereas 41 percent believed abortion should be allowed only in cases of rape or incest. Forty-four percent of Tennesseans in 1992 indicated that the state should make it harder to obtain an abortion.[71] In South Carolina 80 percent held that they opposed abortion under all circumstances, whereas 61 percent of North Carolinians supported abortion under certain circumstances.[72]

With 50 members in the Senate and 120 members in the House of Representatives, the presence of women in the North Carolina General Assembly has not been large enough to have a significant impact on abortion policy or to launch a strong feminist agenda. Typically, women legislators in North Carolina have not been considered strongly feminist. In 1979 three female legislators sponsored a bill that would end public funding of abortions for low-income women. Other than this exception, most women in the General Assembly have chosen to oppose abortion funding more quietly or to support it behind the scenes.

Compared to other states in the South, and even nationally, North Carolina has one of the least restrictive abortion laws. The presence and support of crucial Democratic legislators and particularly the Democratic governor, Jim Hunt, has made the State Abortion Fund possible. Given that Jim Hunt was reelected in 1992 to serve as governor of the state, the support for a liberal abortion policy will most likely continue.

Notes

1. Michael Barone and Grant Ujifusa, *The Almanac of American Politics 1982* (Washington, D.C.: Barone, 1981), 814–15; Michael Barone and Grant Ujifusa, *The Almanac of American Politics 1988* (Washington, D.C.: National Journal, 1987), 871–72.

2. Barone and Ujifusa, *The Almanac of American Politics 1988*, 872; Michael Barone

and Grant Ujifusa, *The Almanac of American Politics 1994* (Washington, D.C.: National Journal, 1993), 936; R. Conrad Stein, *America the Beautiful: North Carolina* (Chicago: Children's Press, 1992), 74–76.

3. Barone and Ujifusa, *The Almanac of American Politics 1994*, 938.

4. H.G. Jones, *North Carolina Illustrated* (Chapel Hill: University of North Carolina Press, 1983), 430.

5. Ruth Ann Strickland and Marcia Lynn Whicker, "Political and Socioeconomic Indicators of State Restrictiveness toward Abortion," *Policy Studies Journal* 20 (Winter 1992): 598–617.

6. Malcolm L. Goggin, "Understanding the New Politics of Abortion: A Framework and Agenda for Research," *American Politics Quarterly* 21 (January 1993): 2–30; James L. Guth, Corwin E. Smidt, Lyman A. Kellstadt, and John C. Green, "The Sources of Antiabortion Attitudes: The Case of Religious Political Activists," *American Politics Quarterly* 21 (January 1993): 65–80.

7. Kenneth J. Meier and Deborah R. McFarlane, "State Policies on Funding of Abortions: A Pooled Time Series Analysis," *Social Science Quarterly* 73 (September 1992): 690–98; Kenneth J. Meier and Deborah R. McFarlane, "The Politics of Funding Abortions: State Responses to the Political Environment," *American Politics Quarterly* 21 (January 1993): 81–101.

8. Raymond Tatalovich and Byron W. Daynes, *Social Regulatory Policy: Moral Controversies in American Politics* (Boulder, Colo.: Westview Press, 1992), 184.

9. Ibid., 204, 208; Barbara Hinkson Craig and David M. O'Brien, *Abortion and American Politics* (Chatham, N.J.: Chatham House, 1993).

10. The new directive interpreted a provision in an appropriations bill passed on 21 October 1993. The language in the bill stated that "None of the funds appropriated under this Act shall be expended for any abortion except when it is made known to the Federal entity or official to which funds are appropriated under this Act that such procedure is medically necessary to save the life of the mother or that the pregnancy is the result of an act of rape or incest." Sally K. Richardson, director of the Medicaid bureau of the Federal Health Care Financing Administration claimed that under this legislative provision, states must fund abortions that are medically necessary and that the HHS interpretation of the law was correct. The directive, issued on 28 December 1993, conflicts with laws or policies in thirty-seven states and consequently some states, such as Utah, plan to resist implementation of the directive until lawsuits challenge it and the administration's interpretation of the Medicaid law is either upheld or clarified.

11. Robert Pear, "States Rebelling at Federal Order to Cover Abortion," *New York Times*, 5 January 1994, A1, A12; Robert Pear, "White House Defends Abortion Order," *New York Times*, 7 January 1994, A16; Melinda Beck, Mary Hager, Eleanor Clift, and Susan Miller, "The President's Tough Choice," *Newsweek* 119 (24 January 1994): 30.

12. Editorial, "So Poor Women Can Choose," *New York Times*, 1 April 1993, A14.

13. Steven V. Roberts and Ted Gest, "New Abortion Battle Lines," *U.S. News & World Report*, 12 April 1993, 30.

14. Editorial, "Abortion Policy Misses Mark," *News and Observer* (Raleigh), 10 December 1977, 4.

15. Judith E. Belsky, "Medically Indigent Women Seeking Abortion Prior to Legalization: New York City, 1969–1970," *Family Planning Perspectives* 24 (May/June 1992): 129–34.

16. Michael W. McConnell, "The Selective Funding Problem: Abortions and Religious Schools," *Harvard Law Review* 104 (March 1991): 1003–4.

17. Miriam K. Slifkin and Janet Allen, "Yes to Public Funding of Abortions," *News and Observer* (Raleigh), 5 February 1978, 3IV.

18. "Court Ruling Shifts Abortion Politics," *Congressional Quarterly Almanac* 45 (1989): 298.

19. Richard Lacayo, "Abortion: The Future Is Already Here," *Time* 139 (4 May 1992): 29; Ellen Whitford, "For Georgia's Poor, Abortion Is a Luxury," *Atlanta Journal*, 22 April 1992.

20. Craig and O'Brien, *Abortion and American Politics*, 1993; Rachele Kanigel and Donna Seese, "Court Allows State Limits on Abortion," *News and Observer* (Raleigh), 30 June 1992.

21. Glen Halva-Neubauer, "Abortion Policy in the Post-*Webster* Age," *Publius: The Journal of Federalism* 20 (Summer 1990): 27–44.

22. National Abortion Rights Action League, *Who Decides? A State-by-State Review of Abortion Rights*, 3rd ed. (Washington, D.C.: NARAL Foundation, 1992). NARAL formulated its rankings by examining the positions of each state's governor and legislative body on legal abortion, using floor votes, surveys, and assessments of abortion rights and anti-abortion organizations. They also examined the restrictions on abortion present in the state at the time and whether the state had responded to *Webster v. Reproductive Health Services* by enacting new restrictions. In their ranking, the higher the number (up to 50), the greater the likelihood that a state would seek to prevent or restrict abortion services.

23. Sagar C. Jain and Steven W. Sinding, "North Carolina Abortion Law 1967: A Study of the Legislative Process," monograph (Chapel Hill: Carolina Population Center, University of North Carolina at Chapel Hill, 1972); David J. Garrow, *Liberty and Sexuality: The Right to Privacy and the Making of* Roe v. Wade (New York: Macmillan, 1994).

24. Ted Vaden, "Other Ways Sought to Fund Abortions," *News and Observer* (Raleigh), 6 August 1977, 1A.

25. "Morrow to Recommend State Funding of Abortion," *News and Observer* (Raleigh), 7 January 1978, 19.

26. Ted Vaden, "Other Ways Sought to Fund Abortions," *News and Observer* (Raleigh), 20 January 1978, 26; Ruth Relos, head, Community Services Branch, Division of Social Services, North Carolina Department of Human Resources, 8 June 1993, personal communication.

27. Ginny Carroll, "Hunt Backs Funding of Abortions by State," *News and Observer* (Raleigh), 20 May 1978, 23.

28. "Abortion Funding Backed," *News and Observer* (Raleigh), 3 June 1978, 34.

29. A.L. May, "Lawmakers Revive Abortion Dispute," *News and Observer* (Raleigh), 2 June 1978, 1, 2.

30. A.L. May, "Panel Clears Controversial Budget Items," *News and Observer* (Raleigh), 2 June 1978, 1, 14.

31. Elizabeth Leland, "Abortion Funding Restricted," *News and Observer* (Raleigh), 5 March 1981.

32. Sherry Johnson, "Pro-Abortion Political Clout Urged," *News and Observer* (Raleigh), 1 February 1981; Rob Christensen, "Battle Brews in North Carolina over New, Stiffer Law," *News and Observer* (Raleigh), 4 July 1989.

33. Stephen R. Kelly, "Abortion Foes Lose Key Vote," *Charlotte Observer*, 11 June 1981.

34. Diane Winston, "Abortion Funding a Divisive Issue for Legislature," *News and Observer* (Raleigh), 1 April 1985.

35. Ibid.; Charles Babington, "Panel Approves Abortion Funding for Poor," *News and Observer* (Raleigh), 29 May 1985.

36. Winston, "Abortion Funding."

37. Ibid.

38. Ann Green, "Abortion Battle Intensified in State," *News and Observer* (Raleigh),

2 June 1985; Katherine White, "State-Paid Abortions Plunge in North Carolina after Program Altered," *Charlotte Observer*, 14 December 1985.

39. John Drescher, Jr., "Abortion Backers Support Funding Law; Foes Cite Abuse by Some Physicians," *News and Observer* (Raleigh), 17 December 1985.

40. Christensen, "Battle Brews in North Carolina."

41. Jim Morrill, "Abortion Rights Groups to Flex Muscle in North Carolina," *Charlotte Observer*, 1 December 1989; Kelly B. Seymore, "Abortion Ruling Builds Support on Both Sides," *News and Observer* (Raleigh), 1 July 1992.

42. Tim Funk, "House Panel Votes to Slash by 78%," *Charlotte Observer*, 15 April 1989.

43. Dennis Patterson, "Legislative Leaders Hope to Nail Down Budget Deal," *News and Observer* (Raleigh), 13 June 1993, 3C; Dennis Patterson, "Lawmakers Reach Tentative Deal to Nearly Triple Abortion Fund," *News and Observer* (Raleigh), 15 June 1993, 3A.

44. Bill Krueger, "General Assembly Finally Resolves Budget Split," *News and Observer* (Raleigh), 8 July 1993, 1A, 10A.

45. The following General Assembly members were interviewed on 23–24 June 1993: Senator Betsy Cochrane, Representative Michael Decker, Representative Ruth Easterling, Senator Ollie Harris, Representative Paul Luebke, and Senator Russell Walker.

46. Christensen, "Battle Brews in North Carolina."

47. Paul Luebke, *Tarheel Politics: Myths and Realities* (Chapel Hill: University of North Carolina Press, 1990), 55.

48. Ibid., 56.

49. Nationwide, a 1989 Harris poll found that 61 percent of Americans supported the *Roe v. Wade* decision, indicating a desire that it not be overturned.

50. In a 1985 ABC News/*Washington Post* nationwide poll, respondents were asked to agree or disagree with the following: "There should be a constitutional amendment banning abortion under most circumstances." A majority of Americans disagreed (54 percent) while 42 percent agreed.

51. Mia Adessa, "Where We Stand on Abortion," *Psychology Today*, October 1989, 10; Dennis A. Gilbert, *Compendium of American Public Opinion* (New York: Facts on File, 1988); Seth Effron, "N.C. Poll: Abortion Wrong, but Keep It Legal," *Greensboro News and Record*, 20 July 1989; Ted Mellnik, "Many in Carolinas Favor Tougher Laws on Abortion," *Charlotte Observer*, 28 June 1989.

52. Ferrel Guillory, "Poll Finds Selective Support for Legal Abortion," *News and Observer* (Raleigh), 26 March 1990; Eloise Salholz, Ann McDaniel, Patricia King, Erik Colonius, David L. Gonzalez, and Nadine Joseph, "Voting in Curbs and Confusion," *Newsweek* 114 (14 July 1989): 16–20.

53. This parallels national opinion on public funding. A 1989 *Newsweek* poll found that 61 percent of Americans nationwide supported a ban on public funding of abortion, except to save a woman's life—34 percent opposed such a ban.

54. Salholz et al., "Voting Curbs and Confusion"; Guillory, "Poll Finds Selective Support"; Chris Geis, "Many Approve of Abortion," *Winston-Salem Journal*, 26 March 1990.

55. Sue Thomas and Susan Welch, "The Impact of Gender on Activities and Priorities of State Legislators," *Western Political Quarterly* 44 (June 1991): 445–56.

56. R. Darcy, Susan Welch, and Janet Clark, *Women, Elections, and Representation* (New York: Longman, 1987); David Hill, "Women State Legislators and Party Voting on the ERA," *Social Science Quarterly* 64 (June 1983): 318–26.

57. Michael E. Berkman and Robert E. O'Connor, "Do Women Legislators Matter? Female Legislators and State Abortion Policy," *American Politics Quarterly* 21 (January 1993): 102–24.

58. In 1967 there was one female legislator (Democrat) in the state Senate and four in the House (three Democrats, one Republican), making up only 2.9 percent of the total state legislature. By 1969 there were two female state senators, one Democrat and one Republican; there was only one Democratic female member in the House. For 1971, there was one Democratic female state senator and two Democratic women in the House. Women made some gains in the 1973 General Assembly with one Republican female in the Senate and nine female legislators in the House (five Democrats, four Republicans)—in total constituting almost 6 percent of the legislature. In 1975, there were two women legislators, both Democrats, in the Senate and fourteen in the House (thirteen Democrats, one Republican).

Women picked up seats in both the Senate and the House in 1977. There were four senators (three Democrats and one Republican) and twenty members of the House (nineteen Democrats, one Republican); in total, women made up 14 percent of the state legislature. Women lost seats in 1979; they had five seats in the Senate (four Democrats, one Republican) and seventeen seats in the House (fourteen Democrats, three Republicans). In 1981, there were three Democratic female senators and nineteen women in the House (fifteen Democrats, four Republicans); in 1983, there were five Democratic female senators and nineteen female legislators in the House (sixteen Democrats, three Republicans). By 1985, there were four female senators (all Democrats) and fourteen women legislators in the House, evenly split between Republicans and Democrats.

In 1987 four female Democrats still served in the Senate; nineteen women were in the House (twelve Democrats, seven Republicans). Women obtained five seats in the Senate in 1989, one Republican and four Democrats, and twenty-one seats in the House (twelve Democrats, nine Republicans)—for a total of twenty-six female legislators constituting 15.3 percent of the legislative body. In 1991, there were five female senators (four Democrats, one Republican) and nineteen female House members (twelve Democrats, seven Republicans). Women gained seats in the Senate in 1993, moving up from five members to seven; they obtained twenty-one seats in the House—in total, they hold 16.5 percent of the seats in the state legislature, the highest percentage of seats held by women since 1967.

59. Greg Trevor, "Abortion Not Seen as Top Issue," *Charlotte Observer*, 5 July 1992.

60. Luebke, *Tarheel Politics*, 55. Women executives in state government, such as Dr. Sarah Morrow, also played an important role in placing public funding of abortions on the state's agenda. Dr. Morrow, secretary of human resources, was responsible for initiating the discussion of public funding and was the first to recommend a State Abortion Fund.

61. Kanigel and Seese, "State Limits on Abortion"; "Abortion Ruling Builds Support."

62. Rachel Brown, "Marches Urge State to OK Abortion Funds," *News and Observer* (Raleigh), 4 June 1978, 17-1.

63. Donna Alvarado, "Anniversary Decision on Abortion Is Marked," *News and Observer* (Raleigh), 23 January 1983.

64. Morrill, "Abortion Rights Groups."

65. Rachele Kanigel, "Abortion-Rights Demonstration Draws Thousands," *News and Observer* (Raleigh), 29 April 1990.

66. Laura Seifert, "Abortion Foes Share Ideas, Discuss Attitudes," *News and Observer* (Raleigh), 2 October 1983.

67. Kathy Tyndall, "Crowd Protests Eleven Years of Legal Abortions," *News and Observer* (Raleigh), 23 January 1984.

68. Green, "Abortion Battle Intensified."

69. Jim Walser, "Abortion Issue Volatile Twelve Years after Ruling," *Charlotte Observer*, 20 January 1985.

70. Frye Gaillard, "Bomb Threat Interrupts Pro-Choice Rally at Church," *Charlotte Observer*, 4 December 1988; Stephen Hoar, "Demonstrations Disrupt Clinics in Raleigh, Chapel Hill, Charlotte," *News and Observer* (Raleigh), 30 October 1988.

71. Paula Wade, "Abortion Survey Finds Positions Strong, Split," *Commercial Appeal* (Memphis), 11 November 1991; Mike Wilkinson, "Abortion Questions Hold Steady—State Poll," *New Sentinel* (Knoxville), 8 November 1992.

72. Schuyler Kropf, "Poll: State's Voters Back Legal Abortion," *News and Courier* (Charleston, S.C.), 9 October 1990.

PATRICIA BAYER RICHARD

7 | Ohio: Steering toward Middle Ground

In the aftermath of *Webster v. Reproductive Health Services, Inc.*, 109 S.Ct. 3040 (1989), political analysts judged some states as "battlegrounds" for abortion policymaking. One of these was Ohio,[1] being neither among those states most hostile to *Roe* nor among those most supportive of that decision.[2] Further, as a competitive two-party state[3] with a diversified economy and population, "an uneasy political equilibrium,"[4] and a legislature typical in many respects,[5] Ohio represents a good target for a qualitative investigation of elements that influence state abortion policy.

Abortion as a Public Issue

Abortion figures as a prominent and divisive issue on the political stage today, although it was off the public agenda for most of this century.[6] When it emerged before some state legislatures in the 1960s, it came as a health and legal reform issue, clearly susceptible to bargaining and compromise. New groups advocating abortion in terms of women's rights or decrying it in terms of its abrogation of a right to life, however, soon joined the debate. Since then, much of the discussion about abortion has been couched in language set by these single-issue activists.

As studies by Luker[7] and Falik[8] reveal, abortion activists hold fundamentally different assumptions and values, not only about the status of the fetus, but also about personhood, motherhood, women's role, and the quality of life. As a result, much is at stake and compromise is difficult for the activist groups that drive the issue into the political arena.

As a public policy issue, abortion has played a role in electoral[9] as well as cultural politics.[10] In an era in which budget deficits constrain new initiatives, issues with symbolic power, such as abortion, offer office seekers and public officials vehicles to reach and mobilize constituencies.

Yet, representative assemblies in the United States primarily function by finding middle ground and satisficing, instead of maximizing, demands. Consequently, many legislators consider abortion an unattractive issue. It arouses strong and divergent emotions. Its salience to some voters leads not only to organized pressures but also to individualized contacts from constituents. It may fracture the legislator's reelection constituency.[11] Moreover, legislators may have deep personal convictions, not necessarily compatible with those of the majority of their constituents.[12]

For these reasons, state legislators may wish that the abortion issue would go away. Since *Webster*, however, state policymaking has increased in importance. A spate of bills has been introduced in state legislatures, the high point occurring in 1990 with 465,[13] although few have passed.

Ohio is among the states that have adopted new laws in the post-*Webster* era. House Bill 108 (HB108), passed in August 1991, was one of twenty-nine "informed-consent" bills introduced in seventeen legislatures that year, of which three were enacted.[14] Based on model legislation provided by the National Right to Life Association, HB108 requires that a woman seeking an abortion wait a minimum of twenty-four hours after she has received information about medical risks, abortion procedures, and probable gestation age of the fetus and has been given materials provided by the state, which she may choose to examine or not, that describe the embryo and fetus and list agencies offering family planning and alternatives to abortion. The legislation was enjoined as a result of court challenges until March 1994, when implementation began.

Past as Prologue

Over the past quarter century during which abortion has been a political issue, Ohio has, in general, lingered behind the initiatives of other states. For example, from 1967 through 1972, immediately prior to the *Roe* decision, while almost half the states altered their abortion laws, Ohio's remained the same.

Between *Roe* and *Webster*, the state took little action. A 1974 law, passed in the wake of *Roe*, provided that no one could be forced to have an abortion, added the guarantee to refuse to perform abortions already in place for private hospitals to public ones, prohibited abortion trafficking, and mandated the "informed consent" of one of a minor's parents or guardians before the minor's abortion. The parental-consent portion of the law was challenged and found unconstitutional in *Hoe v. Brown*, 446 F.Supp. 329 (N.D. Ohio 1976).[15] Efforts to pass a parental notification law began in earnest in the 1981–82 legislative session. In 1985, HB319, requiring parental notification and including a judicial bypass provision, which the earlier legislation had not, passed the legislature. It was upheld in *Ohio v. Akron Center for Reproductive Health*, 110 S.Ct. 2972 (1990).

The other major legislative initiative before *Webster* concerned public funding. In 1979, an anti-abortion funding amendment, the Meshel Amendment, introduced by a Senate Democrat, became part of a budget bill. It proscribed the expenditure of public funds for abortion except to prevent the woman's death or when the pregnancy had resulted from rape or incest, both of which had to be reported to a governmental agency. It thus mimicked the federal Hyde Amendment.

Public opinion in Ohio has reflected the patterns and complexities found in national public opinion. Relatively few want to see abortion outlawed (15 percent in 1981, 12 percent in 1986),[16] but most Ohioans endorse some limitations on the conditions under which abortion should be available. A strong majority supports parental consent (76 percent in 1989).[17]

In the abortion arena, legislators hold the keys to policy change. Thus we here focus on the Ohio General Assembly. We both explore the pattern of support for HB108 and look qualitatively at legislators' understandings of the abortion issue.

The Study

Fifty-six semistructured interviews with legislators took place between April 1990 and February 1991 with a smaller number of follow-up interviews in spring and summer of 1991. In addition to the twenty-five senators and thirty-one representatives, lobbyists and organizers from Ohio Right to Life (ORTL), Planned Parenthood, and National Abortion Rights Action League–Ohio (NARAL-Ohio) and key House and Senate staff members, including the chief executive officer of the Senate and the legislative clerk of the House, were also interviewed. Interviews ranged in length from thirty minutes to several hours, the average interview lasting just under an hour. All respondents were promised anonymity and are not identified by name.

While the interviewees were selected to produce a cross-section of the legislature, with particular attention to geographic and partisan distribution, urban/rural balance, and seniority,[18] female members were oversampled. Of the twenty women in the legislature in 1991 (sixteen in the House and four in the Senate), sixteen of them, thirteen in the House and three in the Senate, participated in the study (see Table 7.1).

Findings

Legislators' Views of Abortion as an Issue

As noted above, since abortion has been framed in ultimate value terms,[19] it has functioned as a condensational symbol,[20] tapping intense emotions. Abortion activists see negotiation as a kind of moral betrayal.[21] In this context, many Ohio

Table 7.1

Characteristics of the Samples, Compared to Senate and House (in percent)

| | Senate | | House | |
	Total (N = 33)	Sample (N = 25)	Total (N = 99)	Sample (N = 31)
Party				
Republican	58	60	40	35
Democrat	42	40	60	65
Sex				
Male	91	88	85	58
Female	9	12	15	42
Urban/rural[a]				
Urban	61	60	70	71
Rural	39	40	30	19
Region of the state				
Northwest	15	20	12	13
Northeast	39	40	38	39
Southwest	21	12	21	16
South/southeast	9	12	11	10
Central	15	16	17	23
Length of time in office				
Earlier than 1985	58	56	69	74
1985 or later	42	44	31	26

a. In the Senate, urban districts are defined as those with two complete counties or less. Rural districts contain up to ten counties. In the House, those districts comprising more than one county are rural.

legislators view the abortion issue as political dynamite with a very short fuse, particularly in circumstances in which legislative action, rather than legislative rhetoric, constitutes the order of the day.

The legislators distinguished abortion from "ordinary legislative issues," where splitting the difference, accommodation, and political benefit reign. Some lawmakers compared it to such other "gut" social issues as the death penalty and gun control.

While members agreed that abortion was a hot issue, some nevertheless ardently advocated legislative action. These legislators shared the activists' perceptions; those with strongly felt positions on abortion tended to see "slippery slopes" from which the abortion policies they opposed removed all wedges. While both avid pro-choice and pro-life legislators displayed such views about the impact of abortion on values and behavior, right-to-life members introduced more apocalyptic visions. Even so, they displayed a certain pragmatism, seeing only modest steps toward their preferred position being taken, at least in the near term. Legislators less intense in their abortion positions commented on the difficulty of negotiating compromise in this arena because of mismatched assumptions, inflexibility, and a general lack of common ground.

Legislative Types

As this suggests, a range of legislative "types" appeared among the lawmakers interviewed. The three belief systems about abortion delineated by Fried were represented.[22]

The pro-choice type emphasizes women's rights, that women can become full human beings only when they can choose not to be pregnant, when they can control their reproduction.[23] It predominated among female legislators and is exemplified by the following quote: "This issue ties to the subservience of women . . . it is a power issue."

Some male legislators expressed this viewpoint as well.

> I don't like abortion . . . but I don't think it's right for government to tell women what they must do, especially for men to do so. (Republican senator)

> I believe deep down that women should have this choice to shape their own lives. (Democratic senator)

A number of legislators articulated the beliefs of the pro-life type: that the fetus is a human being whose right to life cannot be outweighed by the interests of the pregnant woman and that acceptance of abortion signifies value disintegration.[24] For example, a House Republican said that, even in rape cases, "it's still a life," further explaining, "I've met young men and women who are the result of rape and incest . . . they look like perfectly happy, adaptable people." "If you believe it is life, how can you believe it can be [ended]? The pro-choice position is practical, not philosophical" (Republican senator).

Abortion as a symptom of moral decay was a repeated theme. A Republican senator drew an analogy to those Germans during World War II who saw people on the trains but said they did not know what was happening to them: "We know what is happening." Another Republican described abortion as part of a general decline in the certainty of moral boundaries. A Democratic senator spoke of his "deep concern" over "where we are heading"; he would rather not see abortion in the mix as public policy discussion of euthanasia and the right to die proceeds. "More than unborn children are involved" because abortion fits in a context of "public decisions about life and death relative to convenience . . . we keep moving the marker." A Republican representative spoke about abortions for sex selection in terms of a philosophy of if it feels good, do it . . . [we] have to have some way to control people who won't control themselves. There is trouble with so much freedom. People are acting worse than farm animals.

A female legislator said, "When I was in high school, if a girl got pregnant it was like the scarlet letter. Now, people think it's nothing."

The ambivalent type, who sees competing interests in abortion, bases judgment on utilitarian grounds.[25] Many legislators took this balancing approach. Indeed, those who claimed to experience discomfort with activists' "hard line" positions outnumbered the others: "Most of us see the ambiguities, the other side of the argument . . . [this results from] temperament and training," as one senator put it. Representative of the practical concerns central to the ambivalent type's understanding of the issue was a Democratic Representative's statement that "prohibition will not stop abortion." A senator, who said he hoped abortion would be a "last choice," noted that the rich have always been able to obtain abortions, that the deaths from illegal or self-induced abortions have dramatically declined since *Roe*, and that making abortion illegal will not force women to carry an unwanted pregnancy to term. He and others observed that in the days before *Roe*, "every community had a network [which] made arrangements" for illegal abortions.

The desire to find consensus came forward frequently. As a Republican senator put it:

> There is a middle ground. There is a role for government. And for freedom of choice up to a point . . . everything in life is a compromise . . . marriage, divorce, which restaurant you go to, government. . . . When I say I'm neither pro-choice or pro-life, people say—you mean you haven't made up your mind? . . . People don't want to see in gradations.

"When one is in the position to influence a political decision which is morally based, [it is] thorny. In real-world circumstances it is not possible to be ideologically pure," contended a female House member. A Republican who "was in the middle before it was fashionable" saw compromise as intrinsic to the "body politic . . . knowing that the population is divided provides a good reason to compromise . . . [this is] instinctive among political figures . . . I see it as noble [because] it makes democracy work."

For most legislators, abortion has not been a central issue. As one House member put it, "In the legislature, there are approximately ten strong pro-choice people, ten strong pro-lifers, and seventy-nine legislators who wish the issue would go away."

The Impact of Webster

Like Hershey's 1984 study of U.S. Senate campaigns,[26] this study investigated legislators' perceptions of changes in their political environment. Ohio legislators were queried about the impact of the Supreme Court's *Webster* decision.

With few exceptions, legislators interviewed perceived that *Webster* had altered the dynamics of the abortion issue. Before, they said, a legislator could "skate the issue" or be "demagogic," but now, claimed a House Democrat, those who "danced around the issue looking for the public [get] blisters from sitting on the fence."

Although abortion has been on the public agenda for decades, many lawmakers had not seriously examined the question until *Webster*. With a plethora of items vying for attention, "in general we wait until a catastrophe happens" (Republican House member) and "focus on those issues on which you have to make a decision" (Democratic senator). Positions thus varied not only on substantive but also on temporal dimensions, from "I have been against abortion since I knew what it was" to "I never gave it a whole lot of thought until I walked the precincts of my district."

Many legislators evidenced serious soul-searching in arriving at their stance on abortion. For one pro-choice senator, coming to a decision was "a personal struggle . . . I live in fear [about when] I meet my maker . . . I hope it's the right argument." A House member said, "I went through torture" when it became necessary to take a public stand on the question: "In private life, the only question is would you have one?"

A number of legislators reacted to *Webster* by rereading *Roe*. A pro-choice Democrat found the earlier decision persuasive:

> With time I have come to appreciate how much wisdom there is in *Roe*. When all is said and done, it is a landmark which defined the issue as a conflict of rights between the mother and the unborn in which rights gradually shifted from one to the other. The more I've looked at and thought about it, the more I think *Roe* is correct.

For others, the passage of time itself, rather than *Webster*, precipitated a shift in positions.

> I changed my position from one based on life, rape, and incest exceptions to one of "you can't take this basic right away; it's been there too long." . . . This right has been exercised more than 20 million times. It has become inculcated into American lifestyles. . . . In 1974, I would have voted to prohibit abortion. In 1982, I would have supported a prohibition. However, eight more years have passed . . . I want to leave abortion policy right where it is. (Democratic legislator)

Legislators interviewed before the 1990 elections suggested that *Webster* induced some rethinking about the political utility of a pro-life posture. One senator said, "Some took the right-to-life position thinking that there was no real downside; they never dreamed it would come up" as an issue over which state legislators could have real say. "There was no readily observable opposition," said another. Before, explained a House member, "we felt safe . . . you could make a statement without feeling accountable for it." A number of senators, both Democrats and Republicans, said the Republican caucus had backed off pro-life support. As one Republican put it, his colleagues were "trying their hardest to tread water . . . delay is the name of the game." Most saw greater mobilization and intensity about abortion after *Webster*, but less and perhaps shorter lived than first anticipated.

In general, legislators bemoaned their new influence in the abortion policy arena. They saw abortion as "a hassle of an issue," and *Webster* as the last thing that state legislators wanted. According to a pro-life House Republican, "There are likely a significant number of legislators who are favorable to that decision [*Webster*] who are sorry it was made, because now they have to make a decision." In the words of a pro-choice legislator, "Now you really do have to deal with this . . . the question changed."

Influences on HB108 Vote

In the period from Webster until the end of 1993, only one legislative proposal has become law. HB108, known as the "Woman's Right to Know" bill, passed the legislature in August 1991 by margins of 57–38 in the House and 21–12 in the Senate.

A variety of characteristics of all legislators and their districts were explored for their association with voting position on HB108. We assessed the relationships for sex, party, urban-rural character of the district, region of the state in which the district is found, margin of victory in the 1990 election, whether the member is a full-time legislator, terms in office, and race.

Sex

Research suggests that women and men holding legislative office differ in ideology and policy positions in the current era.[27] Sex was significantly related to voting on HB108 in the House, though not the Senate. Among representatives, women opposed HB108 by a $3:1$ margin, while men supported it by $2:1$, a correlation between sex and vote[28] of .31, significant at .01. In the Senate, women split their votes (2–2) and men voted $2:1$ (19–10) for the bill. Controlling for party, sex remains significantly correlated with vote among House Democrats (.29, .02).

Party

The national parties have distinct, opposed positions on abortion, with the Democratic Party's platform endorsing reproductive choice and the Republican Party's platform advocating the right to life of an unborn child. In Ohio, abortion has divided more along party lines in the Senate than in the House.

Party is significantly related to vote in both House and Senate (.35 and .61, respectively, both .01). If we control for sex, the relationship in the House becomes statistically insignificant for women, but remains significant for men (.34, .01). The same is true for the Senate, where *phi* equals .63 (.01) for the men. Sex appears to dominate party as an influence on women's voting on this bill, but, for male legislators, party remains strongly related to vote.

Urban-Rural Differences

Representatives from rural[29] districts were significantly more likely to have voted for HB108 than those from urban districts (.32, .01). In the Senate, legislators with more rural districts voted 10–3 for the informed-consent bill compared to a more closely split vote, 11–9, among those with urban districts.

Intrastate Subcultures

Elazar described three U.S. political subcultures—individualistic, moralistic, and traditional—which reflect varying orientations to politics and the role of government. The traditionalistic approach to politics accepts hierarchies as part of the ordered nature of things; the individualistic subculture has no direct concern with the "good society" but the moralistic does.[30] Ohio, in this classificatory scheme, is primarily individualistic but has moralistic individualistic areas in the northern part of the state and individualistic traditionalistic ones in the southern part.[31]

Region of the state is significantly related to vote in the House (.30, .01), with legislators from the southern part of the state (the individualistic traditionalistic part) most supportive of the informed-consent bill, followed by the northern part (the individualistic moralistic region) and then the central (the "pure" individualistic part). In the Senate, too, those representing the central part of the state were least in favor, but those from the northern and southern regions of the state are essentially equal in their support, and the relationship was not significant.

Electoral Competitiveness

District competitiveness may influence voting in a controversial policy area because members from safe districts are likely to experience fewer cross-pressures. On the other hand, Jewell quoted a four-term Ohio Republican House member who claimed that anti–gun control and anti-abortion constituted his toughest single-issue groups but that he had been "saved" by the diversity of his district.[32]

By a wide margin, the fifty-six legislators interviewed described the right-to-life groups as more visible and better organized than the pro-choice groups. Therefore, it was expected that the safer the district, the more likely the legislator would oppose HB108 because of reduced right-to-life threat to reelection.

This proved true. In the House,[33] those who won their 1990 election by less than 60 percent of the vote went 15–6 for the bill, those who won with 60–69 percent voted 29–19 in favor, while those receiving 70 percent or more split 15–15.

Full-time Legislators

The literature suggests what seems intuitively obvious: that full-time legislators have a greater stake in being reelected.[34] Those who are full-time legislators, based on the argument expressed above, have more to fear from right-to-life groups and therefore were expected to support HB108 more than those who have other occupations.

Although Patterson placed Ohio in the category of a full-time, professionalized legislature,[35] most Ohio legislators list something other than "legislator" or "full-time legislator" as their occupation—about 60 percent in the House and 70 percent in the Senate. No substantial or significant relationship between full-time legislative status and voting position on HB108 existed.

Terms in Office

Those with less seniority may be more vulnerable to defeat and, as a result, may vote more for HB108 than senior members. In neither the House nor the Senate, however, was the relationship significant.

Race

Race continues to bear upon political attitudes and behavior. Blacks tend to be more liberal than whites as well as more Democratic. They were thus expected to oppose HB108 more often than their white colleagues.

Black legislators overwhelmingly opposed HB108. Both black senators and ten of the twelve black representatives voted no, .34 (.05) and .32 (.01) respectively.

Discriminant Analysis

Discriminant analysis was employed to help interpret the ways in which those voting for and against HB108 differed.[36] Table 7.2 shows the standardized coefficients of the variables employed in the discriminant analysis: sex; party; whether the legislator's district is urban or rural; region of the state in which the district is located; election margin in 1990; whether the legislator is full-time; and race of the legislator.[37] The larger the magnitude, the greater that variable's

Table 7.2

Discriminant Analysis of Variables' Contributions to Explaining HB108 Vote

Standardized Canonical Discriminant Function Coefficients

House		Senate	
Sex	.56	Sex	.51
Party	.45	Party	.88
Urban/rural	.33	Urban/rural	.02
Region of state	−.58	Region of state	−.06
Race	−.38	Race	−.25
Full-time rep.	.00	Full-time rep.	−.44
Terms in office	−.19	Years in office	−.33
1990 vote margin	.18		

Note: The discriminant function analysis employed the direct method; all variables passing the tolerance test of .001 were entered.

contribution to the discriminant function. These coefficients indicate that, in the House, region (.58[38]) and sex (.56) contribute most to determining scores on the function (yes or no vote on HB108). In the Senate, party is the most important variable (.88), while sex is second (.51).

The classification of cases by the predictor variables is reasonably high, as Table 7.3 shows. The canonical discriminant functions accurately classify 81 percent of the cases, or legislators, in the House and 85 percent in the Senate.

Influences Shaping Legislators' General Abortion Views and Behavior

The interviews allow exploration into influences shaping legislators' abortion views and behaviors. Here we can look beneath the statistical connections between observable characteristics and votes on a particular bill to try to discern how representatives' abortion positions are formed and maintained.

Personal Values

Values and beliefs constitute cue sources for legislators. Indeed, in their study of voting cues in state legislatures, Songer and his colleagues discovered that the most frequently mentioned influence on decisions in the four legislative chambers investigated was the personal values and opinions of the legislators.[39] This may be especially likely with abortion. Hurwitz found that, on the abortion issue, the majority of his legislative respondents indicated that they would make decisions without seeking information from anyone.[40]

Table 7.3

Classification of Cases by Predictor Variables

House Classification Results

Vote on HB108		No. of Cases	Predicted 1	Group Membership 2
Yes	1	59	47 79.7%	12 20.3%
No	2	40	7 17.5%	33 82.5%

Percentage of "grouped" cases correctly classified: 80.81

Senate Classification Results

Vote on HB108		No. of Cases	Predicted 1	Group Membership 2
Yes	1	21	18 85.7%	3 14.3%
No	2	12	2 16.7%	10 83.3%

Percentage of "grouped" cases correctly classified: 84.85

When asked how they came to their positions on abortion, virtually all respondents referenced their values. The majority of women in the sample articulated reasons that reflected a belief that abortion should be a woman's choice.

> This is a strong belief. . . . Having been born a woman, I feel I have rights to my body. No matter what I do, I have to live a lifetime with it. A man is not bound by that decision the way a woman is. Why should he be able to tie up my life?

Among the men, no single value predominated. Some used the value of life as the basis for their position, while others employed the choice frame.

Personal Experiences

One of the most striking findings of this research is the prevalence and significance of personal experiences in shaping abortion views. For many members, the personal has been political. About a third of the Senate sample and a slightly smaller proportion of the House sample spontaneously responded with personal stories when asked how and when they came to their position on abortion. For example, a senator spoke about the daughter of a good friend of the family dying from an abortion she obtained overseas in the pre-*Roe* era. Another related that an out-of-wedlock pregnancy preceded his marriage. One surmised that, had abortion been available, he, as the last child in a large family, would probably not have been born.

Carroll posits that the logic underlying differences in perspective proceeds not from liberal-conservative ideology but from "sex differences in objective life circumstances and the socialization of women and men to different roles."[41] Reproductive differences stand at the heart of what distinguishes women from men. The gendered realities within which men and women live may shape their abortion perspectives. One female legislator made such a point: "Few legislators look at how these things [abortion laws] play out in people's lives. Most women do. Most women are pro-choice."

Experiences involving pregnancy figured prominently in female legislators' discussions about how they came to their abortion positions. Among the pro-choice female respondents, three mentioned problems in their own pregnancies, two described how life-defining a fear of pregnancy had been for them, and four discussed friends who had had abortions or had given a child up for adoption. A number of these stories were intense and highly personal. Four examples follow.

> I had a spontaneous abortion [that] the doctor thought was illegal.

> I became adamantly pro-choice in 1969. I became pregnant essentially immediately after the birth [of another child]. I suffered a massive uterine hemorrhage. My gynecologist told me he would keep me in bed for four months. He said he couldn't examine me for fear of dislodging the fetus. . . . The doctor said there was a one in ten chance that the baby would be normal. . . . I thought this is crazy that my life is in the hands of everyone else. I have no choice in the matter at all. I am being held hostage by this fetus.

> I don't think that most men understand what it means to have this ongoing concern. . . . I grew up in a religious environment where contraception was frowned upon . . . I'm Catholic. . . . Every month pregnancy was on my mind . . . [it] invaded every aspect of life.

> I had roommate who [got] sepsis [from an illegal abortion] and one who had a kid because she couldn't get an abortion. She gave it up for adoption and has never been the same.

Two of the four pro-life women spoke about having friends who had been unable to adopt a child, an occurrence they attributed to the availability of abortion, and another reflected with nostalgia on a time when, in her view, the onus of out-of-wedlock pregnancy inhibited sexual activity.

While three-quarters of the women brought up personal experiences in telling how they arrived at their abortion positions, only a handful of men did so. One had an experience equally life-shaping to any of the women's:

> I got married when I was nineteen and my wife was eighteen. I don't regret that decision. Abortion was not an alternative. You've probably figured out that [she was pregnant]. This was an important, very personal experience. . . . My life has been better because of it.

For the others, the experience was indirect and not central.

Religion

Studies suggest that religious affiliation influences abortion position.[42] Falik found in her study of abortion activists that pro-choice reflected a liberal, modern, and secular ideology, whereas pro-life arose from a conservative, traditional, and sacred ideology.[43]

Religion figured frequently in shaping abortion positions. For example, counting only specific mentions, half the House sample included this as part of how they came to their abortion position. Of the sixteen, eleven were Catholic; six of them were pro-choice and five pro-life.[44]

The following pro-life and pro-choice statements let the legislators speak for themselves about religious influence.

> I was born into a Catholic family. I had eight years of Catholic education. This led to a position that life is always precious.

> My position is shaped by three factors [including] religious beliefs . . . they are a part of me, the way I think. . . . Women's rights are important to uphold, but in some ways, abortion transcends gender . . . [it is] a religious issue.

> A child is a gift from God. . . . It may be a question of upbringing . . . I went to parochial school.

> My background is very Catholic . . . yet I am not with Right to Life. . . . Tony Celebrezze [the Democratic candidate for governor in 1990] and I are from the same background . . . as a private person, I had been always morally anti-abortion—I still am. . . . As a public person, it is different.

> I am a Catholic . . . I'm not trying to deny the influence of my faith . . . but I represent 110,000 people [who are] a cross-section of believers and non-believers. It was the Catholic myth. I had twelve years of Catholic education, telling me that abortion is murder. I didn't think beyond that. But with *Webster* I have to make a decision.

> My religion is against abortion. But religion is based on free will.

Role Conceptions about Private Values

For some legislators, the relationship between private values and public policies figured importantly in the shape of their abortion views. Some conceived the role of individual beliefs as directly producing public positions. Others saw such beliefs as informing but not determining legislative behavior.

> Legislators are reminded from time to time that they shouldn't let their personal views govern them. I don't think that's possible. . . . My private views *are* my public views. You can't have different private and public stands. . . . You are the same person. (House member)

Another pro-life legislator argued that "it is a fallacy when people say that laws should not be based on some personal moral code."

This position contrasts sharply with the more commonly expressed view, represented by two House members, that distinguished between individual preference and actions and societally mandated ones.

> I am pro-choice and support the rights of women. My personal opinion is anti-abortion. As an individual I oppose abortion but I protect the rights of my constituents to make their own decisions.

> I would never have an abortion, but I can't take away that right from other women. The best way I say it is: I have faith in other women, that in the privacy of their souls, [they will make good decisions].

Party

Party exercises significant influence over legislative behavior. In Ohio, both parties are strong at the local level,[45] while Ohio Republicans are among the strongest of the state parties.[46] The legislative parties figure in members' calculations.

Questions about the role of party on the making of abortion policy brought two categories of response. On the one hand, all respondents agreed that abortion would never be a caucus issue, that is, none of the legislative parties would try to enforce party discipline on such a vote. Despite the national parties' diametrically opposed platform positions on abortion, all legislative caucuses recognize splits within their ranks.

On the other hand, legislators disagreed about whether abortion was a partisan issue. Many claimed that abortion was nonpartisan because some Republicans and some Democrats stood on each side of the issue. Other representatives sized up their caucus and the other party's and perceived different policy preferences predominating. These saw abortion as a party issue, with Democrats pro-choice and Republicans pro-life, though with exceptions.

A variety of indicators indeed show Republican legislators more pro-life than their Democratic colleagues. Sixty-two legislators signed an *amicus* brief supporting Ohio's parental notification law when *Ohio v. Akron Center for Reproductive Health* went to the Supreme Court in the fall of 1989: thirty-four of forty Republican and twenty-one of fifty-nine Democratic representatives and six of nineteen Republican and one of fourteen Democratic senators. Republicans numbered thirty-one among the cosponsors of the 1991 "Woman's Right to Know" bill (HB108), compared to twenty-three Democrats, although Republicans were outnumbered thirty-eight to sixty-one in the House. ORTL consistently endorses more Republicans than Democrats, while the NARAL-Ohio endorses far more Democrats than Republicans.

The connection between party and abortion position has been strongest in the House Republican caucus. In several recent Republican caucus decisions about replacements for vacancies, a pro-life position has functioned as a threshold criterion. According to one appointed Republican, the first question at their party interview pertained to abortion stance. This legislator believed that being pro-life was at the least helpful, if not essential. In another vacancy, the caucus selected a pro-life candidate over a pro-choice one even though several respondents, both legislators and staff, agreed that the political assets of the person chosen were inferior to the other. As one legislator put it, "The issue that won it was the pro-life one."

Sex

Based on earlier research,[47] the women legislators were expected to be more pro-choice than the men and, as a group, more interested in abortion policy. Both these expectations proved true, as the section on personal experiences already suggested.

Female legislators in Ohio were considerably more pro-choice than their male colleagues. All but four of the members of the 118th General Assembly were interviewed; only four of these sixteen took pro-life stances. Only two female representatives (one Democrat and one Republican) and one female senator (a Republican) signed the *amicus* brief discussed earlier and only four cosponsored HB108.[48]

The women had a higher profile on the abortion issue than did the men. About half the male representatives interviewed mentioned female colleagues as sources of information, persuasion, or pressure in this issue area. When asked to identify the key legislators, a set of women's names appeared consistently as the pro-choice ball carriers. In some instances, the response in the House was just "the women." A male legislator suggested that any major (pro-choice) bill would be carried by female legislators because "they can talk from the inside." A woman agreed with this position, calling abortion "a gender issue, an experience issue, an ownership issue." Another noted that it is "considered to be a women's issue. If we don't lead the charge, who will?" Women legislators were far more likely to view the "woman's right to know" (informed consent) legislation as "paternalistic," "insulting to women," and therefore "rankling."

No pro-life woman placed herself in the position of a legislative champion, being a catalyst for changes in Ohio's law. Pro-choice women were more active. The discussion under key legislators, below, expands on these differences.

The women interviewed constituted almost the entire population (81 percent) of female Ohio legislators. If the fraction of women doubled or tripled,[49] and the underlying abortion position distribution remained the same, extrapolating from this sample, pro-choice policy would dominate the Ohio General Assembly.

Constituency

If legislators reflect their constituents rather than their own values on this issue, however, then changing the sex of the legislator would produce no policy difference. Pitkin's ground rules for activity properly described as representation include that the representative must act in the interests of his or her constituents and normally in accord with their wishes.[50] Jewell argues differently, maintaining that how legislators respond to constituents outweighs whether they vote in accord with their wishes.[51] Kingdon claims that the most important generalization about legislators is that they exaggerate the extent to which their views are shared by their constituents.[52]

Conventionally, three representative roles, or approaches to representing constituents, have been elucidated: the trustee, who acts as a free agent, making decisions according to principles, convictions, and conscience; the delegate, who consults with constituents and follows their instructions, even when these run contrary to his or her own judgment; and the politico, who shifts role orientation with issues or circumstances.

In a conflictual policy arena such as abortion, legislators may be most likely to assume a delegate posture, to anticipate what their constituents want. Jewell suggests that state legislators find it difficult in emotional issues to vote against intense constituent opinions.[53] But representatives, especially at the state legislative level, often have little reliable data on constituent views.

Validating Kingdon's forecast, legislators perceived their constituency's position on abortion as consistent with their own. Furthermore, several legislators asserted that only a very few districts had strong enough abortion preferences to make a contrary position by the representative problematic.

Based on "impressions" and "feel for the district" and occasionally on poll data, these representatives believed they were true to their constituencies. Of the fifty-six interviewed, only three, two senators and one representative, perceived a gap between their own abortion position and that of a majority of their constituents.[54] For a great many legislators, though, it was a close call. Very commonly, respondents characterized their districts as narrowly divided or almost evenly balanced. In districts perceived as strongly pro-life or pro-choice, representatives tended to be visible advocates of that position. One of the strongest pro-life legislators interviewed said he recognized that such a strong position was not for everyone, because "not everyone has this type of district."

Fenno discerned that when U.S. House members looked at their constituencies, they saw a nest of concentric circles, moving from the geographic constituency through reelection, primary, and personal constituencies.[55] Jewell and Patterson say that state legislators seem less likely to make distinctions among these various constituencies, perhaps because they are less politically sophisticated or because their districts are smaller and more homogeneous.[56]

Many Ohio legislators' comments revealed a sensitivity to these constituencies. The legislators characterized abortion as a crosscutting issue, with, for example, some ethnic Democratic neighborhoods pro-life and some wealthy Republican neighborhoods pro-choice, hence dividing into their reelection constituencies.

About a dozen legislators, most with pro-life positions, spontaneously brought up various situations of interpersonal cross-pressures, often in their personal constituencies. One pro-life woman spoke about close friends disagreeing with her position, trying to convince her that, if this reproductive right were lost, "we will lose all the other ground gained." Other pro-life legislators said: "I find many of my friends disagree with me on this; it is very hard when people you know disagree strongly"; "we have friends who have had abortions"; "my wife is pro-choice, probably most of our wives are." A pro-choice woman reported that "at the grocery store, at church, I am accosted . . . how can you *do* this? They are incredulous." One legislator thought these countercurrents had utility: "I don't see [legislators] going to the 'rabid side.' "

Legislative Champions

Halva-Neubauer found that legislative champions influenced abortion activity in the three legislatures he investigated.[57] In Ohio, the presence or absence of a prime advocate or two may account for some differences between the House and Senate. When asked who were the movers and shakers in the abortion policy arena, members most consistently named Democratic representative Jerome Luebbers, a pro-life advocate. No other legislator was so closely identified with the issue.

With the incentive for legislative activity falling to those who wish to alter the status quo, the assiduousness of pro-life champions in advancing their cause especially shapes the presence, nature, and progress of legislative proposals. Some representatives rated Luebbers as not especially effective in his role. Other pro-life advocates, however, appeared willing to let him carry the ball. "The women" in the House who were seen as pro-choice supporters appeared to be a bulwark against legislative attempts at severe abortion restrictions.

Interest Groups

While advantage tends to flow to the side protecting current policy, the strength of interest groups matters as well. Among the forty most influential interest groups in the fifty states, Thomas and Hrebenar rank "anti-abortion groups" "most effective" in two states, at the second level of effectiveness in two others, and less effective in forty-four; overall, they tied with tourist industry groups for number thirty-seven.[58] Pro-life groups devoted more time and resources to the state legislatures than did pro-choice groups in the period after *Roe*. Post-*Webster*, groups with a primary interest in abortion policy have increased their activities.[59]

Most Ohio legislators attributed greater lobbying presence and campaign support to the pro-life forces, principally ORTL, but to fundamentalist and Catholic churches and religious broadcasting as well. As part of his response, one pro-choice representative produced a candle he had received recently from ORTL, which read, "If you extinguish the light of even one life, the vision of the entire world is dimmed." The most dramatic difference noted by both pro-life and pro-choice members was in grassroots mobilization and volunteers for campaigns. Here, ORTL outscored pro-choice forces in the views of these legislators.

The amount of heat these groups produced, however, was not seen as overwhelming. A pro-choice Democrat contrasted the few letters he has received about abortion to the hundreds of letters he received on a recent bill that would have required cats, like dogs, to be licensed.

Legislators said they received few visits from lobbyists on the "other side" of the abortion issue from their own. Most seemed to agree with a pro-life Democrat who said, "Those who get pressure are those who don't have a clear position." The lobbyists for ORTL and Planned Parenthood–Ohio and the lead organizer of NARAL-Ohio[60] tended to support this. The PP-Ohio lobbyist thinks of legislators as "friends, foes, and fuzzies" and focuses on the last group, while the ORTL lobbyist has a "core of friends" but will, if she has the time, talk to all legislators.

Legislators commonly complained about the intransigence of the abortion interest groups. A House member with a soft pro-choice position remarked "the 'far left' upsets me too . . . they are not open to many ideas. They also [like ORTL] see this open door thing [and a parade of horrors will follow]." A pro-life senator noted that "when you talk with pro-life persons, if you said you would allow for several exceptions, you would be viewed as a traitor." A House member complained that when members of the insurance committees considered a bill for infertility treatments, including in vitro fertilization, "the pro-life people got involved in that heavily. It's black or it's white . . . nothing in between."

Since the 1990 election, ORTL appears to have been particularly aggressive. At the beginning of the 1991 session both houses considered a living-will bill. Several legislators claimed that ORTL went to the governor in a successful leverage attempt to weaken sections of the bill that it opposed. The ORTL lobbying generating the most heated commentary concerned what one Republican House member characterized as "interference with the internal politics of the caucus." He described lobbyists' activities that affected the caucus decision about candidate selection for a vacancy as "out of bounds."

Leadership

The House Speaker and Senate president exercise considerable power. For example, they make committee assignments and chair their respective Rules Committees. All four legislative parties fund raise for their candidates.[61] Ohio was one of five states in which more than $1 million was raised and distributed in 1984 by legislative parties.[62]

The Speaker, Vern Riffe, clearly ranks first among equals. He has served in the House for eighteen terms and leaves little to chance;[63] he will retire at the end of 1994. Legislators credit Riffe with being true to his word, delivering on promised rewards and punishments. Riffe's campaign funds are extensive and constitute a firm spoke in his wheel of power; his birthday fund raiser brings in a million dollars. He has the ability to shape legislative considerations in the abortion policy area.

Interviews revealed a bipartisan agreement by leaders in both houses to prevent consideration of any abortion legislation in 1990, although several bills were introduced. Members agreed that the decision to forestall abortion legislation had been made primarily because both parties' leaders saw inaction as "membership protection." When the 1991 session began, leadership in both houses gave a green light to the "informed-consent" bill, which passed in the summer of 1991 as HB108. No other piece of abortion legislation emerged.

A strong pro-life legislator contended that "if the leaders were to say, 'let's give it a test, forget all the parliamentary ways of killing it,' I think a strong anti-abortion bill would pass." He was not alone in this view. Yet few legislators of any persuasion on the abortion issue expect Ohio to move aggressively. This partly results from a general reluctance to press the issue, but the Speaker and the Senate president are key players. While most legislators identify both as in the pro-life camp, neither is perceived as a legislative champion on abortion.

As befits a competitive two-party state, Ohio's governorship has alternated between parties for the last several decades. Richard Celeste, a Democrat, completed his second four-year term in 1990; he was ineligible to run again. Celeste, a pro-choice supporter, was succeeded by a Republican, George Voinovich, who, at the outset of his campaign, had modified his life-only exception position to embrace exceptions for abortion also in cases of rape and incest. These changes in the party and abortion position of the governor affected the legislative context.

When Celeste held office, legislators across the abortion spectrum believed restrictive bills would not receive gubernatorial endorsement. Celeste let the 1985 parental notification bill become law without his signature. None of those interviewed thought he would approve a twenty-four-hour waiting period or other elements of what later passed as HB108. Voinovich's victory in 1990 altered the dynamic. As one House member put it, any legislation that "could get a majority of the House and Senate would definitely be signed." Voinovich, however, has provided no encouragement to pro-life legislators to press their hand for further restrictions.

As Halva-Neubauer[64] notes, while agenda-setting studies fixate on actors outside the decision-making process, individual legislators and other public officials can have profound effects. These leaders have critically influenced the handling of the abortion issue in Ohio.

Discussion

In a legislature such as Ohio's, in which no abortion legislation had legislative committee hearings or reached the floor between 1985 and 1991, few behavioral indicators of position existed and those that did were primarily rhetorical. In 1991 the informed-consent bill presented legislators with a real policy option. Few members regarded this bill as extreme. Thus some who were ambivalent types in their abortion stance saw potential utility in providing pregnant women with information about their options, although they worried about precise language and the twenty-four-hour waiting period the legislation imposed. While many ambivalents opposed the bill when it came to a vote, the call was close; another bill seeking to institute restrictions might fit within their abortion worldview.

Steering for Middle Ground

Like the mass public, legislators for the most part reach complex and nuanced abortion positions. Unlike the public, their decisions determine the range of options available to women. This knowledge, along with political considerations and legislative experience, reinforces their search for a middle ground. Ohio legislators have not made policy that satisfies groups active on the issue. Instead, they have operated similarly to how they proceed in nonsymbolic policy arenas, working toward compromise.

This counters the common wisdom about abortion policymaking. Many observers extrapolate from the activists' frame, yielding only black-white alternatives for legislators. Representatives themselves adopt this vision to some extent. Yet, although consensus appears to most legislators beyond reach, legislative results can be viewed as forging a tempered abortion policy structure that stands apart from either untrammeled access or prohibition. Legislators do with this issue what they do with others: find a path that skirts the most politically dangerous territory. In this study, leadership roles, splits in constituencies and in caucuses, a sense that actions will be visible, and the absence of a singularly effective legislative champion all figure in the production of only modest policy changes in Ohio in the post-*Webster* environment. The other chapters in this book reflect on the significance of these factors in other states.

The Personal Is Political

Similarly, the finding of how very political is the personal in this policy arena can be compared with other legislatures. In Ohio, personal experiences frequently grounded legislators' abortion views. In particular, members whose life history called on them to make a decision that bore on reproductive autonomy or the value of life have strongly committed positions on abortion that reflect the choices they themselves made. In effect, their abortion stances can be seen as an attempt to require that others follow their course. More generally, based on this research, legislators extrapolate from their own lives and seek to enact their interpretations of their experiences into law. This qualitative research suggests that not only does the personal experience matter, but also the message the legislator derives from it. For example, the representative who faced a treatment decision when his child was born might have drawn the lesson that individuals should have options, should be able to choose based on their own soul-searching and analysis. Instead, he has sought to ensure that others would select as he did.

Gender Matters

Gendered life experiences form another dimension of how the personal interacts with abortion stance. All female legislators interviewed, regardless of their position, understood the issue in some measure as one they "owned." In this instance, a strong majority of them identified as pro-choice. To the extent that this association between female representatives and abortion position, as well as higher than average level of interest, holds in other legislatures, and at other times, larger cohorts of women in these bodies would alter policy outcomes.

   In the end, though these Ohio legislators would prefer abortion to move off their legislative agenda, they do not expect that it will. Thus they continue to grapple with it, steering a course through a difficult channel.

Notes

The author wishes to acknowledge the support of the Ohio University Research Committee for this research and to thank Karen O'Donnell for her research assistance.

1. E.J. Dionne, Jr., "Foes of Abortion Prepare Measures for State Action," *New York Times*, 5 July 1989, 10, national edition; Larry Martz et al., "The New Political Rules," *Newsweek*, 17 July 1989, 21.

2. Glen Halva-Neubauer, "Abortion Policy in the Post-*Webster* Age," *Publius*, Summer 1990.

3. Malcolm E. Jewell and David M. Olson, *Political Parties and Elections in American States* (Chicago: Dorsey Press, 1988), 25–27; John F. Bibby et al., "Parties in State Politics," in *Politics in the American States*, 5th ed., ed. Virginia Gray, Herbert Jacob, and Robert B. Albritton (Glenview, Ill.: Scott, Foresman/Little, Brown, 1990), 92, 116–17; Malcolm E. Jewell, *Representation in State Legislatures* (Lexington: University of Kentucky Press, 1982), 6; Sally McCally Morehouse, *State Politics, Parties and Policy* (New York: Holt, Rinehart and Winston, 1981), 59.

4. Michael Barone and Grant Ujifusa, *The Almanac of American Politics 1992* (Washington, D.C.: National Journal, 1991), 952.

5. The Ohio General Assembly is typical in both size and terms of office. It has 132 members, 99 in the House and 33 in the Senate; the average size for the lower house is 100 while that for the upper is 38. Representatives have two-year terms, senators four; all but four lower houses have two-year terms, and all but twelve upper houses have four-year terms. Morehouse, *State Politics, Parties and Policy*, 272.

6. James C. Mohr, *Abortion in America: The Origins and Evolution of National Policy 1800–1900* (New York: Oxford University Press, 1978).

7. Kristin Luker, *Abortion and the Politics of Motherhood* (Berkeley: University of California Press, 1984).

8. Marilyn Falik, *Ideology and Abortion Policy Politics* (New York: Praeger, 1983).

9. See, for example, Debra L. Dodson and Lauren D. Burnbauer, *Election 1989: The Abortion Issue in New Jersey and Virginia* (New Brunswick, N.J.: Eagleton Institute of Politics, 1990).

10. Luker, *Abortion and the Politics of Motherhood*; Falik, *Ideology and Abortion Policy Politics*.

11. Richard F. Fenno, Jr., *Home Style: House Members in Their Districts* (Boston: Little, Brown, 1978).

12. Jewell, *Representation in State Legislatures*, 103–4.

13. See various issues of the *State Reproductive Health Monitor*, Alan Guttmacher Institute, New York.

14. *State Reproductive Health Monitor*, 1991, v–vi. Mississippi and North Dakota adopted such bills as well.

15. Howard A. Hood et al., *Abortion in the U.S. VI* (Buffalo, N.Y.: William S. Hein, 1991), 447.

16. "Poll Says Legal Abortions Win Support of Ohioans." *Cleveland Plain Dealer*, 9 July 1981, 18A; "Eighty-Eight Percent of Ohioans Favor Abortion If Mother in Danger," *Cleveland Plain Dealer*, 6 May 1986, 14A.

17. "Seventy-five Percent in Ohio Poll Favor Parental Consent for Abortions," *Cleveland Plain Dealer*, 18 October 1989, 8B.

18. Jewell, *Representation in State Legislatures*.

19. Celeste Michelle Condit, *Decoding Abortion Rhetoric: Communicating Social Change* (Urbana: University of Illinois Press, 1990).

20. Murray Edelman, *The Symbolic Uses of Politics* (Urbana: University of Illinois Press, 1964), 6–7.

21. Marjorie Randon Hershey, "Direct Action and the Abortion Issue: The Political Participation of Single Issue Groups," in *Interest Group Politics*, 2nd ed., ed. Allan J. Cigler and Burdett A. Loomis (Washington, D.C.: Congressional Quarterly Press, 1986).

22. Amy Fried, "Abortion Politics as Symbolic Politics: An Investigation into Belief Systems," *Social Science Quarterly*, March 1988, 137–54.

23. Ibid., 148.

24. Ibid., 148–49, 151.

25. Ibid., 149.

26. Marjorie Randon Hershey, *Running for Office: The Political Education of Campaigners* (Chatham, N.J.: Chatham House, 1984).

27. Sue Thomas, "The Impact of Women on State Legislative Priorities," *Journal of Politics* 53, no. 4 (November 1991); Sue Thomas and Susan Welch, "The Impact of Gender on Activities and Priorities of State Legislators," *Western Political Quarterly* 44, no. 2 (June 1991); Michelle A. Saint-Germain, "Does Their Difference Make a Difference?: The Impact of Women on Public Policy in the Arizona Legislature," *Social Science Quarterly*, December 1989; Susan Welch, "Are Women More Liberal Than Men in the U.S. Congress?" *Legislative Studies Quarterly*, February 1985.

28. The House took two votes on HB108, the first in June of 1991. A minor amendment was added in the Senate, and in August 1991 the House concurred in the revised bill. Four members missed the June vote and eight the August, but none missed both. The dependent measure for the House combines the two votes to achieve a position for each legislator.

29. In the Senate, urban districts are defined as those with two complete counties or less. Rural districts contain up to ten counties. In the House, those districts more than one county in size are coded rural.

30. Daniel J. Elazar, *American Federalism: A View from the States*, 2nd ed. (New York: Crowell, 1972).

31. Ibid., 106–7, 118.

32. Jewell, *Representation in State Legislatures*, 1–2.

33. Because of the small number of Senate seats up for election (16), this relationship was not investigated.

34. Jewell, *Representation in State Legislatures*, 8.

35. Samuel C. Patterson, "State Legislators and the Legislatures," in *Politics in the American States*, 180.

36. William R. Klecka, *Discriminant Analysis* (Beverly Hills: Sage, 1980).

37. Evidence suggests that the linear discriminant function analysis performs reasonably well with dichotomous variables. D.H. Moore, "Evaluation of Five Discriminant Procedures for Binary Variables," *Journal of the American Statistical Association*, 1973, 68.

38. The actual signs of the coefficients are arbitrary. See Marija J. Norusis, *Advanced Statistics for SPSS/PC+* (Chicago: SPSS, 1986).

39. Donald R. Songer et al., "Voting Cues in Two State Legislatures: A Further Application of the Kingdon Model," *Social Science Quarterly* 66 (December 1985).

40. Jon Hurwitz, "Determinants of Legislative Cue Selection," *Social Science Quarterly* 66 (March 1988): 216.

41. Susan J. Carroll, "Gender Politics and the Socializing Impact of the Women's Movement," in *Political Learning in Adulthood*, ed. Roberta S. Sigel (Chicago: University of Chicago Press, 1989), 315.

42. See, for example, Bradley R. Hertel and Michael Hughes, "Religious Affiliation,

Attendance, and Support for 'Pro-Family' Issues in the U.S.," *Social Forces* 65 (March 1987).

43. Falik, *Ideology and Abortion Policy Politics.*

44. These proportions may be skewed by the number of female legislators in this group, four of five of whom were pro-choice.

45. Samuel C. Patterson, "The Persistence of State Parties," in *The State of the States*, ed. Carl E. Van Horn (Washington: CQ Press, 1989), 160.

46. Jewell and Olson, *Political Parties and Elections in American States*, 66.

47. See, for example, Saint-Germain, "Does Their Difference Make a Difference?"; Welch, "Are Women More Liberal Than Men in the U.S. Congress?"; Susan J. Carroll, "Women Candidates and Support for Feminist Concerns: The Closet Feminist Syndrome," *Western Political Quarterly*, June 1984; Susan Mezey, "Does Sex Make a Difference? A Case Study of Women in Politics," *Western Political Quarterly* 31, no. 4 (December 1978); Susan Mezey, "Support for Women's Rights Policy: An Analysis of Local Politicians," *American Politics Quarterly* 6, no. 4 (October 1978).

48. One of the female cosponsors was appointed after the *amicus* brief was filed.

49. Indeed, the number of women increased by 50 percent from the 1991–92 to the 1993–94 General Assembly, from 20 to 30.

50. Hannah F. Pitkin, *The Concept of Representation* (Berkeley: University of California Press, 1967), 164–66.

51. Jewell, *Representation in State Legislatures*, 12.

52. John W. Kingdon, *Agendas, Alternatives, and Public Policies* (Boston: Little, Brown, 1981), 84.

53. Jewell, *Representation in State Legislatures*, 113.

54. The senators, one Republican and one Democrat, took pro-choice positions. The representative, a Democrat, held a pro-life stance.

55. Fenno, *Home Style*, 1–29.

56. Malcolm E. Jewell and Samuel C. Patterson, *The Legislative Process in the United States*, 4th ed. (New York: Random House, 1986.)

57. Glen Halva-Neubauer, "The Success of the Anti-Abortion Agenda in State Legislatures: Lessons from Virginia, Pennsylvania, and Minnesota," paper presented at the annual meeting of the Midwest Political Science Association, Chicago, April 1989.

58. Clive S. Thomas and Ronald J. Hrebenar, "Interest Groups in the States," in Gray et al., *Politics in the American States*, 144–45.

59. Carol Matlack, "Abortion Wars," *National Journal*, March 1991.

60. NARAL-Ohio did not have a lobbyist.

61. Jewell and Olson, *Political Parties and Elections in American States*, 220.

62. Ibid., 219.

63. Alan Rosenthal, "The Legislative Institution: Transformed and at Risk," in Van Horn, *The State of the States*, 86–87.

64. Halva-Neubauer, "The Success of the Anti-Abortion Agenda in State Legislatures," 6.

MARY T. HANNA

8 | Washington: Abortion Policymaking through Initiative

The Supreme Court's decision in the 1989 *Webster* case legitimated the right of states to place some restrictions on abortions. Anti-abortion activists in Louisiana, Michigan, Ohio, South Carolina, and several other states rushed to pass legislation restricting abortion rights in various ways. In Washington State it was the pro-choice supporters who took up the cudgels. Fearful that the Supreme Court might go even further in abridging abortion rights and convinced that there was strong support for such rights in their progressive state, these activists decided to ensure choice, at least for Washingtonians, through the passage of a state initiative. They accomplished this. As we see, however, the struggle was harder and the victory narrower than pro-choice activists expected.

Under the headline "Heady Mixture," a Washington newspaper wrote that the state's voters had been drawn to the polls in large numbers in November 1991 by "initiatives on putting an end to life, pregnancy and the pursuit of politics."[1]

In an off-year election, with no candidates on the ballot except for a few local officials, 67.9 percent of the state's registered voters went to the polls. They were drawn by three path-breaking initiatives. Initiative 553 was the first in the nation to attempt to set term limits not only on state politicians but on national politicians—the state's congresspersons and senators—and to make those limits retroactive. The *New York Times* called Initiative 553 "the most severe term-limits measure ever to go before a state electorate."[2] Initiative 119, termed the "euthanasia" initiative, allowed physicians to help people die, to aid terminal patients who expressed a wish for a painless, voluntary death. The *Times* wrote that Washington voters were "the first in the world to pass electoral judgment on

152

euthanasia."[3] Initiative 120 encoded in state law the most liberal set of abortion rights in the nation.

Although early polls had indicated strong support for term limits and the euthanasia measures, they were both defeated—and by the same margins: 54 percent opposed; 46 percent in favor. The abortion initiative, 120, ended in a dead heat on election day. The yeas and nays were only 6,000 votes apart (with the nays leading) out of the 1,205,796 votes cast. Absentee ballots had to be counted. When these produced a decision favoring the initiative, but only by 4,314 votes, less than one-half of 1 percent of the total vote, state law required a mandatory recount. Not until 24 December, six weeks after the election, were the final results published. Washingtonians had approved the initiative securing abortion rights by 4,222 votes.

The abortion measure was the only one of the three initiatives actually approved, but political commentators and the initiative's supporters were shocked by the narrowness of the win. The National Abortion Rights Action League (NARAL) termed Washington one of four states where abortion would be least at risk if *Roe v. Wade* were overturned.[4] The Catholic Church in Washington thought stopping the abortion initiative so unlikely that it decided to pour most of its money into opposing the euthanasia initiative.[5]

That the abortion initiative did win, even if very late and very narrowly, seems due to four factors. First, the abortion initiative was a fairly radical measure. It went beyond *Roe v. Wade* in permitting public funding for abortions and in setting no real timetable for determining fetal viability, the point at which most abortions are prohibited.

Second, by happenstance more than anything else, it went on the ballot along with two other radical measures. This ensured a long, intense campaign, with extensive lobbying on all sides and unstinting media attention. The radical political triad also brought out an unusually large vote, especially for an off-year election, and, some thought, perhaps a skewed one.

Third, the initiative process in itself may have been a factor in 120's near defeat. Many scholars and politicians argue that the initiative process often gives the edge to opponents rather than supporters of a measure. As political consultant Blair Butterworth said, "It's easier to be loyal to a candidate than to an issue. With an initiative, you don't have that human attachment. The no vote comes easier."[6]

Fourth, abortion rights opponents adopted an unusual strategy. By insisting that even if the initiative was defeated, abortion rights would still be protected by the state's 1970 abortion law, they confused the debate. What really was the "choice" position, and who were its supporters?

We begin our analysis of the 1991 initiative with a discussion of Washington State's political culture. We proceed to a discussion of the complexity involved in the election's political triple play, the convolution of the three initiatives all on the same ballot. Then we examine the supporters and opponents of the abortion initiative and the strategies and tactics they employed. Finally, we assess what has happened in regard to abortion and abortion rights in Washington since the narrow passage of Initiative 120.

Political History

Washington State is one of the younger states in our union, assuming statehood only in 1889. During its earlier history, it gained a reputation for "lusty, gutsy politics, with pronounced strains of populism and radical politics."[7] After World War II, the populist, radical nature of its politics became more muted, but a generally progressive flavor remains. Studies of survey questions regarding personal political ideological leanings and analyses of major public policy decisions consistently categorize Washington as a moderately liberal state.[8] Washington is also a politically bifurcated state, with a tendency toward greater liberalism in the heavily urbanized western part of the state and greater conservatism in the largely rural eastern parts. Three-quarters of the state's population, however, resides in the urbanized west.

When we compare Washington to the nation as a whole from 1980 to 1990—just before the November 1991 elections—we find that Washingtonians are younger, whiter, and better educated than the national average.[9] The state experienced considerable population growth during that decade (and since). Two people moved into the state for every one moving out. While some of this migration was composed of poorer Asian and Hispanic Americans, most of it was made up of young, white, fairly well educated adults, attracted by the state's outdoor recreational lifestyle and the employment opportunities in its high-tech industries.

Political scientist Terrence Cook terms the right to choice in abortion the "locally ascendant" view, "possibly because of the population's low church involvement and relative youth."[10] Washington has one of the lowest levels of religious affiliation of any state. Thirty-one percent of Washingtonians are churchgoers, compared with 49 percent of Americans nationwide. Only Alaska and Nevada have lower rates of church attendance.[11] The Catholic Church, which has played such a large role nationally in the struggle over abortion, is notably weak in Washington. Catholics make up less than 10 percent of the state's population.[12]

A wide open electoral system is a legacy of the state's earlier populist history. The state has a simple method of permanent registration. It provides its citizens easy access to absentee ballots, which are widely used in the state's elections. It is one of only two states (Alaska is the other) that has an open primary, allowing voters to choose a candidate from any party for each position listed.

This is a politically competitive state. A 1988 study showed that 32 percent of

Washingtonians called themselves Republicans, 37 percent Independent, and 31 percent Democrats.[13] Strongly competitive political parties, plus the state's open voting rules, may be responsible for another important fact of Washington's political life—voter turnout in the state remained moderately high even during the troughs of the 1980s.

As long ago as 1912, Washington adopted three important devices of popular control: the initiative, the referendum, and the recall. The recall permits voters to force an unpopular, ineffective, or corrupt official from office. The referendum allows voters to override a law passed by the legislature. The initiative enables voters to enact legislation themselves through the ballot. What concerns us here is the initiative process because that process was used in the November 1991 elections to try to protect abortion rights.

Public opinion polls in the state repeatedly show strong citizen support for the initiative process.[14] Washington has been one of the heaviest users of that process among our states. In Washington the approval rate historically for initiatives has been about 50 percent. Of the 104 initiatives placed on the Washington ballot from the beginning of the process in 1912 until 1990, 53 were approved by voters and 51 failed.[15] Political scientist David C. Nice argues that in Washington state "the combination of high voter turnout, competitive parties and large numbers of independents presents candidates and public officials with a difficult task."[16] One could add that the same factors, plus some of the state's other characteristics discussed earlier, present issue advocates with an equally difficult task in elections on initiatives.

There were many reasons for both opponents and supporters of abortion rights in Washington State to believe that the choice position was "locally ascendant." Washington had been one of the fourteen states in the country to anticipate the Supreme Court's *Roe v. Wade* decision. In 1970 voters approved a statute liberalizing the state's abortion law. Although married women needed the consent of their spouses and minors the consent of a parent, women were permitted abortions up to four months after conception. The law was superseded by the Supreme Court's *Roe v. Wade* decision, but it remained on the books. In 1975 the state supreme court declared a parental-consent rule unconstitutional under both the federal and the state constitutions. In 1984 voters rejected an initiative that would have banned public funding of abortions. The state continued funding abortions for poor women, as it had done since the middle 1970s, even after most federal funding was terminated. Polls taken in the state consistently showed a majority of Washingtonians in favor of choice, and by 1991 Washington was the only state whose entire congressional delegation, Republicans and Democrats, supported abortion rights.

NARAL seemed to have reason to cite Washington as one of the few states where abortion rights were likely to be protected even in the event of *Roe v. Wade*'s overturn. When abortion rights supporters in the state became alarmed by the Supreme Court's 1989 *Webster* decision, allowing state restrictions on abortions, and by the increasingly conservative complexion of the Court, they became convinced that a state law was needed to protect abortion rights. They began the long, and initially sanguine, process of getting an initiative on the Washington ballot.

The Initiative Process

Washington State actually has two forms of initiative, the direct and the indirect. In the direct initiative, at least 8 percent of the electorate that voted in the last gubernatorial election must sign petitions supporting the placement of a proposed law on the ballot. If the requisite number of legal signatures is gathered, the proposed initiative goes before the voters at the next general election. It becomes law if a majority of those voting on the initiative support it. An indirect initiative needs the same kind and number of petition signatures but the validated initiative then goes first to the legislature. The legislature may support it, in which case it becomes law without further action. If the legislature rejects the initiative or amends it, the initiative and the legislature's amendment, if there is one, go before the voters at the next election for their approval or rejection. Between 1912 and 1990, the direct initiative was resorted to almost four times more often than the indirect.

The first public unveiling of the proposed initiative occurred at a fund raiser held at Seattle's Four Seasons Hotel on 22 August 1990. Lee Minto, chair of Pro-Choice Washington, the coalition of women's, civil liberties, medical, and other groups sponsoring the initiative, told her audience that they must raise at least $1 million to put the initiative over. Initiative 120, termed the Reproductive Privacy Act, guaranteed full rights to abortion and provided for public funding for abortions for the poor.

Its chances looked good. Supporters had already gathered two-thirds of the 150,000 signatures needed for the initiative's legal certification. Fund-raising letters had already gone out. The initiative movement had garnered an impressive list of honorary co-chairs including Booth Gardner, the state's governor; Norm Rice, the mayor of Seattle, the state's largest city; and congresspersons Jolene Unsoeld, Norm Dicks, and Jim McDermott. All of these political leaders were Democrats. Later, the King County Council, representing the state's most populous county, also endorsed the initiative by a 5–3 party-line vote, Democrats voting favorably and Republicans opposed. Party politics would not play a major role in the initiative process, but it did appear, here and elsewhere.

By the time petitions were sent to the secretary of state for certification, they contained 242,000 signatures, more than had been gathered for any initiative in the state's history.[17] The euthanasia initiative, sent to the secretary at the same time, contained 223,000 names.

For strategic reasons, the backers of the initiative chose to take the indirect route, sending the initiative to the state legislature rather than directly to the ballot. They argued that the state's House of Representatives was securely in the hands of pro-choice Democrats. Victory, they felt, was certain in the House. Republicans, generally less supportive of choice, controlled the Senate, but only by a single seat. The initiative's promoters hoped that public opinion in the state, so strongly supportive of abortion rights, might force approval of the initiative in the narrowly divided Senate. Legislative acceptance of the initiative would avoid a costly, contentious, statewide campaign in November. And even victory in one house would provide a strong kickoff for a statewide campaign if they were finally forced to go that route.[18]

The strategy backfired. In the backfiring process, several elements came to light that would remain important throughout what indeed became a costly, contentious election fight.

A Virginia-based nonprofit legal center that specializes in pro-life and other conservative social causes, the Rutherford Institute, brought suit, first in a district court and then in the state supreme court. It argued that the initiative should be thrown out because the petitions indicated that the initiative would be presented for a vote of the people, rather than sent to the legislature. The supreme court eventually rejected the suit, but for more than a month and a half in early 1991, energy and money were diverted away from the work of gathering voter support for the initiative. This was only the first of many times when the pro-initiative coalition would be forced to put out brushfires rather than expend effort on advancing their campaign.

What happened in the indirect process also showed that support for the initiative was not as strong as it looked on the surface. There was more divisiveness and tension over the issue among the state's leadership than first appeared.

The state legislature showed little stomach for a legislative struggle over the abortion issue. Senate Majority Leader Jeanette Hayner, a Republican, vowed not to allow the proposal even to come to the Senate floor for a vote. The Democrat-controlled House was considered "a bastion of pro-choice sentiment," but a substantial number of Democratic caucus leaders were both pro-choice and Catholic. If the Senate failed to act on the initiative, it would have to go on the ballot in November. Catholic Democrats, in particular, were not anxious to put themselves publicly on record as pro-choice in what would be a purely symbolic vote. As pro-choice, Catholic Representative Margarita Prentice said, "With the Senate's mind made up it's an exercise in futility."[19] No legislation would be passed; only ammunition provided their opponents for the 1992 elections.

House Speaker Joe King, who at first had strongly urged that legislators vote on the initiative, later declared himself upset at the tactic of bringing it to the legislature rather than directly to the voters. Governor Booth Gardner, supposedly an honorary co-chair of Pro-Choice Washington, insisted in an astonishing statement that he could not remember whether he had signed the petitions for the initiative, as supporters said he did. He also urged that the initiative go directly to the voters. "On an issue of that significance, I think the people ought to go ahead and vote on it. I also think that if they vote on it, they'll put it to rest for a long period of time."[20] At this press conference, the governor was questioned as closely and as much on the euthanasia initiative as on abortion. This was the first real public linking of the two, a linkage that would continue throughout the campaign.

If support proved less sturdy than expected at the state level, the same thing proved true at the national level, although the state's entire congressional delegation was publicly pro-choice. In September 1991 a coalition of pro-choice groups asked the state's congressional delegation to sponsor a Washington, D.C., fund raiser to benefit the initiative. Senator Brock Adams and Representatives Norm Dicks, Jim McDermott, Al Swift, Jolene Unsoeld, and Sid Morrison agreed. The state's other senator, Slade Gorton, Representative Tom Foley (the powerful Speaker of the House), and Representatives John Miller and Rod Chandler refused. Like Gorton and Miller, Speaker Foley said that he simply did not get involved in state politics, although he was already publicly working against the state's term-limitation initiative. Chandler said that he opposed parts of the abortion initiative. These were near party-line divisions. Morrison was the only Republican to agree to the fund raiser and Foley the only Democrat to refuse sponsorship.

Since, in the end, the state legislature refused to act on the abortion rights initiative, it was automatically slated to go on the ballot in November 1991. By early summer, campaigns to win the people over were in full swing by both abortion rights opponents and supporters.

Political consultant Tom Sego explained the flaw in the initiative process that in his opinion makes these citizen-sponsored bills amenable to defeat. "You're in a vacuum, and so you include everything. Your initiative becomes a Christmas wish list."[21] That mistake, he argued, provides opportunities for opponents. All they need do is find the detail that goes one step too far, or can be made to appear to go one step too far, and organize their campaign around that.

Sego seems to be describing what supporters and opponents of Initiative 120 did in Washington State. Abortion rights supporters would certainly disagree that their initiative was a Christmas wish list. They insisted that a team of constitutional experts, lawyers, and doctors spent more than a year refining its language and that it received extensive review by the national-level staffs of the American Civil Liberties Union (ACLU), Planned Parenthood, and the National Organization for Women (NOW). Abortion rights supporters, however, feared a Supreme Court reversal of *Roe v. Wade*. The Court's *Webster* decision had spurred legislative attempts in several states to restrict abortions. By the end of 1991 nine states and the U.S. territory of Guam had passed new restrictions.[22] Eager to protect a woman's right to an abortion, even to a state-funded abortion in the case of poor women, they wrote an initiative which their opponents were quick to claim went beyond the *Roe v. Wade* decision.

The initiative declared that "the state may not deny or interfere with a woman's right to choose an abortion prior to viability of the fetus, or [afterward] to protect her life and health." Viability was to be decided by "the good faith judgment of a physician," based on his determination that "there is a reasonable likelihood of the fetus's sustained survival outside the uterus without the application of extraordinary medical measures." It stated that "if the state provides . . . maternity care benefits, services or information to women through any program administered or funded in whole or in part by the state, the state shall also provide women otherwise eligible for any such program with substantially equivalent benefits, services or information to permit them to voluntarily terminate their pregnancies." The initiative made no mention of the need for either spousal or parental approval of a woman's or minor's abortion.[23]

The Campaign

The meaning of all these clauses formed the battleground for the six months' campaign to approve or reject the initiative. Particularly important were the viability, taxpayer cost, and parental-consent issues. Whether someone other than a doctor might perform abortions became peripherally important. Opponents also made much of the fact that the state already had a law protecting abortion rights, the much more stringent law passed in 1970.

A large number of liberal organizations cooperated to fight for passage of Initiative 120. These included state chapters of Planned Parenthood, NARAL, the League of Women Voters, NOW, and the ACLU. Also active were the Religious Coalition for Abortion Rights and the Washington State Medical Association. They came together under an umbrella organization called Yes on 120. The fight against the initiative was conducted mainly by Human Life of Washington, the state's largest anti-abortion organization, and the Catholic Church. Fundamentalist Protestant groups were also active.

The two sides adopted notably different strategies. Some members of some of the groups fighting for the abortion rights initiative also supported 119, the euthanasia initiative. The state's medical association opposed 119. Given the division in their ranks regarding the two initiatives, the abortion rights organizations focused their energies exclusively on 120, and tried hard to keep the two initiatives separate. Although the Catholic Church put twice as much money and rhetoric into fighting the euthanasia initiative, it and Human Life of Washington saw both these initiatives as "life issues." They therefore tied them together and fought them as a package whenever possible. For example, 200,000 leaflets were distributed in eastern Washington just a few days before the election. One side urged citizens to vote no on 119 and the other, to vote no on 120.

Op-ed pieces published in the *Seattle Times* in mid-October outlined the arguments each side made throughout the campaign. The piece opposing the initiative was written by State Senator Linda Smith, a Republican. She asked readers to "picture a serpentine of cars with Canadian, Oregon and California license plates crossing the Washington border." If this initiative is passed, with its lack of a residency requirement and its public funding for abortions, she warned, Washington would become the abortion capital of the United States. (Others, linking the abortion and euthanasia initiatives, referred in speeches to Washington's becoming the "fly and die" state.) Public schools with maternity programs would have to provide taxpayer-supported abortion services under this initiative, Smith argued. Children could be taken out of school for abortions without their parents' knowledge or consent. Under this initiative (with its reference to "medical assistants"), medically unlicensed persons "could perform part or all of the actual abortion," as long as they were acting under the general direction of a physician. (Possibly even by telephone, some opponents later suggested.)

"Perhaps most alarming," Smith wrote, this initiative allows abortions "nearly up until the time of birth" because it defines fetal viability as a fetus "capable of sustained survival outside the womb without the use of medical technology." Smith reminded readers that "even full-term babies can require special medical procedures."

The senator ended by denouncing supporters of the measure for saying that if 120 did not pass, women might no longer have the right to an abortion. That was not true, she insisted. It would only mean a return to Referendum 20 (the state's 1970 abortion rights law), which guaranteed abortions but with safeguards—abortions performed by licensed physicians in a state-approved medical facility, parental consent in the case of minors seeking abortions, and a ninety-day residency requirement for abortions in the state "to ensure that Washington does not become the 'drive thru' abortion site for the nation."[24]

The column written in support of 120 was by Joan Fitzpatrick, professor of constitutional law at the University of Washington. She argued that the initiative must be passed because "if *Roe* is overruled, Washingtonians will be subjected to outdated and highly restrictive [state] abortion laws that were enacted between 1854 and 1970." No abortions, except to save the life of the mother, would be allowed past sixteen weeks, even though, she noted, serious fetal defects are often not found that early. The 1970 law would also require spousal consent to an abortion and contains a clause requiring parental consent for minors, already ruled unconstitutional by the state's supreme court. Fitzpatrick insisted that Initiative 120 would simply incorporate *Roe v. Wade* into state law. "[It] does not allow an unlimited right to an abortion." Instead, its interpretation of the Supreme

Court's definition of viability is "very conservative." "A fetus is not viable if he or she would never leave an intensive care unit of a hospital (where 'extraordinary' care is given)." Very few abortions are performed in Washington after the twenty-fourth week—only 4 out of almost 31,000 in 1989. Further, she countered, Initiative 120 specifically requires that only licensed physicians perform abortions. "Anyone else who performs an abortion on another is guilty of a felony."

Fitzpatrick rejected the claim that the initiative would mean vastly increased spending for state taxpayers. The clause providing that a woman eligible for maternity care must receive substantially equal benefits if she chooses an abortion would not mean equal amounts of state money in both cases, but equal access and treatment. "Abortions cost far less than maternity care leading to a birth," and state rules regarding income eligibility for maternal care would be extended to those seeking an abortion. The initiative would not "pay for abortions for wealthy women."

Fitzpatrick concluded by charging that "opponents of 120 know that Washington is a solidly pro-choice state. The campaign against 120 has thus resorted to one principal tactic: distortion of the truth . . . in order to confuse and scare voters."[25]

These two columns summed up the major arguments made by both sides. They also demonstrated the way the campaign would be waged by each side. Opponents of the measure, like opponents of initiative measures in general, struck hard in emphasizing every seemingly radical or potentially problematic section of the measure. In a pamphlet setting out guidelines for letters to newspapers to be sent by initiative supporters, pro-choice leaders urged that "letters should stress *our* themes."[26] By October and November 1991, however, abortion rights leaders and supporters were spending most of their time and energy responding to opposition charges instead of making independent arguments of their own for the initiative.

Archbishop Thomas Murphy, leader of the Seattle Archdiocese and Washington's most prominent churchman, crisscrossed the state in September and October, arguing against both the euthanasia and the abortion initiatives. He urged Washingtonians to vote against both initiatives because "they share the common ground of attacking the value of life either in the womb of the mother or in a terminally ill situation."[27] He particularly attacked what he described as Initiative 120's change in the definition of fetal viability. Surprisingly for a Catholic bishop, Murphy also repeated, in a somewhat oblique way, the fact that failure of 120 would not mean the absence of all abortion rights in the state but would merely mean reinstatement of the more restrictive 1970 law. "Initiative 120," he said, "would eliminate all existing Washington State laws on abortion. It would eliminate the ability of the state to place responsible restrictions on abortion practice."[28]

During September, as well, the Catholic Church launched voter registration drives, erecting tables in church vestibules to sign up voters. Don Hopper, in charge of the project for the Seattle Archdiocese, acknowledged that it was an unprecedented action for the church in Washington and that "certainly our doing it this year has the two [euthanasia and abortion] initiatives as a focus."[29] Initiative supporters replied with some equanimity that adding voters to the rolls was always a good thing. Indeed, they themselves were also actively trying to register new voters, especially young people on the college campuses of the state.

On 6 October, both Catholic and conservative Protestant anti-abortion activists held "Life Chain" rallies in a number of cities and towns. They lined the more heavily traveled streets with demonstrators holding signs protesting abortion and the initiative. In the small city of Walla Walla, demonstrators lined nine blocks. In Tacoma, a larger, industrialized city, they lined fourteen blocks. Pictures showing the demonstrators and their signs (*Abortion Kills Children*) and stories about the "Life Chain" were printed in most of the state's newspapers.

A small group of pro-choice clergy met in response to the "Life Chain" and, especially, to Archbishop Murphy, who was continuing his travels and speeches opposing the initiatives. The thirty-five clergy and lay people were associated with the Religious Coalition for Abortion Rights. Their spokesperson, the Reverend Flora Bowers, a Methodist minister, denounced the language being used to fight the abortion initiative as "dishonest" and "manipulative."[30]

The charge that abortion rights opponents were waging a "dishonest" and "manipulative" campaign grew louder and more impassioned as the initiative's opponents aired a series of dramatic, hard-hitting television ads.

In early October a thirty-second campaign spot ran on seventeen stations across the state. It depicted two middle-class couples at a barbecue. In it one man says, "I'm all for women's choice. I just don't like the government tell'n me I have to pay for it." "Yeah," says a second man. "They wanna raise our taxes by—what—60 million dollars? So we can pay for all those abortions . . . maybe even for wealthy women." One of the wives exclaims, "That's highway robbery."[31]

The ad highlighted one of the most potent charges made by the anti-initiative forces. Pointing to the clause in the initiative that states that if the state provides maternity-care benefits to eligible women (as Washington State does), it must provide equal benefits to women seeking abortions, anti-initiative supporters argued that since Washington had spent $62 million on maternity benefits for poor women in the previous year, it would be obliged to spend an equivalent amount for abortions if the initiative passed.

Belle Taylor McGhee, spokeswoman for Yes on 120, denounced the ad as "a red herring. The ad is patently false."[32] Abortions, she said, cost a fraction of what services leading to a live birth cost. (Washington spent $2.6 million on abortions for the poor in 1990.) She denied that the initiative would or could cost taxpayers the large sums of money claimed. The initiative intended only to ensure parity in treatment and services. It did not mandate equal sums of money. Kate Gibbie, director of the state's Department of Health, also insisted that state eligibility standards would rule out tax-funded abortions for wealthy women. The sum of $60 million in additional taxes to pay for abortions, though, was raised over and over in the campaign, both on television and in newspaper reports.

Other television ads followed, a flurry of them in the days just before the election. One argued that if the initiative passed, schools could "set it up and take a child out of school for an abortion and the parent would not have to be notified."[33] Reverend Flora Bowers of the Religious Coalition for Abortion Rights called the ad "a real scare tactic."

Just as the man in the barbecue ad insisted that he was all for choice, an ad widely run the week before the election promised that a no vote on the initiative would still be a vote for choice and abortion rights because it would reinstate the 1970 law. This law allowed abortion but kept some controls over how the abortion decision was made, controls, the ad insisted, that many people wanted.

Initiative supporters agreed that this ad and this argument hurt their vote. It used the watchword "choice" against them. As Seattle political consultant Blair Butterworth explained, "It was really confusing at the end. You had the pro side saying this was a pro-choice issue and the other side saying we are [for choice], too, but this is a pig in a poke."[34]

Supporters of the initiative brought in political leaders to refute the ads. They sent speakers to club meetings and public forums across the state to argue against the questions and anxieties raised by the ads regarding taxpayer costs, vulnerable schoolchildren, unlimited abortion up to the moment of birth, and the other issues. They quickly put together an ad that ran the last weekend before the election in which citizens shook their heads over the anti-initiative ads and said, disgustedly, "They'll say *anything* to take away your choice."[35] David Mitchell, political consultant to the initiative movement, conceded, however, that "it was impossible to fight them on each and every charge."[36] "They wrote a sloppy law," Mary Jo Kahler, spokeswoman for the opposition, rejoined. "We did a good job of raising questions about their main themes."[37]

The campaign was bitter and costly, with more than $1.5 million spent on both sides. In the end, absentee ballots made the difference.

Although the initiative was trailing by about 6,000 votes at the end of election day, 5 November 1991, about 200,000 absentee ballots still had to be counted. Both supporters and opponents agreed that the fact that the outcome depended on absentee ballots probably meant the initiative would pass. Although voters can mail in absentee ballots until midnight on election day, most actually mail in their ballots much sooner. This means that these absentee voters would not have been affected by the last-minute anti-abortion ads. Even though conventional wisdom says that absentee voters tend to be older, often conservative people, in recent elections in Washington more and more younger, working voters have been attracted by the convenience of voting by mail.[38] These are precisely the voters polls showed most likely to support abortion rights. Finally, a third of the 200,000 absentee ballots came from urbanized, liberal King County. Almost 60 percent of the county's voters who had turned out on election day had voted in favor of the initiative. If the support ratio for the initiative continued in the absentee ballots from this populous county, the measure would pass. It finally did win by a scant 4,222 votes.

The Aftermath of the Vote

The close vote on the abortion rights measure in a state where choice was considered the "locally ascendant" position seems to reflect the four factors cited earlier: that the initiative was a radical measure, certainly in comparison to abortion rights legislation under consideration in many other states; that the effect of the initiative's radical nature was compounded by the fact that, seren-dipitously, it turned up on the same ballot as the pioneering term-limits and euthanasia measures; that the initiative process favors those forces opposing a measure, a factor of which 120 opponents took full advantage; that both support-ers and opponents claimed to be for "choice," confusing voters and establishing a new strategy that anti-abortion activists, including the Catholic Church, might adopt in other places in the future. The postelectoral analyses of 120 supporters and opponents and of political analysts and journalists in the state all point to these factors as important in the campaign. Polling data bear them out.

Although polls taken early in the campaign demonstrated majority support for abortion rights (as well as for term limits and euthanasia), polls taken im-mediately before the election showed that support had slipped, especially among late deciders. Elway Research conducted a statewide poll for the *Seattle Times* over the three days just before November 5. The poll showed that among the 80 percent of voters who had made up their minds on the abortion issue more than a month before the election, 60 percent favored the initiative. Among voters who had decided only in the week before the election, 70 percent intended to vote against it.[39]

"My sense is that they [120 backers] assumed Washington was overwhelm-ingly pro-choice and decided to argue the issue on its merits," said consultant Blair Butterworth, who had earlier run a pro-choice campaign in Nevada. "They took the high road, and the one thing we've learned working this issue is to expect the other side to take the low road."[40] Supporters charged their opponents with taking the low road; opponents accused supporters of "writing a sloppy bill." There is some truth to both accusations.

Abortion rights supporters insisted that theirs was the opposite of a sloppy bill. One of the initiative's drafters, University of Washington law professor Stewart Jay, even insisted that 120 improved on *Roe v. Wade*'s language, which he called "too vague."[41] There was no doubt, however, that rights supporters in Washington State focused almost exclusively on the goal of providing women with the widest possible abortion rights with the fewest possible restrictions. Washington's seemingly pro-choice climate encouraged them to write an initiative that would do that. Their initiative therefore relied on a doctor's judgment alone, rather than a timetable or fetal testing, to determine viability. It abjured any form of consent, spousal or parental, and it included public funding for the poor. The initiative, without any of the restrictions in the 1970 state abortion law, provided ammunition for its opponents. It made it easy for opponents to raise the red flags that the initiative process itself so well accommodates. The issues raised so strongly—public funding for abortions, the absence of parental consent for minors, the moral qualms involved in the viability question—are issues that numerous surveys show divide Americans across the country.[42] Raising these issues has caused restrictive abortion legislation to be passed in some states and has doomed liberal abortion rights legislation in others. The gamble that Washington State abortion rights activists took in writing their wide-open initiative paid off in the end, but it was a close call.

The Elway poll indicated the effect these emotional issues may have had on sectors of the Washington electorate. First, late deciders, those most exposed to the campaign speeches and ads raising questions about this liberal initiative, with its few restrictions, in the end were much more likely to oppose it. The poll also showed that churchgoers opposed the initiative by 2–1 or better. Fifty-seven percent of all voters opposed to the initiative cited "moral reasons" to explain their opposition. After moral reasons, voters cited their belief that the state's existing abortion law was adequate and that no new law was needed.[43]

Both opponents and supporters were convinced that the fact that the abortion rights initiative was on the same ballot with term limits and, especially, the euthanasia measure affected the outcome. On election night, while the "no" votes were still in the lead, an abortion opponent and state representative, Duane Sommers, predicted the initiative's defeat. He conceded to reporters, however, "I think if 120 was on the ballot by itself, it probably would have passed."[44] Representative Jennifer Belcher, an abortion rights supporter, confessed, "People were very nervous that 120 wouldn't pass, but no one wanted to say that publicly. We were concerned that other issues on the ballot would bring out conservative voters."[45]

The Elway poll again bore out the gut reactions of political campaign leaders. Just as voters opposed to Initiative 120 said "moral reasons" guided their response, voters opposed to euthanasia gave moral reasons for their objections, for example, their belief that "life is sacred."[46] Churchgoers opposed euthanasia as well as abortion rights by 2–1 or better (Catholic and conservative Protestant churches actively campaigned against both initiatives as "life" measures).

While we can analyze the campaign and the reasons for its surprisingly close conclusion, it is important to note that the abortion rights initiative *was* approved. Washington in the end did maintain its liberal attitude toward abortion, even if narrowly. Following Connecticut, Maryland, and Nevada, Washington became the fourth state in the nation to incorporate liberal abortion rights into state law in reaction to the concerns raised by the Supreme Court's 1989 *Webster* ruling.

After the tumult of the 1991 campaign and the vote, Washington has continued to maintain its generally liberal attitude toward abortion. No real effort has been mounted in the state to overturn the new abortion rights law. The issue played a minuscule role during the 1992 elections in the state. And in April 1992 Washington became one of the few states in the nation to pass a bill prohibiting interference with health-care facilities providing abortions.

Notes

1. "Heady Mixture," *Spokane Spokesman-Review*, 6 November 1991, A1.
2. "State of Washington Rejects a Plan to Curb Incumbents," *New York Times*, 7 November 1991, B16.
3. "Voters Turn Down Mercy Killing Idea," *New York Times*, 7 November 1991, B16.
4. Barbara Hinkson Craig and David M. O'Brien, *Abortion and American Politics* (Chatham, N.J.: Chatham House, 1993), 281.
5. "Hot Topics to Fill Ballot in November," *Seattle Times*, 25 July 1991, C1.
6. "Voters Say: 'Not So Fast,' " *Seattle Times*, 6 November 1991, A2.
7. Hugh Bone, "The Political Setting," in *Political Life in Washington*, ed. Thor Swanson et al. (Pullman, Wash.: Washington State University Press, 1985), 7.
8. Elizabeth Walker, "Interest Groups in Washington State," in *Government and Politics in the Evergreen State*, ed. David C. Nice, John C. Pierce, and Charles H. Sheldon (Pullman, Wash.: Washington State University Press, 1992), 43.
9. Terrence E. Cook, "The Political Setting," in Nice, Pierce, and Sheldon, *Government and Politics*, 7–8.
10. Ibid., 10.
11. Ibid.
12. Felician A. Foy, ed., *1993 Catholic Almanac* (Huntington, Ind.: Our Sunday Visitor Publishing Division, 1992), 433.
13. David C. Nice, "Political Parties in Washington," in Nice, Pierce, and Sheldon, *Government and Politics*, 71.
14. Hugh A. Bone and Herman J. Lugan, "Direct Democracy in Washington," in Nice, Pierce, and Sheldon, *Government and Politics*, 113.
15. Ibid., 106.
16. Nice, "Political Parties in Washington," 73.
17. "Legislators Lukewarm to Abortion Initiative," *Seattle Times*, 1 February 1991, C1.
18. "Political Strategy on Abortion-Rights Initiative Backfires," *Seattle Times*, 21 March 1991, A1.
19. Ibid., A8.
20. "Gardner Wants Abortion, Aid-in-Dying Votes," *Seattle Times*, 23 January 1991, D4.

21. "Initiative Measures Must Fight Long Odds," *Seattle Times*, 11 November 1991, A4.

22. Craig and O'Brien, *Abortion and American Politics*, 280.

23. Washington Office of the Secretary of State, *Voter's Pamphlet: State General Election, November 5, 1991*, Edition No. 1, 30–31.

24. Linda Smith, "Should Abortion Laws Be Revised? No," *Seattle Times*, 13 October 1991, A17.

25. Joan Fitzpatrick, "Should Abortion Laws Be Revised? Yes," *Seattle Times*, 13 October 1991, A17.

26. American Civil Liberties Union of Washington, "Guidelines for Letters to the Editor," 2. Mimeograph.

27. Thomas Murphy, "Washington State's November Ballot: Euthanasia and Abortion," *Origins: Catholic News Service Documentary Service* 21 (17 October 1991): 299.

28. Ibid., 301.

29. "Church Joins the Campaign," *Seattle Times*, 21 September 1991, A1.

30. "Pro-Choice Clergy Rally to Initiative," *Seattle Times*, 9 October 1991, B1.

31. "Anti-120 Ad Denounced as a Lie," *Seattle Times*, 4 October 1991, C1.

32. Ibid.

33. "Did 120 Opponents Use 'Choice' to Win Votes?" *Seattle Times*, 7 November 1991, A1–2.

34. Ibid.

35. Ibid.

36. Ibid.

37. Ibid.

38. "Initiative 120 Backers Claim Victory," *Seattle Times*, 13 November 1991, D1–2.

39. "Absentee Ballots to Decide Abortion Measure," *Seattle Times*, 6 November 1991, D1, 3.

40. Ibid.

41. "Abortion Rights Measure Wins, Barely, in Washington State," *New York Times*, 22 November 1991, B17.

42. Craig and O'Brien *Abortion and American Politics*, chap. 7.

43. "Morality, Freedom of Choice Clash in Decisions on 119, 120," *Seattle Times*, 6 November 1991, D1–2.

44. "Washington Said No, but Showed Lots of Initiative," *Spokane Spokesman-Review*, 7 November 1991, A1, 9.

45. Ibid.

46. "Morality, Freedom of Choice," D1–2.

MICHAEL A. RUSSO

9 | California: A Political Landscape for Choice and Conflict

Californians make up 13 percent of the American population. Thus much of America is defined by California. Yet, in more recent times, understanding what is going on in the state is increasingly difficult. Its size, diversity of population, and conflicts—whether contests over water rights in the Central Valley or disputes among rival gangs in South-Central Los Angeles—demonstrate that California is a complex state of mind.

The nation views painful video images of California that focus on urban unrest and the fragile environment: Rodney King, Polly Klaas, Lyle and Erik Menendez, the all-too-frequent hillside firestorms, Mexicans attempting to cross the border at San Diego, and the ever-present potential for disaster in a state defined by the energy and edges of geological fault lines.

To make sense of this, writers such as Joan Didion, Richard Rodriguez, and Kevin Starr wrestle with California's identity and different dreams.[1] They say that California is undergoing a social and multicultural redefinition—much like the one the United States underwent during the 1890s, a decade of adjustment to the closing of the frontier and the fixing of New York and Chicago in the minds of Americans.

For the time being, California's fractious parts do not add up to a whole. Proposals to divide the state, to set term limits for elected officials, and to manage the pervasive cynicism within the social and political fabric reflect the frustration among Californians. So what finally emerges from California's present uncertainty may ultimately shape America's social and political character.

One area in which California is truly a bellwether is the legalization of abortion. In 1967 California was one of the first states to make abortion legal, and it

168

remains a solidly pro-choice state. More abortions take place in California than in any other state. In 1992 the Field poll reported that 75 percent of the adult public either advocate no change in the existing abortion laws (41 percent) or favor legislative actions that would make it easier to obtain abortions (34 percent).[2] Even if the Supreme Court had overturned *Roe v. Wade*, abortions would have remained legal under the state's privacy laws. And little real political power exists to change this situation because of the Democrat-controlled statehouse. Nonetheless, conflicts between pro-choice and anti-abortion forces in the state are real and further demonstrate the divisions and frustrations in the social and cultural landscape.

Pro-choice candidates win statewide and federal elections, but opposition from grassroots political alliances of anti-abortion groups with the Christian Right can cost votes. According to a recent Field poll, 21 percent of all California adults consider themselves among the Religious Right, whereas 54 percent do not qualify as religious by the poll. The remainder of California adults, the so-called religious moderates, represent 25 percent of the adult population. These voters often provide the margin of victory or defeat in close electoral contests.[3]

Californians are highly individualistic; they are more libertarian, a smaller percentage of them are Catholic, and they are less religious and more unchurched than the rest of the nation. Factors such as these shape the abortion debate and create the potential for the abortion issue to be mobilized by both the right and the left. Like New York, California is a large political arena; big money, costly campaigns, and a wide range of media markets add up to a high degree of complexity in statewide elections. The electorate is racially diverse, and there are large business and special interests and a highly professionalized state legislature.

In 1992 California elected two women to the U.S. Senate. That election powerfully demonstrated the ability of the women's political network to mount campaigns using issues of gender and choice to gain advantage for women candidates perceived by voters as "agents of change."

Clearly, Dianne Feinstein and Barbara Boxer won on the basis of a weakened California economy and record levels of unemployment in the state. Nevertheless, the almost harmonic convergence of issues and especially the fierce public discussions of gender—the fiasco over the confirmation hearings of Clarence Thomas, the May 1991 *Rust v. Sullivan* Title X regulations (the so-called gag order at federally sponsored clinics), and the potential for the Supreme Court to overturn *Roe v. Wade*—kept Clinton well ahead of Bush in statewide polls and ultimately brought more women into federal and state office.

In February 1994 State Treasurer Kathleen Brown announced her candidacy for governor. Both her father and her brother are past governors, so she can be considered a leading contender. Whether Brown is capable of drawing on the same issues is unpredictable; nonetheless, women in state politics have an impressive record. Another feature in the 1994 governor's race that merits attention is the role of pro-life Republicans and how their disenchantment with Republican governor Pete Wilson could influence his reelection in a close contest.

Given the unique features of California's political culture, what history governs its discourse about abortion? What are the pressure points, conflicts, and legislation proposed by pro-choice and pro-life activists? What are the potential outcomes for politicians and citizens? How does the issue of abortion translate into the social and political fabric of the state?

The History of Legal Abortion

The liberalization of California's abortion laws took place in the 1960s amid that decade's social and cultural upheaval. For over a hundred years, California's penal code had defined abortion as a crime unless a physician determined it necessary to save the life of the mother. But by the 1960s, the firm moorings that had anchored this law gave way to changes in medical science, the professional role of physicians, the "sexual revolution," and the demands of the women's movement. By 1973 these factors led to a legal recognition in California that a woman had a "constitutional right" to abortion under the state's privacy laws.

Berkeley sociologist Kristen Luker wrote one of the most important books on this topic, *Abortion and the Politics of Motherhood*.[4] Her account of the history of abortion policy is vital in attempting to understand the present debate in the state. Luker closely examines the chief constituencies for change in California: the professional organizations of physicians who in the early 1960s sought to reform abortion laws, and the growing women's movement that toward the end of the decade called for the repeal of all abortion laws. Both groups had a marked effect on the shape and scope of changes in the state law, as well as determining the climate of opinion about abortion policy.

The first public discussion about abortion in California took the form of state legislative hearings from 1961 to 1964. These hearings resulted from divisions within the medical establishment over strict versus broad interpretation of the existing laws. For example, did the mental health of the mother constitute grounds for a physician to recommend abortion? Survey data of the time show that abortion was illegal in California only if the existing laws were strictly and narrowly interpreted.[5] Nevertheless, among doctors, hospitals, and medical organizations, there was neither much formal public policy on abortion nor any genuine coherence in the practice and availability of abortions.

The public hearings brought about a range of conflicting responses. Physicians who advocated a broad interpretation of the law wanted additional legislation to assure the continuance of abortion as a safe medical procedure. A second group of physicians, those who adhered to a strict interpretation of the law, argued that advances in medical science should have had the effect of decreasing the actual number of legal abortions. Thus the early phase of public discussion focused on the moral boundaries of therapeutic abortion and the problem of criminal abortion.

News events stimulated public interest in the abortion issue and marshaled groups who advocated liberalizing California's restrictive abortion laws. The Sherri Finkbine case in 1962 and an epidemic of rubella (German measles) in 1964–65 became catalysts for statewide and national controversy and set the stage for the legislative and judicial responses.

Sherri Finkbine was an Arizona housewife who had taken thalidomide, a tranquilizer, in the early stages of her pregnancy. Because of a discovery in Europe that the drug caused birth defects, she requested an abortion. In an effort to warn women about the dangers of the drug, Finkbine and her husband brought their situation to the attention of the media. The public disclosure generated explosive publicity when hospitals and physicians refused to perform the abortion. Finally, Finkbine was forced to go to Sweden for the procedure.

According to Kristen Luker, this case caught the public's imagination.[6] First, the case forced people to define exactly what circumstances in principle constituted grounds for abortion. Second, it forced doctors to define exactly what they were doing when they performed an abortion. Third, because the case involved possible birth defects, it forced into the open the fundamental disagreement about whether an embryo/fetus represented a "real" person or merely a potential person. Thus the controversy in the Finkbine case foreshadowed the serious medical, legal, and moral dilemmas ahead.

One year later, a rubella epidemic in California placed the problem squarely in the hands of physicians and soon polarized the medical, public health, and legal communities. Did exposure to rubella constitute sufficient grounds for an abortion under existing laws? While physicians continued to perform abortions during the epidemic, the 1964 state legislative hearings brought more calls for the legal protection of abortion. Medical doctors wanted a clarification of the legal status of certain abortions—health, rape, and fetal indications. Lawyers and especially public health officials had a long-standing concern with the problem of illegal abortions. Lastly, women in far greater numbers came into the debate; the rubella epidemic and the Finkbine case provided vivid testimony of how abortion personally and directly confronted women.

Following the 1964 hearings, the California Committee on Therapeutic Abortion (CCTA)—an advocacy group composed of lawyers, physicians, social workers, and public health professionals—became the first professional organization to call for the repeal of the 1872 law and support for a reformed abortion law, the Beilenson bill. Neither the 1961 nor the 1964 version of the bill was able to get out of legislative committee.

Once again, news events drew public attention to abortion and assisted the CCTA in mobilizing support for the reform bill. In 1966 the California State Board of Medical Examiners charged nine doctors with formal disciplinary action for performing rubella-related abortions. The decision backfired. Highly publicized hearings and testimony from some 2,000 physicians who formed a nationwide group in support of the "San Francisco Nine" resulted in a state ready for change in its abortion laws.[7]

In 1967 California's state legislature passed the Therapeutic Abortion Act (Health and Safety Code, secs. 25950–58), which allowed the termination of pregnancy by a qualified doctor in a hospital certified by the American Hospital Association when the continuance of the pregnancy would "gravely impair the physical or mental health of the mother" or when the pregnancy was the result of rape or incest. The act provided that "in no event shall the termination be approved after the 20th week of pregnancy." Luker concluded, "A mere six years after its first proposal, a variation of the 'Scandinavian type' or 'middle way' law was passed. Though it did not permit abortion on demand, it offered considerable protection to the medical profession."[8]

Restriction on the state's presence between doctor and mother was the most significant aspect of the new law; in practice, this allowed abortion even in difficult cases involving rubella and thalidomide. At the time, California governor Ronald Reagan insisted that he would veto the bill unless its reference to abortion for "fetal indications" was dropped. Not covered in the law was the moral and legal status of the congenitally damaged embryo, thus keeping open this aspect of the debate.

What had been proposed in the 1960s as compromise legislation and a "middle way" launched a rapid sea change in social consequences. The number of abortions in the state rose dramatically, from 5,018 in 1968, the first year under the new law, to more than 100,000 annually by 1972—representing a 2,000 percent increase in the number of abortions performed in California. In California, "abortion on demand" was soon to become the practice.[9]

At the same time, the abortion debate shifted from a reform argument among professionals to a call by women's organizations—the National Organization for Women (NOW), the National Abortion Rights Action League (NARAL), the Society for Humane Abortions (SHA)—for the repeal of all abortion laws. As Harvard educator Carol Gilligan has suggested, women were speaking in a different voice; they talked openly about birth control and sexuality, and, in a language of moral rights, they laid the groundwork for the idea that women had a right to use abortion to control their lives.

Thus the demand for the repeal of abortion laws was tied to an expanded role for women in public life. As Kristen Luker noted: "It allowed women to argue . . . that although childbearing was important, it was not the single most important thing in a woman's life . . . it vitiated the arguments of employers that only certain jobs were 'good for a woman.' In a society that had recently experienced a nationwide upheaval over civil rights, such discrimination would be difficult to justify."[10] The California courts agreed.

In 1969 the California Supreme Court became the first in the nation to strike down an abortion law (Penal Code 274). Under due process, in *People v. Belous*, the court recognized that a woman possessed the constitutional right "to life and to choose whether to bear children." The judges rejected the argument that the state had a compelling interest in the "embryo and fetus" equal to or greater than the mother's right to choose. The court added: "The law has always recognized that the pregnant woman's right to life takes precedence over any interest the state may have in the unborn." With its ruling on abortion and its pioneering laws in areas such as criminal prosecution, consumer rights, and personal injury, the California court was soon to become one of the most influential forces in American law.[11]

In 1972, three months before the landmark U.S. Supreme Court decision in *Roe v. Wade*, Californians approved an amendment to the state constitution that specifically added the right of "privacy" to the other inalienable rights of individuals. Here, the rights guaranteed by the state constitution did not depend on those guaranteed by the U.S. Constitution. These amendments formed the basis for the constitutional right of choice and became the conceptual framework for any further legislative and judicial analysis of abortion in California. Even if the U.S. Supreme Court overturned *Roe v. Wade*, abortions would remain legal in California under the state constitution and privacy laws.

By November 1972, the California Supreme Court had invalidated nearly all the provisions of the 1967 Therapeutic Abortion Act. In *People v. Barksdale*, the court found that the crucial statutory language of the 1967 law was "vague and obscure." Terms such as the "mental health of the mother" did not meet the minimum standards of due process; consequently, the 1967 law was found unconstitutional. During the past twenty years, the California state legislature has not acted to amend the 1967 law. Thus the state's current abortion law is the creation of the court's ruling. The only remaining constitutional regulation of abortion in California today is the requirement that an abortion be performed by a licensed physician in an accredited hospital.[12]

The Present State of Mind

Merriam-Webster defines a *guerrilla* as "one who engages in irregular warfare, esp. as a member of an independent unit carrying out harassment and sabotage." This may be an apt description for the present state of mind and conflict over abortion—a form of "guerrilla politics." In the two decades of social and political skirmishes over parental notification by minors, Medi-Cal funding for low-income women, and laws to assure access to clinics, the abortion issue has remained on the periphery of the political agenda in California. Since social, ethical, and symbolic values are critical in the abortion debate, such key players as the Roman Catholic Church, the anti-abortion movement, and the Democratic Party have little hope for honest, open discussion.

Instead, each side has just enough force to permit such citizen groups as California Abortion Rights Action League (CARAL), Planned Parenthood, the California Prolife Council, and Operation Rescue to offset any genuine victories for the opposing camp. While abortion may not play a controlling or decisive role in state politics, it can provide a vantage point from which to test political alliances and listen to undercurrents of political discourse.

The Church and Abortion Politics

In November 1989 Archbishop Roger L. Mahony of Los Angeles spoke before an assembly of Roman Catholic bishops in Baltimore. The Roman Catholic Church represents the single largest organization opposed to legal abortion in the United States. Several weeks earlier, Mahony's Los Angeles residence had been the site of violent abortion rights demonstrations; an effigy of a mitered bishop, bearing a close likeness to the archbishop, was burned at the front door. Mahony provided the best summary of the situation facing the bishops:

> I think that we, as Catholics, in our public moral stance on most pro-life issues, stand increasingly alone. We may be the only major population-segment in our country and the nation-wide institution so fully committed to defend and protect the rights of the unborn. We may, in reality, be the only moral conscience in our country willing to proclaim this publicly. The weeks and months ahead are going to be difficult and painful as we are attacked on many sides by those who look to quick solutions for pivotal basic moral issues. We need to be courageous, and even heroic, in our beliefs and in the proclamation and practice of those beliefs.[13]

Mahony's idea of church against society seemed almost defiant as he challenged the bishops to take up abortion as a personal cause. Much in the same fashion earlier that year, at the "Let Them Live L.A." week, Mahony spoke at the Central Baptist Church in Pomona to 2,000 to 3,000 anti-abortion activists. His appearance with Randall Terry endorsed Operation Rescue and forged an unaccustomed alliance between the Catholic Church and Protestant fundamentalists.

In his role as the archbishop of the largest Catholic archdiocese in the country, Mahony represents a church whose members are widely diverse in ethnic, educational, economic, and political makeup. Randall Terry's militancy speaks to a select audience and often places him at odds with local police and judges. At present, a number of bills before the California legislature would curtail the protest activities of Operation Rescue and similar anti-abortion organizations.[14]

Following the 1989 *Webster* decision, conservative bishops like Mahony took the issue of abortion as a test of their moral authority, especially among Catholic pro-choice candidates who were up for election in statewide contests. But if the idea was that through dramatic political stands a prelate could seize the moment and have the "whole world watching" on the evening newscast, such ploys failed. San Diego Bishop Leo T. Maher's public denouncement of pro-choice Catholic Lucy Killea simply flopped; it helped elect Killea, the Democratic candidate, in what was considered a safe Republican senatorial district.

Clearly, church leaders had mixed results in affecting elections and the Maher/Killea incident firmly demonstrated that Catholics do not passively follow their bishops on abortion. Such political tests are reminders of the complications that arise when leaders of tax-exempt religious organizations enter the political arena, especially the Catholic Church, whose social teachings include immigration and welfare reform, the problems of health care, and abolition of the death penalty.

The California Catholic Conference has the task of forwarding the bishops' agenda in Sacramento. Julie Sly, associate director of communications for the conference, described for me the work of the California conference, and the precise role Catholic bishops have in affecting public policy:

> The Conference is really the bishops. And a lot of times people think the Conference is the staff. So there is some confusion that way. There have been occasions, three or four years ago, during the Maher incident, when more radical pro-life people felt that we [the staff] did not do enough on abortion. I recall one bishops' meeting where there was a fairly heated discussion about it. However, at least my experience with the bishops is that they are more comfortable in the role of teacher and pastor. This can vary from bishop to bishop. They are a little more cautious now as I think some of them have been burned.[15]

At times, the church's views do not correspond with the views and actions of individuals or groups in the anti-abortion movement. Although firmly supported by the Catholic hierarchy, the campaign against legal abortion in the state represents a complex blend of secular and religious visions about abortion. Groups within the movement conflict over specific plans of action, especially among those members who would ban all abortions. A realistic political program, however, one that truly challenges the dominant political culture, requires a legislative agenda that aims at making abortion less accessible to women and less acceptable to citizens generally.

The Anti-Abortion Movement in California

The California Prolife Council is the main lobbying arm of the anti-abortion forces in the state, with offices and staff in Sacramento. Secular in tone, this organization approaches abortion policy from a civil rights perspective and is an affiliate of the Washington, D.C.–based National Right to Life. The primary goals of the organization include advocating laws that restrict abortion, marshaling public support, and identifying pro-life candidates for state and federal office. At hearings before the California legislature, the organization has advanced measures that would restrict state funding of abortions, enforce parental consent for minors, ban fetal experimentation, reinstate a conscience clause for hospital employees, gather statistics on the number of abortions statewide, and propose an informed-consent law for those having abortions. Additionally, the Prolife Council provides counseling to women who seek an alternative to abortion.

The strategy is to keep the issue of abortion before the public, the legislature, and the courts. Jan Carroll, the legislative director of the council and associate western director of the National Right to Life Committee, explained, "It's our job to keep passing these kinds of restrictions in order to entice the courts to take another look at them." She told me, "In the states we believe that most people are against most abortions, and eventually that will bear out in legislation."[16]

For the past fifteen years, the Prolife Council has been instrumental in advocating restrictive language to the California state budget in an attempt to ban Medi-Cal funding of abortions. But the American Civil Liberties Union has been successful in its legal challenge, reinstating funds based on a 1981 state supreme court ruling in *Committee to Defend Reproductive Rights v. Myers*. In the 1990–91 legislative year, after the *Webster* decision, the budget amendment proposed by Senator John Doolittle (R-Rocklin) and Assemblyman Phillip Wyman (R-Tehachapi) was seen as a test on where each California legislator stood on abortion. Doolittle's amendment failed in the Senate by 12 to 24; Wyman's amendment failed in the Assembly by 30 to 36. Here the anti-abortion legislative agenda in the statehouse must draw support primarily from legislators such as Senator Donald Rogers (R-Bakersfield) and Assemblyman Tim Leslie (R-Sacramento), and occasional coalitions with powerful Democrats, such as David A. Roberti, the president pro tempore of the Senate. Tests over abortion are few, however, and bills rarely get out of committee because pro-choice forces in the Democratic Party dominate the all-important Health Care Committees in both Senate and Assembly.

In 1987, the California state legislature passed a parental-consent law (AB2274) requiring minors to obtain parental or court permission for an abortion. Because of a restraining order, the state has never enforced the law, which is pending review before the First Appellate Court of San Francisco. The law is a potent political bombshell, and because of the potential for a highly publicized court battle, few politicians want this matter resolved. Nonetheless, in oral argument on 7 April 1994 Republican attorney general Dan Lungren appealed this injunction. The three justices on the court will issue an opinion shortly. Individuals I interviewed held to the idea that, whatever decision is rendered, the various sides to the case will petition for an appeal before the California Supreme Court.

In California, a "pro-life" candidate is more often a "pro-family" conservative Republican candidate. Whereas some candidates consider themselves "pro-life," others may use the term "pro-family." The various factions within the pro-life movement share a conservative political agenda but sometimes differ on legislative strategy. For example, the California Right to Life Educational Fund in Pleasant Hill and the Right to Life Political Action Group in Santa Barbara link abortion to a broad array of legislation initiatives dealing with sex education, unlawful sexual intercourse, and self-esteem (also called "community empowerment laws"). The religious and moral concerns of these organizations are allied nationally to American Life League and the powerful "family values" agenda of Pat Robertson's Christian Coalition, and Lou Shelton's Traditional Values Coalition. In any event, the key leaders in the pro-life movement agree that the future of their cause resides in the Republican Party.[17]

During the 1992 election cycle, California "pro-family" conservatives distributed over 4.5 million "nonpartisan" voter guides through 15,000 California churches and, combined with Christian television and radio stations, bypassed the mainstream media and traditional party institutions. The Allied Business PAC, the primary vehicle for conservative contributions, contributed over $1.6 million to campaigns through the primary and general elections of 1992. This included support from such businessmen as Howard Fieldstead Ahmanson, Jr., of Orange County, heir to the Home Savings and Loan fortune. As a result of the "pro-family"/"pro-life" coalition, conservative candidates won eighteen of thirty-two congressional races, nineteen of thirty-one Assembly races, and three of six Senate races. In city councils and on school boards, some forty "pro-family" candidates won office.

As a grassroots political movement, the anti-abortion organizations have a clear political agenda in identifying candidates, mobilizing voters with direct-mail campaigns, and targeting specific contests on school boards and town councils. Reflecting on the role of the anti-abortion movement in state elections, and specifically Republican politics, Jan Carroll commented to me,

> California defies category. If you come with the perspective that this is a liberal state, you really haven't seen all that's here, especially the ability of grassroots movements to have an effect on elections. I keep wondering how many times we have to demonstrate to the Republican Party that we don't want candidates like Wilson. Regularly in the primaries we defeat the lukewarm candidates they seem to hand us . . . candidates like John Seymour.
>
> You can't get people to be enthusiastic about a [pro-choice] candidate who doesn't support what they [pro-life] support. So if they don't show up [on election day], it's just as bad as if they voted against the candidate. And if the grassroots folks aren't satisfied—the people who are going to do the work for the candidate—politically it's a darn hard road to haul.

The leadership of the pro-life movement in California appears committed to a grassroots political agenda, thereby maintaining a voice in state politics. This strategy may not change abortion policy or win statewide or federal elections, but it buys time, commands attention, and, most of all, builds a local political apparatus. The calculation here is the readiness to be part of a larger endeavor, namely, the chance in 1996 that the anti-abortion movement might reestablish itself nationally in presidential candidacies of Jack Kemp, Dan Quayle, or William Bennett.

Women and the Politics of Choice

To assess the politics of abortion in California, I interviewed Susan Kennedy, the executive director of the state Democratic Party. She is the former executive director of the California Abortion Rights Action League (CARAL). I asked her about the political strategy of the anti-abortion movement in the state. She commented: "With the escalation of violence on the local level, and the activities in local elections, the anti-choice community is planting the seeds for a reversal down the road. And it's very difficult to guard against. . . . But I think the strategy that the anti-choice community is using is very effective."[18]

Whereas the anti-abortion movement has the task of keeping the issue of abortion fresh in the mind of citizens—a rhetoric of agitation—the pro-choice forces have an altogether different rhetoric, that is, one of integration. This is an argument of balance, concern for women, and the need to stabilize, unify, and reinforce the dominant political culture of the Democratic Party. The campaign to maintain abortion rights is more defensive in tone, resulting in a less ambitious legislative agenda. A strategy of electing more women to local, state, and federal office appears to be the best guarantee of abortion rights. On this point, Susan Kennedy responded,

> There is a base minimum this country will not go beyond because we have the technology to keep abortion safe. . . . I think we will never revert back to the period prior to 1973. The more that women are involved in politics raises that minimum base level of security because you will have people to say why something is really bad legislation, or why something should or should not happen.
>
> From a personal perspective, the more of our mothers, sisters and wives are in public office the more they influence husbands, sons, and brothers not to be so receptive to the anti-choice message. That will also increase our base level of security.

By 1989, the turmoil over abortion and the widespread belief that the U.S. Supreme Court could reverse *Roe v. Wade* provided the impetus for women's organizations nationally to mobilize for political action. In California, there were concerns about access to clinics, the harassment of women and physicians, and the potential for violence at clinic sites. Leaders in the pro-choice movement expressed the need to strengthen abortion rights with legislative proposals that would extend medical facilities in some of the thirty-eight counties of the state that do not have clinics, secure the training of physicians in medical schools, permit testing of RU-486 (the French "abortion pill"), and provide greater protection for the safety of both women and doctors. Omnibus or proactive proposals to clarify state laws on abortion further or to protect abortion rights have failed. Thus, the call to action among pro-choice women to run for public office may be among the more salient features and the long-term legacy in the politics of abortion.

For example, in the late 1980s the California Abortion Rights Action League (CARAL) doubled its membership. In its campaign to assure abortion rights for women, CARAL in northern California increased from 44,000 members in 1986 to 85,000 by 1990. For the first time, women's political organizations—National Organization for Women, Planned Parenthood, National Women's Political Caucus, and the Hollywood Women's Political Committee—met together in a "political summit" essentially to raise money for women candidates, but also to select key races for special attention and discuss how to prepare women for tough campaigns. The abortion rights cause brought great numbers of women into politics and defined a new type of Democratic candidate such as Tricia Hunter, who won election in 1990 as a "pro-choice Democrat," in a conservative San Diego assembly district. With little support for pro-choice women in the Republican Party, naturally women took the high ground in the Democratic Party—the arena for women in state politics.

In both statewide and local races, such women candidates as Dianne Feinstein, Anna G. Eshoo, and Debra Bowen came into the mainstream of Democratic Party politics. Opinion polls showed that women were perceived as agents of change, as more honest in an era of greater scrutiny of government officials, and as candidates of choice regardless of party affiliation.[19] Susan Kennedy described this phenomenon as a wave or a crest and noted that "it's not going to repeat itself just by virtue of the fact that it's been done before. However, it did put more women into mainstream politics. . . . So when the wave sweeps people back out, we will have more women left on the shore." The best evidence so far of women taking hold of the political establishment is the development of a "farm bench" of women candidates and new sources of financial support for women candidates.

Kennedy explained, "Back in 1991, a year before the election, I sat in a meeting in the proverbial 'smoke-filled room' with a bunch of elected officials and political hacks. They were deciding who was going to run for various open Assembly seats in California. In case after case, where there was an opening, I heard the phrase: Don't we have any women?" As party officials in California tapped women candidates for crucial races, the sources for campaign money changed. Before the 1992 election cycle, women tended to rely on monies from women's political organizations; now, as incumbents, women could draw support from important leaders such as Assembly Speaker Willie Brown and the mainstream interests, the traditional financial base of party support. In large arena states such as California, where a credible candidate for the U.S. Senate must be capable of raising upward of $10 million, sources of money for women candidates in a close race could be the decisive factor.

I asked Susan Kennedy how abortion figures in statewide campaigns, and how an appeal for abortion rights can assist a Democratic candidate. She recalled the 1992 Senate race in which Barbara Boxer won a razor-thin victory over Republican Bruce Herschensohn, who was strongly favored by the anti-abortion movement. Boxer's election was the result of an aggressive voter registration effort and her standing among pro-choice women. Kennedy commented,

> You cannot take it [abortion] out of the main picture of a campaign because there are people out there who would not have voted for Bruce Herschensohn if he were pro-choice; and there are those who would not have voted for Barbara Boxer if she were anti-choice. But [as voters] they're not thinking about it anymore—they know she's okay—it doesn't register on the scale. These are the kinds of issues that blend into the persona of the candidates.
>
> So in the 1992 election, abortion is a major reason why Barbara Boxer won. She effectively used abortion on a statewide level. It certainly did not overcome the importance of the economy. But a .04 percent margin of those who based their decision on abortion, or even 1 percent—some races in the state are lost by a 2 or 3 percent margin. So 1 percent—that's a lot.
>
> Abortion will be a cutting-edge issue that is marginal. And by marginal I don't mean insignificant—I mean when you have a close race an issue like abortion or immigration can push a race over the top. Or you could lose a race, depending on who the electorate is.

The issue of abortion may not play a controlling or decisive role in state politics; nonetheless, there is the potential during a campaign that abortion can be mobilized by candidates of the right or the left. Barbara Boxer's 1992 Senate victory is an example of how abortion politics works in a close election, at the margins—a form of "guerrilla politics." Moreover, the Boxer election underscores a particular geography whereby pro-choice states such as California, New York, Florida, and Washington become crucial to the abortion rights cause. No matter what decision might be rendered by the U.S. Supreme Court on abortion, these states would keep it legal.

In the real world, one fact marks the abortion debate in California and the nation: Bill Clinton and the Democrats recaptured the White House in 1992. All the political warfare over Supreme Court nominees and the expectations of a possible reversal of *Roe v. Wade* can be seen differently today. Not that abortion is settled—rarely do such controversial matters find complete resolution. Instead, at the moment, we have a sufficient pause to consider how abortion has become so much a part of the social and political discourse of our time, and how it impacts on the lives and careers of church leaders, pro-life and pro-choice activists, and women candidates for public office.

Notes

1. Joan Didion, "California: The Golden Land," *New York Review of Books* 40, no. 17 (21 October 1993).

2. "Large Majority of Californians Favor Pro-choice Position on Abortion," *California Poll*, 29 May 1992.

3. "Religion and Politics," *California Opinion Index*, September 1993.

4. Kristin Luker, *Abortion and the Politics of Motherhood* (Berkeley: University of California Press, 1984).

5. Ibid., 69.

6. Ibid., 78.

7. Laurence H. Tribe, *Abortion: The Clash of Absolutes* (New York: Norton, 1990), 38.

8. Luker, *Abortion and Politics of Motherhood*, 88.

9. Ibid., 94.

10. Ibid., 121.

11. David J. Garrow, *Liberty and Sexuality: The Right to Privacy and the Making of Roe vs. Wade* (New York: Macmillan, 1994).

12. Julie Sly, "Commenting on the Current Status of Abortion Law in California/Implications of *Webster* Ruling," California Catholic Conference, 6 July 1989; and Raymond J. Leonardini, Esq., "Current Status of Abortion Law in California," Memorandum to California Catholic Conference, 23 May 1989.

13. "Debate and Vote on Abortion Resolution," National Conference of Catholic Bishops/United States Catholic Conference, Official Proceedings, November 7, 1989.

14. Nell Bernstein, "Sidewalk Wars," *California Lawyer*, September 1993.

15. Interview with Julie Sly, California Catholic Conference, 23 September 1993.

16. Interview with Jan Carroll, California Prolife Council, 12 October 1993.

17. Mark Nollinger, "The New Crusaders: The Christian Right Storms California's Political Bastions," *California Journal*, January 1993.

18. Interview with Susan Kennedy, California State Democratic Party, 12 October 1993.

19. "Election '92," *California Journal*, December 1992, 576.

MARYANNE BORRELLI

10 | Massachusetts: Abortion Policymaking in Transition

Fiercely restrictive of abortion before *Roe v. Wade* (1973), the Massachusetts legislature passed pro-life legislation over the objections of a pro-choice governor in the mid-1970s. By the early 1990s, however, the legislature was cautiously supporting pro-choice policies. The shift from challenging the *Roe* decision to acquiescing in its provisions is extraordinary. How could this happen?

Close study of Commonwealth abortion politics during the post-*Roe* years yields two hypotheses. The first, which I endorse, suggests that changes in the mass political culture have influenced electoral races and abortion policy debates. Specifically, as the Roman Catholic Church, the dominant pro-life institutional actor, lost political authority within the Commonwealth, Catholic legislators began to endorse pro-choice laws; and Catholic legislators predominate in this legislature. Presuming that the legitimacy of law depends on popular support, this approach presents the authoritative allocation of values as an ultimately democratic undertaking. It also stresses the power of the legislative branch, the dominant partner in the lawmaking process, to set the Commonwealth political agenda.

A more elite-driven theory of political development attributes the new direction in Massachusetts abortion law to pro-choice executives and judges. This second hypothesis notes that Massachusetts governors, almost without exception, have been pro-choice during the post-*Roe* years. Similarly, Commonwealth justices have upheld *Roe* standards when the legislature did not. Their efforts alone, however, do not account for the change in public opinion and the increased strength of the Commonwealth pro-choice movement. Instead, executive and judicial activism helped create a political environment that facilitated popular adoption of a pro-choice position. At the same time, the political culture played its part in elite behaviors, the liberal tenor of other Commonwealth social policies easing the way for their pro-choice stance.

This chapter details developments in Commonwealth abortion politics and policies. Scholars routinely stress the endurance of a political culture, but this text investigates how it may change. What does it mean when people alter their most fundamental beliefs and rewrite their most controversial laws?

Massachusetts Abortion Law in the Courts

Massachusetts, before the *Roe* decision, prosecuted medical practitioners and others for aiding women to "procure a miscarriage." An abortion was "lawfully" performed only if a doctor acted in "good faith" to preserve the life or health of the woman.[1] The law did not go unchallenged, but Commonwealth justices rejected claims that it expressed the moral judgment of one religion; that it extended beyond the proper protection of public health, safety, or morals; that it interfered with a doctor's judgment and a patient's rights; that it invalidly proscribed free speech; that its punishments were cruel and unusual; or that it violated freedom of choice in private morality.[2] Self-evidently, the justices accepted and endorsed the pro-life intent of the law. Over 80 percent of the women seeking abortions left the state to have the procedure.[3]

Massachusetts state legislators viewed *Roe* as setting exceptions to the rule that abortion was unlawful; they did not accept the decision as naming and protecting "reproductive rights." In fact, the legislators wrote their own law to protect doctors and hospitals who "conscientiously objected" to abortion.[4] Where *Roe* was silent—procedural guidelines, fetal rights, informed consent, minor access—the legislature imposed strict regulations.[5] There was no difficulty passing these statutes over the pro-choice governor's objections, the strength of resistance to *Roe* placing the Commonwealth in the subset of states that "challenged" that ruling.[6] The restrictions duly provoked pro-choice litigation. The state judiciary, however, did not immediately abandon its earlier pro-life perspective.

Framingham Clinic, Inc. v. Board of Selectmen of Southborough (1977) challenged laws that barred an abortion clinic from locating in an area zoned for medical offices. The five justices of the Supreme Judicial Court (SJC), the highest court in the Commonwealth, ruled for the clinic. Citing *Roe*, the court described the right to terminate an abortion as a protected and "fundamental" right of privacy at its "apogee" in the first trimester of pregnancy. Citing *Planned Parenthood of Missouri v. Danforth* (1976), the court then maintained that the state retained some regulatory powers during even these months. Weighing these rulings, the SJC concluded that the zoning laws constituted unjustified discrimination and were unduly burdensome of women's rights but that some regulation of first-trimester abortions was acceptable.[7] In 1979, however, the Commonwealth's parental-consent requirements were disallowed in the now-famous Supreme Court case *Bellotti v. Baird*.[8] Later amended to the letter of the Court decision, Commonwealth law now requires that both parents consent to the minor's abortion, with provision for the absence or loss of one parent, and provides a judicial bypass.[9] Planned Parenthood litigation against these standards, which are among the most restrictive in the nation, has not been successful: federal courts in 1981 and 1989 ruled the parental-consent–judicial-bypass arrangement constitutional.[10] *Planned Parenthood League of Massachusetts v. Bellotti* (1981), however, was a partial pro-choice success. Though the court accepted most of the Commonwealth's stipulations for informed consent, it rejected the twenty-four-hour waiting period and the fetal description requirement.[11] By the early 1990s, the contest over minor access/parental consent had returned to the state legislature, pro-choice and pro-life lobbies recommending markedly different standards to the lawmakers.[12]

The *Framingham Clinic, Baird,* and *Planned Parenthood* (1981) cases were pro-choice victories because they constrained pro-life legislative initiatives. Policymaking by litigation, though, is inherently reactive, ceding control of the policy agenda to the opponent. Moreover, these rulings balanced pro-choice and pro-life values, allowing the state legislature to regulate abortion closely. *Moe v. Secretary of Administration and Finance* (1981) instead obliged legislators to secure reproductive rights through the Commonwealth budget.

In *Moe*, the SJC ruled that the Commonwealth Declaration of Rights gave greater protection to a woman's right to terminate a pregnancy than did the federal Constitution. Massachusetts was consequently obliged to provide public funding for all medically necessary abortions, lest women's rights be burdened by economic considerations.[13] Though pro-life lobbies legislatively blocked public funding for non-Medicaid abortions,[14] *Moe* distinguished Massachusetts as a potentially pro-choice state. Additional evidence that the judiciary was assuming a more pro-choice stance came in civil rulings on clinic blockaders.

Planned Parenthood filed suit against Operation Rescue in 1989, seeking an injunction that would halt pro-life clinic demonstrations. As these protests consumed town resources, and as law enforcement officials found the protesters increasingly difficult to manage, it became electorally and legally expedient for the Office of the Attorney General of the Commonwealth to enter the case.[15] This case ultimately yielded the only statewide injunction against clinic blockaders in the nation, with terms of up to two and one-half years for recalcitrant offenders.[16] The attorney general vigorously implemented the injunction, and over a dozen Operation Rescue members served time in county houses of correction. Their sentences averaged twelve months, far longer than the jail terms imposed in other states.[17]

Meanwhile, Planned Parenthood and the Massachusetts Coalition for Choice lobbied for a medical facilities access act. Though the bill raised some constitutional questions, it became law during the 1993 legislative session.[18] A more detailed study of this process is given later in the chapter; for now, one should note that the SJC injunction was only one among several factors influencing the legislators. More important, the legislative history of this act suggests that the Massachusetts electorate and legislature are testing a new political ethic in abortion policymaking.

The lasting strength and legitimacy of law depends on the democratic polity that supports its implementation. The reader's attention is now directed to that more complex set of power relations.

Of Reputations and Realities: The Pro-Choice and Pro-Life Lobbies on Beacon Hill

The political culture of a state creates and confines citizen expectations, setting and curbing elite agendas. Because a political culture is foundational and enduring, the strongest indicator of a state's post-*Casey* abortion law could be its pre-*Roe* abortion law. The legal trends discussed in the previous section suggest that Massachusetts contradicts this expectation. Post-*Roe* court rulings, while protecting pro-life government interests, defend access to abortion as a fundamental right, dictate state funding, and restrain clinic blockaders.[19] During these same years, the Commonwealth political culture experienced an ideological revolution, moving from a decisively pro-life position to a "mixed" pro-choice/pro-life stance. The sources of this change are numerous and are best uncovered through study of the sociopolitical agendas of the pro-choice and pro-life movements.

In 1986, a ballot referendum for a pro-life amendment to the Commonwealth constitution brought pro-choice groups together to form the Campaign for Choice. After defeating the proposal, the pro-choice lobby continued to pool its resources. Renamed the "Coalition for Choice," it began to focus on legislative politics in 1987. Coalition activities were directed by a steering committee of the seven larger organizations: Black Women for Policy Action, the Civil Liberties Union of Massachusetts (CLU, a state affiliate of the ACLU), Mass. Choice (a state affiliate of NARAL), Planned Parenthood League of Massachusetts (a state affiliate of Planned Parenthood Federation of America), and the Massachusetts chapters of the National Organization for Women (NOW), the League of Women Voters, and the Religious Coalition for Abortion Rights (RCAR).[20] Each group drew a distinctive set of people into the network, generating new policy debates. NOW leadership pushed the coalition to the left, arguing for unrestrictive abortion policies, and NOW members mobilized to counter pro-life demonstrations.[21] The League of Women Voters and the CLU contacted state officeholders. CLU and Planned Parenthood litigated test cases.[22] Mass. Choice and its political action committee undertook electoral politicking.[23] In designing legislative proposals, Black Women for Policy Action, RCAR, and Planned Parenthood spoke for women of color, the clergy, and medical professionals.[24]

Coalition partnerships, however, were accompanied by significant inefficiencies. Following an unsuccessful effort to place a pro-choice constitutional amendment on the ballot in 1989, internal criticisms were so strong that the coalition undertook a searching self-study. By 1993 discussions within the network had produced a five-page "Proposed Consensus Document" articulating moderate policy recommendations and political strategies.[25] Additionally, the steering committee was expanded by two seats, held in rotation by smaller coalition groups. Provisions for adding new permanent members to the steering committee were made, and greater discretion was extended to subcommittees.[26] Whether this outreach capitalizes on the diversity of the pro-choice movement or merely controls its dissidents will not be immediately evident. At the least, for good or bad, this reorganization will permit the coalition to present a more united front to state government and to pro-life opponents.

If political circumstances dictate coalition building among pro-choice interests, they oblige pro-life groups to stress their mutual independence. Though a number of denominations have endorsed the pro-life agenda, the Roman Catholic Church is the leading pro-life religious actor in the Commonwealth. Archbishop Bernard Cardinal Law of Boston has always argued that abortion must be the first concern of his church. Viewing the outcome in *Roe* as comparable to the *Dred Scott* decision, Law encourages political activism and discourages civil disobedience.[27] Writing for the archdiocesan newspaper one week after the murder of abortion provider Dr. David Gunn, the cardinal described both this killing and the pro-choice movement as proof that a "culture of death" pervaded the United States.[28] The cardinal then defined the mission of the pro-life movement in contrasting terms.

> In the final analysis, the challenge of the pro-life movement is to change hearts. While there is a legitimate role for political efforts, the real challenge is to bring about a shift in societal attitudes. This cannot be done by the manipulation of judicial and political power, as the proponents of abortion have sought to do. They have failed. Try as they might, they cannot and will not silence the pro-life movement. Power is all the proponents of abortion have on their side; their reasons cannot finally persuade human hearts.[29]

Though the cardinal cautions against violence in pro-life demonstrations, pro-choice advocates are identified as the unremitting oppressors.

Even as these messages reflect the archbishop's sincere commitment to his teaching mission, they reveal why the Massachusetts pro-life movement is so strongly identified with Roman Catholicism. The wider political influence of this church dates back over a century to the rise of machine politics in the Commonwealth, an event of enduring significance.

When I first started [in the 1970s], on the day of an important vote about abortion or parochial schools, you would see a lot of parish priests in the State House. . . . You see, the Irish Catholics had a very strong [voter] turnout, which was reflected in delegations to the legislature. The Italians were there as diversity, but they were intimidated. The Irish Catholics were a very difficult bloc that it was tough to crack. (Norma Shapiro, chair, Massachusetts Coalition for Choice and Legislative Liaison, Civil Liberties Union of Massachusetts.)[30]

The Massachusetts Catholic Conference was formally incorporated in 1969 to serve as "the official representative of the four Roman Catholic Dioceses of the Commonwealth on public policy issues relating to the spiritual well-being of concerned and compassionate citizens."[31] Representing parishioners but caring for citizens, the Conference implicitly sought to extend church authority deep into Commonwealth politics. In the 1990s, pro-choice advocates challenged this mission, becoming one of the forces that obliged the church to change its political strategies.

These public debates over church-state relations were precipitated by Governor Weld's 1990–91 abortion reform proposals. Viewing the governor's endorsement of unrestricted access as extreme, Law concluded there was "a direct contradiction between participation in the sacramental and public life of the church and support or acceptance of the continued evil of abortion."[32] *Boston Globe* reporters immediately surveyed Catholic state legislators, the majority in the state legislature. Approximately 54 percent rejected Law's assertion that "to be prochoice is to be proabortion," and 52 percent described themselves as pro-choice. Pro-choice Catholic sentiments and allegiances within the legislature were thus publicly exposed.[33] Political beliefs were also changing in the electorate. In a state that was approximately 49.5 percent Catholic, 76 percent of voters surveyed believed that "in general, a woman should be able to obtain an abortion." [34] A new culture of religion and politics was emerging.[35] At the national level, U.S. bishops acknowledged that faith-driven lobbying was unlikely to achieve pro-life victories. Hoping that a campaign questioning the morality of abortion would be more persuasive, the bishops changed their appeals.[36] As Law joined in this effort, Catholic pro-life lobbying in the Commonwealth became less controversial, though no less assertive.

Other pro-life organizations within the Commonwealth also extend this message of abortion as a moral concern, seeking to draw nonchurchgoers and non-Catholics into membership. Nevertheless, church-affiliated and unaffiliated organizations share a common political agenda, have overlapping membership lists, and pool leadership resources. For example, the Massachusetts Citizens for Life (CFL) is the dominant nonchurch organization in pro-life electoral and institutional politics. Gatherings of this organization have been addressed by Cardinals Law and O'Connor; the CFL legislative director has spoken to parish groups.[37]

Survey and election data suggest pro-life appeals to Massachusetts voters are not winning adherents. In 1986 a pro-life ballot referendum recommended a constitutional amendment to restrict abortion and abolish public funding. It was narrowly defeated, with 58 percent of voters opposing and 42 percent favoring its passage.[38] Pooled data from the American National Election Survey, collected during election years from 1988 through 1992, indicated a further erosion of pro-life support and the gradual strengthening of the pro-choice movement. Only 9 percent of Massachusetts respondents, compared to 14 percent in the other forty-nine states, believed that abortion should never be legal. In contrast, 40 percent (32 percent in the other states) believed abortion should be legal in all circumstances, and 51 percent (55 percent in the other states) held a "mixed" pro-choice/pro-life position. By this measure, Massachusetts public opinion on abortion is among the most liberal in the country, a circumstance that prevails when its citizens are queried on parental consent (45 percent pro-life, 34 percent "mixed," 23 percent pro-choice in Massachusetts; 57 percent pro-life, 25 percent "mixed," 18 percent pro-choice in other states) and public funding (26 percent pro-life, 49 percent "mixed," 26 percent pro-choice in Massachusetts; 28 percent pro-life, 38 percent "mixed," 25 percent pro-choice in other states).[39] But only 7 percent of Massachusetts voters use abortion as a litmus test for candidates.[40] In 1990, the most recent election for which data are available, this worked to the disadvantage of the pro-choice movement. Districts that opposed the 1986 pro-life referendum elected approximately 33.3 percent of pro-life senators, 55.9 percent of pro-life representatives; in contrast, districts that supported the referendum elected only 4.5 percent of the pro-choice senators, 5.1 percent of the representatives.[41] By this measure, the pro-choice movement needs to reorder the political priorities of its voters. The pro-life movement, in its turn, must expand its power base, particularly among state lawmakers.

Currently, the pro-life network in the state legislature is largely a product of historic allegiances. The twelve senators and sixty-eight representatives listed as pro-life by the CFL in 1992 were disproportionately self-identified as Roman Catholic. Roman Catholics were overrepresented in the pro-life listing (83.3 percent of pro-life senators, 67.5 percent of all senators; 88.2 percent of pro-life representatives, 60.4 percent of all representatives), while Protestants were underrepresented (none among pro-life senators, 12.5 percent of all senators; 11.8 percent of pro-life representatives, 18.2 percent of all representatives). The one senator and three representatives who self-identified as Jewish were all pro-choice leaders. More recently elected and younger legislators were pro-life in proportionate numbers. Women were underrepresented among pro-life legislators (16.7 percent of pro-life senators, 22.5 percent of all senators; 11.8 percent of pro-life representatives, 22.5 percent of all representatives).[42] Legislators' personal beliefs thus seem to influence their abortion policy decisions.

Many pro-choice districts allow their legislators considerable independence, reelecting senators and representatives with whom they disagree. Still, abortion is an unpredictable and controversial issue that engenders a strong subjective sense of risk among legislators, a conclusion proven in legislative interviews. Consider the following commentary by Cheryl Jacques (D-Needham), a senator in her first term. A white woman in her early thirties, Jacques is the Senate co-chair of the Judiciary Committee, which has jurisdiction over abortion, and is widely regarded as a pro-choice advocate from a pro-choice district.[43]

> I didn't consider myself a pro-choice candidate . . . and I also felt from going door-to-door that abortion was not *the* issue. . . . I prefer that government not play that role in people's lives—it's a libertarian position, though I don't like that term. Anything involving lives and bodies is not something that government should be involved in. Abortion is such a private and personal decision—I wouldn't want someone to make it for me. And then there is the practical problem [if abortion is illegal] of what to do to women who have made a horrible, emotional decision and broken the law. . . . It's a difficult question because you want to separate church and state, but it's hard because this is such a personal moral decision. . . . People [voters] are also becoming sick of abortion—you need more than this to evaluate someone's ethics. The economy and such issues are a better guide. Because the pro-choice label—to be pro-abortion is the most horrible thing . . . you see, I would refer to myself as pro-personal responsibility.[44]

Though one would expect the congruence of Jacques's position with that of her district to reduce the senator's sense of risk, these explanations are extended and elaborate. Jacques may also be precise in her comments because she is the first self-identified Roman Catholic to be the primary sponsor of a reproductive-choice act.[45]

Senator Jacques states that moral decision making invariably creates a place for the church in the state: A church offers guidance to the individual confronting ethical dilemmas and seeking to do good. This presentation at once provides and delimits a political role for any church. It also attempts to reconcile, without directly prioritizing, the contradictions in the senator's religious affiliation and policy position. Pro-life Catholic legislators confront the different problem of defending the similarity of their religious and political ideals.

> Religion is not an issue for us—it's more an issue for pro-choice because [abortion] relates to the basis of the faith. Certain things are fundamental to faith. . . . [Senator] White would consider himself strong in faith but his abortion view is based in human rights. There is life from conception and therefore a duty to protect life. . . . It's a civil rights issue and his duty as an elected public official. (Jim Burke, administrative assistant to State Senator W. Paul White)[46]

> It's a strong commitment that I've always had—it probably goes back to parochial school and I've lived with it all my life. My district is strongly

> pro-life, strongly Catholic. There are three active Catholic churches . . . and several Baptist churches and an active Citizens for Life chapter. I feel very comfortable with this position—I've run on it, been challenged on it. For me, pro-life means that I don't want to see the fetus killed and I feel that the fetus is an unborn child. . . . No exceptions. Abortion is the taking of life. (State Representative Kevin Poirier.)[47]

In Senator White's office (D-Dorchester), fluency in Roman Catholic terminology extended to the staff, whose explanation of political obligation echoed the secularized pro-life movement. Representative Poirier (R-N. Attleboro) stresses the similarity of his life experience to that of his constituents, concluding that his duty is to voice their shared beliefs legislatively. Non-Catholic members advertise their abortion stance with a similar awareness of the Catholic cultural presence.[48] Church influence over political dialogue, however, is a poor substitute for control of the policy agenda.

Also contributing to legislators' caution in abortion policymaking is the pro-choice editorial policy of the *Boston Globe*.[49] The paper is a formidable watchdog, naming pro-choice legislators who attend pro-life forums and publicizing confidential conversations in the attorney general's office.[50] In legislative, mayoral, and gubernatorial campaigns, reporters consistently accent the candidates' abortion position.[51] "I would speak for forty-five minutes on the economy," complained one challenger, "and abortion would have the higher profile." During the election years 1990 and 1992, the *Globe* printed 252 and 329 abortion-related articles, respectively, and virtually all endorsed the pro-choice agenda. This is formidable advertising for the movement and contributes to a sense that its power is on the rise.

Some readers might argue that the pro-choice and pro-life lobbies should devote themselves to electoral politics, changing the legislators in order to change the law. Both movements have targeted and endorsed candidates, the Coalition for Choice working to elect a pro-choice Senate.[52] Interest groups publish newsletters and arrange media events.[53] Stretched to sustain their legislative initiatives, however, neither lobby has the resources to build powerful political action committees (PACs) within the Commonwealth. Mass. Choice and CFL PACs encourage donors and others to volunteer in endorsed campaigns. Even this support is provided only to unreservedly pro-choice or pro-life candidates: a Mass. Choice candidate supports public funding and advocates the removal of all restrictions on minors seeking abortions; a CFL candidate believes that life begins at conception and seeks to protect every human life until natural death.[54] Though CFL does criticize pro-choice legislators, Mass. Choice targeting has had a higher profile. Six "mis-representatives" were targeted in 1992; four senators were defeated, though not entirely by pro-choice activism.[55] One pro-life senator was defeated by an also-targeted pro-life representative, hardly a pro-choice victory.[56] Another senator lost to a challenger who conducted an anti-incumbency campaign.[57] The last two senators lost by 1.05 percent and 1.1 percent of the vote.[58] These outcomes oblige one to agree with Senator Jacques: abortion is not "*the* issue" for voters, perhaps in part because the movements lack the resources to make it so. Also limiting the lobbies' electoral opportunities are the legislators, who have deliberately centralized their campaign staffs and fund-raising efforts.

The complex historical processes at work within the Commonwealth warn against equating political culture and Roman Catholic Church activism. Massachusetts is, after all, overwhelmingly Democratic and liberal in its social policy. It also has a significant proportion of working and professional women. All these circumstances contribute to creating a more pro-choice policy environment.[59] Still, the presence of the Roman Catholic Church as the institutional leader of the Commonwealth pro-life movement decisively influences pro-choice and pro-life political strategizing. One is left to wonder how these factors are experienced during legislative debates—is religion and culture a subtext or is it actively referenced? What is the "tone" and "feel" of statehouse politics? Who exercises power and on what terms? The next section tests the preceding conclusions about Commonwealth politics by examining the legislative behaviors that surrounded two abortion bills in the 1993 legislative session.

Power as Strategy and Substance: The 1993
Reproductive Choice and Clinic Access Bills

Because abortion legislation rarely came to a floor vote in the late 1980s and early 1990s, lobbyists felt they "basically had to take [the legislators'] word for it, that they were anti-choice or pro-choice."[60] During the 1993 session, however, two abortion rights bills came out of committee and sparked considerable action within the chambers. The Reproductive Choice Act was debated and amended in the House, ending the legislative session in the Committee on Third Readings; the Medical Facilities Access Act passed by voice vote in the House and was debated for three weeks in the Senate before being passed. Both bills were the product of a newly aggressive pro-choice movement, whose leaders referred to the Reproductive Choice Act as a "disaster" and the Medical Facilities Access Act as an achievement.[61] This combination of failure and success reflected differences in the subject matter and politics of each bill, the intricacies of legislative negotiations in the House and Senate, and the ability of pro-choice and pro-life lobbyists to capitalize on legislators' uncertainties.

The Reproductive Choice Act

The Reproductive Choice Act ran contrary to every accepted practice for developing pro-choice legislation. Written by Representative Susan D. Schur (D-

Newton), it was presented to the Coalition for Choice within two weeks of its submission deadline. Because bills are routinely unsuccessful on their first submission, coalition lobbyists accepted the imperfections of this proposal and returned to their own agendas.[62] Schur was left to pursue her policy ambitions independently.

Schur, an established pro-choice leader in the House, backed by a strongly pro-choice district, was then a seventh-term legislator and a senior member of the Judiciary Committee.[63] When that committee issued an unfavorable report on her bill, she persuaded the Judiciary co-chair to motion that the House substitute the bill for the committee report. This rarely used parliamentary maneuver obliged legislators to vote for or against the bill without having been briefed.[64] With Schur insisting that her bill only eliminated archaic statutes, the House voted in its favor, 95–52.[65] This outcome, remembered the Mass. Choice lobbyist, was entirely unexpected.

> We had one hour's notice and so we didn't have the time to talk to everyone. [Speaker] Flaherty could have delayed [the vote], but Schur was running for mayor and there was a lot going on in her life—she felt that she had the votes and wanted to go for it. And she had been doing pro-choice for years. And then we didn't really understand the vote, as there were anti-choice people supporting abortion. We thought, "Perhaps this is an overwhelming tide."[66]

Debate on the bill was scheduled for the following week. In the interim, the pro-life lobby documented the weaknesses in Schur's argument and Cardinal Law held a press conference condemning her proposal as "the most extreme pro-abortion bill ever presented to the Massachusetts legislature."[67] Mother's Day gave added impetus to pro-life grassroots mobilization.[68]

Meanwhile, pro-choice lobbyists and representatives prepared an amendment to win over lawmakers with "mixed" positions.[69] Their strategy was to co-opt moderate objections while minimizing discussion. Speaker Flaherty initially agreed to open floor debate by recognizing the amendment sponsor. Valerie Barsom (R-Wilbraham), however, requested permission to give her "maiden" speech and House rules dictated that she speak first.[70] Pro-choice strategists consoled themselves that Barsom had campaigned as pro-choice and would therefore support the bill. Instead, she offered a contrary amendment.[71] The crucial section of the bill is given below, first as proposed by Schur and then as amended by Barsom.

> Notwithstanding any other general or special law to the contrary, the right of a woman to choose to terminate a pregnancy before 24 weeks or at any time if such termination is necessary to protect her life or health, shall not be restricted by any laws, ordinances, or regulations.[72]

> The right of a woman to choose to terminate a pregnancy *before viability* or twenty-four weeks *whichever occurs first,* or at any time if such termination is

necessary to protect her life or health, shall not be *unduly burdened* by any laws, ordinance or regulations.[73]

Pro-choice momentum disintegrated. Pro-life and "mixed" legislators challenged the mother's health clause as endorsing third-trimester abortions. Also questioned was the impact of the law upon parental consent for minors, conscientious objection by doctors and hospitals, and regulations for public health. Pro-choice arguments lacked credibility—the representatives and the coalition were sponsoring bills that would liberalize the law in precisely those ways that were occasioning concern.[74] Barsom, as was her right, refused to yield the floor, so the pro-choice amendment could not be advanced.[75] In statehouse hallways, pro-choice and pro-life lobbyists openly argued the bill's provisions.[76]

Ultimately, the Barsom amendment was approved by a vote of 83–71, twenty-six of the legislators who initially favored the pro-choice bill supporting its pro-life revision. Newer members predominated among those who changed their vote, but several long-standing pro-choice and pro-life legislators also equivocated. Quite simply, the pro-life lobby raised enough questions that lawmakers found the Barsom amendment appealing. The legal implications of its language, borrowed from the *Casey* decision, were not always recognized, though many who endorsed the amendment favored regulating abortion.[77] The following retrospectives suggest some of the assessments made after the two roll-call votes.

> That was Barsom's maiden speech. It was a heavy, gutsy action. But she was a legislative aide before coming into the legislature [as a member] and is also a young attorney. She is a Republican, so the Speaker doesn't have much control over her. Actually, no one has much control over her. But she is pro-choice for what she advocates, and she felt the Schur bill was not right. (Kevin Poirier, a pro-life and senior Republican representative)[78]

> The problem was that we were voting in the dark. This thing [the Schur bill] was sprung on us last week. People were not ready for the debate. So, people were left voting on the side of caution. (Peter V. Forman, the pro-choice Republican minority leader; voted for the Barsom amendment)[79]

> The Schur bill was a disaster—we did whatever we could to slow it down. But the bill that is now in the [Committee on Bills in the] Third Reading is still unacceptable. . . . But we appreciated Barsom and her efforts to weaken the bill. The bottom line is that it not reach the governor's desk. . . . You have to use the strategies and so forth when the numbers aren't there [in the legislature]. (Gerald D'Avolio, executive director, Massachusetts Catholic Conference)[80]

Because Barsom had presented herself as pro-choice throughout the floor debate, pro-choice organizations immediately held a "lobbying day" to clarify the meaning of their label.[81] The amended Schur bill ended the 1993 session in the Committee on Third Readings. Immediately resubmitted for consideration in the new session, the 1994 proposal testified to pro-choice learning. The new bill is three sections long (the old was fourteen) and the claim to reproductive choice is narrowed to meet legislators' stipulations regarding minors, medical practitioners, and public health. Sponsored by Representative David B. Cohen (D-Newton), this bill is on the agenda of the Coalition for Choice, though it is not a first priority.[82]

The Medical Facilities Access Act

Commonly referred to as the "clinic access bill," this act was signed into law by Governor William F. Weld on 4 November 1993; it is the first piece of pro-choice legislation ever passed by the Massachusetts legislature. While a strong pro-choice lobbying effort was integral to passage of the bill, the silence of influential pro-life organizations and the societal fears generated by then-current events also contributed to its success. The legislative process surrounding the clinic access bill therefore contrasts strongly with that of the Reproductive Choice Act.

The injunction obtained by Planned Parenthood against Operation Rescue was a pro-choice victory, but it was never deemed sufficient: an injunction is directed against named individuals and organizations, while a law can be invoked against any blockader. The effort to pass such legislation began even before the injunction was handed down. Coalition for Choice lobbyists, pro-choice legislators, and the attorney general's office negotiated the language of the bill, which was first submitted in the late 1980s. Each year, in response to committee hearings and reports, the text was refined. By December 1992, when the bill was submitted for consideration in the 1993 session, it was cosponsored by ten senators and twenty-one representatives; it had become a top legislative priority for the coalition.[83]

The 1992 elections saw both the House and Senate become potentially pro-choice chambers: Mass. Choice estimated that seventy-five representatives were pro-choice, sixty-one pro-life, and twenty-four "mixed," with twenty-four senators pro-choice, twelve pro-life, and four "mixed."[84] Still, pro-choice advocates accented public safety issues in presenting their bill, hoping to distance it from abortion controversies. The bill was subsequently assigned to the Criminal Justice Committee rather than the Judiciary Committee, an important jurisdictional change. Then, just two weeks before the committee hearing, abortion provider Dr. David Gunn was killed by a man with ties to the pro-life movement. Suddenly, as media coverage stressed, clinic violence was very much a public safety concern.[85] Pro-choice witnesses wore black armbands to the hearing and the bill's principal sponsor, Representative David Cohen, testified to the increasing harassment of Massachusetts clinic workers: "One demonstrator kept saying to

clinic personnel, 'I just saw someone with a gun. Are you afraid?' "[86] Public
attitudes and political pressures pushed legislators to take action. The silence of
the Citizens for Life and the Massachusetts Catholic Conference, neither of
which endorsed civil disobedience, did not help the pro-life organizations, who
argued against the bill on First Amendment grounds.[87]

The clinic access bill received a favorable report from its committee and was
quickly passed by voice vote in the House. "A lot of legislators didn't want their
fingerprints on that one," said one member. The bill arrived in the Senate in early
May. Legal memoranda from the attorney general of the Commonwealth, the
Civil Liberties Union of Massachusetts, and the Coalition for Choice defended it
as constitutional.[88] During the three weeks of Senate debate, special care was
taken to ensure pro-choice majorities on votes to amend, lest the bill be delayed
in conference committee. According to Norma Shapiro, Chair of the Coalition
for Choice,

> We had a solid twenty-seven votes, with nineteen Democratic, so even the
> [pro-life] Senate president was hard-pressed to delay action, given the strong
> vote. There were fourteen roll-call votes on anti-choice amendments, delays,
> and parliamentary procedures. We never had less than twenty-four votes—and
> we lost only due to absences. There were no changed votes. . . . The coalition
> divided the Senate up so each lobbyist called five senators or so, every one to
> three days. And we worked with the Republican minority leader so he was
> prepared for the motions should anything come up. He wasn't a floor leader—
> we were just covering all the bases.[89]

The final Senate vote was twenty-seven in favor, twelve opposed.[90] The Senate
president, Democrat William Bulger, left the floor during a break in the debate
and did not return for the vote.[91]

Henceforth, any person who "knowingly obstructs entry to or departure from
any medical facility or who enters or remains . . . so as to impede the provision
of medical services, after notice to refrain from such obstruction or interference"
can be punished by a fine and/or time in jail. Repeat offenders will receive
higher fines and sentences.[92] Though all pro-choice lobbyists and senators celebrated passage of the bill, some hailed it as indicative of future developments,
while others wearily acknowledged the special circumstances that allowed its
success.[93] Pro-life lobbyists angrily noted that what had been debated as a public
safety measure was now proclaimed a pro-choice *coup* in the *Boston Globe*.
They also expressed their doubts about the constitutionality of the act. Pro-life
senators and their staffs were equally outspoken.

> We are very much opposed to people chaining themselves to clinics or to
> committing violent acts, but then to go beyond all trespass law, well. . . . You
> see that if someone feels strongly enough to picket, to go to jail, then to really
> break you, there is an extra law on the books. . . . This is a vindictive, politi-
> cally correct law put on the books to go after one group in the Commonwealth.

> This country was founded on free speech—this was a very drastic step and it just boggled our minds.[94]

The clinic access bill is an uncontested addition to the Massachusetts General Laws and at least one pro-choice senator has written to her constituents that "we have won the legislative battle for clinic safety."[95] The judicial battle may begin in the not-so-distant future.

There are no simple lessons to be drawn from these case studies. Evidently the pro-choice and pro-life movements are equals in political strength and sophistication. When fully mobilized, each has the ability to counter the other. This equality represents an increase in power for the pro-choice movement and a loss for the pro-life movement: In twenty years, the legislature has gone from overriding a pro-choice governor to giving serious consideration and even approval to pro-choice bills. Now, both pro-choice and pro-life lobbies are working to protect and expand their bases of political support. A desire to encourage pro-choice legislative leadership was at the core of that lobby's acceptance of Susan Schur's entrepreneurial activities—disciplining her efforts would have consumed valuable resources and her proposal initially seemed unlikely to advance. Because lobbyists cannot afford the appearance of disorganization or weakness, however, pro-choice and pro-life networks within the Commonwealth can now be expected to weigh any opportunity against existing alliances and resources.

These case studies do prove the unpredictability of chamber dynamics and societal perceptions. The Reproductive Choice Act revealed that subjective risk does not necessarily motivate legislators to research the issue. Many representatives voted for the Barsom amendment without recognizing the legal implications of its "undue burden" language. In this policy area, as in many others, members rely on their colleagues for voting cues. Confronted by two women, both with strong legislative credentials and both claiming to be pro-choice, the House majority endorsed what seemed the more incremental, but still pro-choice, change. Cue giving was no less important in the Medical Facilities Access Act, extraordinary efforts being made to sustain a pro-choice voting bloc. Here the concern was as much to threaten the pro-life Senate president with pro-choice strength as to reassure senators that their commitment to the movement would secure valued legislation.

Massachusetts politics makes no allowances for participants' limitations. As one lobbyist acknowledged with a shrug, "The rules [of debate] are used by both sides and both claim abuses of the rules. The rules are to be used in whatever way to win. . . ."[96] Schur and Barsom used their expertise in chamber rules to advantage themselves in the zero-sum game of policymaking. Both legislative histories evidence the lobbies' ability to use recent events and grassroots activities to their advantage. In the Reproductive Choice proceedings, pro-life lobbies sponsored a letter and telephone campaign in honor of Mother's Day; during committee hearings on Medical Facilities Access, pro-choice witnesses wore black armbands as a reminder of the Gunn killing. In an environment partially characterized by decision makers' subjective fears, the appearance of public unity or popular concern can be determinative, setting the context in which cues will be interpreted and causing one equal to be perceived as stronger (or weaker) than another.

The previous section concluded that the political culture of the Commonwealth, especially its Roman Catholic character, conditions much of the strategy and substance in abortion policymaking. These case studies have overlaid that sociopolitical understanding with lobbyists' calculations of legislative coalitions and vulnerabilities, with members' assessments of electoral and political risks, and with issue leaders' sophistication in chamber procedures. Nothing, however, alters the earlier presentation of abortion policymaking as rooted in culture and consequently subject to all the variabilities of societal evolution. In the mid-1990s, pro-choice and pro-life networks each retain the power to determine the other's future.

Conclusion

Massachusetts politics are a contest for control of persons, policies, and institutions. This is an intimate profession in which success is contingent on one's demonstrated ability to use power to punish or to reward. These practices are inherited from a history of machine politics, a polite term for the class, ethnic, and racial conflicts that have dominated the Commonwealth. Political change comes slowly in this environment, informal power being redistributed only with great difficulty. This is no less true in abortion politics. The Commonwealth has restricted abortion since 1845, and the Roman Catholic Church has sustained a pro-life philosophy among many voters. And yet the Massachusetts electorate and elected elites have moved from a pro-life stance to a "mixed" position, a development benefiting the pro-choice lobby in the post-*Roe* years.

This chapter has detailed attitudinal changes and continuities in the social, religious, and political alliances that create abortion politics in the Massachusetts Commonwealth. The most significant occurrence is the diminished political authority of the Roman Catholic Church. This ideological and institutional change allowed pro-choice sentiment to surface in the legislature, giving that movement greater access to the state policy agenda. Though the Roman Catholic Church remains a powerful socializing agent within the Commonwealth, its new political circumstances are evident in the character of its lobbyists' appeals: morality and reason, not faith, now structure their logic. Legislators—Catholic legislators especially—acknowledge church influence in their rhetoric, but their actions prove an independence from its standards. A new political ethic is at work in the Commonwealth.

Historical and current political circumstances dictate different political strategies for pro-choice and pro-life lobbies. The pro-choice movement embraces coalition building, pooling scarce resources to build much-needed alliances. Initially protecting its agenda through litigation, pro-choice lobbies have gradually moved from countering pro-life proposals to securing passage of a controversial bill.[97] Pro-choice legislators have acquired crucial leadership positions. Both chairs of the Judiciary Committee, for example, are now pro-choice. This achievement is not unqualified, however. The remaining senators on the committee are pro-life and the majority of representatives are pro-choice, the legislative subsystem reflecting the priorities of pro-life Senate and pro-choice House leadership.[98] Pro-life lobbies, meanwhile, advertise their organizational independence from the Catholic Church on behalf of attracting a wider constituency. Different philosophies regarding political activism also dictate this strategy, the Massachusetts Catholic Conference and Citizens for Life rejecting the civil disobedience practiced by Operation Rescue and others. Within and amid these tensions, pro-life organizations have informally shared membership and leadership resources on behalf of protecting their traditional Catholic power base.

All these activities are set in the context of a liberal Democratic polity. Party affiliation, though, does not structure Massachusetts abortion debates—consider Republicans Weld (who wishes to remove all restrictions) and Barsom (who endorses the "undue burden" standard of *Casey*) or Democrats Bulger (the pro-life Senate president) and Flaherty (the pro-choice Speaker of the House). Still, the Commonwealth's strong presumption in favor of a liberal agenda contrasts with its more conservative abortion law, a tension exacerbated when the Supreme Judicial Court concluded that the state constitution obligated Massachusetts to provide public funding for Medicaid abortions. The weight of this liberal social policy tradition certainly did not hinder attitudinal change in favor of the pro-choice movement.

Legislators, meanwhile, would prefer not to confront abortion issues. Because even cloakroom conversation on the topic is limited, lobbyists face a formidable task in socializing members. As the case studies demonstrated, activists have achieved mixed results in this endeavor. Not infrequently elected by voters who disagree with their abortion position but do not accord the issue a high priority, legislators teeter between minimal objective and high subjective electoral risk. Not surprisingly, members prefer smaller policy revisions and watch their colleagues for cues. This is a dangerous practice in a political system that is unsparing, tough, and fast paced.

The changes identified in this study are likely to continue, albeit slowly, in future legislative sessions. Though the popular and legislative shift from challenging *Roe* to acquiescing in its provisions is greater than that in other states, Massachusetts legislators are moderates. It was the ambiguity of the "undue

burden" language that made Barsom's reproductive choice amendment intuitively appealing. Further evidence that change will be piecemeal is the fate of
the Schur bill. Like Weld's abortion reform packages, this bill was partially
defeated by its own complexity. Passage of a pro-choice bill will be most likely
when its provisions are specific and comprehensible to the members, especially
to those with "mixed" positions. Pro-life lobbyists are thus in the situation once
endured by pro-choice activists, matching pro-choice legislative proposals and
working to halt contrary legislation in committee.

The judicial and executive branches remain important to abortion policies
and politics. Both set a pro-choice standard for the Commonwealth. The
legislature is unlikely to liberalize abortion law further than the court already
has, passage of the Medical Facilities Access Act following from singular
political and societal events. Similarly, Massachusetts has had an almost un-
interrupted series of pro-choice governors since *Roe*. A pro-choice governor
is therefore an assumed element in Massachusetts abortion politics. A pro-life
governor would rework the equations of power, changing policy expectations
if not altering the political culture. He or she would also, presumably, recast
the ideological profile of the judiciary, altering standards for civil rights
appeals in abortion conflicts. Still, some would argue that Weld has been
unusually strong in his support of pro-choice policies, contributing to movement confidence and strength. Pro-choice lobbies within Massachusetts, however, remember that Weld was a member of the Reagan administration and
describe him as a newcomer to their cause. It seems most accurate to conclude that Weld's activism on abortion contributes to his liberal credentials
within the state. His pro-choice stance, in conjunction with his fiscal conservatism, also causes some moderate Republicans to view him as a potential
presidential candidate.[99] This national profile at once frees and motivates
Weld within the Commonwealth, his political ambitions not being tied to this
constituency. The governor's abortion reform proposals have never received
a favorable report from the Judiciary Committee.

Massachusetts resembles other states in its shift from judicial to legislative
abortion politics.[100] Here, that evolution was decisively influenced by the Commonwealth political culture. Elite decision making at once reflects and influences this popular belief system. The pace of change in the Massachusetts
political culture is unusual, particularly in regard to the political fortunes of the
Roman Catholic Church. Nonetheless, I would not wish to suggest that the
Commonwealth has left its past behind. Edwin O'Connor's classic of the 1950s,
The Last Hurrah, seemed a nostalgic bow to a lost political ethic, and yet it is an
ethic that surfaces in today's statehouse rhetoric and behavior. So also are abortion policies certain to continue in their equivocations. Though the Commonwealth may ultimately become pro-choice, for now it is safest to note that it
inches along in transition.

Notes

A number of interviewees requested that their comments be kept in confidence; I extend my thanks to those listed below and to others for generously sharing their experiences and expertise.

1. *Massachusetts General Laws Annotated*, chap. 272, sec. 19. I am indebted to Damon J. Borrelli for his help in researching Massachusetts statutory and case law.

2. *Commonwealth v. Brunelle*, 361 Mass. 6 (1972).

3. Barbara Hinkson Craig and David M. O'Brien. *Abortion and American Politics* (Chatham, N.J.: Chatham House, 1993), 76.

4. *Massachusetts General Laws Annotated*, chap. 112, sec. 12I.

5. *Massachusetts General Laws Annotated*, chap. 112, secs. 12L, 12M, 12O, 12P, 12R, 12S, 12T.

6. I am indebted to Glen Halva-Neubauer for his analysis of state responses to the *Roe v. Wade* ruling. See Glen A. Halva-Neubauer. "The States After *Roe*: 'No Paper Tigers,' " in *Understanding the New Politics of Abortion*, ed. Malcolm L. Goggin (Newbury Park, Calif.: Sage, 1993), 167–90.

7. *Framingham Clinic, Inc. et al. v. Board of Selectmen of Southborough et al.*, 373 Mass. 279 (1977).

8. *Bellotti, Attorney General of Massachusetts, et al. v. Baird et al.*, 444 U.S. 887 (1979).

9. *Massachusetts General Laws Annotated*, chap. 112, sec. 12S. Charles P. Kindregan, Jr., and Monroe L. Inker, *Massachusetts Practice*, vol. 3, *Family Law and Practice* (St. Paul: West, 1990), secs. 2288–89.

10. *Planned Parenthood League of Massachusetts et al. v. Bellotti et al.*, 641 F.2d 1006 (1981). *Planned Parenthood League of Massachusetts et al. v. Bellotti et al.*, 868 F.2d 459 (1st Cir. 1989).

11. *Planned Parenthood League of Massachusetts et al. v. Bellotti et al.*, 641 F.2d 1006 (1981).

12. *Boston Globe*, 24 January 1991, 26. "An Act Relative to Consent and Counseling for Certain Minors," first reading text, 1994.

13. *Mary Moe and Others v. Secretary of Administration and Finance and Others*, 382 Mass. 629 (1981).

14. *Boston Globe*, 5 May 1993, 1, 26.

15. *Boston Globe*, 15 June 1992, 17. *Planned Parenthood League of Massachusetts, Inc. et al. v. Operation Rescue et al.*, 406 Mass. 701, 703–705 (1990). Attorneys general in other states have refused to seek such injunctions. See *Time* 22 March 1993, 47. In Massachusetts, the attorney general's office stated that Commonwealth civil rights law compelled action. See *Massachusetts General Law*, chap. 12, sec. 11H. The attorney general also retained some control over its political-legal agenda by entering early in the case proceedings, Massachusetts law being set in the trial court. See *Bartley v. Phillips*, 317 Mass. 35, 42 (1944).

16. *Planned Parenthood League of Massachusetts, Inc. et al. v. Operation Rescue et al.*, 406 Mass. 701 (1990). *Boston Globe*, 5 March 1993, 27, and 15 March 1993, 15.

17. See the following issues of the *Boston Globe*: 23 January 1992, 65, 68; 23 May 1993, 21, 28; 1 July 1993, 18; 27 March 1992, 23; 3 September 1992, 77; 5 March 1993, 27; 5 May 1993, 1, 26; 10 December 1993, 1, 21; 1 July 1993, 18; 4 May 1993, 23. See also *Pilot*, 26 March 1993, 2, 14.

18. H2936, "An Act Relative to Medical Facilities Access."

19. *Framingham Clinic, Inc. et al. v. Board of Selectmen of Southborough et al.*, 373 Mass. 279 (1977). *Mary Moe and Others v. Secretary of Administration and Finance and*

Others, 382 Mass. 629 (1981). *Planned Parenthood League of Massachusetts, Inc. and Others v. Operation Rescue and Others*, 406 Mass. 701 (1990).

20. Melissa Kogut, lobbyist, Mass. Choice, telephone interview with the author, November 1993. Dorothy Lohman, public affairs coordinator, Planned Parenthood League of Massachusetts, telephone interview with the author, November 1993. Norma Shapiro, chair, Massachusetts Coalition for Choice and legislative liaison, Civil Liberties Union of Massachusetts, telephone interview with the author, November 1993. *Boston Globe*, 4 November 1986, 23, and *Boston Globe*, 7 November 1986, 23, 26.

21. "An Act Relative to Consent and Counseling for Certain Minors," first reading text, 1994. Melissa Kogut, telephone interview with the author. Dorothy Lohman, telephone interview with the author. Norma Shapiro, telephone interview with the author.

22. Joan Andersen, women's issues/reproductive rights specialist, League of Women Voters of Massachusetts, telephone interview with the author, November 1993. Norma Shapiro, telephone interview with the author. For an example of CLU and Planned Parenthood litigation, see *Mary Moe and Others v. Secretary of Administration and Finance and Others*, 382 Mass. 629 (1981).

23. Melissa Kogut, telephone interview with the author.

24. Norma Shapiro, telephone interview with the author.

25. *Boston Globe*, 13 December 1990, 64, and *Boston Globe*, 29 December 1990, 30. Norma Shapiro, telephone interview with the author. Coalition for Choice, "Proposed Consensus Documents for Coalition for Choice Building Project," 24 August 1993.

26. Norma Shapiro, telephone interview with the author.

27. *Commonweal* 111, 23 March 1984, 163–65. *Origins*, 6 September 1984, 184–86. *Pilot*, 26 March 1993, 2, 14. *Boston Globe*, 5 October 1992, 15. Several priests have been arrested for their role in Operation Rescue; they are not priests of the archdiocese and have not received the services of archdiocesan legal counsel, circumstances that one observer described as "a quiet shunning, a very subtle diplomacy." See also *Boston Globe*, 19 October 1991, 26. The cardinal recommended that Operation Rescue appeal the then-recent court injunction against clinic blockaders, obeying its dictates in the meantime.

28. *Pilot*, 26 March 1993, 2, 14.

29. Ibid.

30. Norma Shapiro, telephone interview with the author.

31. Mission Statement, Massachusetts Catholic Conference, 25 August 1992. See also *Overview*, the monthly newsletter of the Massachusetts Catholic Conference.

32. *Boston Globe*, 11 October 1992, 13, 16.

33. *Boston Globe*, 9 October 1991, 16; 9 October 1991, 1, 16; 6 October 1991, 1, 27.

34. *Boston Globe*, 5 September 1990, 24. See also *Boston Globe*, 26 July 1992, 8.

35. William G. Mayer, assistant professor of political science, Northeastern University, telephone interview with the author, November 1993. Kevin Poirier (R-N. Attleboro), state representative, telephone interviews with the author, November and December 1993. Norma Shapiro, telephone interview with the author.

36. Archbishop Joseph Cardinal Bernardin was a strong advocate of this approach to abortion politics. See the following issues of *Origins*: 17 October 1985, 306–8; 30 October 1986, 349; 2 February 1984, 568; 22 October 1987, 348–49; 12 April 1990, 747.

37. Arlene Champoux, legislative director, Massachusetts Citizens for Life, telephone interview with the author, November 1993. *Origins* 14 (1 November 1980): 213–313. *Boston Globe*, 20 January 1992, 15, 26, and *Boston Globe*, 21 January 1992, 18.

38. *Boston Globe*, 4 November 1986, 23, and 7 November 1986, 23, 26.

39. I am indebted to Clyde Wilcox for his analysis of the survey data relating to Massachusetts and national public opinion on abortion policies. Warren E. Miller, Donald R. Kinder, Steven J. Rosenstone, and the National Election Studies, *American National*

Election Study: Pooled Senate Election Study, 1988, 1990, 1992 [computer file], 3rd release (Ann Arbor, Mich.: Inter-University Consortium for Political and Social Research [distributor], 1993). See also Barbara Norrander and Clyde Wilcox. "State Differences in Attitudes toward Abortion," paper presented at the annual meeting of the American Political Science Association, Washington, D.C., September 1993. Malcolm L. Goggin and Christopher Wlezien, "Abortion Opinion and Policy in the American States," In *Understanding the New Politics of Abortion*, ed. Malcolm L. Goggin (Newbury Park, Calif.: Sage, 1993), 190–202. Jeffrey E. Cohen and Charles Barrilleaux. "Public Opinion, Interest Groups, and Public Policy Making; Abortion Policy in the American States," in Goggin, *Understanding the New Politics of Abortion*, 206.

40. *Boston Globe*, 9 November 1986, 46, and 5 September 1990, 24.

41. *Pro-Life Reference Journal, 1992–93* (Boston: Massachusetts Citizens for Life). *Boston Globe*, 9 November 1986, 46.

42. *The Massachusetts Political Almanac*, vol. 1, *The Legislature* (Centerville, Mass.: Center for Leadership Studies, 1993). *Pro-Life Reference Journal, 1992–93*.

43. *Massachusetts Political Almanac*, vol. 1, *The Legislature*.

44. Cheryl Jacques (D-Needham), state senator, telephone interview, November 1993, emphasis in the original.

45. Ibid., *Massachusetts Political Almanac*, vol. 1, *The Legislature*.

46. Jim Burke, administrative assistant to State Senator W. Paul White, telephone interview with the author, November 1993.

47. Kevin Poirier, telephone interviews with the author.

48. Confidential interviews conducted by the author, November 1993.

49. The influence and bias of media coverage relating to abortion was analyzed in a series of articles written by David Shaw. Shaw interviewed *Globe* reporters, and several of the trends identified in his article are evident in the Boston paper's coverage. See the following issues of the *Los Angeles Times*: 1 July 1990, A1; 2 July 1990, A1; 3 July 1990, A23; 3 July 1990; 4 July 1990, A1.

50. See the following issues of the *Boston Globe*: 22 January 1992, 40; 7 June 1992, 25, 29; 4 September 1992, 18; 11 September 1992, 26; 8 October 1992, 46; 28 October 1992, 1, 24; 29 October 1992, 21, 28; 31 October 1992, 13 19; 1 November 1992, 37; 11 December 1992, 75.

51. See the following issues of the *Boston Globe*: 5 September 1990, 21, 28; 19 September 1990, 43; 23 October 1990, 27; 17 August 1993, 12; 19 August 1993, 29, 32.

52. Norma Shapiro, telephone interview with the author.

53. See *Boston Globe*, 23 April 1992, 5; *MCFL News*, November 1992.

54. Arlene Champoux, telephone interview with the author. Melissa Kogut, telephone interview with the author.

55. Arlene Champoux, telephone interview with the author. *Boston Globe*, 23 April 1992, 5, and 28 May 1992, 32; *Massachusetts Political Almanac*, vol. 1, *The Legislature*.

56. *Massachusetts Political Almanac*, vol. 1, *The Legislature*; *Boston Globe*, 23 April 1992, 5, and 28 May 1992, 32.

57. For a discussion of the Locke-Jacques campaign from within the district, see the *Needham Times* and *Needham Chronicle* throughout the summer and fall of 1992. Note the parallels between the Jacques campaign and the 1990 Weld gubernatorial campaign, both races stressing political change and yet being claimed more narrowly as pro-choice victories.

58. *Massachusetts Political Almanac*, vol. 1, *The Legislature*.

59. Each of these factors has been weighed and compared by a number of scholars. For a survey of this research, see Goggin, *Understanding the New Politics of Abortion*.

60. Confidential interview conducted by the author, November 1993.

61. Norma Shapiro, telephone interview with the author.

62. Ibid.

63. Joe Carleo, legislative assistant to State Representative Susan D. Schur, telephone interview with the author, November 1993. Melissa Kogut, telephone interview with the author. *Massachusetts Political Almanac*, vol. 1, *The Legislature*.

64. Joan Andersen, telephone interview with the author. Gerald D'Avolio, executive director, Massachusetts Catholic Coalition, telephone interview with the author, November 1993. Dorothy Lohman, telephone interview with the author. Rachel Schumacher, administrative aide to State Representative David B. Cohen, telephone interview with the author, November 1993. Norma Shapiro, telephone interview with the author.

65. *Boston Globe*, 5 May 1993, 1, 26, and 6 May 1993, 40.

66. Melissa Kogut, telephone interview with the author.

67. "Information and News Release: Statement of Massachusetts Bishops on Reproductive Choice," Massachusetts Catholic Conference, 8 May 1993. Arlene Champoux, telephone interview with the author. Norma Shapiro, telephone interview with the author. See also *Pilot*, 7 May 1993, 18; *Boston Globe*, 9 May 1993, 21, 24.

68. Melissa Kogut, telephone interview with the author.

69. Rachel Schumacher, telephone interview with the author. Norma Shapiro, telephone interview with the author.

70. *Boston Globe*, 11 May 1993, 22. Norma Shapiro, telephone interview with the author.

71. Rachel Schumacher, telephone interview with the author. Norma Shapiro, telephone interview with the author.

72. H3239, "An Act Relative to Reproductive Choice," original second reading text, 1993, chap. 111I, sec. 2.

73. H3239, "An Act Relative to Reproductive Choice," amended second reading text, 1993, chap. 111I, sec. 2. Italics added.

74. Rachel Schumacher, telephone interview with the author. Norma Shapiro, telephone interview with the author. See also "Information and News Release: Statement of Massachusetts Bishops on Reproductive Choice."

75. *Boston Globe*, 12 May 1993, 23, 29.

76. Confidential interview conducted by the author, November 1993.

77. *Boston Globe*, 11 May 1993, 22, and 12 May 1993, 29. See also *Pro-Life Reference Journal, 1992–93*; *Massachusetts Political Almanac*, vol. 1, *The Legislature*. Dorothy Lohman, telephone interview with the author. Kevin Poirier, telephone interviews with the author. Norma Shapiro, telephone interview with the author.

78. Kevin Poirier, telephone interviews with the author.

79. *Boston Globe*, 12 May 1993, 23, 29.

80. Gerald D'Avolio, telephone interview with the author.

81. *Boston Globe*, 12 May 1993, 23, 29. "H3239: An Act Relative to Reproductive Choice," prepared by Planned Parenthood League of Massachusetts for the Coalition for Choice, 1993. "*Roe* vs. *Wade* and the Myth of 'Abortion on Demand,' " prepared by Mass. Choice for the Coalition for Choice, 24 June 1993. "The Meaning of 'Undue Burden,' " prepared by the Massachusetts chapter of the National Organization for Women, 1993.

82. "An Act Relative to Reproductive Choice," first reading text, 1994.

83. David B. Cohen, "Fact Sheet; An Act Relative to Medical Facilities Access, House Bill 2936," 1993. Mass. Choice, "Fact Sheet; Clinic Access, S225 and H2936," 1993. Joan Andersen, telephone interview with the author. Robert Gill, legislative director for State Senator Lois G. Pines, telephone interview with the author, November 1993. Cheryl Jacques, telephone interview with the author. Dorothy Lohman, telephone

interview with the author. Rachel Schumacher, telephone interview with the author. *Boston Globe*, 5 May 1993, 1, 26.

84. *Boston Globe*, 6 November 1992, 25, 27. Melissa Kogut, telephone interview with the author.

85. See the following issues of the *Boston Globe*: 11 March 1993, 3; 13 March 1993, 3; 19 March 1993, 27; 28 March 1993, 75. See also *People*, 29 March 1993, 44–46; *Newsweek*, 22 March 1993, 34–35; *Time*, 22 March 1993, 44–47.

86. *Boston Globe*, 26 March 1993, 26, and 22 March 1993, 1, 8. Joan Andersen, telephone interview with the author. Melissa Kogut, telephone interview with the author. Rachel Schumacher, telephone interview with the author.

87. *Boston Globe*, 25 March 1993, 28, and 26 March 1993, 26.

88. Memo from Scott Harshbarger, attorney general of the Commonwealth, to the Massachusetts State Senate, 2 June 1993. Memo from Civil Liberties Union of Massachusetts, signed by Staff Attorney Sarah Wunsch and Legislative Specialist Norma Shapiro, to the Massachusetts State Senate, 2 June 1993. Memo from Massachusetts Coalition for Choice, signed by Chair Norma Shapiro, to the Massachusetts State Senate, 1 July 1993.

89. Norma Shapiro, telephone interview with the author.

90. "House No. 2936; House Action, Senate Action," Legislative Reporting Service, Inc., 1993. *Journal of the Senate*, 7–8 June 1993. "State Senate Votes on Clinic Access," Planned Parenthood League of Massachusetts, 1993.

91. Dorothy Lohman, telephone interview with the author. Norma Shapiro, telephone interview with the author.

92. H2936, "An Act Relative to Medical Facilities Access," third reading text, 1993.

93. Melissa Kogut, telephone interview with the author. Cheryl Jacques, telephone interview with the author.

94. Jim Burke, telephone interview with the author.

95. Letter to constituents, State Senator Lois G. Pines (D-Newton), 12 November 1993.

96. Gerald D'Avolio, telephone interview with the author.

97. Throughout the 1970s and 1980s, the pro-choice movement could not pass its legislation and therefore settled for matching pro-life proposals. Pro-life bills sought to ban abortion for sex selection, to establish a commission to study alternatives to abortion, to prohibit the use of public funds for abortions, and to amend the constitution. Pro-choice bills included proposals to distribute information regarding reproductive health services and access to contraceptives; to liberalize minor access to abortion; and to amend the constitution. This strategy of responding to one bill with another was discussed in a telephone interview with Norma Shapiro. H2936, "An Act Relative to Medical Facilities Access."

98. *Pro-Life Reference Journal, 1992–93. Massachusetts Political Almanac*, vol. 1, *The Legislature*.

99. See the following issues of the *Boston Globe*: 22 May 1992, 21, 25; 7 August 1992, 10; 11 August 1992, 15.

100. Glen A. Halva-Neubauer. "The States After *Roe*: 'No Paper Tigers,' " in Goggin, *Understanding the New Politics of Abortion*, 167–90. Suzanne Staggenborg, *The Pro-Choice Movement: Organization and Activism in the Abortion Conflict* (New York: Oxford University Press, 1991).

JAMES R. KELLY

11 | Beyond Compromise: *Casey*, Common Ground, and the Pro-Life Movement

The end of the Republican Reagan-Bush era marks, among other things, the end of one of the many stages in the decades-old controversy over legal abortion. Belatedly following worldwide trends, American fiscal conservatives, especially those used to dominating Republican Party inner circles, can no longer be expected to join with moral conservatives in seeking the recriminalization of abortion. After the 1992 election, during which President Clinton received the unanimous backing of legal abortion advocates while former President Bush claimed the almost unanimous support of the organized opposition to legal abortion, the recriminalization of abortion, the mirror-image "right-to-life" goal and "pro-choice" fear, already seemed a phrase of the past.

President Clinton appointed Ruth Bader Ginsburg, a strong supporter of abortion rights, to the Supreme Court, and the Republicans were promising a "big tent" on abortion. On 15 December 1992 a group of prominent Republican moderates, calling themselves "the Republican Majority Coalition," announced that in the next presidential election the Republicans would be "inclusive." R.W. Apple, Jr., of the *New York Times* noticed that the coalition's founders had included no abortion opponents in the group. In terms of the systematic study of abortion sentiment, this cannot count as surprising. Francome found that British Conservatives, like the Republicans, first opposed legal abortion and then enthusiastically accepted it.[1] There's a straightforward logic to it: When a government supports restrictive abortion laws, it implicitly endorses interference with "private solutions" to problem pregnancies, making it difficult for the same government to defend the proposition that, after birth, it cannot "interfere" by helping the babies (and their mothers) it did not want aborted. Before the *Casey* decision, Republican support of a Human Life Amendment raised no difficult problems involving such issues of consistency, since only the Court and not the president could weaken *Roe*. It is worth noting that six months after the 1989 *Webster* decision (which upheld St. Louis abortion regulations requiring viability tests and prohibiting elective abortions at public hospitals), three distinct Republican political action committees (PACs) were formed specifically to raise funds for Republicans who favored Medicaid-funded abortions.

Abortion Politics after the Reagan-Bush Era

Republican Party fiscal conservatives can be expected to continue to attract the votes of working- and lower-middle-class moral traditionalists by supporting their "social" issues when they require, like school prayer or the teaching of creationism, no significant tax revenues for social programs. But it would be premature to conclude that *all* debates about abortion with a distinctive Republican-Democratic flavor are concluded. Indeed, after the Bush defeat, the great majority of social-movement organizations carried on exactly as before. Debates continued about the federal government's funding abortion for women below the poverty line and state restrictions such as parental notification of a minor's abortion. The Clinton proposals for health-care reform raise the issue of government funding for nontherapeutic abortions that have been prohibited by the Hyde Amendments declared constitutional in *Harris v. McCrae* (30 June 1980). These are familiar abortion disputes, and they were contested in familiar ways even after *Casey* and the Republican loss of the presidency.

No right-to-life group has opposed health reform, but all have protested classifying elective abortion as "health care." Still, in terms of lingering Republican Party–abortion opposition ties, it should be noted that throughout the summer and fall of 1993 the publications of major social-movement organizations opposing abortion, such as the *National Right to Life News* and the *American Life League's All About Issues* never explicitly acknowledged that some changes were necessary so that more Americans would have health insurance. By contrast, the U.S. Bishops and the Catholic Health Association of the United States (the national organization representing 600 hospitals and more than 1,500 other centers providing long-term or specialized health care) opposed including abortion as health care *but* strongly supported health reform, adding that "the needs of the poor have a special priority."[2]

There are some pretty obvious reasons for the continuity in abortion politics in the post-*Casey* and post-Reagan/Bush era. Not only are many of the immediate issues familiar replays of past contests, but the new ones have a strong impact on state and local areas, where the movement may still hope to remain an important presence. Michael Griffin's 10 March 1993 murder of Dr. David Gunn outside the Pensacola Women's Medical Service and Rachelle Shannon's 27 August attempt to murder Dr. George Tiller outside his Wichita, Kansas, abortion clinic give special urgency to efforts to pass legislation (the Freedom of Access to Clinic Entrances bill) making violence committed at abortion clinics a federal offense with greatly increased jail sentences and fines.

All known social-movement organizations protested their opposition to violence in defense of fetal life.[3] *Feminists for Life* held a rally on 7 April in downtown Rochester, New York, to "condemn the violence against David Gunn, to demonstrate our continuing dedication to non-violence, to express our grief over this tragic and senseless act." Communications director Nancy Myers of the *National Right to Life Committee* (NRLC), the oldest, largest, and most prestigious of the social-movement organizations opposing legal abortion, complained that "for two days after the shooting, no national television program quoted a mainstream pro-life spokesperson—not once."[4] She noted that "Nightline" presented as a "typical" pro-lifer a man named John Burt, identified as a former Ku Klux Klan member. Burt knew Griffin, but Myers observed that "Burt does not represent any pro-life group."

On 24 January 1993 the Supreme Court (*NOW v. Scheidler*) ruled that the Racketeer Influenced and Corrupt Organization Act (RICO), which involves huge fines, forfeiture of property, and prison terms of up to twenty years, can be applied to abortion protesters. On 26 May 1994 President Clinton signed into law the Freedom of Access to Clinic Entrances (FACE) bill, under which offenders face fines of up to $100,000 and a year in prison for a first conviction and up to $250,000 in fines and three years in prison for subsequent offenses. On 30 June 1994 the Supreme Court (*Madsen v. Women's Health Center*) ruled that a thirty-six-foot buffer zone separating abortion protesters from an abortion clinic entrance and driveway did not violate their first amendment free speech rights. While these cumulative judgments against local abortion protest will impede the aggressive Operation Rescue type of civil disobedience, the history of abortion protest strongly suggests that alternative forms of direct mobilization will continue. Under the right circumstances, the movement can draw on deep and ready reservoirs of protest that are constantly replenished by repugnance to the principle that direct killing of unwanted life can be safely integrated into law and policy. The media does not highlight, and so outside observers do not notice, that all the grassroots organizations that arose to combat legal abortion have always included opposition to infanticide and euthanasia in their work. This is a dimension that ensures the movement's ability to rally large numbers of volunteers and donations, especially from the strong religious base that sees both abortion and assisted suicide as interrelated attacks against the sacredness of human life. During November 1992, as Clinton defeated Bush, the *National Right to Life News* reported with pride that after the mobilization of right-to-life groups, California voters defeated a bill by 54 to 46 percent that would have legalized "physician-assisted death," allowing doctors, by injection or drug, to cause a patient's death if asked to do so. In the first of a NRL News series, Burke Balch, the NRLC state legislative director, recalled that "from its founding, the pro-life movement has been committed to the defense of all innocent human life whether born or unborn, young or old, 'normal' or disabled."

So far, the defeat of Bush and the election of Clinton have made surprisingly little difference in the tactics or thinking of the movement opposing abortion. There has been no diminution in levels of contribution or volunteers reported by national groups. Notwithstanding this continuity, it remains true that substantive fears about the legality of abortion are irrevocably gone and that this salient fact will eventually affect movement thinking. The movement must now exist without the promise of anything close to the victory it has for almost three decades defined as essential and reachable. That promise and that era are gone. This is a new era for abortion politics and abortion discourse. Even a *New York Times* editorial acknowledged "that a basic abortion right is fairly secure."[5] Justice Harry A. Blackmun, the principal author of *Roe*, told reporters that constitutionally protected legal abortion is "now a settled issue with this Court."[6]

It cannot be said that mainstream right-to-life reflection has come to grips with the central facts in this new era, namely the *Casey* decision and the Bush defeat. The central concern at the June 1993 annual NRLC convention was how to keep the Republican Party, their political ally since the 1979 Reagan campaign, in the fight against abortion. But it is important to note that there was very little cheering for William J. Bennett's recommendation that the movement seek the "middle ground" and welcome into the Republican "big tent" even those who accept some legal abortion. Right-to-life activists have never cheered when the politically savvy have pointed them in directions that explicitly involve them in moral compromise. If activists say they oppose abortion because it kills an innocent human life, how can they accept the direct killing of some fetuses in cases of rape, incest, and fetal deformity? While political strategists shrewdly maneuvering for enhanced election odds can promote some "middle ground," grassroots abortion opponents cannot. For a new era, abortion politics requires a new vocabulary. The latest effort on the periphery of both pro-life and prochoice social movements to achieve one bears close watching. Its name is "common ground." If it does not move from the periphery to the mainstream of abortion discourse, the collective achievement of any "moral equilibrium" in the unresolvable political, legal, and personal debate over abortion cannot be expected. The term "common ground" began before the *Casey* decision and the Democratic 1992 presidential victory. The argument of this chapter is that if the *Casey* decision is viewed in terms of the Governor Casey arguments (see below), then the grassroots emergence of a "common ground" conjoining pro-life and pro-choice activists can begin to advance toward the center stage of abortion discourse. In the new era of abortion politics it makes sense to scrutinize the emergence of a common ground and to begin to discuss its possible future. Abortion politics will not cease; the only question is whether it can be conducted in such a way that a moral equilibrium no longer seems so hopeless that increasing violence followed by increasing limits on the right of dissent are considered as inevitable consequences of the insoluble issue of legal abortion.

Casey's Arguments

Among the several themes struck by Governor Robert P. Casey of Pennsylvania before and after he approved the abortion law passed by the Pennsylvania legislature was that any bill restricting abortion should also explicitly and directly acknowledge that the mother considering an abortion had correlative claims on the state restricting her. It is significant that Governor Casey vetoed an earlier abortion law passed by the Pennsylvania legislature precisely because it did not explicitly link the interests of mother and fetus. In his veto message, he wrote:

> Finally, I must note that our concerns cannot end with protecting unborn children, but must extend to protecting, and promoting the health, of *all* our children, and their mothers. The right to life must mean the right to a decent life. Our concern for future mothers must include a concern for current mothers. Our respect for the wonders of pregnancy must be equaled by a sensitivity to the traumas of pregnancy. This Administration has called for significantly increased support for child and maternal health programs, for education, for rape counseling and support services.

Casey's 17 December 1987 veto of Pennsylvania's first Abortion Control Act[7] dramatically captures the difference between his and the Reagan-Bush approach to abortion legislation: "And we will continue to advance more programs born of the recognition that our moral responsibility to mothers and children does not end at birth. *Those proposals deserve to receive the same overwhelming vote of approval in the Legislature that this bill received"* (italics added). Casey invited the legislature to search with him for a "strong and sustainable Abortion Control Act that forms a humane and constitutional foundation for our efforts to ensure that no child is denied his or her chance to walk in the sun and make the most out of life." Casey insisted on a bill that did not merely restrict abortion but that sought to expand its communal implications.

In subsequent addresses Casey emphasized the connection between opposing abortion and supporting women and their families.

> We believe in a country and a society which cares for both the mother and the child . . . we have got to work as a society to eliminate the crisis and not eliminate the child. . . . To give women a real choice: health care, school lunch programs, nutritional programs, the Women, Infant and Children's nutritional program that we have been pushing hard in Pennsylvania. That's important.

Child care, family and medical leave so people can understand their responsibilities and not have to choose between their job and their family.[8]

In a speech entitled "Children First, Before and After Birth," Casey opposed a
policy adopted in some states to reduce welfare costs by refusing additional aid to
women having a child while on public assistance. "My response to that was, 'Not in
Pennsylvania. It's not going to happen here.' And it didn't happen in Pennsylvania.
Because it's wrong. . . . We didn't just refuse to cut assistance to women and
children. We increased it. Because when times are tough, women and children need
more help, not less."[9] In his speeches linking abortion restrictions with the traditional
positions taken by the Democratic Party, Casey boasted that he successfully supported welfare reforms that emphasized job training and jobs, such as a youth
apprenticeship program and a "school equity" program to help schools in districts
with a low tax base. "The best welfare reform of all," he said, "is a job."

Casey also noted other programs in Pennsylvania related to his strong pro-life
position: legislation providing comprehensive, affordable health care for children
whose families are not poor enough to qualify for medical assistance but who
cannot afford health insurance on their own; increases in the Women, Infants and
Children Program; new programs for comprehensive prenatal and postnatal care;
increased funds for mammograms and cancer screening for low-income women;
loan funds for housing for low-income families; tripled state funding for domes-
tic violence and rape-crisis programs; a $4 million statewide adoption program
that, besides continuous attention to the facts about abortion, included "advocacy
of a New American Compact in this country which seeks to involve all public
and private institutions in a fight for policies and programs to offer women
meaningful alternatives to abortion and to offer children and families the help
they need to live decent, healthy and happy lives."

At a St. Louis University conference on abortion and public policy Casey
described his own efforts to be a governor "faithful both to his prolife convictions and to his oath to uphold the constitution" by drawing on the classical
virtue of prudence:

Prudence we all know to be a virtue. Classical thinkers rated it the supreme
political virtue. Roughly defined, it's the ability to distinguish the desirable
from the possible. It's a sense of the good, joined with a practical knowledge
of the means by which to accomplish the good. A world in which every unborn
child survives to take his first breath is desirable. But we know that such a
world has never been. And prudence cautions us never to expect such a world.
Abortion is but one of many evils that, to one extent or another, is to be found
at all times and places. . . . But the point is that after facing up to such facts,
the basic facts of our human condition, prudence does not fall silent. It is not
an attitude of noble resignation; it is an active virtue . . . it doesn't capitulate.
It's tolerant, but not timid. . . . Prudence asks: "If there is no consensus, how
do we form one? What means of reform are available to us?"[10]

Prudence Unheard

Casey petitioned the convention committee and the party chairman but was not allowed to address the 1992 Democratic National Convention that nominated Bill Clinton. John Leo wrote that Casey was "graphically humiliated by the abortion lobby. One of his political enemies, a woman who had fought many of his programs in Pennsylvania, was brought on-stage at the convention and pointedly honored as a 'Republican for Choice.' "[11] It was clear that Casey did not expect that the national Democratic Party would stop supporting legal abortion. In an article entitled "What I Would Have Told the Democrats," Casey argued for a diversity in the party, acknowledging that while he thought the "unborn child has a fundamental right to life. . . . I recognize that many people hold strongly to an opposing view."[12] He recommended that "the party should have explicitly rejected abortion on demand and endorsed the principle that voters, through their elected representatives in the states, would have the right to enact reasonable regulations restricting abortion, such as those in the Pennsylvania law just upheld by the Supreme Court in *Planned Parenthood v. Casey*." Casey's argument that a retreat from an "abortion-on-demand" position would attract "Reagan democrats" back into the party was not without some warrant.[13]

Paradoxical Abortion Politics Lead to Common Ground

The post–Reagan/Bush era political losses of abortion opponents are obvious, but those of the pro-choice movement are not. If they do not become clear, common ground will not enter mainstream abortion discourse. Although it seems an odd assertion, only the continued vitality of the right-to-life movement makes it at all likely that government and policy elites will define abortion solely as *a neutral* personal "choice" rather than *a rational* public solution to any problem pregnancy requiring social assistance. In the context of a principled pro-choice position it is worth recalling that the first movement to make abortion legal cannot be characterized as "pro-choice." Historically, the first organized support for legal abortion came from the Malthusian League and the eugenics movement.[14] More recently, Staggenborg found that the founders of the National Association for the Repeal of Abortion Law (NARAL) were mostly "single-issue activists with backgrounds in the family planning and population movements."[15] She reports a large overlap in the memberships of NARAL and Zero Population Growth.[16] The paradox of the next stage of abortion politics is that both principled abortion opponents *and* supporters—that is, pro-choice as well as right-to-life activists—face disappointing political futures. A not unlikely future is more abortion and less choice. For *both* the pro-life and pro-choice principles require considerable social and economic restructuring, and both are expensive. Neither principled pro-life nor pro-choice activists can expect much political support in an era defined by individualism, consumerism, and ever fiercer international competition for ever scarcer resources. The link between the futures of the pro-life and pro-choice movements is no longer unilinear. Unlike in the past, as the fortunes of one weaken, the fortunes of the other no longer inevitably rise. The convenient academic term for such complicated nonlinear and intertwining inter-relationships is *dialectical*. This new dialectically shared fate of the abortion movement and countermovement is also morally ironic: a diminishment of the vitality of the movement opposing abortion will result in *less* real choice, especially among economically disadvantaged women, because there will be less pressure for government to treat abortion as a "neutral choice" and more fiscal pressure to regard abortion as a rational public policy solution. Similarly, some pro-life activists[17] have reluctantly come to realize that in a political and social order strongly affected by the dominance of economic considerations, cooperative efforts that made it more likely that women would feel they realistically *could* choose birth rather than abortion would represent a solid and difficult achievement.

New Paradox, New Terms

Any argument asserting a dialectical and paradoxical link between the fates of the pro-life and pro-choice movements cannot immediately seem plausible to either. The abstract terms "dialectical" and "paradoxical" do not help. A more concrete term is needed that accurately captures these new paradoxical and ironic qualities in a way that adversaries on both sides can employ. For the paradox asserts, and it is worth repeating, not a shared morality, which is why compromise is not possible, but a shared pro-choice/pro-life political fate, which is why a constantly shifting truce—or, perhaps, a series of negotiated truces—is possible.

The Distinction between Middle-Ground Compromise and Common-Ground Truce

As mentioned earlier, right-to-life activists have never applauded when political insiders have pointed them in directions that explicitly involve moral compromise. As opponents have always been quick to point out, if activists oppose abortion because it kills a human life, they can hardly accept abortion even in the relatively rare cases of pregnancy by rape or in cases of fetal deformity. Moral compromise would represent the irretrievable loss of a morally significant public witness to what they insist is the foundation for the evolving good society: that each form of developing human life has an equal right to life and that this right is neither earned by promise of achievement nor granted by a parent nor the government. From the long-run perspective, "middle-ground" strategies would insufficiently repair the movement's political and legal losses and permanently jeopardize the cultural impact of its moral argument that all forms of human life—from "womb to tomb," to use the movement's phrase—have inalienable rights. Another approach, and another phrase, is needed that guards the centrality of the morality of the pro-life argument yet does not entirely remove the movement from the pragmatic political and legal engagements required to remain a public presence as opposed to a sectarian witness. This will be difficult. Several prominent liberal commentators on the abortion controversy have inspected and dismissed the term. For example, Anna Quindlen in a column pointedly entitled "Going Nowhere" and Ronald Dworkin in his widely reviewed book about abortion and euthanasia, entitled *Life's Dominion*, dismissed any hope that common ground can be found between the two sides of the abortion debate.[18] Dworkin's inability to find any distinction between "common ground" and "moral compromise" showed the formidable difficulties awaiting those attempting to move "common ground" to center stage in abortion discourse.

Like Dworkin, leaders of prominent social-movement organizations opposing abortion have regarded "common ground" as a euphemism for morally compromising "middle-ground" political efforts to end the abortion controversy. No official representative of a social-movement organization opposing abortion has promoted "common ground." The *National Right to Life* president, Wanda Frantz, warned activists in NRLC's 3,000 chapters that "common ground" was a "clever pro-choice" strategy seeking "to gain acceptance of the pro-abortion position as morally equivalent (or morally superior!) to the pro-life position." Randall Terry likened common ground to blacks negotiating with the Ku Klux Klan and Jews cooperating with Nazis. In a special issue of *Sisterlife*, the quarterly of *Feminists for Life*, Marilyn Kopp defended the "common-ground movement" while Mary Bea Stout had doubts.[19] So, does "common ground" have a future? First, we should briefly review its past.

Just What Is "Common" in "Common Ground"?

Although the authoritative *Oxford English Dictionary* provides no definition, "common ground" is not a neologism. Although he never defined the term, or even referred to it in his text, J. Anthony Lukas used "common ground" as the title of his book about the decade-long dispute over legally forced integration of the Boston school system.[20] We might say that the emergent sense of common ground is that of public adversaries publicly cooperating even as they remain publicly divided. Most important, they cooperate without compromising—or even seeking to compromise—their conflicting principles. In the abortion controversy, common ground describes cooperation that stems precisely from the pro-life and pro-choice principles that irrevocably divide the two movements. Thus, common ground is more morally complex than its semantic cousin, "common cause," which also describes the momentary alignments of two adversaries, such as Germany becoming the ally of France to combat the nineteenth-century sea power of Great Britain. When adversaries describe their surprising cooperation by the term "common ground," they want us to know that their cooperation betrays or even softens no principle. While "compromise" and "middle ground" can with honor appear in the same sentence as "common cause," their appearance with "common ground" signals either an outsider's misunderstanding or an insider's moral laxity. For the entire point of the phrase "common ground" is to proclaim publicly that these specific cooperative acts performed with adversaries blur no principle or violate any integrity. It is not at all certain that a term of such subtlety will quickly find common usage. Indeed, the phrase is in constant danger of trivialization. The 22 March 1993 *New York Times* news summary described "an interest in restaurants" as the ice-breaking "common ground" found by President Clinton and German chancellor Helmut Kohn at their first state meeting. There are far deeper reasons to be doubtful that the term common ground will prevail in abortion debates.

Whose Common Ground?

Abortion opponents have questioned the timing and the source of the application of "common ground" to abortion politics. The phrase first appeared in the early 1990s in books and articles by prominent proponents of legal abortion. Although they acknowledged they were pro-choice, the first "common-ground" authors described their efforts as sympathetically portraying *both* sides of the abortion controversy in search of an honorable compromise. The most prominent authors were Harvard law professor Laurence H. Tribe, who at one time suggested the First Amendment as the locus for abortion rights, and PBS commentator and essayist Roger Rosenblatt, who characterized himself as "conventionally pro-choice."[21] In his *Abortion: The Clash of Absolutes*, Tribe employed the term "common ground"; in *Life Itself: Abortion in the American Mind*, Rosenblatt tried "uncommon ground." Both acknowledged that the obvious humanity of the fetus was a significant dimension of even legal debate about abortion, both recognized that opponents of abortion could not simply be dismissed as religionists or as opponents of gender equality, and both sought a conciliatory tone. Both succeeded more in tone than in substance. Tribe entitled his penultimate chapter "In Search of Compromise," and there he mostly rejected "*Casey*-type" state restrictions, such as informed-consent provisions and parental notification. Rosenblatt's phrase "legally permit but discourage" anticipated Clinton's 1992 campaign promise to make "abortion safe, legal and rare." Rosenblatt concluded only that "it is time for Congress to make a law like *Roe v. Wade* that fully protects abortion rights but legislates the kind of community help like sex education that would diminish the practice."[22] Abortion opponents reading such "common-ground" books would find it hard not to agree with Dworkin's pessimistic judgment that authors promoting common ground inevitably urge "compromise . . . on terms that protect what they themselves believe to be fundamental principles of justice."[23]

A Short and Distorted Media Life

"Common ground" had a fleeting existence in the media, peaking during the 1992 election campaign and then virtually disappearing. Michael Griffin's 10 March 1993 murder of Dr. David Gunn during a protest at a Pensacola, Florida, abortion clinic seemed to disqualify any sober use of the phrase in reporting about the abortion controversy. But just before the 1992 election of Clinton, the term burst into the major print media. The same handful of examples was transformed into what quickly seemed to be a nascent national movement capable of competing with the older, established abortion adversaries. Stories appeared in *USA Today*, the *Los Angeles Times*, the *Washington Post*, the *Boston Globe*, the *Christian Science Monitor*, *Glamour*, and numerous local media, such as the *St. Louis Post-Dispatch*, the *Kansas Star*, the *San Jose News*, the *Oregonian*, and the *Cleveland Plain-Dealer*. The first national media account explicitly employing "common ground" that I know of is Tamar Lewin's 17 February 1992 front-page *New York Times* article entitled "In Bitter Abortion Debate, Opponents Learn to Reach for Common Ground." Lewin reported the "breakthrough" common ground event that began in St. Louis on 12 July 1990 with Andrew Puzder, a "pro-life" lawyer; Loretto Wagner, a past president of Missouri Citizens for Life; B.J. Isaacson-Jones, director of St. Louis Reproductive Health Services; and Jean Cavender, also of Reproductive Health Services. In my judgment, the chronologically first example of common ground in the abortion controversy also illuminates its emergent moral characteristics. The empirical record, admittedly slight, suggests that when these characteristics are missing, common ground does not take root.

The Still Seminal Common Ground

First, its origins were the grassroots. The St. Louis "common-ground" breakthrough came closely after the Supreme Court's 3 July 1989 5–4 *Webster* decision, which upheld Missouri abortion legislation prohibiting public hospitals from performing elective abortions and requiring viability testing at twenty weeks. Soon after, Andrew Puzder, who had helped draft the Missouri law, wrote an op-ed essay in the *St. Louis Post-Dispatch* suggesting that when states pass laws that restrict abortion, both opponents and proponents of legal abortion suddenly have a shared interest in reducing the number of abortions by cooperating to reduce the need for abortion. B.J. Isaacson-Jones read the article and called Puzder. After a few satisfactory conversations, they widened the group to include activists with proven movement loyalties. Loretto Wagner, for example, had organized the first St. Louis mass protest against *Roe* and had served for more than a decade as coordinator of the city's participation in the annual 22 January "March on Washington" protesting *Roe.* She had been arrested a dozen times for civil disobedience outside abortion clinics. She had also founded two shelters for women with problem pregnancies.

In her many interviews, Wagner's first point is always that common ground "is not meant to be a compromise." St. Louis common ground involved no long discussions about the reasons for opposing or supporting legal abortion. Nor did it directly seek mutual respect, although that was a by-product. The St. Louis rationale for common-ground efforts was not conversion, contestation, or compromise; it was not even dialogue. Simply put, the pro-life side wanted to save fetal lives, and the pro-choice side wanted to ensure choice, and both sides found that in some cases each side could best do this by cooperating with the other. Wagner listed some of the ways they found:

> We need to relieve some of the pressures that cause many women to choose abortion and to make it possible for a kinder society for them and their children. There are many things we can agree on: more and better quality pre- and postnatal care, providing more access to treatment of substance abusing mothers and their children, welfare reforms, day-care, affordable housing, adoption, improved recruitment of foster parents, helping women find jobs and educational opportunities. Neither side wants to see poor women economically compelled to have abortions.[24]

Wagner's last sentence is crucial to understanding common ground and how abortion adversaries can be cooperative and uncompromising at the same time. Common-ground participants are not likely to be *anti*-abortion and pro-*abortion*; they are likely to be *pro*-life and pro-*choice* in the sense that common ground involves assisting women and supporting social policies that reduce the pressure on women to abort. It would seem that among opponents of abortion, "common-ground" support would come from groups following what is called, since Joseph Cardinal Bernardin's 6 December 1983 address at Fordham University, the "consistent ethic of life." The consistent ethic of life finds connections between the oppositions to abortion, capital punishment, militarism, and poverty.[25]

Wagner suggested still another way of understanding how common ground was the antithesis of compromise. Common ground involved, through mutual challenge, a deepening of pro-life and pro-choice principles rather than their accommodation. Referring to Isaacson-Jones's successful efforts to include adoption among the services offered by Reproductive Health Services to women with unwanted pregnancies, Wagner observed that with the stimulus of common ground, "maybe clinics would live up to their own [pro-choice] expectations." Similarly, common ground should stimulate abortion opponents to be consistent in their pro-life principles. For the sake of integrity, abortion opponents must respect the entirely appropriate pro-choice challenge to consider, precisely in terms of loyalty to their pro-life principle, whether their historically specific kinds of public opposition to abortion have contributed to reducing the pressures on women to abort and to consider whether they have omitted other promising activities and practices. For integrity, legal abortion activists must respect the entirely appropriate pro-life common-ground challenge to consider, precisely in terms of loyalty to their principle of pro-choice, whether their public promotion of legal abortion has always contributed to increasing the reproductive freedom of women and whether they have omitted other promising activities and practices aimed at reducing the pressures on women to abort. Reciprocal common-ground challenges encourage abortion opponents to show the ways they are pro-life as well as anti-abortion and legal abortion supporters to show how they are pro-choice rather than pro-abortion.

It is worth reviewing, as a benchmark, the five properties of common ground developed by the breakthrough group in St. Louis. They can serve to understand better the reasons why other common-ground efforts have not shown similar success. St. Louis Common Ground (1) resulted from a combined pro-life and pro-choice initiative; (2) it publicly distinguished its aims from moral compromise and political accommodation; (3) common-ground participants continued their movement activisms and kept their movement credentials; (4) they agreed to focus on reducing the pressures on women to abort; (5) and they were able to cooperate by locating overlaps between a pro-life consistent ethic approach and the pro-choice distinction between reproductive choice and legal abortion. Not all five properties are found in the common-ground examples brought to prominence by the media between the Bush and Clinton administrations. Indeed, some of the most significant examples that had them were not included by the media. A main reason was that the media sought to assimilate "common ground" into "pluralism."

Assimilating Common Ground into Moral Pluralism

Media interest in common-ground efforts waxed during the 1991–92 presidential campaign and waned immediately after Clinton's election. During that brief period of prominence almost all reports referred to the same handful of "common-ground" initiatives, although only St. Louis originally used that term. Interestingly enough, each of the others derived from a pro-choice initiative and none of them explicitly characterized its focus as reducing the pressures on women to abort. Unlike the St. Louis emphasis, those that followed focused mostly on dialogue aimed at mutual understanding. My judgment is that the media placed "common ground" into the more accessible category of "pluralism," which they interpreted as learning to live with differences about abortion.

The media most often referred to two kinds of common-ground efforts, and here are two examples of each: grassroots-initiated efforts at dialogue, and professionally led efforts at conflict mediation. Recently there has been some overlap between the two.

The two local efforts reported in media stories in the early 1990s about common ground were initiated by legal abortion activists: Magi Cage, who directed a Wisconsin abortion clinic, and Peggy Green, a San Francisco-based activist. Cage said she wanted to "improve respect for diversity" and "to lessen the gridlock on social legislation" associated with Wisconsin abortion politics. Her approach was circuitous. She brought together pro-choice and pro-life legislators, one from each party, who in turn contacted two leaders each from opposing abortion activist groups. With the help of a professional facilitator, they formed a "focus" or screening group for the state legislative leaders trying to steer family policy and school policy legislation between pro-choice and anti-abortion political shoals. They lasted only thirteen months and disbanded in the fall of 1992.

The longevity of the San Francisco common-ground attempt is similarly precarious. Their main achievement so far has been a three-day retreat held at the end of March 1992. The retreat announcement focused on dialogue: "Our opponents see our slogans, know our loves, feel our sadness. They haven't heard our stories. They don't know why we care." Besides dialogue, San Francisco Common Ground located areas for pro-life/pro-choice cooperation, specifying "the relationship between teenage pregnancy and low self-esteem, the lack of services for pregnant women, the lack of support for working mothers." They concluded that "in all these areas we can work together." But, so far, they haven't.

Enter the Professionals

The pre-Clinton 1990s also marked the late entrance of conflict-resolution professionals into the abortion controversy. In September 1991 the Family Institute of Cambridge (FIC), a Massachusetts family therapy group trying to adapt therapeutic techniques to public controversy, initiated its Public Conversations Project. Six months later, Search for Common Ground, described by its founder John Marks as "social entrepreneurs" seeking "innovative ways" to "reframe contentious issues and to develop viable policy alternatives," added the Common Ground Coalition for Life and Choice to its roster of projects.

Unlike grassroots groups, these professional mediators came to the abortion controversy with ready frames of references and prepared methodologies. The Family Institute of Cambridge found parallels between the "stuck" conversational processes in dysfunctional families and the "stalemated" polemics of abortion adversaries. FIC initiated a highly structured process of dialogue intended to enable abortion opponents to seek understanding rather than victorious debate. Usually four activists, but no organizational leaders, from each side were recruited and instructed to speak from personal experience. No critical responses to each other's reflections were permitted, only questions for clarification. FIC staff report that the more than twenty FIC-facilitated dialogues show some success.[26] If the FIC mediation were to result in any extra-experimental consequences, their likely direction would seem to be toward a depolarization of abortion politics facilitated by professional conflict-resolution professionals.

While the Family Institute staff does not disclose to participants their own positions on legal abortion, the two directors of the Common Ground Coalition for Life and Choice (CGCFLC) do. Mary Jacksteit publicly describes herself as pro-choice, and Adrienne Kaufman, O.S.B., a religious from the Order of St. Benedict, describes herself as pro-life. CGCFLC's goals are explicitly wider than dialogue. They propose to "reframe" the abortion controversy so that abortion adversaries "can find a basis on which they can collaborate on specific projects." Indeed, CGCFLC envisions an ambitious national network of local groups "working with a common-ground approach to abortion." On 5–6 March 1993 CGCFLC sponsored a national meeting of local common-ground efforts. Attending were the familiar ones reported by the media (from St. Louis, Wisconsin, San Francisco, Cambridge, and Buffalo). In his preface to Search for Common Ground's 1992 annual report, which goes by the same name as the organization, President John Marks describes its approach as "enlightened self-interest": "We are convinced that adversarial ways of dealing with conflict are inadequate and that alternatives exist. We promote 'win-win' approaches. The idea is to find solutions that maximize the gain of involved parties. We believe that once adversaries recognize that they share interests, they can often work together and become partners in satisfying mutual needs" (p. 4). So far, the Common Ground Coalition for Life and Choice has been involved in one grassroots effort, in Buffalo, New York. They were invited by the Council of Churches after Operation Rescue's April–May 1992 "Spring of Life Campaign" gave new and public intensity to the community's and the churches' many disagreements over legal abortion. The Buffalo Coalition for Common Ground has sponsored two weekend workshops, and its steering committee (twenty-two individuals who formally represent no abortion social-movement organization) in September 1992 circulated a Mission Statement:

> Buffalo Coalition for Common Ground is a voluntary association dedicated to the promotion of cooperative alternative approaches for addressing problems that deeply divide the Greater Buffalo Community. Without requiring persons of different views to abandon their principles or activities, the goal of the Buffalo Coalition for Common Ground is to diminish polarization through (1) identifying mutual concerns; (2) creating models for collaboration, among persons of different views, for finding solutions that benefit the community; (3) promoting and facilitating, as needed, projects undertaken by collaborative partnerships that develop.

Toward the Future

Before the 1992 election, the media coverage reported common ground in the less challenging but more familiar categories of dialogue, pluralism, and inclusion. Indeed, two exceptionally clear examples of authentic common ground were never included in media reports, nor were their participants invited to national meetings of "officially" designated common-ground efforts. Neither called itself "common ground," and neither was primarily interested in depolarizing the abortion controversy by accommodating it to the normal political processes of compromise. The media could not assimilate either effort in the category of pluralism. In both instances, principled pro-life and pro-choice activists joined to reduce the growing pressures on women to abort. The first example shows how grassroots common-ground efforts that remain in the voluntary private sector can begin at any time, in any place, and in any political climate. The second shows the formidable difficulties even powerful common-ground coalitions face when they move beyond voluntarism and into the political arena.

In February 1992 a grassroots group composed of six pro-life and six pro-choice women published the *North Carolina Piedmont Area Directory of Pregnancy Support Services*, a sixty-four-page comprehensive guide to available state and community services for pregnant women needing medical, financial, housing, and legal assistance, family counseling, and child care. The *Directory* contained special sections for working mothers and college students. The project's founder, Joanna A. Ellis-Monaghan, a member of *Feminists for Life*, explained that "it's really hard to track down these resources. They're there, but they're not all together. . . . A newly pregnant woman trying to contend with the physical and emotional demands of pregnancy often doesn't have time or strength to hunt for these resources and this can have a powerful impact on her decision of whether or not to abort her pregnancy." In her published advice for other pro-life activists Ellis-Monaghan explains that "although the *Directory* does not actually discourage or prevent other organizations from referring for or performing abortions, these agencies *are* distributing the directories to their clients. Thus women who contact these organizations have a much better chance of getting life-affirming information and immediate access to concrete, comprehensive support for pregnancy and afterward than they would have previously." She explained that, without pro-choice cooperation, "you may end up putting a lot of work into a directory and finding out that only pro-life crisis pregnancy centers and some churches will use it."[27]

To my mind, the most significant (unnamed) common ground happened in New Jersey when official representatives of the New Jersey chapters of the National Organization for Women and the American Civil Liberties Union joined with the leadership of New Jersey Citizens for Life, the New Jersey Right to Life Committee, the New Jersey State Catholic Conference, the U.S. Catholic

Conference, and others, including the Educational and Legal Defense Fund of the National Association for the Advancement of Colored People and the Puerto Rican Legal Defense and Educational Funds, to protest a New Jersey welfare reform bill, the Family Development Act (FDA), which was passed by the state legislature and signed into law by Democratic governor Jim Florio on 21 January 1992. While the act contained several provisions agreeable to almost all partisans (such as mandated job training, better coordination of state services, and the removal of the "marriage penalty"), pro-life and pro-choice (but not Planned Parenthood or the National Abortion Rights Action League) organizations formed a coalition to protest the bill's novel "additional child provision (ACP)." Contrary to its title, ACP was intended to make more certain that in New Jersey there would be *fewer* additional children born to women below the poverty level. The phrase "additional child provision" actually meant "no additional welfare provisions." Henceforth, New Jersey would provide no medical assistance or any increase in family benefits to a woman who became pregnant while receiving welfare. For such a women, "choice" now included choosing between abortion and even deeper family poverty. NOW and ACLU representatives objected that in New Jersey women now had to trade their reproductive rights for welfare assistance. Abortion opponents objected that the ACP would cause more abortions. Bishop James McHugh and the New Jersey Catholic Conference protested that "combined with the state's policy of paying for abortion, the state, in effect, will coerce poor women to have an abortion as a cost-saving measure."[28] Other states actively considering a New Jersey approach to welfare reform include California, Kansas, Louisiana, Wisconsin, and Wyoming. More state reforms modeled after New Jersey's "additional child provision" are likely. President Clinton appointed Florio as chairman of a national task force, the State and Local Task Force on Welfare Reform. Reluctant taxpayers are not likely to protest measures such as New Jersey's "additional child provision," especially those who causally link race and poverty. The New Jersey NAACP notes that black (48 percent) and Puerto Rican women (28 percent) are disproportionately affected by the ACP. In his televised reelection campaign ads, New Jersey Governor Jim Florio featured his signing of the "additional child provision." His successful Republican opponent, Christine Todd Whitman, also supported the provision.

Confronted by powerful forces driven by considerations of taxes, poor women, welfare costs, and, probably, race, even a formidable common-ground coalition failed, although a lawsuit continues. This is worth thinking about, especially in terms of other common-ground efforts that intend to move beyond the familiar category of dialogue and pluralism. A likely direction in American society is more legal abortion with less choice, especially for poorer women but also for the many millions of working- and middle-class women precariously balancing the conflicting demands of work and family. If common ground is narrowly aimed at increased toleration and respect for pluralism, it cannot be expected to contribute much to counter a near-dominant economism that systematically subverts both pro-life and pro-choice principles by subordinating all family-related concerns to issues of economic efficiency and increased productivity. The legitimacy of modern societies increasingly rests on the demonstrated ability of elected national officials to satisfy ever-increasing consumer needs. A polity whose legitimacy is practically achieved by this forever escalating criterion is especially threatened by any sizable populations that, by the criterion of economic efficiency, are unproductive and may be even superfluous. Abortion adversaries will not quickly see such economism as a common threat to both their principles and even less quickly acknowledge it as a shared test of their conflicting but now politically linked loyalties. Perhaps after their abandonment by Republican fiscal conservatives, abortion opponents, shown by polls to be less affluent than legal abortion supporters, will again publicly draw the connection between economic reform and pro-life principle.[29] In turn, a greater number of pro-choice activists might publicly distinguish the principle of reproductive choices from the population-control activists committed to the self-interested premise that population control is the major key to world stability. Without constant critique, a consumer society whose public moral discourse is pretty nearly exhausted by an "equality" defined almost entirely as "equal opportunity" cannot be expected to remain effectively "abortion neutral" in fact as well as slogan. Some attention by activists, opinion molders, and scholars to the nascent moral category of common ground and the fledgling groups seeking to define it can contribute to such efforts.

Notes

1. Colin Francome, *Abortion Freedom: A Worldwide Movement* (Boston: George Allen & Unwin, 1984), 210.
2. The Catholic Health Association, *Setting Relationships Right: A Proposal for Systemic Healthcare Reform* (Saint Louis: The Association, 1993), x; *Catholic Trends* 24, no. 5 (25 September 1993), 1.
3. Helen Alvare, *Origins*, 25 March 1993, 701; Judie Brown, "American Life League," letter to members, 5 April 1993; *National Right to Life News*, 30 March 1993.
4. Nancy Myers, "Hitting a New Low in Bias," *National Right to Life News*, 30 March 1993, 4.
5. *New York Times*, 19 July 1993.
6. *New York Times*, 9 November 1993, B8.
7. Robert Casey, "To the House of Representatives of the Commonwealth of Pennsylvania: Veto of the Abortion Control Act of 1987," 17 December 1987.
8. 8 July 1992 address at Boston College.
9. Robert P. Casey, "Children First, Before and After Birth," 3 March address at a conference sponsored by the U.S. Catholic Conference, Department of Social Development and World Peace, the Campaign for Human Development, Catholic Charities U.S.A., and Catholic Relief Services, in *Origins* 22, no. 40 (18 March 1993): 696–99.
10. Robert P. Casey, "A Law without Honor," 11 March 1993 address to the confer-

ence on Abortion and Public Policy at St. Louis University, *Human Life Review* 19, no. 2 (1993): 54–64.

11. *U.S. News & World Report*, 19 October 1992, 27.

12. Robert P. Casey, "What I Would Have Told the Democrats," *Wall Street Journal*, 31 July 1992. See also "The Democratic Party and Abortion," Casey's 11 May presentation to the National Press Club, Washington, D.C., in *National Right to Life News*, 14 June 1993, 4; "Abortion and the Democratic Party," 2 April address to the University of Notre Dame Law School, in *Origins* 22, no. 1 (1992): 10–13. Address to the Catholic League Mid-West Regional Dinner, 25 September 1992, in *Catholic League Newsletter*, December 1992, 7–10.

13. Cf. Alan I. Abramowitz, "It's Abortion, Stupid: Policy Voting in the 1992 Presidential Election," paper delivered at the annual meeting of the American Political Science Association, 2–5 September 1993.

14. Francome, *Abortion Freedom*, 59, 64; also see Peter J. Donaldson, *Nature against Us: The United States and the World Population Problem, 1965–1980* (Raleigh: The University of North Carolina Press, 1991); Dennis Hodgson, "The Ideological Origins of the Population Association of America," *Population and Development Review* 17, no. 1 (March 1991): 1–34; Betsy Hartmann, *Reproductive Rights and Wrongs* (New York: Harper & Row, 1987); and Kurt W. Back, *Family Planning and Population Control* (Boston: Twayne, 1989).

15. Suzanne Staggenborg, *The Pro-Choice Movement: Organization and Activism in the Abortion Conflict* (New York: Oxford University Press, 1987), 25.

16. Ibid., 19.

17. Paige Comstack Cunningham, *A Strategic—and Caring—Agenda for the Next Four Years*, Americans United For Life newsletter, 1 May 1993; also see her *European Abortion Laws Put America to Shame*, Americans United For Life newsletter, August 1993, 1; Mary Ann Glendon and George Weigel, "Catholic Politicians Must Fight Abortion," *Newsday*, 8 May 1990; also see Mary Ann Glendon, "Life after Roe: Widening the Discussion," *Church*, Winter 1993, 5–9.

18. Anna Quindlen, "Going Nowhere," *New York Times*, 23 June 1993; Ronald Dworkin, *Life's Dominion* (New York: Knopf, 1993).

19. Wanda Frantz, "The President's Column," *National Right to Life News*, 9 March 1993; Randall Terry, *Operation Rescue Newsletter*, Summer 1993; Marilyn Koop, "Uncommon Cause, Common Ground," and Mary Bea Stout, "Abortion Defenders Bearing Gifts," *Sisterlife*, Summer 1993.

20. J. Anthony Lukas, *Common Ground* (New York: Knopf, 1985). Still, the title fits. With enormous empathy, Lucacs captures the backgrounds animating the different positions of the key players in the controversy and the poverty common to the black and white families directly affected by the ruling. In effect, the book argues for analyzing equal rights in a substantive framework larger, and even more challenging, than the legal equality formally achieved through the courts.

21. Laurence H. Tribe, *Abortion: The Clash of Absolutes* (New York: Norton, 1990); Roger Rosenblatt, *Life Itself: Abortion in the American Mind* (New York: Random House, 1992).

22. Rosenblatt, *Life Itself*, 9–10 and 178.

23. Ronald Dworkin, *Life's Dominion* (New York: Alfred A. Knopf, 1993), 9.

24. Telephone Interviews with L. Wagner, 19 March and 31 March 1993.

25. James R. Kelly, "Toward Complexity: The Right-To-Life Movement," in *Research in the Social Scientific Study of Religion* (Greenwich, Conn.: JAI Press, 1989), 1: 83–107.

26. Carol Becker, Laura Chasin, Richard Chasin, Margaret Herzig, and Sally Ann

Roth, "Fostering Dialogue on Abortion," *Conscience* 13, no. 3 (Autumn 1992), 2–9.

27. From a communication sent by Ellis-Monaghan in response to inquiries about the *Directory*.

28. Bishop James T. McHugh, "New Jersey Opts to Punish the Poor in 'Welfare Reform,'" *The Monitor* (newspaper of the Camden Diocese), 27 February 1992, 14.

29. James R. Kelly, "Learning and Teaching Consistency: Catholics and the Right-to-Life Movement," in *The Catholic Church and the Politics of Abortion: A View from the States*, ed. Timothy A. Byrnes and Mary C. Segers (Boulder, Colo.: Westview Press, 1992).

12 | The Pro-Choice Movement Post-*Casey*: Preserving Access

The central issue for the pro-choice movement in the 1990s is preserving access to abortion. Access here means the safety of abortion clinics and the availability of abortion to all women. Pro-choice advocates view as one of their chief objectives the inclusion of abortion coverage in national health insurance plans and the extension of poor women's eligibility for Medicaid funding of abortion. They also place top priority on safety issues including prevention of clinic violence and harassment of clinic personnel. To be sure, abortion rights activists still worry about the outright recriminalization of abortion. But after the victory of President Clinton in the 1992 elections and the Supreme Court's decision in *Planned Parenthood of Southeastern Pennsylvania v. Casey*, their concerns are directed more to issues of clinic safety and abortion availability.

At the same time, pro-choice advocates do not think that the right to abortion enunciated in *Roe v. Wade* is fully secure. They worry that the Supreme Court has subjected a woman's constitutional right to burdensome restrictions and state regulations. They therefore continue to favor codifying *Roe* as the law of the land through congressional approval of the Freedom of Choice Act (FOCA) and through state laws such as those passed by Connecticut in 1990 and Maryland in 1991 and 1992.[1] Pro-choice advocates also seek opportunities to challenge state regulations mandating informed consent and twenty-four-hour waiting periods as unduly burdensome to women. Nevertheless, FOCA has receded in importance as issues of abortion access and clinic safety have come to the fore.

This chapter reviews recent efforts of the pro-choice movement to preserve access to abortion. The first section describes pro-choice reaction to the *Webster* and *Casey* decisions. Pro-choice advocates anticipated the Supreme Court's deci-

225

sion in *Webster* by mobilizing activists for two major marches in Washington in 1989 and by coordinating the presentation of *amicus* briefs to the Court in *Webster*. They expected *Webster* to be damaging to their position and prepared a strong media campaign for the state elections and legislative maneuvering that followed the Court's ruling. The 1992 Supreme Court decision in *Casey* also evoked strong criticism from pro-choice advocates, who viewed the Court's decision as seriously weakening the fundamental right to abortion. They reacted to *Casey* by redefining the issue from abortion narrowly conceived to the broader concept of reproductive rights, and by mobilizing for the 1992 presidential election campaign. Proclaiming that the Court was one vote away from reversing *Roe*, movement organizations worked actively to ensure the election of pro-choice Democrat Bill Clinton as president.

The second section reviews briefly the impact of Clinton administration decisions on access to abortion. Through executive orders, Supreme Court nominations, and cabinet appointments, the Clinton administration has reversed policies inherited from the Reagan and Bush administrations and has generally altered the parameters of abortion politics. At the same time, as a result of the Clinton victory in 1992, the pro-choice movement has suffered to some extent from complacency and loss of momentum, as well as disagreement over the Freedom of Choice Act.

The third section of this chapter examines pro-choice reaction to the continuing problems of clinic violence and harassment of clinic personnel. After a brief look at the statistics on clinic vandalism, we review recent Supreme Court decisions, lower court decisions awarding compensatory and punitive damages to abortion clinics, and congressional passage of the Freedom of Access to Clinic Entrances Act (FACE). We also examine the problem of continuing harassment of abortion physicians and other clinic staff. The National Abortion Federation and other groups in the pro-choice movement worry about a shortage of physicians trained and willing to perform abortions and have taken steps to remedy this deficiency. Access to RU-486, the French abortion pill, actively sought by the Clinton administration, may make it easier for nonclinic and nonsurgical physicians to perform abortions.

The fourth and final section examines Medicaid funding of abortion coverage for poor women and inclusion of abortion in any future national health insurance program. Congressional regulation of Medicaid abortions has been broadened under the Clinton administration, but individual states are challenging the right of the federal government to set standards for the state's portion of Medicaid funding. The debate over inclusion of abortion coverage as a basic benefit in any national health plan continues to be fierce and bitter. There are compelling arguments on each side of the debate, and it is difficult to predict how this will be resolved.

This chapter concludes with comments about future directions of the pro-choice movement. In order to do this we need to be clear at the outset what we

mean by "pro-choice movement." Staggenborg describes the pro-choice movement as "a remarkable reform movement that succeeded first in legalizing abortion and later in remaining mobilized to become a significant force in American
politics."[2] Initially begun in the period from the 1930s through the 1950s, the
original movement was a loose organization of professionals including physicians who feared prosecution for performing illegal therapeutic abortions, demographers worried about overpopulation, public health officials concerned
about maternal mortality from illegal abortions, social workers concerned about
family poverty, and police officials disturbed by illegal abortionists' defiance of
anti-abortion laws. Staggenborg's fascinating sociological account of the development and maintenance of this reform movement shows how the movement
began to attract a critical mass of supporters as a result of the social-protest
movements of the 1960s and the family planning movement that had become
institutionalized by the 1960s. The civil rights struggle, the antiwar protest, and
later the women's liberation movement provided key constituents for pro-choice
organizations, including women, students, and clergy. Likewise, the network of
Planned Parenthood clinics and the Clergy Consultation Service on Abortion
provided an organizational base as well as a tactic—"abortion referrals"—that
helped mobilize movement participants.

Although *Roe* was a signal victory for pro-choice advocates, the movement
did not decline after *Roe*, but survived, according to Staggenborg, for two reasons: it developed formalized organizational structures and professional leadership; and it countermobilized in response to increasing threats from a developing
right-to-life movement. Today, pro-choice advocates and activists are drawn
from a variety of major organizations, including the Planned Parenthood Federation of America (PPFA), the National Organization for Women (NOW), the
National Abortion and Reproductive Rights Action League (NARAL), the Religious Coalition for Abortion Rights (RCAR), the National Abortion Federation
(NAF), Catholics for a Free Choice (CFFC), the Center for Reproductive Law
and Policy in New York City, the National Women's Health Network, and a
variety of other organizations, such as the American Civil Liberties Union
(ACLU), the League of Women Voters, the American Association of University
Women, and the Women's Law Project. Planned Parenthood, NOW, NARAL,
CFFC, and RCAR have affiliated organizations in many states. In addition, the
pro-choice movement includes many statewide organizations such as Right to
Choose in New Jersey, Pro-Choice Arizona, Coalition for Choice in Massachu-
setts, and Pro-Choice of Washington.

Pro-Choice Reaction to the *Webster* and *Casey* Decisions

As we noted in the introduction to this volume, *Webster* and *Casey* returned
some regulatory initiative to the states and thus refederalized the abortion issue.

The struggle over abortion law and policy is now conducted at both national and state levels, with increasing attention given to state attempts to regulate abortion. This development has presented a real challenge to both the pro-life and pro-choice movements. After *Webster,* the pro-life movement was ready with model laws for state legislatures to consider. The pro-choice movement reacted with two strategies. First, they sought to redefine the abortion issue, to frame it in terms of the locus of decision making—individual women or state governments. Second, they sought to broaden the scope of conflict from courts to legislative and electoral struggles.

Pro-choice organizations were moderately successful in both strategies. They had prepared for the *Webster* decision by redefining the central issue in abortion politics as the right to decide, and by organizing a massive media campaign to get out the message. They also broadened the scope of conflict. At the national level, pro-choice advocates made use of the federal courts, including the Supreme Court, and they aggressively pursued congressional legislation to make access to abortion safer and more widely available. They also organized massive marches both before and after the *Webster* decision. In April 1989 they brought more than 300,000 pro-choice supporters to Washington to show their strength; the following November, another 150,000 descended on the nation's capital. Simultaneously, pro-choice activists organized large "Mobilize for Women's Lives" rallies in more than 150 cities and towns across the United States—from Maine to Missouri to California, where 50,000 Los Angeles marchers caused a gigantic traffic jam.[3] Between the April march in Washington and the November rallies in various states, pro-choice advocates struggled to adjust to the new post-*Webster* politics of abortion where state politics mattered.

Pro-choice organizers also had initial successes in the 1989 and 1990 state elections. NOW and NARAL actively participated in the 1989 New Jersey and Virginia gubernatorial elections, which pitted pro-choice Democrats against pro-life Republicans. In each state, the pro-choice candidate won—Governor Jim Florio in New Jersey and Governor Douglas Wilder in Virginia. Also in 1989, pro-choice activists in Florida created enough pressure at a special legislative session to defeat Governor Bob Martinez's proposed restrictions on abortion.

In the 1990 state elections, governors' seats in the large populous states of Florida, Texas, and California shifted from anti-abortion to pro-choice hands, and NARAL claimed at least partial credit for these pro-choice victories. According to NARAL researchers, the 1990 elections increased the number of governors who favored keeping abortion legal from sixteen to twenty-seven, and the number of state legislative bodies that favored keeping abortion legal from twenty-three to forty-five.[4] Pro-choice organizers were also heartened by the actions of four states—Connecticut, Maryland, Nevada, and Washington—that passed laws liberalizing abortion after *Webster*. The Connecticut General Assembly acted in 1990 to legalize all abortions prior to viability (in effect writing

Roe into state law), but required counseling for minors under the age of sixteen. Maryland passed a similar measure in 1991 which was approved by voter referendum in 1992 by a 2–1 margin. Nevada voters passed a similar codification of *Roe* by a ballot initiative in 1990. And Washington voters passed the Reproductive Privacy Act in 1991, which provides that a woman has a fundamental right to reproductive choice.[5]

Nevertheless, the political context and climate in 1989–92 was not altogether favorable for the pro-choice movement. Following *Webster,* pro-choice organizations lobbied for congressional passage of less restrictive abortion laws. Both houses of Congress voted to allow the District of Columbia to use its tax revenues to pay for poor women's abortions, only to have the measure vetoed by President Bush. In October 1989 the president vetoed a Labor–Health and Human Services appropriations bill that broadened Medicaid funding to cover abortion in cases of rape and incest. He also made clear his intention to veto any reproductive rights bill or Freedom of Choice Act that Congress sent to him.

For its part, the Supreme Court upheld Ohio and Minnesota parental notification statutes in 1990, and in 1991, in *Rust v. Sullivan,* the Court upheld a 1988 Reagan administration Health and Human Services regulation (the "gag rule") banning abortion counseling in any federally funded family planning clinic.[6] President Bush's nominations of David Souter and Clarence Thomas to the Supreme Court further alarmed pro-choice advocates. Amid heightened speculation that *Roe* would be overturned, the Court announced that it would hear a challenge to Pennsylvania's 1989 post-*Webster* restrictive law in the case of *Planned Parenthood of Southeastern Pennsylvania v. Casey* (1992).

In *Casey,* the Court both reaffirmed a woman's right to abortion and permitted states to restrict that right. At issue were provisions of the 1989 Pennsylvania Abortion Control Act that required parental consent, spousal notification, abortion counseling by a physician as a prerequisite for obtaining a woman's informed consent, and a mandatory twenty-four-hour waiting period before an abortion could be performed. A badly splintered Supreme Court upheld legal abortion as stated in *Roe*, but also upheld most of the Pennsylvania restrictions (spousal notification excluded). Needless to say, pro-choice advocates were not pleased with the Court's ruling and disputed those who characterized the *Casey* decision as a reaffirmation of abortion rights. They expressed concern over the extent to which *Roe* was redefined. In its ruling the Court rejected *Roe's* trimester framework for balancing the interests of the woman and the government. The Court also lowered the standard of review for the constitutional right of privacy where abortion is concerned. The time-honored standard used by the *Roe* Court was "strict scrutiny," under which a state law infringing on a constitutional right is valid when there exists a "compelling governmental interest" for its enforcement. *Casey* lowered this standard so that a state law could be upheld as long as it did not impose an "undue burden" on the woman.

Pro-choice activists regard the restrictive provisions upheld in *Casey* as cruel and humiliating laws, designed to deny women their constitutional right through harassment, red tape, and delay. They view such provisions as particularly burdensome for women of modest income, who often must travel long distances to abortion clinics and who must therefore bear higher costs because of the mandatory twenty-four-hour waiting period. In a letter to the *New York Times*, Congressman Don Edwards (D-Calif.) noted that "Mississippi's 24-hour waiting period has enabled protesters to record the license plate numbers of women's cars parked at clinics, obtain their names and addresses, and harass them and their families at home. Anti-abortion groups have gone as far as informing a woman's neighbors of her decision to have an abortion."[7]

Some pro-choice organizations reacted to *Casey* by broadening their agendas. Two groups in particular, NARAL and RCAR, changed their names and redefined their goals to include sex education, prevention of teen pregnancy, and access to family planning. NARAL changed its name from the National Abortion Rights Action League to the National Abortion and Reproductive Rights Action League, while retaining its acronym. In addition to its traditional work for safe, legal abortion, NARAL will focus on sexuality education, improved contraception, and increased access to pre- and postnatal care. As part of its ongoing electoral and campaign efforts, the organization will also respond to the increase in Religious Right activism in school board races. The Religious Coalition for Abortion Rights (RCAR), an association of thirty-five member organizations dedicated to voicing support from the religious community for reproductive rights, also revised its agenda in order to support women's reproductive health and freedom as well as abortion rights. RCAR changed its name to the Religious Coalition for Reproductive Choice to reflect its expanded mission more accurately: "to ensure that every woman is free to make decisions about when to have children according to her own conscience and religious beliefs, without government interference."[8]

There were only a few political options open to pro-choice organizations after *Casey*. They could lobby Congress to pass the Freedom of Choice Act (FOCA), knowing full well that President Bush would veto the bill. They could collect empirical data showing that the provisions of the Pennsylvania law (a model for laws in fifteen other states) were, in practice, unduly burdensome for women; but this kind of lawsuit would take several years. Or they could work hard to ensure the victory of a pro-choice president in the 1992 elections, in hopes that such a president would change the ideological complexion of the Supreme Court and reverse some of the restrictive anti-abortion laws enacted during the Reagan-Bush years.

As we know, pro-choice advocates chose to concentrate their energies on this third option. NARAL, NOW, and other organizations worked actively to support Democrat Bill Clinton, who argued throughout the campaign that abortion should be "safe, legal, and rare." Pro-choice organizers were aided by political action committees (PACs) such as the Democratic-oriented EMILY's List (Early Money Is Like Yeast) and the Republican WISH List (Women in the Senate and House), two fund-raising groups that directed money solely to the campaigns of candidates who supported a woman's right to decide. Pro-choice groups also benefited from the record number of women candidates who ran for Congress in 1992—a majority of whom were pro-choice. Although the economy may have been the most important issue of the 1992 race, pro-choice activists declared that, after *Casey*, *Roe* was dead, and stressed the necessity of electing a Democratic, pro-choice president who would reverse the ideological drift of a conservative Supreme Court.

The Clinton Administration and Abortion Policy

This political strategy of the pro-choice movement was successful. The election of President Clinton in November 1992 generally altered the parameters of abortion politics and changed the climate to one more favorable to abortion rights supporters. In presidential policymaking and appointments, the Clinton administration clearly has taken steps to improve access to abortion.

Immediately after his inauguration in January 1993, President Clinton signed five executive orders reversing restrictive abortion policies inherited from the Bush administration. He reversed the ban on abortion counseling in federally funded family planning clinics; overturned the moratorium on federally funded research involving the use of fetal tissue; ordered a study of the current ban on import of RU-486, the French abortion pill, for personal use; revoked the prohibition on abortions in military hospitals; and voided the "Mexico City policy," which forbade U.S. foreign aid funds to agencies promoting abortions.[9] The president signed these executive orders on 22 January 1993, the twentieth anniversary of *Roe v. Wade*. Since 22 January is the day pro-life activists annually hold their "March for Life" in Washington, the symbolic significance of Clinton's actions was not lost on either right-to-life advocates or, for that matter, pro-choice advocates.

President Clinton also underscored a commitment to broaden access to abortion through his cabinet and subcabinet appointments. Attorney General Janet Reno is an outspoken critic of clinic violence and testified during her confirmation hearings that, under her direction, the Justice Department would vigorously protect the right of access to abortion clinics. Surgeon General Dr. Joycelyn Elders is a strong supporter of legalized abortion, sex education, and contraceptive dissemination as ways to combat widespread teenage pregnancy. Secretary of Health and Human Services Donna Shalala has supervised negotiations with the French manufacturer of the abortion pill RU-486 to bring the drug into the United States for testing; she has also testified regularly on Capitol Hill in support of legislation such as the Freedom of Access to Clinic Entrances Act (FACE) and the inclusion of abortion coverage in any national health plan. Clinton also appointed Walter Dellinger to be assistant attorney general for the Office of Legal Counsel; while at Duke University, this constitutional scholar wrote numerous articles and *amicus* briefs developing the legal theories that support a woman's constitutional right to choose abortion.

In addition to cabinet appointments, of course, President Clinton has thus far been presented with two opportunities to nominate justices to the Supreme Court. In 1993, he appointed Ruth Bader Ginsburg, a firm abortion rights advocate, to fill the seat vacated by Justice Byron White. In May 1994, he appointed Stephen G. Breyer to fill the seat vacated by Justice Harry Blackmun. Breyer is a moderate liberal with impeccable legal credentials who is regarded as prochoice. As a federal judge on the U.S. Court of Appeals for the First Circuit, Judge Breyer dissented from a 1989 decision that challenged the constitutionality of a state law requiring parental consent for a minor's abortion. At the same time, Judge Breyer found unconstitutional the "gag rule" that prohibited federally financed clinics from counseling women on abortion.[10] Since Breyer has few rulings on abortion-related cases, pro-choice advocates have been cautious in their praise of his nomination. Nevertheless, the general view is that, in naming Breyer to the High Court, President Clinton has kept his 1992 campaign promise to appoint only justices who would support *Roe v. Wade.*

It seems safe to say that Clinton's judicial nominations will change the ideological complexion of the Supreme Court on abortion law. At the same time, the issues before the Court no longer involve the relatively simple question of whether *Roe* will be preserved. Instead, they are complex issues, such as whether protesters can block clinics or whether federal laws against racketeering can be used against direct action anti-abortion groups such as Operation Rescue. President Clinton has appointed two Supreme Court justices who are liberal centrists and careful jurists. It is not easy to predict how they will rule in some of the complex reproductive rights cases that may come before the Court in the near future.

In addition to the appointments he has made, President Clinton's administration has developed several policy initiatives generally welcomed by pro-choice advocates. On 26 May 1994 he signed the Freedom of Access to Clinic Entrances Act (FACE), a federal law that prohibits the use or threat of force or physical obstruction to deny anyone access to abortion clinics.[11] On 16 May 1994, after sustained political pressure from the Clinton administration, Roussel Uclaf, the French manufacturer of the controversial abortion pill RU-486, agreed to donate the pill's patent rights to the Population Council, a nonprofit contraceptive research group in New York.[12] The Population Council will begin clinical trials immediately, find an American company to produce the pill, and eventually apply to the Food and Drug Administration to license the drug as safe and effective. The advantage of RU-486 is that it presents women with a nonsurgical alternative to abortion. Because it can be prescribed discreetly in the offices of private physicians, it also offers an alternative to running the gauntlet of clinic blockades and protests.[13]

Passage of the FACE law and the agreement to import RU-486 represent major victories for pro-choice groups. As Eleanor Smeal of the Fund for the Feminist Majority noted, "With a one-two punch, the Clinton administration has increased abortion access dramatically."[14] Again, the difference a change in the presidency can make is obvious. The Bush administration banned the importation of RU-486 in 1992. President Clinton overturned the ban in 1993, and over a fourteen-month period in 1993–94, his administration actively pressed for an agreement with the French manufacturer of RU-486 to speed U.S. development of the drug.

At the same time, it would be foolish to minimize what Staggenborg has called the cyclical nature of victories and defeats for both the pro-life and pro-choice movements in the long political struggle over abortion policy in the United States. According to the cycle of action and reaction, mobilization and countermobilization, defeat reinvigorates a movement, whereas victory tends to engender complacency and loss of momentum. The *Webster* and *Casey* decisions reinvigorated the pro-choice movement to organize and mobilize to defend *Roe*. By the same token, the electoral victory of a pro-choice president in 1992 appears to have left many Americans under the impression that abortion rights are no longer at risk in the United States. Pro-choice organizations thus face a twofold challenge: how to sustain membership and momentum in the favorable climate of the Clinton presidency, and how to develop new strategies to accommodate an increasingly complex abortion debate that has moved beyond simple questions of legality to complex issues such as federal funding and parental notification.[15]

Problems for the Pro-Choice Community: Clinic Safety

Clinic violence and harassment of clinic personnel clearly pose major problems to abortion providers and women seeking access to abortion. The National Abortion Federation, a membership association of abortion providers, reports that since 1977 there have been more than 1,500 violent acts at abortion clinics nationwide. These include 37 bombings, 87 cases of arson, 178 death threats, 31 burglaries, 91 assaults, 300 bomb threats, 567 incidents of vandalism, and 2 kidnappings. There have been 525 clinic blockades and 31,230 arrests of protesters at abortion clinics. The cost of such blockades to city and county law enforcement officials between 1988 and 1993 totaled more than $3 million. Between 1992 and May 1994, the cost to abortion clinics of noxious chemical vandalism (use of tear gas and butyric acid) at clinics was $853,050.

Clinic staff have also been the victims of violent and disruptive actions. In

July 1994, Dr. John B. Britton and his volunteer escort, James H. Barrett, were shot to death outside a women's clinic in Pensacola, Florida. In March 1993 Dr. David Gunn was shot and killed at another abortion clinic in Pensacola. Yet another incident occurred in August 1993, when Dr. George Tiller was shot twice and wounded outside his clinic in Wichita, Kansas. Since 1993, NAF has tabulated 192 incidents of stalking, defined as the persistent following, threatening, and harassing of an abortion provider, staff member, family member, or patient *away from* the clinic. In addition, clinic personnel are regularly subjected to harassing phone calls and hate mail (more than 1,400 such incidents have been reported to NAF since 1991).[16] Ironically, some extremists in the anti-abortion movement now argue that killing abortion doctors is justifiable homicide, mandated by the Bible. This is the view of Paul Hill, a former Presbyterian minister and anti-abortion protester, who was charged with the 1994 shootings in Pensacola. Hill was indicted by federal authorities on charges of violating the Freedom of Access to Clinic Entrances law and by Florida officials on murder charges.

Pro-choice organizations have taken legal action at federal and state levels to combat clinic blockades and violence. Initially, protesters were arrested for violating state trespass laws and ordinances against disturbing the peace. In state courts, lawsuits have been filed against clinic blockaders such as Operation Rescue. But the first line of attack for pro-choice advocates has been federal courts, since clinic disruption occurs in many states and has the character of a nationwide problem.

Initially, federal courts enjoined Operation Rescue and other groups from blockading clinics under an 1871 law, the Ku Klux Klan Act, which prohibits conspiracies to deprive people of their civil rights. Ultimately, this question of whether federal courts may enjoin anti-abortion protesters from impeding access to clinics was appealed to the Supreme Court. In early 1993, in *Bray v. Alexandria Women's Health Clinic,* the Rehnquist Court ruled that abortion clinic operators could not invoke the Ku Klux Klan Act of 1871 in suing those who block women's access to abortion clinics.[17]

A year later, however, in January 1994, the Court ruled unanimously that clinics could invoke the federal racketeering law (RICO) to sue violent anti-abortion protest groups for damages. The issue in *NOW v. Scheidler* did not concern abortion itself, but was about how broadly to interpret a major federal law, the Racketeer Influenced and Corrupt Organizations Act (RICO). In an eight-year-old lawsuit, the National Organization for Women (NOW) had accused Operation Rescue and several other groups and individuals of running a nationwide conspiracy to drive abortion clinics out of business through a campaign of intimidation, bombings, and other violent acts. Since the Court has ruled affirmatively on the applicability of RICO (to clinic blockades), NOW must go back to federal district court in Chicago and prove that the disruptive acts were part of a "pattern of racketeering activity" undertaken by the groups named in the lawsuit.[18]

The Supreme Court's decision in the RICO case gives abortion clinics a potentially powerful legal weapon—including the prospect of triple damages—to combat and possibly deter the violence that has made it increasingly risky and expensive for the clinics to keep their doors open. The ruling also means that federal judges may invoke RICO to issue injunctions against pro-life protests and clinic blockades. Thus, from a pro-choice perspective, the Court's decision in *NOW v. Scheidler* seems to compensate for the 1993 decision in *Bray* that clinic operators cannot invoke the 1871 Klan law to sue those who block women's access to abortion clinics.

Moreover, the *Bray* ruling and the murder of Dr. David Gunn led to an effort in Congress to provide more federal protection for women seeking abortions and ultimately to passage of the Freedom of Access to Clinic Entrances law. As mentioned earlier, FACE was passed by the House and Senate and signed by President Clinton in May 1994. FACE makes it a federal crime to use or attempt to use force, threats, or physical obstruction to injure, intimidate, or interfere with anyone providing or receiving abortions and other reproductive health services. The legislation defines "interfering" as restricting a person's ability to move and "physical obstruction" as making access to a clinic impossible or unreasonably difficult. Examples of such nonviolent acts of physical obstruction include chaining protesters to doorways and staging sit-ins.

FACE subjects protesters to jail time and stiff fines if they block access to clinics. The law imposes a fine of up to $10,000 and a jail term of up to six months for first-time offenders convicted of "nonviolent physical obstruction"; subsequent convictions carry greater penalties. For violent actions (where someone is injured), the penalty for a first offense is one year in jail and a fine of up to $100,000; again, subsequent convictions carry larger penalties. FACE also allows abortion clinic employees and clients to sue protesters in federal court for damages stemming from violations of the law, and empowers federal judges to enjoin protesters and fine those who violate an injunction.[19]

The clinic protection bill elicited broad support from both parties in Congress. The Senate approved the bill 69–30, following a 241–174 favorable House vote. Its relatively speedy passage through Congress and into law was expedited, no doubt, by a Democratic administration. But the legislation was also propelled by a spate of unusually violent attacks in 1993, including several firebombings of abortion clinics and the slaying of Dr. Gunn in Florida. It represents a triumph for pro-choice advocates, who have labored for years to bring what they regard as an increasingly lawless anti-abortion movement under the jurisdiction of federal judges and marshals.

Pro-life advocates are highly critical of the law, arguing that the measure was intended less to quell anti-abortion violence than to rob that movement of a hallowed protest tactic wielded historically with great success by more liberal causes: peaceful civil disobedience. They also contend that the law violates First

Amendment rights to free speech and freedom of religion. Immediately after President Clinton signed the bill into law, two anti-abortion groups filed suit in federal court, seeking an injunction against its enforcement until the court has time to consider its constitutionality. The American Life League sought to prevent the new law from taking effect. The American Center for Law and Justice, an anti-abortion public interest law firm affiliated with the evangelist Pat Robertson, filed suit on behalf of Operation Rescue and Randall Terry, contending that the law violates the religious freedom of these protesters and "shows the ever-growing anti-Christian persecution that is coming from our government."[20]

Pro-choice attorneys defend the law, saying it punishes behavior, not speech. In fact, the new law explicitly exempts from punishment any conduct shielded by the First Amendment's free speech and assembly clause, such as peaceful picketing, chanting, and passing out leaflets. Moreover, they argue, courts have never held sit-ins and blockades to be acts of free speech. Sit-ins were always recognized as civil disobedience—that is, the violation of law with the expectation of arrest and jail for one's illegal actions. What is new about the FACE clinic protection law are the much heavier fines and jail terms this law imposes (in contrast to the $100 fines and overnight jail stays that traditional sit-ins frequently carry). Pro-choice advocates justify these more severe penalties by differentiating a sit-in at an ordinary building from a blockade of an abortion clinic. In their view, access to an abortion clinic involves a woman's constitutional right to privacy and must remain unimpeded under protection of federal law, whereas acts of ordinary trespass involve different kinds of rights and can be enforced locally.

A strong indication of how courts may adjudicate the free speech of anti-abortion protesters was provided by the Supreme Court at the conclusion of its 1993–94 term. In *Madsen v. Women's Health Center,* the Court, in a 6–3 decision written by Chief Justice Rehnquist, ruled that a state judge did not violate the First Amendment when he ordered protesters to demonstrate quietly and keep at least thirty-six feet from a Florida abortion clinic. The chief justice, citing Florida's interests in assuring public safety, public order, and the health of patients, said the thirty-six-foot buffer zone "burdens no more speech than necessary to accomplish the governmental interest at stake." At the same time, the Court struck down stricter restraints, including a ban on protesters trying to speak to patients within three hundred feet of the clinic, as excessively curbing of rights of free speech.[21]

Coming a month after passage of the Freedom of Access to Clinic Entrances Act, the Supreme Court's decision gives timely guidance to judges who must implement the new law safeguarding clinics. As mentioned above, FACE provides federal remedies, including injunctions and criminal penalties, for riotous and violent protests at abortion clinics. With constitutional challenges to the new law already filed and possibly headed for the Supreme Court, the justices' decision in *Madsen* indicates that broad constitutional attacks on the new law are likely to fail. In short, *Madsen* and FACE are significant victories for pro-choice advocates seeking to protect access to abortion.[22]

It appears that with strong federal legislation and strong state court rulings, clinic violence and disruption (blockades) may decline if not cease, although peaceful clinic protests will probably continue. Much depends on the consistent application of heavy penalties to violators. It should be noted that pro-choice advocates have successfully sued protesters in state courts. In May 1994, a Texas jury ordered abortion protesters to pay $204,000 in actual compensatory damages to Planned Parenthood of Southeast Texas for conspiring to disrupt operations at Houston abortion clinics during the 1992 Republican National Convention. In addition, two protest groups in the case, Operation Rescue and Rescue American-National, were ordered to pay more than $1 million in punitive damages to Planned Parenthood. In another case, the U.S. Supreme Court refused to consider an appeal of an $8.2 million damage award by an Oregon jury to a clinic in Portland.[23]

These civil awards are the largest ever won against the anti-abortion protest movement. Smaller monetary awards, based on actual damages only, have been levied in Kansas, California, and New York State. Health-care providers have had difficulty in collecting the funds, however. At the same time, clinic violence and disruption in these states has declined since the awards were made. Thus, pro-choice advocates believe that the threat of large monetary damages might do far more than the threat of jail to deter many abortion opponents from blocking access to clinics and harassing clinic personnel and patients.

Problems for the Pro-Choice Community: Abortion Availability

If the advent of a Democratic administration in Washington in 1993 has enabled pro-choice organizations to secure legislation protecting access to abortion clinics, it has also magnified opportunities for pro-choice advocates to realize one of their most cherished goals: the availability of abortion to all women regardless of their socioeconomic status. Currently, the principal vehicle for achieving equity in reproductive health care is expanding the Medicaid program that funds health care for the indigent. Since 1977, anti-abortion groups have successfully restricted Medicaid funding of abortion for low-income women through passage of the Hyde Amendment (named after its sponsor, Representative Henry Hyde, Republican from Illinois). But since the Clinton administration came to power, a quiet battle has been under way to roll back restrictions on federal financing of the abortions of low-income women. This continuing effort consists of two principal initiatives: expanding Medicaid coverage and including abortion in any future national health insurance program.

Federal Financing of Poor Women's Abortions
through Medicaid

Jointly funded by federal and state governments, the Medicaid program is designed to provide comprehensive medical services to low-income individuals. Under Medicaid, the federal government establishes a minimum standard of covered medical care. While states are free to use their own funds to expand their health programs, they cannot drop below the standard set by Congress. States are free not to participate in Medicaid, but once a state opts to take part, it must cover at least those services that make up the federal package of covered care. States that do not comply risk losing their entire federal Medicaid budgets.

The struggle over Medicaid began almost immediately after Clinton's inauguration and has preoccupied pro-choice groups throughout 1993–94. In reality, this campaign is a dress rehearsal for the main event—the debate over inclusion of abortion coverage in national health reform. In April 1993, President Clinton's first budget proposed dropping the ban on federally financed abortions. On 30 June 1993, however, the House of Representatives, by a vote of 255–178, approved a modified version of the Hyde Amendment, which extended Medicaid coverage to rape and incest survivors but failed to broaden coverage for all women.[24] On 28 September 1993, the Senate, by a vote of 59–40, rejected a committee amendment that would have ended the sixteen-year virtual ban on Medicaid coverage of abortion.[25] What emerged from Congress, then, was a slight expansion of Medicaid coverage to include cases of rape and incest as well as life endangerment; since 1981, government-financed abortions have been legal only if the pregnancy threatened the woman's life. President Clinton signed the appropriations bill on 21 October 1993. Two months later, the Health Care Financing Administration (HCFA), the federal agency that oversees Medicaid, issued a directive requiring states to pay for abortions for low-income women made pregnant by rape or incest.[26]

Several states balked at the new federal directive, saying that it conflicts with provisions of their state constitutions or statutory laws and that, in any case, Congress intended funding in cases of rape and incest to be optional, not mandatory, for the states. State Medicaid directors claimed that the federal government did not consult them before issuing the order, and that the directive was issued improperly, with no opportunity for public comment.[27] In a letter to President Clinton in January 1994, Governor Robert Casey of Pennsylvania announced that he would not comply with the administration's order and said that the federal government had exceeded its authority in trying to override Pennsylvania's state law permitting such payments only when the rape or incest had been reported to local law enforcement or health officials. In March Governor Casey filed a lawsuit in federal district court seeking to enjoin the federal directive and asserting that the administration's interpretation of federal Medicaid law required him to flout state law.[28] In a related development, in February 1994,

Congressman Jay Dickey (R-Ariz.) introduced a bill to allow states to decide whether or not to provide Medicaid coverage of abortions in cases of rape or incest. Dickey claimed that the federal policy requiring coverage of such abortions represents an "unfair and illegal burden" to the many states not yet in compliance with the new HCFA directive.[29]

Despite the protests by some state Medicaid directors, the Clinton administration is standing behind the HCFA interpretation of the 1993 Hyde Amendment approved by Congress. Medicaid officials insist that their reading of the law is correct and that Congress intended to require states to pay for abortions when pregnancies resulted from rape or incest. They contend that states are required to cover abortions that are medically necessary and that, by its action last year, Congress added abortions for rape and incest to the category of medically necessary abortions. Finally, they insist that the federal directive is in accord with the decisions of four federal courts of appeal holding that Medicaid programs must cover all abortions eligible for federal reimbursement.[30]

It is estimated that the new Medicaid policy would require Medicaid coverage for only about 1,000 abortions a year. Since we are not talking about a large number of abortions, the controversy over the Clinton administration directive apparently has symbolic importance for the various parties to the argument. Expanding Medicaid coverage in even a small way seems to be a kind of dress rehearsal for the larger expansion of coverage promised in a national health insurance reform. There is also the reality that the previous version of the Hyde Amendment, which prohibited federal financing of abortions except for life-endangered pregnancies, was in effect for almost fourteen years and that many states adjusted their Medicaid programs to that federal standard. The Center for Reproductive Law and Policy (CRLP) reports that statutes, regulations, or constitutional amendments in thirty-one states mirror the previous version of the Hyde Amendment. These states, especially Arkansas and Colorado, where the near bans on Medicaid coverage for abortion were adopted as amendments to their state constitutions, need time to bring state law into accordance with the new federal standard.[31] To help these states do this, CRLP has filed suit in federal district courts in Arkansas, Colorado, Louisiana, North Dakota, Oklahoma, Pennsylvania, and Michigan, challenging these states' virtual prohibition on Medicaid funding and arguing that their laws are invalid because they conflict with the version of the Hyde Amendment adopted by Congress as part of the most recent federal Medicaid budget. In five other states—Florida, Minnesota, Montana, Texas, and West Virginia—CRLP has challenged Medicaid funding restrictions in state courts.[32]

It appears that pro-choice attorneys are seeking to establish a track record of court decisions that can be used to support federal financing of abortions in some cases. This strategy may be preparatory to anticipated legal challenges, should abortion be eliminated from any future health-care plan.

Federal Financing of Abortions through
National Health Insurance

The battle over Medicaid coverage of abortion is merely a prelude to the much greater policy debate over inclusion of abortion in any future national health insurance program. The position of pro-choice advocates is clear on health-care reform. They favor a plan with a defined benefits package, which must be spelled out clearly and explicitly, and which must include abortion coverage. Officials of pro-choice organizations such as NARAL, Planned Parenthood, and NOW have indicated that these groups will not support health-care reform unless it includes abortion coverage as part of the basic benefits package.[33]

President Clinton's health plan, proposed in September 1993, does include abortion coverage as part of its basic benefits package. The word "abortion" does not appear in the plan. The term "pregnancy-related services" is used to designate a range of health services for women: contraception, Pap smears, mammograms, family planning, prenatal care, and abortion. The idea is to provide complete health coverage for women. Abortion is treated as a health issue and a health decision.

What the Clinton health plan would do, of course, is to restructure health-care financing and blur existing lines between the middle class and the poor. The Clinton plan envisions folding most Medicaid recipients, and the government money for their care, into the same regional alliances (insurance pools) as everyone else, with access to the same basic benefits. Employers and individuals will pay the vast majority of insurance premiums under this national managed-care system. But tax money would be used to subsidize the premiums of small companies and those that pay low wages, as well as for low-income people now receiving Medicaid benefits and for an additional 37 million people who are now uninsured. This unified system with subsidies for the poor would largely erase the line between federal and private money in the health insurance system. And it would give abortion rights supporters a goal they have sought for seventeen years: a health system that does not differentiate between the well-to-do and the poor in access to abortion. It would render obsolete the current two-tiered system with its restrictive Hyde Amendments.

Comments made thus far by President and Mrs. Clinton outline the arguments being used for inclusion of abortion in the health plan. One argument is that the plan maintains the status quo, the coverage that exists for most women right now, which extends to pregnancy-related services including abortion. Pro-life forces argue that it is misleading to think that this plan continues the status quo because poor women, previously dependent solely on Medicaid-restricted funds, will now have access to abortion. Abortion rights advocates counter that since the majority of health insurance plans already cover abortions, any effort by the government to strip the national plan of abortion coverage would amount to a major reduction in benefits and a government intrusion into the rights of patients.

A second argument made by the Clintons for inclusion of abortion coverage in the health plan is that hospitals, doctors, and other health-care workers who do not wish to in any way condone or provide or participate in abortion would have a conscience exemption. Such a conscience clause would allow them to choose not to perform the procedures. Nevertheless, right-to-life advocates insist that even under the new plan taxpayers would still be supporting the abortions performed, even though federal financing would make up only a tiny part of the overall spending on health care (most of it would be paid for by employers, insurers, and individuals).

There may not be any satisfactory answer to the objections of those who say they do not want their tax dollars connected to abortion services in any way, particularly since the Clinton health plan would mix together and blur the lines between federal and private monies. In fact, even under our current two-tiered system, tax dollars are used to fund abortions for federal government employees, abortions performed in military hospitals, and abortions for poor women whose pregnancies result from rape or incest or are life threatening. So there may be no satisfactory way to ease the consciences of anti-abortion advocates concerned that their tax dollars are being used to fund abortions. Nevertheless, the Clintons emphasize that health providers who object to abortion on moral grounds will not be required to condone or participate in abortion or to violate their conscience beliefs. Moreover, the Clintons have stressed that the basic benefits package would also expand family planning services to prevent the need for abortion.

The deeper opposition of pro-lifers to inclusion of abortion coverage in national health insurance could be reduced to two fundamental points: (1) abortion is not health care, but is an unjustifiable destruction of human life; and (2) since all benefits would be federally mandated under the Clinton health plan, the inclusion of abortion would amount to a government endorsement of the procedure. The intractability of the abortion conflict is illustrated by the response of pro-choice advocates to these objections: (1) abortion is an issue of reproductive health, involving physicians and routinely taking place in medical settings; and (2) failure to cover abortion would amount to government disapproval of the procedure. Since it is impossible for government to be neutral on this issue, it is best to leave decision making to the individual, and this the Clinton health plan does.

In my judgment, this review of arguments about inclusion of abortion in national health insurance illustrates the narrow range of discussion and the complexity of a unified system of health care in the United States. Ultimately, this issue is a question of values, involving considerations of distributive justice and equality for poor people and respect for the religious and conscience beliefs of those deeply opposed to abortion on moral grounds. More immediately, this issue will be resolved practically—through politics. Those who organize and bring pressure to bear most effectively on Congress and the administration will prevail. As abortion rights supporters and abortion opponents mobilize for the big battle, each side must make a judgment about how far it will push and where it will compromise (if, indeed, it will compromise at all). In any case, the mix of largely private monies with a small amount of government Medicaid funds will make it virtually impossible to restrict federal money the way the Hyde Amendment now does.

It is difficult to predict how this battle over health-care policy will turn out. Right-to-life forces have been bombarding Congress with telephone calls and postcards urging their representatives to exclude abortion coverage from the plan. Pro-choice groups have also mobilized grassroots supporters to lobby Congress; on 18 May 1994, abortion rights supporters tied up the congressional switchboard with calls for inclusion of abortion coverage. As of this writing, all four congressional committees that produced versions of a health-care bill resisted attempts to eliminate abortion coverage.[34] All sides expect a fierce floor fight over abortion in both the House and the Senate, however. Most congressional observers expect this issue to test severely the ability of congressional leaders to produce acceptable health-care legislation.

Conclusion

This review of the fortunes of the pro-choice movement post-*Casey* indicates how professionalized and well organized the movement is and how much it relies on specialized litigational interest groups such as the CRLP and lobbying organizations such as NARAL to continue the struggle to protect women's reproductive rights and preserve access to abortion. Initially, after *Webster* in 1989, the pro-choice movement geared itself for political mobilization and campaigning in statewide elections in 1989 and 1990. Through state affiliates, NARAL, NOW, Planned Parenthood, and RCAR were successful in electing pro-choice governors and state representatives. In the wake of *Casey,* however, pro-choice organizations seem to have relied on specialized legal assistance and professional lobbying to secure legislation protecting clinics from disruption and expanding Medicaid coverage for low-income women.

What emerges clearly from this review is how important the White House is to abortion politics and policy. The shift from the Bush presidency to the Clinton administration improved considerably the chances of pro-choice advocates to see their proposals enacted into law. Having a pro-choice president matters—in Supreme Court appointments, on the importation of RU-486, in clinic protection laws, and on federal directives to states on Medicaid coverage of poor women's abortions. Of course, state politics matters also, but this review shows, I think, how the federal government can set the tone on abortion policy for the nation as a whole.

Congress is generally more responsive to grassroots lobbying, and it is here, I think, on the issue of abortion funding in Medicaid programs and health-care plans, that pro-life forces may have an advantage over their pro-choice counterparts. But it is still too early and too difficult to tell whether a new national health plan will include abortion under its basic benefits package.

Finally, there are no indications that the intensity of abortion politics will decrease in the near future. Pro-choice organizations are deeply concerned about welfare reform and the coercive use of contraceptives such as Norplant. They will continue searching for empirical evidence that post-*Casey* state regulations, such as informed consent and mandatory waiting periods, are "unduly burdensome" to women—in order to challenge the new standard of review enunciated by the Supreme Court in *Casey*. And they are growing increasingly concerned about the aggressive campaigning of Religious Right activists for seats on local school boards in order to set school policies on sex education, contraception, and AIDS prevention. In other words, the culture wars will continue, and the political struggle over abortion policy on the federal and state level shows no signs of abating.

Notes

1. Telephone interview with Leslie Meyers, Legislative Affairs Department, National Abortion and Reproductive Rights Action League (NARAL), 16 May 1994. On Connecticut, see Spencer McCoy Clapp, "Leading the Nation after *Webster:* Connecticut's Abortion Law," in *The Catholic Church and the Politics of Abortion: A View from the States,* ed. Timothy A. Byrnes and Mary C. Segers (Boulder, Colo.: Westview Press, 1992), 118–36. On Maryland, see chapter 3 by Eliza Newlin Carney in this volume.

2. Suzanne Staggenborg, *The Pro-Choice Movement: Organization and Activism in the Abortion Conflict* (New York: Oxford University Press, 1991), 148. See also David J. Garrow, *Liberty and Sexuality: The Right to Privacy and the Making of Roe v. Wade* (New York: Macmillan, 1994); and Kristin Luker, *Abortion and the Politics of Motherhood* (Berkeley: University of California Press, 1984).

3. Barbara H. Craig and David M. O'Brien, *Abortion and American Politics* (Chatham, N.J.: Chatham House, 1993), 307–8.

4. *Who Decides? A State-by-State Review of Abortion Rights,* 3rd ed. (Washington, D.C.: NARAL Foundation, 1992), i.

5. For Maryland and Washington, see chapter 3 by Eliza Newlin Carney and chapter 8 by Mary Hanna in this volume.

6. See *Hodgson v. Minnesota,* 497 U.S. 417 (1990); *Ohio v. Akron Center for Reproductive Health,* 497 U.S. 502 (1990); and *Rust v. Sullivan,* 111 S.Ct. 1759 (1991).

7. Representative Don Edwards (D-Calif.), "Roe's Legacy Is Hardly Secure," *New York Times,* 24 April 1994, 16.

8. Center for Reproductive Law and Policy (CRLP), *Reproductive Freedom News* 3, no. 1 (14 January 1994), 6–7.

9. See *Origins* 22, no. 34 (4 February 1993): 574.

10. *New York Times,* 17 May 1994, A14. See also CRLP, *Reproductive Freedom News* 3, no. 10 (27 May 1994): 2. As we go to press, Judge Breyer has indicated at his Senate confirmation hearings his support for *Roe v. Wade* as settled law, but he has

refused to comment on specific details of state abortion laws that might come under future Supreme Court scrutiny. *Boston Globe*, 13 July 1994, 12.

11. *Star-Ledger*, 27 May 1994, 1, 4. *Congressional Quarterly*, 30 April 1994, 1070, and 7 May 1994, 1131. See also *New York Times,* 13 May 1994, A1, A22; *Star-Ledger*, 13 May 1994, 1, 5.

12. *New York Times*, 17 May 1994, A1, A16; *Star-Ledger*, 17 May 1994, 1, 3.

13. An RU-486 abortion is by no means a one-step, hassle-free procedure. RU-486 can be used only in the earliest stages of pregnancy (within the first forty-nine days), and it requires three or four visits to a doctor's office. See Katharine Q. Seelye, "Enter RU-486, Exit Hype," *New York Times*, 22 May 1994, E16.

14. *Star-Ledger*, 27 May 1994, 4.

15. See Eliza Newlin Carney, "Those Winds of Change Are Tricky," *National Journal* , 15 May 1993, 1176–77.

16. Statistics provided to the author by the National Abortion Federation, May 1994. See also *New York Times*, 30 July 1994, 1, and 13 August 1994, 6.

17. Craig and O'Brien, *Abortion and American Politics*, 315, 355.

18. These include Operation Rescue and its founder, Randall Terry; the Pro-Life Action League and its founder, Joseph Scheidler; the Pro-Life Direct Action League, Project Life, and several other individuals. NOW filed the original lawsuit on behalf of two abortion clinics: the Delaware Women's Health Organization in Wilmington and the Summit Women's Health Organization in Milwaukee. See *New York Times,* 25 January 1994, A1, A17; also *Star-Ledger,* 25 January 1994, 1, 6, 7.

19. *New York Times*, 13 May 1994, A1, A22; also *Star-Ledger,* 27 May 1994, 1, 4; also *Reproductive Freedom News* (a publication of the Center for Reproductive Law and Policy), 3, no. 9 (13 May 1994): 6.

20. *Star-Ledger,* 27 May 1994, 4. As of this writing, abortion opponents have filed seven lawsuits in federal courts (in Arizona, California, the District of Columbia, Florida, Louisiana, Virginia, and Wisconsin) challenging the constitutionality of the FACE law. Federal judges have dismissed two of those lawsuits. See CRLP, *Reproductive Freedom News* 3, no. 12 (24 June 1994): 2. In addition, in July 1994, abortion opponents from Operation Rescue, Rescue America, and the Pro-Life Action Network were arrested for blocking clinic entrances in Little Rock, Arkansas. It is expected that they will be charged with violating FACE, the very law they were protesting. *New York Times*, 9 July 1994, 10.

21. *New York Times*, 1 July 1994, A1, A16–17.

22. Telephone interviews with Fran Avallone, executive director, Right to Choose (major pro-choice organization in New Jersey), 17 May 1994 and 3 July 1994.

23. *New York Times,* 7 May 1994, 10, and 10 May 1994, A1, A16. See also CRLP, *Reproductive Freedom News,* 3, no. 9 (13 May 1994): 2–3, 5–6.

24. *Congressional Quarterly Weekly Report* 51, no. 27 (July 3, 1993): 1735–39.

25. *New York Times,* 29 September 1993, A19.

26. *New York Times,* 25 December 1993, 1, 10; and 26 December 1993, 23. See also CRLP, *Reproductive Freedom News* 3, no. 1 (14 January 1994): 5–6. HCFA is part of the Department of Health and Human Services, headed by Secretary Donna Shalala.

27. *New York Times,* 5 January 1994, A1, A12; also, 19 January 1994, A12.

28. The following information may help explain Governor Casey's challenge to, and refusal to comply with, the Clinton administration's Medicaid directive. While purporting to cover abortions in cases of life endangerment, rape, and incest, Pennsylvania law is more restrictive than the Hyde Amendment because it requires a two-physician certification of life endangerment, as well as onerous reporting requirements for survivors of sexual abuse. Pennsylvania's Abortion Control Act allows Medicaid coverage only if a rape or incest survivor personally reports the crime and the perpetrator's name to law

enforcement personnel, or when two doctors certify that a woman will die if she does not obtain an abortion. Because current federal law requires Medicaid coverage of abortions in cases of rape, incest, or life endangerment—without dangerous reporting and certification requirements—pro-choice advocates argue that the Pennsylvania provisions conflict with federal law. This is the rationale behind the complaint filed on 11 January 1994 in which CRLP and Women's Law Project attorneys urged a federal district court to enjoin Pennsylvania's virtual ban on abortion coverage for Medicaid-eligible women. It should be noted that, under the new Medicaid directive, definitions of rape and incest are to be determined by state law. Moreover, states may impose "reasonable reporting or documentation requirements." According to Medicaid officials, however, states must ensure that these requirements do not deny or impede Medicaid coverage and that a physician may waive the requirement if he or she certifies that a woman is unable, for physical or psychological reasons, to comply. See *Reproductive Freedom News,* 3, no. 1 (14 January 1994): 2–3, and vol. 3, no. 7 (15 April 1994): 3. See also *New York Times,* 5 January 1994, A1, A12.

29. CRLP, *Reproductive Freedom News,* 3, no. 5 (11 March 1994): 4; also vol. 3, no. 6 (1 April 1994): 3; see also *New York Times,* 19 January 1994, A12.

30. *New York Times,* 5 January 1994, A1, A12. CRLP, *Reproductive Freedom News,* 3, no. 1 (14 January 1994): 5.

31. For example, Barbara D. Matula, the Medicaid director in North Carolina, said the federal directive had not created a problem in her state. North Carolina has been using its own money to pay for abortions in cases of rape or incest, and now the federal government will share the cost, she said. But she noted: "States are divided on this issue. There are states for which this directive presents legal problems, and they are quite rightly exercised about it. They have to change their laws, and they don't have enough time to do so. There are other states like North Carolina that don't have a problem. We all have concerns about the process, the fact that we were not consulted before the directive was issued." *New York Times,* 19 January 1994, A12. See also chapter 6 by Ruth Ann Strickland in this volume.

32. CRLP, *Reproductive Freedom News* 3, no. 12 (24 June 1994): 3.

33. Telephone interview with Leslie Meyers, Legislative Affairs Department, National Abortion and Reproductive Rights Action League (NARAL), 16 May 1994.

34. *New York Times,* 14 July 1994, A16.

TIMOTHY A. BYRNES

Conclusion: The Future of Abortion Politics in American States

The ten case studies that make up the heart of this book have offered us a tremendous amount of information concerning the politics of abortion in the American states. They have described the very different ways in which various states have approached the issue of abortion. They have offered explanations for the diverse outcomes that have emerged from these processes. And in many cases they have pointed to general directions in which abortion policy is likely to move in the future. My task, in this concluding chapter, is to build on these case studies by viewing them collectively rather than individually. Here I am not so interested in a particular state, but in what these ten states, as a group, tell us about the past, present, and future of abortion politics in the United States.

I approach this task in two closely related ways. First, I examine the tremendous diversity represented by these ten states and their politics of abortion. I point to the very different policies that states have adopted in this regard and to the perhaps surprisingly diverse political processes that produced those policies. Second, I use the findings of the ten case studies to offer a series of explanations for the differences across states in terms of their abortion policies. Why do these states differ so dramatically? What particular attributes of the ten states account for these differences?

My explanatory analysis draws on previous work in this field. A number of excellent studies using aggregate data have identified the key factors that explain the variation in state abortion policies.[1] Most of the variables I examine are similar to those examined by others. The difference between this analysis and others, indeed the fundamental distinguishing feature of this collaborative proj-

246

ect, is that I am working with material drawn from in-depth case studies. Jeffrey Stonecash has trenchantly pointed out the limitations of studying state politics through the use of statistical indices of all fifty states. "Because it is difficult and very costly to get data on all 50 states," he argues, "we often have to look where the light is (i.e., where data can be acquired relatively easily) and accept less than satisfactory results."[2] These results, Stonecash maintains, often do not reflect the rich, complex political circumstances that pertain in the American states. The cases included in this volume tried to capture as much as possible of this richness and complexity of state politics. In fact, taken as a whole this volume establishes that the case-study method is a very valuable way of examining the political phenomena that have played such powerful roles in framing abortion policy across the country.

Defining Difference

The first and clearest conclusion we can draw from reviewing our representative sample of cases is that the politics and law of abortion in America differ tremendously from state to state. In clear, emphatic detail, the case studies reveal the different policies that states have adopted toward abortion and the very different processes that have produced those policies. Most obviously, some states have tried to restrict access to abortion after *Webster* and *Casey* and others have not. Louisiana and Pennsylvania, to cite the two clearest examples, took the Supreme Court's decisions as invitations to curtail sharply the availability of abortion in their borders. Washington and Maryland, in contrast, took the decisions as portents of the future and acted to insulate women in their states from further erosions of federal abortion rights in the future. In whatever direction a given state moved, it is indisputable that states now have more freedom to regulate abortion than they had before 1989 and that states are acting on this freedom to frame policies that fit most comfortably with their particular historical, social, and political circumstances.

Glen Halva-Neubauer has argued elsewhere that *Roe v. Wade* federalized, but did not nationalize, abortion policy in the United States.[3] A national constitutional right to abortion, he argues, did not eradicate state government jurisdiction over abortion. Instead, it limited that jurisdiction and inaugurated a dialogue between state legislators and governors, on the one hand, and the federal judiciary, on the other. These ten case studies serve in a sense as an indication of the current state of that dialogue. Some states respond to the court's openings with restrictions; some respond with liberalizations; and some find it difficult to respond immediately as political forces unleashed by the openings contend with each other in the state legislature, governor's mansion, or state political process at large.

Beyond the obvious and wholly expected differences in policy is the tremendous diversity in process uncovered by our case studies. Louisiana and Pennsylvania, again, are clear examples of straightforward legislative processes. In both states, the legislatures passed restrictive abortion laws, one with the governor's signature, one over the governor's veto. But in other states, the process is not nearly so simple. Even among states where the voters themselves had the opportunity directly to set policy, the diversity of approach was impressive. In Arizona, citizens voted on a referendum that would have restricted abortion through an amendment to the state's constitution; in Maryland, the state legislature first passed a statute protecting the right to abortion and then, as a result of an anti-abortion petition drive, put that statute before the people in a statewide referendum; and in Washington State, a pro-choice petition drive placed an "indirect initiative" before the state legislature. Then, once the legislature refused to act on it, the initiative was acted on by the voters in a statewide ballot.

Some of our cases also highlighted the contemporary vitality and significance of the various state judicial systems. Of particular interest are such states as California and Massachusetts, which have state constitutional rights to privacy that are more explicit, and therefore less assailable, than the national right. John Kincaid has defined "the new federalism" as "the willingness of state courts to exercise their long dormant authority to base the protection of individual rights on independent interpretations of state constitutional rights rather than U.S. constitutional rights."[4] Something like this has already occurred in Massachusetts with regard to state funding of abortion, and it seems likely that California's right to privacy would insulate the right to abortion in California from both federal court decision and state legislative action. Indeed, abortion would seem to be a key aspect of this "new federalism," and the role of state courts on this issue bears close watching in the future.[5]

Those of us who deal with federalism in undergraduate classrooms often need to convince our students, at first, of the continuing viability and significance of the concept. California really is different from Louisiana, I have often said, not only socially and economically, but politically, legally, and even constitutionally. The case studies in this book certainly offer vivid support for that contention. The states themselves, their political cultures, their institutional settings and their political processes, continue to vary greatly over 200 years after the drafting of the Constitution. And those differences, at the moment at least, are graphically illustrated by their various policies on abortion.

In *Federalist 39* James Madison assured partisans of state power that the U.S. Constitution created a national government of "enumerated objects only, and [left] to the several states a residuary and inviolable sovereignty over all other objects."[6] In time, of course, Madison's notion of dual federalism has given way to less stark and more sophisticated formulations of intergovernmental relations; it is now questionable at best to consider any aspect of state sovereignty truly "inviolable." Nevertheless, one aspect of that sovereignty, legislative and judicial initiative on the issue of abortion, has clearly moved back to the states in the last five years. The effects of this development should not be overstated, but they have, in ways that are deeply significant to millions of women, shifted emphasis from United and placed it on States.

Accounting for Difference

More important than the description of difference is the explanation of it. What accounts for the fact that American states have responded so differently to their enhanced initiative on the issue of abortion? As I stated earlier, a number of studies have already offered answers to this important question. These studies identified key independent variables and related them to the dependent variable of state-level abortion policy. The contributors to this volume have relied on many of these same variables, and their conclusions are in some instances quite consistent with conclusions drawn from aggregate studies. As a collectivity, however, the contributors to this volume approached the question much more inductively. The editors supplied them with a series of variables, which I discuss below, but our main instructions were for each contributor to examine closely the politics of abortion in his or her state and identify those dimensions, or variables, that best explain the outcome in the particular state. Here, having assessed all the case studies carefully, I pull these explanations together and offer a more general account for the diversity of abortion policy in American states.

The variables we discussed with our contributors, and those that proved most powerful in explaining particular outcomes, fall into two broad categories. The first is what I have chosen to call contextual variables, aspects of a given state that set a specific context in which particular abortion policies are set. More specifically, these contextual dimensions or variables are (1) the state's policies on abortion before *Roe v. Wade*, (2) the state's political culture, and (3) its public opinion on legal abortion. The second category, political variables, is composed of those aspects of the state's political life that are likely to have a direct and tangible effect on a given piece of abortion legislation or public policy. Included in this category are (1) the strength of various abortion-related interest groups, particularly groups related to religious institutions or movements; (2) the role of the governor; (3) the nature of party politics in the state; and (4) the influence of female legislators on the state's abortion policies.

Over the course of this conclusion I take each of these variables in turn and discuss the degree to which they help explain the diversity of contemporary abortion policy depicted so vividly in chapters 1–10. This chapter, and the book, ends with some comments on the degree to which our collective findings can point to the trajectory that abortion policy is likely to take in the future.

Contextual Explanations

Pre-Roe, Post-Webster

The simplest, and in some ways the best, explanation for a given state's contemporary policy toward abortion is that state's policy toward abortion before 1973. "Past is prologue," one might hypothesize; the more restrictive a state was before *Roe*, the more restrictive that state is likely to be after *Webster*. Our case studies offer substantial support for this hypothesis, but they also counsel caution in applying it, and clearly indicate its explanatory limitations.

Our ten states' policies on abortion pre-*Roe* fell into the following four categories.[7]

Abortion Legal for Any Reason:	Washington State
Abortion Legal to Protect the Physical and Mental Health of the Pregnant Woman:	California, Maryland, North Carolina
Abortion Legal Only to Save the Pregnant Woman's Life:	Arizona, Massachusetts, Minnesota, Ohio
No Legal Abortion:	Louisiana, Pennsylvania

Again, a quick review of the results of the case studies reveals that this past is indeed quite a prologue, particularly at the poles. Pennsylvania and Louisiana, the most restrictive before *Roe*, have taken the most restrictive actions since *Webster*. And Washington State, the most unrestrictive before *Roe*, has passed the most liberalized and protective policy since *Webster*. Moving in from the poles, the consistency is less remarkable, but still instructive. California, Maryland, and North Carolina, all home to liberalized abortion law before *Roe*, are now home to liberal abortion law in the 1990s. In contrast, Minnesota, Massachusetts, and Ohio, quite restrictive before *Roe*, are now on uncertain ground, "shifting" or "steering" toward some middle position.

These findings, all in all, lend support to the notion that *Roe v. Wade* short-circuited a process whereby the fifty American states were headed in the 1970s to continued diversity in terms of their receptiveness to legal abortion. Indeed, these findings suggest that while *law* concerning abortion was affected powerfully by *Roe v. Wade*, the *politics* of abortion may not have changed all that dramatically in many places over the past two decades. Some states were very resistant to abortion rights then, and many of those same states remain resistant now.

That said, this hypothesis should not be oversold. For one thing it does not account for all our state case studies. Arizona, in particular, stands out as a state that does not fit this pattern. Arizona was quite restrictive before *Roe*, but as we have seen, its people handily defeated an anti-abortion initiative in 1992. For that matter, the whole group of states under the heading "abortion legal only to protect the woman's life" seems to be drifting in the pro-choice direction. None of these states—Minnesota, Massachusetts, or Ohio—seems likely to pass the kind of firmly restrictive statute that their pasts might predict.

This hypothesis also should not be oversold because our case studies have revealed just what a blunt instrument it is. What if the people of Washington State, instead of passing Initiative 120 by 4,222 votes, had voted it down by a similar margin? Would we then have to adjust our findings accordingly? Hanna's case study makes clear that the referendum in Washington was a very complex affair that was influenced by a number of factors, some of which had nothing to with abortion. Her analysis suggests that simple categorizations such as this, though surely helpful in drawing aggregate conclusions, should be used with extreme caution when accounting for particular outcomes in a given state or predicting outcomes in similar states.

Finally, the "past is prologue" hypothesis is, in the final analysis, intellectually unsatisfying. It is not so much an explanation for outcomes as it is a surrogate for some *other* aspect of the states that was present both before 1973 and after 1989. In short, identifying a fairly consistent historical pattern should not be confused with accounting for that pattern. To provide such an account we must look at other contextual facets of the states and to the particular political processes that surround the issue of abortion.

Political Culture

Many of our contributors have used the term *political culture* very loosely as a synonym for political context or political setting. That was fine for their purposes as they strove to set the scene for the politics of abortion in their respective states. Here in the conclusion, however, I use the term much more carefully and restrict it to Daniel Elazar's definition of political culture as "the particular pattern of orientation to political action in which each political system is imbedded."[8] Elazar identified three different political subcultures—individualist, traditional, and moralist—and argued that each American state was characterized by some combination of these three. In the individualist political culture, government is viewed in utilitarian terms and "both politicians and citizens look upon political activity as a specialized one, essentially the province of professionals."[9] Traditionalist political cultures, in contrast, are rooted in a "paternalistic and elitist conception of the commonwealth."[10] In these systems political power is confined to "a small and self perpetuating group drawn from an established elite who often inherit their 'right' to govern through family ties or social position."[11] Finally, in moralist cultures politics is geared toward the creation of the good society. Government is considered a "positive instrument with a responsibility to promote the general welfare."[12]

As Halva-Neubauer has pointed out, Elazar conceived political culture as an indicator of political style and process rather than an explanation of policy outcomes. Nevertheless, since outcomes are the primary concern of this volume, we look to see if there is any consistent relationship between political culture and state-level policy on abortion. Susan Hansen included political culture in her multiple regression analysis of abortion in the states and found no significant relationship, but we are interested in seeing whether there is any pattern among our sample of representative states.[13]

The political cultures of our states were classified by Elazar as follows:

> Arizona: Traditionalist-Moralist
> California: Moralist-Individualist
> Louisiana: Traditionalist
> Maryland: Individualist
> Massachusetts: Moralist-Individualist
> Minnesota: Moralist
> North Carolina: Traditionalist-Moralist
> Ohio: Individualist
> Pennsylvania: Individualist
> Washington: Moralist-Individualist

Hansen hypothesized that a moralist political culture would lead to *anti*-abortion policies, but the pattern here, if there is one, runs in exactly the opposite direction. The most firmly pro-choice states (California, Washington, North Carolina) have a powerful moralist element to their political culture. Indeed, the most interesting case in this regard is North Carolina. This arguably most pro-choice southern state is also the *only* member of the old Confederacy with a moralist political culture. And our other moralist cultures, Massachusetts and Minnesota, are both with varying speeds drifting away from restrictive anti-abortion policies. What is going on here?

Hansen's claim was that a moralist political culture would lead to "moralist" policies, as commonly understood, and that the government would prohibit abortion as a way of building a "good society."[14] While superficially plausible, this hypothesis is based on a limited reading of Elazar's categorization. The point is not that certain states will adopt policies that are *moral*; instead, it is that moralist conceptions of the government's role in public life will be deeply rooted in a given state. These conceptions, I hasten to add, could just as easily cohere around individual freedom and a limited role for government policy as they could around policies designed to impose one moral vision or another on the population. Indeed, Elazar himself has concluded that the former is in modern-day America much more likely to be true than the latter. Speaking specifically of policy on abortion, Elazar held that there has apparently been a shift "from a moralist stance against certain kinds of behavior to an equally fervid moralist endorsement of the freedom to engage in such behavior. If," he continued, "abortion was considered immoral forty, or even twenty years ago, today those moralist people who support the right to freely choose abortion tend to view anybody who favors limitations on abortion as, in a sense, rejecting the true faith."[15]

It seems that we have identified something like this shift across a fairly broad spectrum of cases. The moralist political culture may underlie the firm pro-choice inclinations of Californians and North Carolinians. An evolving notion of moralism and its relationship to governmental policy may explain the changes we have observed in Massachusetts and Minnesota. And this freedom-oriented conception of moralist culture may account for the fascinating events in Arizona recounted by Daniel O'Neil. Barry Goldwater and other conservatives opposed Proposition 110 because it was inconsistent with their convictions concerning the proper role of the government in individual private lives; it was unworthy, in short, of a state characterized by a moralist political culture.

Just as with the historical hypothesis, however, we have to be cautious about our claims for political culture. It, too, is a very blunt explanatory instrument, and it does not neatly explain the substantial variation across our sample of cases. I believe we have uncovered an interesting pattern of developments in moralist political cultures, but much work remains to be done. A good place to continue, it seems to me, is the role of public opinion on abortion policy in a given state. Our most basic, some might say simplistic, conceptions of democracy would lead us to expect that the more a state's public expresses opposition to abortion, the more likely that state would be to outlaw it.

Public Opinion

The literature on public opinion and state policy differences, of course, is a testament to how inadequate such simple notions of democracy are. Indeed, largely because of the paucity of reliable state-level data, it is only relatively recently that scholars have established a tangible relationship between public opinion and policy outcomes in the American states. Wright, Erikson, and McIver found in 1987 that states that have populations with liberal political orientations will tend toward the adoption of liberal policies.[16] The process of applying this general conclusion to the specific policy of abortion, however, has proved considerably difficult for a number of reasons. First, Wright, Erikson, and McIver measured general policy liberalism. It is not at all clear that such a general measure can accurately predict any single policy outcome, much less a policy outcome on an issue such as abortion, which might not align itself neatly on an ideological spectrum. "Abortion policy," after all, is a very complex set of policies having to do with availability, funding, parental involvement, and so on.[17] State ideological indices might be related to some but not all of these specific policies.

Despite these difficulties, a good deal of interesting and suggestive analysis has been done recently on the relationship between public opinion and state-level abortion policy. Goggin and Kim, working with a forty-two-state data set that included over 1,500 respondents in each state, found that "state abortion policy does follow state public preferences, although the effect of abortion opinion is mediated by the preferences of the state political actors that make abortion policy."[18] Using a somewhat more complex model, Goggin and Wlezien concluded that state publics react "thermostatically" to the policies formulated by political elites. If those policies are more restrictive than the public wants, for example, then the public will be likely to resist further restrictions on the access to abortion.[19] Not exactly how one describes democratic process to an eight year old, perhaps, but indicative of an important relationship between attitude and policy.

In fact, based on Cohen and Barrilleaux's classification of state public opinion on abortion, it appears that our sample of states is quite supportive of a hypothesis relating opinion to policy in this area.[20] California, one of our most firmly pro-choice states, for example, was characterized by Cohen and Barrilleaux as a "consensus" pro-choice state, with at least a net 36 percent advantage of pro-choice over pro-life respondents among its citizenry.[21] Pennsylvania, in contrast, exhibits only a "majority" pro-choice public opinion (5 percent to 15 percent differential between pro-choice and pro-life), while middle-ground states like Minnesota, Massachusetts, and Ohio all cluster in a category Cohen and Barrilleaux called "landslide" (net 16 percent to 35 percent pro-choice).[22] In terms of our cases, however, these data should be viewed with caution. First, two of our most clear-cut cases, Louisiana and Washington, were not included in Cohen and Barrilleaux's classification. Moreover, it is not clear what these data on public opinion refer to exactly, or which specific policies related to abortion they might best explain. It is also interesting to note in this regard that every one of the states included in Cohen and Barrilleaux's typology was characterized as "pro-choice" in terms of public opinion. It is the degree of "pro-choiceness" (to coin an unwieldy term) that differs.

The primary aim of this volume, however, was not to delve into this conceptual and methodological thicket. The case studies report on public opinion in most instances, but they focus primarily on the processes through which that opinion was "mediated" by policymakers and other political elites and transformed into policy on abortion. As a group, the contributors to this volume acknowledge the significance of public opinion on state-level policy outcomes. But also as a group, they have chosen to leave close analysis of this variable to aggregate analysis, where it can be most useful in leading to broad, albeit limited, conclusions. The case studies in this volume have focused most pointedly on the political institutions and procedures that process that opinion, along with a number of other factors, into policy. Following that lead, then, I now turn to some of those institutions and procedures.

Political Variables

One of the descriptive benefits we have derived from our case studies is a look into the very complex institutional and political settings of the American states. To repeat a point I made earlier, these chapters illustrate graphically how much the states differ, one from another, despite all the nationalizing and centralizing forces at work in American politics today. At this juncture, I want to highlight some of these categories of difference and ask how the particular constellation of political relationships in a given state influences policy. Perhaps, however, I have got this the wrong way around. As Theodore Lowi argued, now three decades ago, the particular set of political relationships that revolve around a given issue may be a function of the *type* of issue under discussion.[23] Lowi identified four policy types—distributive, regulatory, redistributive, and constituent—and argued that the significance of a given political actor or a given political relationship depended on the type of policy being debated or enacted. Regulatory policy would involve a different political process, for example, than would distributive, redistributive, or constituent policy. Politics follows policy, as the aphorism now has it.

Raymond Tatalovich and Byron Daynes have campaigned for a fifth category: social regulatory policy.[24] They, along with others, believe that Lowi's typology does not capture the distinctive political relationships and processes that cohere around such issues as prayer in schools, pornography, affirmative action, and perhaps most starkly, abortion. My intention here is not to join the debate over whether social regulatory policy is subsumed into Lowi's original classification. Instead, my intention is to take Tatalovich and Daynes's category of social regulatory policy and apply it to the formation of abortion policy *in the states*.[25]

Tatalovich and Daynes deal only with *national* social regulatory policy. Indeed, one of their contentions is that "federalism is important to social regulatory policy because historically the states had jurisdiction over most of these issues."[26] We, in this collaborative work, have tried to understand what takes place when that federalism is reinvigorated, when a policy over which the states have "historically" had jurisdiction is returned, at least in part, to state legislatures, governors, and state court systems. What are the most significant political institutions and political relationships when it comes to the making of state-level abortion policy?

Interest Groups

A good place to start drawing this map of state-level abortion politics is with interest groups. Tatalovich and Daynes, who rightly focused a great deal of attention on the role of interest groups in the setting of social regulatory policy, wrote that "single issue groups are the lobbies that most increase public aware-ness and the political significance of social regulatory policy."[27] Tatalovich and Daynes were making this observation about social regulatory policy at the na-tional level, but our contributors certainly found the same to be true of abortion policy in the states. In case after case, we find the key actor in the making of abortion policy to be abortion-related single-issue interest groups, and in many instances we find the relative strength of these groups and the relative effective-ness of their legislative strategies to be the key explanation for the particular policy that ultimately emerges.

At one level, these findings are not at all surprising. James Madison predicted in *Federalist 10* that the size and diversity of the American republic would diminish the influence of any given "faction." But as Thomas and Hrebenar have argued, it is entirely possible that "the lack of economic and social diversity in the states would lead to their domination by a few interests or a single all-powerful interest."[28] Indeed, in their review of the interest communities of all fifty states, Thomas and Hrebenar did find that a few organized interests were often at the heart of a given state's politics.[29] By and large, abortion-related groups were not counted among these (in two they were), but following Lowi, and Tatalovich and Daynes, it makes perfect sense for such groups to dominate the subset of a state's politics devoted to social regulatory policy generally or abor-tion policy specifically.

What is interesting about the role of abortion-related interest groups in abor-tion politics, then, is not their influence—that is wholly unremarkable—but the type of interest that has emerged as most influential. Whereas distributive poli-cies are driven by "clientele" interests, and redistributive policies by "peak" associations, I think it is fair to say that our case studies have established that abortion policy is characterized by the prominent role of "religious" groups. In state after state we find religious organizations, primarily but by no means exclu-sively the Catholic Church, at the center of opposition to abortion and therefore at the center of the legislative and political battles over abortion policy.

The relationship between religion and abortion policy would seem, on the face of things, to be straightforward. Some churches—Catholic, Mormon, and evangelical Protestant in particular—include opposition to abortion as one of the central tenets of their faiths. These churches have been prominent supporters of the right-to-life movement at both national and state levels.[30] Similarly, on the individual level, the connection between religious belief and religious practice, on the one hand, and attitudes toward abortion, on the other, is well estab-lished.[31] Scholars trying to document the relationship between religion and abor-tion policy at the state level, however, have focused, as Stonecash would expect them to, where the light is, where the data are most readily available. For exam-ple, by controlling for a large number of other factors, Susan Hansen was able to conclude that the percentage of a state's population that belonged to the Mormon or Catholic Church correlated with a state's restrictiveness on abortion.[32] And somewhat more broadly, Strickland and Whicker found a link between percentage belonging to "conservative religions" and restrictions on abortion.[33] These findings, though certainly suggestive and interesting, do not exhaust the very complex relationship between religion and public policy in the states.

Our case studies tried to capture some of this complexity by examining the roles of religious groups and institutions in the politics of abortion and attempting to gauge the impact these groups had on the policy of a given state. It is clear, for example, after reading Christine Day's analysis, that the unique constellation of religious forces in Louisiana is a key factor in that state's enduring resistance to legal abortion. It is equally clear that the unusual prominence of the Pennsylvania Catholic Conference has played an important role in producing the many Abortion Control Acts in that state. Moving in from the pro-life pole, of course, we find a great amount of variation across states in the degree to which religious groups and institutions involve themselves in the politics of abortion, and an even greater variation in the degree to which those groups find success once engaged.

It is also true, of course, that religious groups are much more active in opposition to legal abortion than in defense of it. The religious nature of the interest-group spectrum is, on the whole, one-sided. Nevertheless, religious organizations are among the most important players in the state-level interest-group communities that have formed around this issue. They are important players in pro-life states such as Louisiana and Pennsylvania. But they are also deeply involved, albeit in a steeply uphill battle, in Washington, California, Arizona, and Maryland. Anyone seeking to understand the politics of abortion in a given state would be well advised to pay very close attention to what one might call the constellation of organized religious interests in that state.

The Role of the Governor

Another aspect of a state's politics that is deserving of close attention in this regard is the role of the state's governor. As Thad Beyle has written:

> At the top of each state's political and governmental hierarchy is the governor—the person who personifies the state to many. He or she is seen as the most powerful political personality in most states; the state legislature, the state bureaucracy, the state press, the state's politics, and the state's policies are affected by, or bear the imprint of, the governor.[34]

Given the central role that governors play in many states, it is easy to see why Halva-Neubauer included the position of the governor, in conjunction with the positions of legislative leaders and "champions," as an important, albeit not definitive, explanation for state-level variance in post-*Roe* abortion policy.[35] Indeed, the governor appears to have played a very important role in several states included in this volume. Strickland placed great importance on Governor Hunt's support for and protection of public funding of abortion in North Carolina; Halva-Neubauer, not surprisingly, emphasized the effect that individual governors have had on abortion policy in Minnesota; and, according to our case studies, Governor Casey in Pennsylvania, Governor Weld in Massachusetts, and Governor Roemer in Louisiana have all been central players in abortion politics in their states.

It is interesting to note, however, that the significance of the chief executive in state-level abortion politics differs from the role that Tatalovich and Daynes ascribed to presidents in *national* social regulatory policy. Tatalovich and Daynes argue that "presidents do not exert decisive leadership to change social regulatory policy" and that any presidential steps in this area are usually little more than "symbolic gestures."[36] This may be a bit of a misunderstanding in the case of abortion when one considers the influence of presidential appointments on the national Supreme Court. Nevertheless, it is true that President Ronald Reagan, our most clearly pro-life president since *Roe v. Wade*, never did "exert decisive leadership" in a legislative sense to have national abortion policy changed substantially.

A number of reasons suggest themselves for this difference between nation-level and state-level executives. The obvious one is that legislative initiative, since *Roe* and especially since *Webster*, has clearly been in the hands of state governments. While the U.S. Supreme Court was defending the right to abortion, state legislatures were trying to whittle away at that right and governors were either abetting or frustrating those efforts. Governors are important players in state-level abortion legislation, in other words, because governors are important players in all state-level legislation. Indeed, in the light of the Court's decision in *Casey*, state legislative battles over abortion and the governors' central role in them will only take on greater significance as the states try to work out just what an "undue burden" is.[37]

Second, recent scholarship has suggested that state-level electorates, responding perhaps to this matter of jurisdiction, are more interested in abortion than national electorates are, and that voters are "willing to cross party lines to support the [gubernatorial] candidates who support their positions."[38] Governors are by necessity very sensitive to the views and voting preferences of their constituents. They may involve themselves in political and legislative battles over abortion because they have calculated that it is in their interest to do so. At the least, it is now increasingly difficult, after *Casey*, for some governors to get away with the argument that their position on abortion is not relevant because access to abortion is protected by the U.S. Constitution.[39]

Party Politics

Many of the contributors to this volume have paid close attention to the role of political parties—their organizational structures, ideological dispositions, and their competition with one another—in the making of abortion politics. Indeed, the nature of partisan competition over abortion was one of the factors we asked our contributors to examine, and it is not surprising that it proved so important in a number of states. Nevertheless, this is another aspect of the politics of abortion that must be approached with great care and with an eye to the various permutations that can and do arise.

Tatalovich and Daynes found the party dimension of *national* social regulatory policy to be much more straightforward. "Republicans," they noted, "exploit social regulatory policy to mobilize conservative voters whereas Democrats are constrained not to abandon liberalism."[40] Something like this dynamic may be at work in such states as California and Maryland, and the Democratic Party's solid control of those states may therefore account for the solidly pro-choice policies adopted. But, on the whole, forwarding Tatalovich and Daynes's party-ideology argument to state-level abortion policy is dangerous, and in some instances downright inappropriate, for a number of reasons.

First, and perhaps most obviously, the Democratic Party in some states is not "constrained not to abandon liberalism." Far from it. In a number of southern states, Louisiana among them, the Democratic Party is actually quite conservative, at least on issues such as abortion, and the fact that the state is home to a powerful Democratic Party is no indication whatever that the state is likely to pursue pro-choice policies. Second, the issue of abortion continues to cut across standard definitions of conservative and liberal in often confounding ways. Is Pennsylvania's Governor Robert Casey, a Democrat, necessarily a "conservative" because he is a staunch foe of abortion? Is Louisiana's Buddy Roemer a "liberal" because he vetoed, on fairly technical grounds, a bill limiting access to abortion? Just these two examples, and there are many more, make the point that "liberal" and "conservative" are complex labels that are not always clearly related to abortion. In fact, even some of the most ardently anti-abortion leaders of the Catholic Church have at the same time taken a number of "liberal" positions on issues as diverse as labor relations, foreign policy, and protection of the environment.

This is not to argue, of course, that there is no partisan division over abortion, or that that division does not have important implications for public policy on abortion. Strickland's treatment of North Carolina suggests, for example, that even among some southern states, the partisan differences can be determinant. And Nossiff's interesting historical examination of Pennsylvania's Democratic Party may help explain why sometimes those differences can be muted or short-circuited in a given state. But O'Neil's analysis of events in Arizona shows us again just how difficult it is to draw general conclusions in this regard. Just as moralist political culture can, and apparently does, cut both ways on abortion, so conservatism, even within the Republican Party, does not necessarily lead to a pro-life stand on abortion. The role that Barry Goldwater played in Arizona in defining conservatism in the context of the abortion issue is fascinating and may well repeat itself in other states in the future.

At the least, attempts to infer a given state's abortion policy on the basis of that state's partisan politics ought to be based upon some detailed knowledge of the parties in that state. This is the type of analysis that Strickland, Halva-Neubauer, Day, Nossiff, and O'Neil have provided here.

Female Legislators

It is a truism to say that legislators are significant actors in the making of legislation. Of course they are, and state legislative politics and procedures were central elements of almost every case study reported in this volume. What was distinctive about this legislative activity, however, was the particular role played by women in the legislative process. Given that abortion policy affects women in a particular and pointed way, women have often been leading figures in state-level efforts to defend the right to abortion. We saw this phenomenon at work in California, Louisiana, Washington, Maryland, Massachusetts, and Ohio.

These findings are consistent with studies of the role of female legislators in general, and with aggregate studies of the effect of female legislators on state-level abortion policy specifically. Sue Thomas and Susan Welch studied a twelve-state sample of legislatures and found that women "as evidenced by their self-assessed priority legislation, by their committee assignments, and by their proudest accomplishments, give more priority to issues relating to women, children, and families, while men were more likely to focus on issues of business and commerce."[41] The increased number of women in state legislative bodies creates "a larger potential support network for women who push issues of importance to them."[42] And since "the burdens to women of maintaining a home and career have become publicly more evident," women can be expected to pay more attention than they did in the past to the particular legislative concerns of their gender.[43] Thomas and Welch quoted U.S. representative Barbara Kennelly on this point: "My business is to get legislation through. My added business is to get legislation through to help women."[44]

Given this general tilting of legislative priorities toward "women's issues," it is not surprising that aggregate studies of state-level abortion policy have found that the proportion of women in a legislative body correlates significantly with that body's likelihood to defend access to abortion. Susan Hansen, for example, found that "it is the proportion of women in the state legislature, rather than other indicators of support either for liberal policies or for women's rights in general, that emerges as a consistent predictor of the continuation of abortion access guaranteed by *Roe*."[45] Using a somewhat finer instrument, but arriving at a very similar conclusion, Berkman and O'Connor found that the "greater the number of women, the more likely the state will not require parental notification."[46] In fact, "the presence of women Democrats explains far more variation across states than measures of Democratic Party strength or the several measures of state public opinion."[47]

Patricia Bayer Richard's interviews with legislators in Ohio give us deeper insight into the cause of these correlations. Many women she spoke with were passionate about what they saw as their special representational responsibilities. Advancing the interests of women and defending access to abortion were clearly major priorities for these women, and those priorities were expressed in ways one would not expect to hear from men. In addition, our state case studies, particularly at the poles, once again support the aggregate findings. Washington, with a large percentage of female legislators, is firmly pro-choice, while Louisiana and Pennsylvania, with very few female legislators, may be classified as our most pro-life states.

As always, of course, we must be careful that we do not inappropriately apply aggregate-level conclusions to individual circumstances. In a number of our states, women legislators were central actors in abortion policymaking, but not always in a simple or straightforward way. Women in Maryland, for example, were indispensable early proponents of liberal abortion law, but they later retreated from the front lines of the legislative battle so as not to present a convenient partisan target for their opponents. And in Massachusetts and North Carolina, women have been deeply involved on both sides of this contentious issue. In almost all cases, however, careful examination of the details of the politics of abortion has revealed central involvement in the issue on the part of female legislators, particularly in defense of abortion rights.

This raises the interesting matter of pro-choice activists adopting the political *strategy* of electing more women to state legislatures for the express purpose of moving policy in a pro-choice direction. Russo argued convincingly that this is happening in California, and Hansen remarked more generally that "electing more women to state legislatures reduces the number of abortion restrictions adopted."[48] In this instance, at least, political science meets politics.

Conclusion

Perhaps the last phrase of the preceding section could serve as the central theme of this volume: political science meets politics. By using and building on the classifications, categories, and variables offered by political science, the case studies included here have added substantial detail to our understanding of the *politics* of abortion in American states. These studies have taken us inside the politics of ten disparate states and showed us the relationships, processes, and circumstances that have resulted in a diversity of state-level policy on abortion. These studies have also identified a number of patterns and outcomes that have helped us to generalize from these ten cases, and perhaps improve the accuracy of our predictions about states not included here.

At the least, we have offered a road map for the study of abortion politics in American states. Taken together, the cases argue that anyone seeking to understand the politics of abortion in a state, or to predict the future course of abortion policy in a state, would be well advised to examine the state's policy toward abortion before *Roe v. Wade*; the state's political culture; public opinion of legal abortion within the state; the role of anti-abortion interest groups, particularly those that can be classified as religious; the role of the state's governor; and the presence, number, and influence of female members in the state's legislature.

Aggregate, fifty-state studies help us to understand the broad patterns on this issue. And drawing from those studies, we asked our contributors to examine closely the variables discussed above. But we also asked the contributors to try to capture what aggregate studies cannot capture so well: the nature of the political relationships and processes found in the states and how those relationships and processes had transformed aggregate classifications into policy. There are a number of things we can know about the politics of abortion in the *states*, emphasis on the plural, and many of them have been discussed here. But there are some very important aspects of the politics of each state that can be understood only by careful attention to that state. In chapters 1 through 10, quite naturally, we have tilted away from the general and toward the particular. We have done so with the conviction that in examining the particular, we would be able to identify important generalities. Those generalities, reported here, may not lead us to confident explanations or predictions of specific outcomes across all fifty states. But they do afford us a more detailed understanding of the contextual and political factors that will, in the future as in the past, shape abortion policy in the American states.

Notes

1. See, for a number of examples, the chapters under the heading "State Abortion Policy and Politics," in *Understanding the New Politics of Abortion*, ed. Malcolm L. Goggin (Newbury Park, Calif.: Sage, 1993).
2. Jeffrey M. Stonecash, "Observations from New York: The Limits of Fifty State Studies and the Case for Case Studies," *Comparative State Politics* 12 (1991): 1–9.
3. See Glen Halva-Neubauer, "Abortion Policy in the Post-*Webster* Age," *Publius: The Journal of Federalism* 20 (1990): 32.
4. John Kincaid, "State Court Protections of Individual Rights under State Constitutions: The New Judicial Federalism," *Journal of State Government* 61 (1988): 163.
5. For an illustrative example, see Rebecca M. Salokar, "The First Test of *Webster's* Effect: The Florida Church," in *The Catholic Church and the Politics of Abortion: A View from the States*, ed. Timothy A. Byrnes and Mary C. Segers (Boulder, Colo.: Westview Press, 1992), 48–70.
6. Alexander Hamilton, James Madison, and John Jay, *The Federalist Papers*, ed. Clinton Rossiter (New York: Mentor, 1961), 245.
7. These categories are drawn from Barbara Hinckson Craig and David M. O'Brien, *Abortion and American Politics* (Chatham, N.J.: Chatham House, 1993), 75.

8. Daniel J. Elazar, *American Federalism: A View from the States*, 2nd ed. (New York: Crowell, 1972), 84–85.

9. Ibid., 95.

10. Ibid., 99.

11. Ibid.

12. Ibid., 97.

13. Susan Hansen, "Differences in Public Policies toward Abortion: Electoral and Policy Context," in Goggin, *Understanding the New Politics of Abortion*, 235.

14. Ibid., 228. Hansen, relying on Halva-Neubauer, does acknowledge that the moralist political culture might cut both ways on the question of abortion.

15. Daniel J. Elazar, *Cities of the Prairie Revisited: The Closing of the Metropolitan Frontier* (Lincoln: University of Nebraska Press, 1986), 107.

16. Gerald C. Wright, Jr., Robert S. Erikson, and John McIver, "Public Opinion and Policy Liberalism in the American States," *American Journal of Political Science* 31 (1987): 980–1001.

17. A similar argument is made in Michael B. Berkman and Robert E. O'Connor, "Do Women Legislators Matter? Female Legislators and State Abortion Policy," in Goggin, *Understanding the New Politics of Abortion*, 269–70.

18. Cited in Malcolm L. Goggin and Christopher Wlezien, "Abortion Opinion and Policy in the American States," in Goggin, *Understanding the New Politics of Abortion*, 191.

19. Ibid., 201.

20. See Jeffrey E. Cohen and Charles Barrilleaux, "Public Opinion, Interest Groups, and Public Policy Making: Abortion Policy in the American States," in Goggin, *Understanding the New Politics of Abortion*, 203.

21. Ibid., 206.

22. Ibid.

23. Theodore J. Lowi, "American Business, Public Policy, Case Studies, and Political Theory," *World Politics* 16 (1964): 677–715.

24. See Raymond Tatalovich and Byron W. Daynes, *The Politics of Abortion: A Study of Community Conflict in Public Policy Making* (New York: Praeger, 1981), 218–30; and Raymond Tatalovich and Byron W. Daynes, eds., *Social Regulatory Policy: Moral Controversies in American Politics* (Boulder, Colo.: Westview Press, 1988).

25. My use of Lowi and Tatalovich and Daynes in this way was suggested by Glen Halva-Neubauer, "Legislative Agenda Setting in the States: The Case of Abortion Policy," Ph.D. dissertation, University of Minnesota, 1992.

26. Raymond Tatalovich and Byron W. Daynes, "Conclusion: Social Regulatory Policymaking," in Tatalovich and Daynes, eds., *Social Regulatory Policy*, 223.

27. Ibid., 211.

28. Clive S. Thomas and Ronald Hrebenar, "Interest Groups in the States," in *Politics in the American States: A Comparative Analysis*, 5th ed., ed. Virginia Gray, Herbert Jacob, and Robert Albritton (Glenview: Scott, Foresman, 1990), 123.

29. See Ronald J. Hrebenar and Clive S. Thomas, *Interest Group Politics in the American West* (Salt Lake City: University of Utah Press, 1987); *Interest Group Politics in the Southern States* (Tuscaloosa: University of Alabama Press, 1992); *Interest Group Politics in the Midwestern States* (Ames: Iowa University Press, 1993); and *Interest Group Politics in the Northeastern States* (University Park: Pennsylvania State University Press, 1993).

30. See, on the Catholic Church, Timothy A. Byrnes, *Catholic Bishops in American Politics* (Princeton: Princeton University Press, 1991); and Byrnes and Segers, *The Catholic Church and the Politics of Abortion*.

31. See, in particular, Elizabeth Adell Cook, Ted G. Jelen, and Clyde Wilcox, *Between Two Absolutes: Public Opinion and the Politics of Abortion* (Boulder, Colo.: Westview Press, 1992), 93–130.

32. Hansen, "Differences in Public Policies toward Abortion," 238.

33. Ruth Ann Strickland and Marcia Lynn Whicker, "Political and Socioeconomic Indicators of State Restrictiveness toward Abortion," *Policy Studies Journal* 20 (1992): 613.

34. Thad L. Beyle, "Governors," in Gray, Jacob, and Albritton, *Politics in the American States*, 201.

35. Halva-Neubauer, "Abortion Policy in the Post-*Webster* Age," 33.

36. Tatalovich and Daynes, "Social Regulatory Policymaking," 216.

37. It is true, of course, that the powers of the governor vary substantially from state to state. For an aggregate analysis of the institutionalized powers of American governors, see Beyle, "Governors," 228.

38. Elizabeth Adell Cook, Ted G. Jelen, and Clyde Wilcox, "Issue Voting in Gubernatorial Elections: Abortion and Post-*Webster* Politics," *Journal of Politics* 56 (1994): 198.

39. For a more detailed discussion of this phenomenon, see Timothy A. Byrnes, "The Cardinal and the Governor: The Politics of Abortion in New York State," in Byrnes and Segers, *The Catholic Church and the Politics of Abortion*, 142–48.

40. Tatalovich and Daynes, "Social Regulatory Policymaking," 216.

41. Sue Thomas and Susan Welch, "The Impact of Gender on Activities and Priorities of State Legislators," *Western Political Quarterly* 44 (1991): 453.

42. Ibid., 447.

43. Ibid.

44. Ibid., 446.

45. Hansen, "Differences in Public Policies toward Abortion," 242.

46. Berkman and O'Connor, "Do Women Legislators Matter?" 275.

47. Ibid.

48. Hansen, "Differences in Public Policies toward Abortion," 242.

About the Editors and Contributors

MaryAnne Borrelli is Assistant Professor of Government at Connecticut College, where she teaches courses in American national institutions and women in politics. She contributed "The Consistent Life Ethic in State Politics: Joseph Cardinal Bernardin and the Abortion Issue in Illinois," to *The Catholic Church and the Politics of Abortion: A View From the States* (1992).

Timothy A. Byrnes teaches political science at Colgate University in Hamilton, New York. He has written *Catholic Bishops in American Politics* (1991) and has co-edited *The Catholic Church and the Politics of Abortion: A View from the States* (1992).

Eliza Newlin Carney is Staff Correspondent of the *National Journal* in Washington, D.C. Her article on the 1992 Maryland referendum, "Abortion-Rights Test," appeared in the 10 October 1992 issue of that weekly.

Christine L. Day is Associate Professor of Political Science at the University of New Orleans. She is the author of *What Older Americans Think: Interest Groups and Aging Policy* (1990). Her article on a 1990 Louisiana anti-abortion bill vetoed by the governor appeared in *The Catholic Church and the Politics of Abortion: A View from the States* (1992).

Glen A. Halva-Neubauer is Dana Assistant Professor of Political Science and Director of the Urban Studies Program at Furman University, Greenville, South Carolina. His previously published work has appeared in *Publius* and in *Understanding the New Politics of Abortion*.

Mary T. Hanna holds the Miles C. Moore Chair of Political Science at Whitman College in Walla Walla, Washington. She is the author of *Catholics and American Politics* (1979) and of many articles on religion and politics in the United States.

James R. Kelly is Professor of the Department of Sociology at Fordham University. His articles on the pro-life movement have appeared in the *Review of Religious Research*. He wrote "Learning and Teaching Consistency: Catholics and the Right-to-Life Movement," in *The Catholic Church and the Politics of Abortion: A View from the States* (1992), and contributed an essay on the right-to-life movement in *The New Dictionary of Catholic Social Thought* (1994).

Rosemary Nossiff is Assistant Professor of Political Science at Rutgers University Newark, where she teaches American government and politics. Her article, "Why Justice Ginsburg Is Wrong about States Expanding Abortion Rights," appeared in *PS*, June 1994. Her doctoral dissertation at Cornell University compared pre-*Roe* abortion politics in New York and Pennsylvania.

Daniel J. O'Neil is Professor of Political Science at the University of Arizona in Tucson, Arizona, where he teaches courses in comparative government and religion and politics. He wrote *Church Lobbying in a Western State: A Case Study of Abortion Legislation* (1970) and numerous articles on North American and European politics.

Patricia Bayer Richard is Professor of Political Science and Dean of University College at Ohio University in Athens, Ohio. Her work on electoral politics and on public policy and reproductive technologies has appeared in such journals as the *Western Political Quarterly*, the *Social Science Quarterly*, and the *Women's Studies Quarterly*, and in numerous books.

Michael A. Russo is Professor and Chair, Department of Communications, at St. Mary's College of California. In 1991 he was a Fellow at the Joan Shorenstein Barone Center on the Press, Politics and Public Policy at Harvard University, where he wrote "The Church, the Press, and Abortion: Catholic Leadership and Public Communication."

Mary C. Segers is Professor of Political Science at Rutgers University in Newark, New Jersey, where she teaches political theory, religion and politics, and women and politics. She coauthored *Elusive Equality: Liberalism, Affirmative Action, and Social Change in America* (1983), and has written numerous articles on abortion politics and public policy. She edited *Church Polity and American Politics: Issues in Contemporary Catholicism* (1990) and coedited *The Catholic Church and the Politics of Abortion: A View from the States* (1992).

Ruth Ann Strickland is Associate Professor, Department of Political Science and Criminal Justice at Appalachian State University in Boone, North Carolina. Most of her published works have focused on selected public policy issues and abortion politics.

Index

Abortion
  rates in United States, 71, 80
Abortion clinics
  laws on access to, 40, 54, 118, 166, 207,
    226, 232–37
  violence at, 34, 206–7, 226, 230, 233–37
  See also individual state entries
Abortion Justice Association (AJA), 20
Abortion law
  and conscience exemption, 183, 193, 241
  and "convenience" abortions, 36
  and counseling in federally funded
    clinics, 34, 229, 231–32
  and fetal defects, 19–20, 30, 36–37, 54,
    105, 107, 160
  and fetal disposal, 29, 34
  history of, 1–10
  and incest, 19, 30, 33, 36–37, 69, 73–76,
    78, 85, 90, 105, 107, 110–11, 129,
    172, 238–39
  and informed consent, 8–10, 22, 25–26,
    29, 40–42, 44–45, 54, 58, 118, 184,
    229
  and kickbacks, 54, 60, 62–63
  and maternal health (mental or physical),
    19–20, 54, 78, 107, 110–11,
    172–73, 250
  and maternal life, 36–37, 54, 69–70,
    73–75, 79, 85, 107, 110–11, 129,
    160, 170, 238, 250
  and parental consent, 4, 22, 25, 70, 79,
    112, 118, 128, 155–60, 165, 176,
    184, 193, 229, 232

Abortion law *(continued)*
  and parental notification, 8, 10, 33, 39,
    54, 58, 60, 62–63, 128, 142, 147,
    229, 260
  and physician liability, 41
  and public funding, 22–23, 25, 33–34,
    55, 64–65, 70, 85–86, 89, 104–12,
    119–20, 129, 153, 155–56, 159–60,
    162, 165, 184, 198, 215, 226,
    237–42, 248
  and rape, 19–20, 30, 33, 36–37, 54, 69,
    73–76, 78, 85, 90, 105, 107,
    110–11, 129, 172, 238–39
  and residency requirement, 4, 160
  and southern states, 106
  and spousal consent, 4, 9, 22, 25, 155,
    159–60, 165
  and spousal notification, 4, 26, 229
  and trimester framework, 5, 7, 229
  and "trusted adult" bill, 39
  and undue burden standard, 10, 25–26,
    41, 58, 69, 78, 183–84, 193, 196,
    198–99, 229–30
  and viability of fetus, 6–7, 9, 32, 34, 44,
    110, 153, 159–61, 165, 192, 215,
    228–29
  and waiting period, 8–10, 26, 40, 79,
    128, 184, 229–30
  See also individual state entries
Abortion reform movement, 3–4, 16,
  19
Action League for Life, 119–20
Adams, Brock, 158

Welch, Susan, 260
Weld, William F., 187, 194, 198–99, 258
Welfare reform, 220–21
Wellstone, Paul, 38
Whicker, Marcia Lynn, 257
White, Byron, 10, 232
White, Paul W., 189–90
Whitman, Christine Todd, 221
Wilcox, Clyde, 69–70, 80
Wilder, Douglas, 228
Wilke, John, 4
Wilson, Pete, 170, 177
Winn, Robert, 73
Wlezien, Christopher, 254

Woman's Right to Know bill. *See* Ohio, Woman's Right to Know bill
WomenElect, 110, 118–19
Women Exploited by Abortion, 119–20
Women's Health Organization, 118
Women's Law Project, 227
Women's Pavilion Clinic, 120
Wright, Gerald C., 253
Wyman, Phillip, 176
Wynn, Albert, 63

Young Women's Christian Association (YWCA), 94

Zero Population Growth, 211